UNITED NATIONS CONFERENCE ON TRADE AND DEVELOPMENT

FDI and Tourism:
The development dimension

East and Southern Africa

UNITED NATIONS
New York and Geneva, 2008

Note

UNCTAD serves as the focal point within the United Nations Secretariat for all matters related to foreign direct investment, as part of its work on trade, finance and development. Through its Division on Investment and Enterprise (DIAE), UNCTAD also assists developing countries to attract and benefit from FDI and to build their productive capacities and international competitiveness. The emphasis is on an integrated policy approach to investment, technological capacity building and enterprise development.

The term "country" as used in this study also refers, as appropriate, to territories or areas; the designations employed and the presentation of the material do not imply the expression of any opinion whatsoever on the part of the Secretariat of the United Nations concerning the legal status of any country, territory, city or area or of its authorities, or concerning the delimitation of its frontiers or boundaries. In addition, the designations of country groups are intended solely for statistical or analytical convenience and do not necessarily express a judgement about the stage of development reached by a particular country or area in the development process. The reference to a company and its activities should not be construed as an endorsement by UNCTAD of the company or its activities.

The boundaries and names shown and designations used on the maps presented in this publication do not imply official endorsement or acceptance by the United Nations.

The following symbols have been used in the tables:

Two dots (..) indicate that data are not available or are not separately reported. Rows in tables have been omitted in those cases where no data are available for any of the elements in the row.

A dash (-) indicates that the item is equal to zero or its value is negligible.

A blank in a table indicates that the item is not applicable, unless otherwise indicated.

A slash (/) between dates representing years, e.g., 1994/95, indicates a financial year.

Use of a hyphen (-) between dates representing years, e.g., 1994-1995, signifies the full period involved, including the beginning and end years.

Reference to "dollars" ($) means United States dollars, unless otherwise indicated.

Annual rates of growth or change, unless otherwise stated, refer to annual compound rates.

Details and percentages in tables do not necessarily add to totals because of rounding.

The material contained in this study may be freely quoted with appropriate acknowledgement.

UNCTAD/DIAE/IA/2008/6
UNITED NATIONS PUBLICATION
Sales No. E.08.II.D.28
ISBN 978-92-1-112761-4
ISSN 1818-1465

JAN 2 1 2009

Acknowledgements

This report is part of the UNCTAD research and policy analysis project, *FDI in Tourism: the Development Dimension*. The East and Southern African phase of the project was made possible with generous financial support from the International Development Research Centre (IDRC), Canada.

This report has been prepared by Diana Barrowclough and Hafiz Mirza under the overall guidance of Anne Miroux. It is based on desk research and fieldwork lead by Ramesh Durbarry (Mauritius), Happy Fidzani (Botswana), Moses Ikiara (Kenya), Josephat Kweka (United Republic of Tanzania) and Francis Nsonzi (Uganda). Stephen Gelb and Kate Rivett-Carnac (South Africa) also contributed to an early phase of the research. We also acknowledge with thanks the intellectual support and encouragement given by Basil Jones and Susan Joekes (IDRC) and Mondher Sahli (University of Victoria); editing by Praveen Bhalla, final research assistance by Rosie Pinnington and desktop publishing by Teresita Ventura.

Finally, UNCTAD thanks the government officials, tourism practitioners, investors, and civil society groups and individuals who helped at various stages of the project, giving their time and expertise generously, and agreeing to be interviewed. Drafts of country studies and preliminary findings have been reviewed and disseminated at national and international workshops, and we also thank participants for their comments.

Current Studies on FDI and Development

The UNCTAD Series on *Current Studies on FDI and Development* was launched in 2005. It aims to contribute to a better understanding of transnational corporations and their activities, and especially their impact on development. The series also aims at stimulating discussion and further research.

Titles in the series include:

1. UNCTAD (2005), *TNCs and the removal of textiles and clothing quotas.* (New York and Geneva: United Nations).
2. UNCTAD (2006), *Measuring restrictions on FDI in services and transition economies* (New York and Geneva: United Nations).
3. UNCTAD (2007), *The universe of the largest transnational corporations* (New York and Geneva: United Nations).
4. UNCTAD (2007), *FDI and tourism: the development dimension.* (New York and Geneva: United Nations).
5. UNCTAD (2007), *Elimination of TRIMS: The experience of selected developing countries* (New York and Geneva: United Nations).
6. UNCTAD (2008,), *FDI and tourism:the development dimension –East and Southern Africa* (New York and Geneva: United Nations).

Contents

Part A: FDI and Tourism in East and Southern Africa

Boxes

Figures

Part B: County Case Studies

Box

Figures

Tables

IV. Mauritius country case study **119**

V.   United Republic of Tanzania country case study 159

Boxes

Figures

Tables

Abbreviations

APTA	American Public Transport Association
AUTO	Association of Uganda Tour Operators
BEDIA	Botswana Export Development and Investment Authority
BIDPA	Botswana Institute for Development Policy Analysis
BOI	Board of Investment (Mauritius)
CCA	Conservation Corporation Africa
CEDA	Citizen Entrepreneurial Development Agency
COMESA	Common Market for Eastern and Southern Africa
CSR	corporate social responsibility
EAC	East African Community
EIA	environmental impact assessment
EIU	Economist Intelligence Unit
EPZ	export processing zone
EU	European Union
FAP	Financial Assistance Policy (Botswana)
FDEI	foreign direct equity investment
FDI	foreign direct investment
FIAS	Foreign Investment Advisory Service (World Bank)
GATS	General Agreement on Trade in Services
GDP	gross domestic product
GOK	Government of Kenya
HATAB	Hospitality and Tourism Association of Botswana
HRA	Hotel and Restaurants Authority (Kenya)
IATA	International Air Transport Association
ICT	information and communication technologies
IFSC	International Financial Services Centre
IRS	Integrated Resort Scheme (Mauritius)
ISO	International Organization for Standardization
IVTB	Industrial and Vocational Training Board (Mauritius)
KIA	Kenya Investment Authority
KIPPRA	Kenya Institute for Public Policy and Research Analysis
KTB	Kenya Tourist Board
kVa	kilovolt-ampere
LDC	least developed country
MFA	Multi-Fibre Arrangement
MICE	meeting, incentives, conference and exhibition
MNRT	The Ministry of Natural Resources and Tourism
MOTTI	Ministry of Tourism, Trade and Industry
NDP	National Development Plan
NEMA	National Environmental Management Authority
NGO	non-governmental organization
SACU	Southern African Customs Union
SADC	Southern African Development Community
SSA	sub-Saharan African
SME	small and medium sized enterprise
TAWICO	Tanzania Wildlife Corporation
TFDI	foreign direct investment in tourism
TILA	Tourist Industry Licensing Act (Kenya)
TIC	Tanzania Investment Centre
TNC	transnational corporation
TTCI	Tourism and Transport Consult International (Kenya)
TUGATA	The Association of Uganda Travel Agents
UCOTA	Uganda Community Tourism Association
UBOS	Uganda Bureau of Statistics
UIA	Uganda Investment Authority
UNCTAD	United Nations Conference on Trade and Development
UWA	Uganda Wildlife Authority
WTTC	World Travel and Tourism Council
WTO	World Trade Organization
ZIPA	Zanzibar Investment Promotion Agency

PART A

FDI and Tourism in
East and Southern Africa

I. FDI and Tourism in East and Southern Africa, an analytical overview[1]

Executive summary

Many developing countries are looking to tourism as a potentially promising avenue for economic and human development. This is a relatively new position for some countries, and reflects the rapid increase in tourism in terms of both numbers of arrivals and revenues for several economies in recent years. Traditionally, tourism was placed below manufacturing or agriculture, since it was not seen as a significant or appropriate source of growth. In contrast, today, a "quiet but significant reappraisal" is taking place, which values tourism as a potential means of earning export revenues, generating large numbers of jobs – including for young people and women – promoting economic diversification and a more services-oriented economy, helping to revive declining urban areas and cultural activities, and opening up remote rural areas. For example, there is now growing research on what is called "pro-poor tourism" that is gaining mainstream support through the donor and development-assistance communities.

FDI is one of the routes through which developing countries can carry out tourism, but the dynamics of FDI in this dynamic sector, and its implications, have been relatively little studied. There is very little empirical information about the extent of tourism-related FDI in the global economy or its overall impact. Because tourism is an industry that needs to be managed carefully, with or without FDI, and because FDI poses special challenges and concerns, this report aims to provide information and analyses that will assist policy-makers to design policies that most support their development objectives and strategies.

The first chapter provides a synthesis of country case studies on the developmental impact of FDI in the tourism industry for five East and Southern African countries: Botswana, Kenya, Mauritius, Uganda and the United Republic of Tanzania. Subsequent chapters describe the experiences of each country, case by case. The studies constitute the second phase of a wider global project on the subject, conducted by UNCTAD (box 1). It is hypothesized that FDI in the tourism industry may interactively amplify the development impacts that are associated with both tourism and FDI. Given the potentially footloose nature of FDI and the sensitivity of tourism to exogenous shocks, it is critical for low-income countries such as those in Africa to examine the development dimension of FDI in order to be able to devise a strategic policy for maximizing and sustaining its positive impacts and minimizing its negative ones.

The study first highlights the main findings with respect to the development impacts of TFDI in the five countries on income, employment, technology and skills transfer, wages, and linkages, as well as the social and environmental impacts among others. It then examines the salient policies that are in place, identifying those that have hindered and promoted TFDI.

The East and Southern African findings support the findings of the study at the global level (UNCTAD, 2007). Firstly, all the countries in the study were found to be broadly open to tourism FDI, as compared to the policy stance several decades ago when the norm was rather to be explicitly closed to tourism FDI. However, there are a variety of stances, and some countries have adopted policies to attract TFDI (e.g. Mauritius, the United Republic of Tanzania and Uganda), while others (Kenya and Botswana) have a more restrictive approach.

In terms of the impact of tourism FDI, the East and Southern Africa experience also conformed with the wider picture found in the global studies. First, and perhaps most importantly, TFDI inflows have contributed to a sustained increase in both arrivals and revenues from international tourism by enhancing the service delivery and supply capacity (especially accommodation provided by international hotel chains) of these countries. Secondly, the evidence shows that TFDI has become an important means for the tourism industry to benefit from the transfer of skills, technology and standards, and could contribute to raising the tourism sector's productivity and competitiveness. This appears to be more significant in countries that are relatively new to tourism or to FDI.

Thirdly, the studies found that the impact of TFDI was mixed, contributing to significant linkages in some countries and not in others. The impact appears to be sensitive to the structure and level of development of a particular country, among other factors. Fourthly, although most of these countries have incentives and policies for TFDI, little is known about their effectiveness. The studies indicate a need for more transparency, for example with regard to access to land, fiscal and financial incentives and the legal framework. There appears to be a need to promote investment opportunities through a central agency to facilitate implementation and to cut bureaucracy. Fifthly, there is scope for countries, especially bordering countries, to jointly promote tourism and TFDI in the region through regional integration schemes. Finally, on the basis of a preliminary survey of the social impacts of TFDI, it appears that social impacts relate more to the characteristics of tourism as an industry, rather than to ownership – foreign or local – in particular. However, in many cases, benefits emerging from corporate social responsibility seem to be closely associated with FDI.

In summary, the key message from the country case studies is that both policy and non-policy initiatives to make the tourism industry amenable to increased FDI are key to sustaining its development role.

Box 1. The UNCTAD project, FDI in Tourism

These East and Southern Africa country case studies are part of a wider UNCTAD research and policy analysis project on the role and impact of TNCs in global tourism. Themes in the global project included: the extent of TNC activity; the role and implications of non-equity compared to equity modes of participation; South-South tourism and investment; and the linkages between hotel groups and their host countries. The project aimed to provide much-needed information to help policy-making in countries that wish to benefit more from international investment in tourism.

A number of in-depth country studies were conducted during the project, to gain evidence of the trends and impact of FDI and TNCs *in situ*. Each used the same methodology and questionnaires to enable cross-country comparisons, and additional questions were added specific to each country context. The approach compared domestically owned with foreign-owned hotels and enterprises in the same activity and of similar quality. Questions were asked about employee numbers, salaries, training and other human resource policies, and also about procurement linkages, imports of goods and services, use of expatriates and financial arrangements.

The countries were selected with the aim of gathering a broad range of experiences. They included landlocked countries, LDCs, island economies, countries with a long history of FDI and those with a short history, as well as countries with policies that were welcoming to mass tourism and those that followed a more niche-oriented strategy. In the first phase of the work, the following countries were covered: Bhutan, the Dominican Republic, Kenya, Morocco, Sri Lanka, Tunisia and the United Republic of Tanzania. Some of the countries share similar sources of comparative advantage in tourism but different policy histories, and hence offer an opportunity to partially isolate the contribution of FDI or of different policy stances.

In the second phase of work, with generous support from the International Development Research Centre (IDRC) of Canada, parallel research was conducted in East and Southern Africa. The research carried out by country researchers Ramesh Durbarry, Happy Fidzani, Moses Ikiara, Josephat Kweka and Francis Nsonzi. A third phase of research has now begun in West Africa, also with the support of the IDRC

The full list of countries examined in the UNCTAD project to date are listed in box table 1 below. The research approach focused on questionnaires and interviews, to supplement and extend available official data. Interviewees included investors and hotel managers, firms that supplied hotels, transport firms, tour operators and agencies, public policy makers, and social groups with an interest in tourism and development. Typically, at least 40 to 50 interviews were conducted in each country; for example, in Mauritius, 48 hotel managers and 20 tour operators and related enterprises were interviewed.

Questions were asked about tourist demand, capital formation, human resource and employment effects, use of technology and technology transfer, corporate and competitiveness impacts, and impacts on the value-chain as measured through procurement practices. Questions were also asked about the environment and corporate social responsibility. In addition, interviewees were asked open questions and given the opportunity to elaborate more freely on issues.

/...

Box I.1. The UNCTAD project, FDI in Tourism (concluded)

In most countries, the population of foreign enterprises was relatively small, and in some cases almost all firms could be interviewed. In others, a sample was selected, favouring the four- and five-star classifications where FDI was most likely to occur. Domestic firms were selected at a similar size and level as the foreign ones; however, this was not always possible, as foreign firms are frequently larger and operate in a higher price bracket. In some countries, there was considerable debate on whether non-indigenous citizens should be described as "local" or "foreign", and how to treat individual owners (e.g. did a South African owning a bed-and-breakfast facility in the United Republic of Tanzania count as FDI?). For the most part such small operations were excluded from the global study, although they were reported on in the East and Southern African studies.

Firms ranged in size from small family operations to large enterprises (including hotels employing hundreds of people and operating hundreds of rooms). The relevant markets were mostly in the upper and middle price ranges; few foreign firms operated at the low-price end of the market. The locations of enterprises interviewed included capital cities, coastal resorts and wildlife areas.

In some countries, interviews were also conducted with local residents and non-governmental organizations (NGOs), in order to get a preliminary sense of the livelihood impact of tourism FDI (following the pro-poor tourism approach advocated by the Overseas Development Institute). In Mauritius, for example, this meant that 50 interviews were conducted with tourism employees, local residents and other individuals whose lives are affected by tourism activities , in addition to the interviews with investors and policymakers.

Box table I.1. Phase 1 and II sample group countries

Tourism strategy/FDI experience	Long history of tourism FDI	New to tourism FDI
Relatively mass market approach	Kenya South Africa Tunisia	Dominican Republic Mauritius
Relatively niche market approach	Morocco Sri Lanka	Bhutan Botswana United Rep. of Tanzania Uganda

This three-part UNCTAD study is the first comprehensive and systematic investigation of its kind. We were assisted in our research by governments, investment agencies, public and private sector institutions, and local and foreign investors who generously gave of their time and shared their experiences with us in interviews and follow-up discussions, in addition to providing data. However, the opinions expressed here are those of UNCTAD and the country researchers, and should not be seen as representative of any country's official policy.

Detailed information about the project and its methodology is presented in UNCTAD (2007).

A. Introduction

Many sub-Saharan African (SSA) countries have taken policy measures to promote their tourism sector with the intention of attracting more investment so as to maximize its potential as a growth sector. It is estimated that in some developing countries, tourism is already worth more than traditional commodity-based or manufacturing exports in terms of export revenues and share in GDP. Furthermore, since tourism has started to attract more FDI (see box I.2 for definitions of FDI), the sector has become an important avenue for reducing the resource gap in developing countries by contributing to gross capital formation, and skills and technology transfer, and by creating jobs, thereby reducing poverty. Tourism is also one of the sectors with potential for "shared growth", given its ability to employ unskilled labour and establish linkages with many other sectors of the economy. Thus the development dimension of FDI in the tourism industry is considered to be much broader than that of other competing sectors for FDI such as mining. On the other hand, the long and cross-cutting nature of the tourism value chain means that any negative effects of tourism FDI will also be very widespread. Tourism is an industry that requires a careful approach, with or without FDI; and when FDI is involved there can be additional concerns and challenges.

This chapter provides a synthesis of country case studies on the development impacts of FDI in tourism for six East and Southern African countries: Botswana, Kenya, Mauritius, South Africa, Uganda,

and the United Republic of Tanzania. The case studies sought to present evidence on the scale and trends in tourism FDI, and on its development impacts. The working hypothesis was that FDI in the tourism industry may interactively amplify the development impacts associated with both tourism and FDI – both negative and positive. It is hoped that the analysis will help inform policy-making with a view to maximizing and sustaining the positive impacts of TFDI and minimizing the negative impacts.

The case study countries were selected with a view to enabling a comparative analysis of different country contexts. Some countries have much older tourism industries (e.g. Kenya, Mauritius and South Africa) and others have younger tourism industries (e.g. Botswana, Uganda and the United Republic of Tanzania). Some countries can offer diversified tourism attractions such as wildlife and beach experiences (Kenya and South Africa), while others have limited tourist attractions: either a beach (Mauritius) or wildlife (Botswana and Uganda). Botswana, Mauritius and South Africa have higher levels of development compared to, Kenya Uganda and the United Republic of Tanzania (which also belong to the same regional economic grouping).

This chapter is organized as follows: section B presents findings on patterns and trends in FDI in the case study countries; section C analyses the impact of TFDI on the respective economies; Section D examines the institutional and policy framework and Section E summarizes the main conclusions and policy implications.

Box I.2. What is – and is not – foreign direct investment?

FDI occurs when an investor resident in one country (the source country) acquires ownership in and a significant influence over the management of an enterprise or productive asset in another country (the host). This may involve creating a new enterprise (greenfield investment) or changing the ownership of an existing enterprise (via a merger and or acquisition). This definition is usually taken to mean a minimum of a 10 per cent equity stake, although it is of course possible to control a firm or assets with less, and even without an equity share. One practical problem discovered through the UNCTAD research project is that there are a large number of foreigners residing in host countries in which they own and run hotels. While this may be an important source of investment capital for a developing country, strictly speaking it is not FDI.

FDI is measured in two different ways: FDI stocks and flows, and the operations and activities of foreign affiliates in host countries. Financial FDI data are compiled according to the concepts used for balance of payments (flows) and international investment position (stocks) statistics, while information on the activity of foreign affiliates is typically collected through surveys. This publication uses both forms of measurement.

FDI *flow* data for a country are usually provided on an annual basis. They give a sense of the dynamism of foreign investment because they are composed of: (i) the flow of equity capital (the foreign investors' purchase of shares in a tourism enterprise in a host country); (ii) reinvested earnings (the foreign investors' share of earnings not distributed by dividends or remitted home); and (iii) intra-company loans.

FDI *stock* data, by comparison, give a consolidated rather than a dynamic picture, being the sum of: (i) the value of the capital and reserves held by a foreign investor in a host country, including the value of retained profits: and (ii) the net indebtedness of foreign affiliates. Like flow data, stock data are also provided on an annual basis. It is preferable to use stock data for many analytical purposes, in part because equity flows in or out of a country can be distorted by one or two large projects in any given year. However stock data are not always available. Also, in many countries they are estimated simply by cumulatively adding the FDI flow data – which defeats the purpose, as they may overestimate or underestimate the true value of the stocks held.

Ideally, both measures are needed, using flow data to understand why the stock values have increased or decreased in any given year. For example, stock values could increase, even if there were no new inflows, if long-held assets were revalued upwards because of a real-estate boom, for example, or the increased profitability of the company. As a general rule, the more developed the economy the better the FDI data. The United States, for example, provides among the most comprehensive FDI data. For many countries, including some that appear to be increasingly significant sources of outward investment in developing countries, the data on FDI in tourism is still largely lacking.

This publication uses both stock data and flow data, but also particularly focuses on other ways of measuring the scale and scope of FDI activity, such as the level of employment in foreign affiliates or the number of hotels affiliated to a TNC.

The latter is especially important in tourism given the fact that many TNCs are reducing equity in "their" hotels, or even hold no equity at all while still maintaining a managerial or overseeing role through a management or franchising contract (allowing them to still maintain control over the company). Moreover, because the impact of a TNC depends upon a whole package of elements including technology, managerial techniques and access to world markets, in addition to equity capital, non-equity modes of having a presence are considered as important in many circumstances.

Source: UNCTAD (2007).

B. FDI patterns and trends

In most low-income SSA countries, FDI has become a major source of investment capital. Total FDI constitutes a significant share of GDP in the United Republic of Tanzania and Uganda (the two low-income countries in the sample) compared to Botswana, Kenya, Mauritius and South Africa (figure 1). In 2000, the share of FDI in GDP was significantly higher for the United Republic of Tanzania and Mauritius reflecting a one-time investment (especially in mining in the case of the former, and in telecommunications in the latter).

Figure 1. FDI inflows as a percentage of GDP, 2000 and 2004

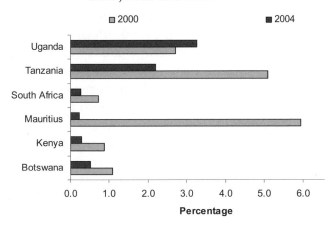

Usually, TFDI is a small fraction of total FDI and this was the case also in the countries studied.

In Botswana, FDI inflows in total FDI increased steadily from 3.5 million pula in 1997 to 10.4 million pula in 2001, followed by a constant decline to reach 4.2 million pula in 2004. The steady increase in FDI, especially up to 2001, can be associated largely with the Botswana Government's Financial Assistance Policy (FAP) that guaranteed financial assistance to investors (both local and foreign) in tourism as well as other selected sectors.

The case study found, however, a different pattern for the trend in tourism (hospitality) FDI inflows: except for the years 2000 and 2004, TFDI inflows generally displayed an upward increase, although its share in total FDI stock was quite small (ranging between 0.2 per cent and 2 per cent between 1997 and 2004).

In Mauritius, the Government's efforts to promote export-oriented FDI inflows in the 1970s started showing impressive results in the 1980s, and more so towards the middle of the decade, with increased FDI going especially to the textile and garment manufacturing export processing zone (EPZ), and later into the banking, telecommunications and tourism. Despite considerable fluctuations, annual FDI inflows grew rapidly, particularly from the second half of the 1990s: from an annual inflow of 1,164 million rupees in 1997, to 2,368 million rupees in 2005. Based on this trend the country has been extremely successful in attracting foreign investment capital. In tourism in particular, the study found evidence of a similar pattern of strong growth in FDI, with more foreign capital directed towards the construction of world-class hotels and villas under the Integrated Resort Scheme. Prior to that, investment codes guided investment in tourism to ensure against overcapacity in the sector. These codes were somewhat restrictive and appeared to favour growth of local investments over foreign investments. Despite these policies, investments in new hotels by both national and foreign investors grew rapidly. The share of inward FDI flowing into the tourism sector was estimated to be 19.1 per cent of total FDI in Mauritius in 2005 and 36.1 per cent in 2006, and the study found that further increases are anticipated.

Kenya's experience appeared to be somewhat different. Comparing the findings of the country studies, it appears that while Botswana, Kenya and Mauritius have had long-standing open-door policies towards foreign capital inflows, Botswana and Mauritius seem to have had more success in attracting FDI inflows than Kenya. Kenya recorded high (though fluctuating) FDI growth rates between 1970 and 1979, but experienced a rapid decline in the 1980s, reaching as low as $0.39 million in 1988. A sharp recovery occurred in 1990, only to be followed by another protracted decline until about the second half of the 1990s. Estimated annual average FDI inflows into Kenya during the period 1996–2003 were around $39 million a year compared to those to Uganda and the United Republic of Tanzania, which were $220 million and $280 million respectively. It seems therefore that Kenya has largely been bypassed by the global surge in FDI into developing countries experienced in the 1990s. Since the beginning of the 2000s, recorded inflows have improved, mainly due to new investments by mobile phone companies and for financing electricity generation activities. Between 1997 and 2004, the tourism sector (mainly the hospitality industry) is estimated to have attracted about 10.7 per cent of projects with foreign participation approved by the Kenya Investment Authority. Given the lack of more specific information on actual inflows and FDI stocks, this seems to be the most reasonable estimate of the sector's share in the country's FDI inflows in the specified period.

According to the findings of the country study, Kenya's low level of inward FDI relative to its immediate neighbours and other developing countries, reflects in part its lack of significant progress, including what were described as "stop-go" economic reforms, concerns about corruption, poor growth performance, deterioration in the quality of infrastructure and rising labour costs. Also, it lacks the mineral resources that have been a magnet for FDI in other African countries. For Botswana and Mauritius, incentives appear to have played an important (though not decisive) role in foreign firms' decision to invest. But the existence of well working institutions, and supportive and predictable policies and efforts to improve infrastructure facilities, were seen as having played an even greater role.

The case study for the **United Republic of Tanzania**, on the other hand, shows that the country had relatively more protectionist policies based on import substitution until the beginning of the 1980s. Thereafter, the introduction of liberalization policies in the 1980s and other structural reform measures, including greater moves towards privatization in the 1990s, created opportunities for more capital inflows. Concerted reform efforts in the 1990s and various incentives offered by the Government to investors also contributed to success in attracting more FDI. Foreign capital inflows into the United Republic if Tanzania between 1995 and 2004 are estimated to have amounted to over $2.4 billion, compared with a total of only $90 million between 1990 and 1995. The leading recipient industries have been mining and tourism, with their shares in total FDI inflows averaging 30 per cent and 14 per cent respectively. Recently however, the usefulness of incentives in ensuring that benefits from FDI accrue more widely to the local economy and contribute to poverty reduction has been called into question. The country study found that such incentives do not necessarily facilitate linkages that enable the local economy to reap more benefits.

Uganda promoted and achieved high inflows of FDI before 1970, but these were followed by a sharp decline in the 1970s and 1980s in all sectors of the economy, including the tourism sector. The country case study found that the negative perception of the Ugandan investment environment arose from political instabilities, including the expropriation of Asian investors' assets and their expulsion from the country in 1972. Following improvements in the political and investment climate in the early 1990s, FDI inflows rebounded during the period 1993–2004, recording an average annual growth rate of 30 per cent.

Specific initiatives to improve the investment climate included the establishment of an investment code protecting investors' rights in 1991, the return of properties confiscated from Asians during the 1970s,[1] and the revoking in 1992 of preferential trade agreement preferences being conditional on majority domestic ownership (Reinikka and Collier, 2001).

These went a long way towards restoring investor confidence in Uganda. However, foreign investment in the country's tourism sector has been quite small. In 2000,[2] the market value of foreign direct equity investment (FDEI) in the accommodation and tourism sector was

estimated to be \$1.2 million, accounting for about 0.17 per cent of total FDEI stocks (Bank of Uganda, 2002). Survey respondents and interviews indicated that the improvement in FDI inflows into Uganda in the 1990s and beyond, notwithstanding declines recorded in some years, affirmed the important role political stability plays in attracting foreign capital.

The findings of the country case studies reiterate more general UNCTAD findings that tourism FDI is typically a small proportion of total FDI, whether measured by inward flows of FDI or by stocks (UNCTAD, 2007). However, the relatively low levels of capital inflows, compared to total FDI, does not mean that they are insignificant in the host countries. As indicated in both the East and Southern African country case studies and in the global phase of the project, FDI has become a significant source of investment capital in the tourism sector. This is especially marked in countries where tourism is being emphasized as a new sector of growth (in this case, Botswana, Uganda and the United Republic of Tanzania).

C. Development impact of tourism-related FDI

The approach adopted in the case studies in discerning the specific impacts of tourism-related FDI is to distinguish the economic effects of tourism firms by ownership (i.e. foreign and domestic).[4] The evidence in the country case studies suggests that the development impact on the tourism industry may be determined by various combinations of three main (among other important) factors. First, and more importantly, is the policy environment, including policy reforms that trigger further inflows of FDI (both generally, and in the tourism industry). This can be broadened to include the perception that the foreign and domestic private sectors will effectively benefit from each other, which can help to create a welcoming environment.

The second set of factors that emerged in the country case studies that determine the impact of tourism-related FDI is the level of development (and maturity) of the tourism industry in a particular country. In economies where tourism is a mature sector, as in Kenya, Mauritius and South Africa, the extent and nature of the impact of TFDI differed from those of less mature countries (such as Botswana, Uganda and the United Republic of Tanzania). In the former countries, the tourism industry has built confidence in local sourcing, resulting perhaps in stronger and wider linkages with the domestic economy than in the latter countries, where a larger proportion of sourcing is from abroad (due to the lack of locally available quality supplies).. The country studies suggest that the more mature the industry, the higher is the level of confidence in domestic private suppliers and their capacity to meet the industry's demands. Consequently there will be greater linkages of TFDI with the local economy, resulting in a positive impact.

Third, it appeared that geography also plays an important role in influencing the nature of impact in two ways. One is in terms of natural resource endowment, where countries can be distinguished by the extent to which they can offer beach versus wildlife (safari) or other natural tourist attractions (or a combination of the two). It is important to note that the impact of the latter type of tourism product (wildlife/natural resource attraction) appeared to involve a greater engagement with local communities in terms of sourcing and corporate social responsibility. This was usually associated with foreign more than domestic investments. Furthermore, it is in this type of tourism that most impacts appeared to be felt in the immediate vicinity, compared to for example beach or business (urban) tourism, where impacts are spread more widely.

Finally, the country studies indicate that regional integration may make a real difference for the development dimension of TFDI. Countries in the study are members of various regional groupings, including the Southern African Customs Union (SACU), the Southern African Development Community (SADC), the East African Community (EAC) and the Common Market for Eastern and Southern Africa (COMESA). These issues could not be discussed in much detail in the country case studies, in part because the integration process in the blocs is still relatively recent. However, TFDI benefits appeared to accrue to both FDI source and destination countries. For firms in countries that are important sources of TFDI, such as Kenya and South Africa, benefits of scale can occur as they increase their linkages within their home country (Kenya or South Africa) in order to provide services or goods that are needed by affiliates in neighbouring countries. From the perspective of the host countries (e.g. Uganda or the United Republic of Tanzania) FDI can bring potential benefits, and also the regional bloc as a whole may become more attractive for further FDI flows.

The following section describes the findings of the country studies in terms of a number of key impact indicators (following the approach used in UNCTAD, 2007). Overall, the foreign firms appeared to produce larger scale impacts than did domestic firms with respect to each of the indicators studied, which is perhaps what one would expect given their larger size and greater capital value. However, it is important to note that in countries where domestic firms had reached a certain scale, or where supportive policies existed to enhance local potential, and where the forging of linkages between local and foreign firms was relatively easy, such differences were less notable (eg, Kenya).

1. Contribution to earnings

That high-income countries dominate receipts from international tourism, and total global tourist arrivals is no longer a subject of dispute. The Organisation for Economic Co-operation and Development (OECD) estimates that almost two thirds of all international tourism in 2003 arrived in developed countries, whereas Africa accounted for only 4 per cent of total international arrivals, and 3.7 per cent of global tourism receipts. But given the marginalization of Africa in global trade (with only 2 per cent of global export receipts), tourism has made an important contribution as a major source of export earnings in all the studied countries (figure 2a), reaching about one third of export revenues in Mauritius and the United Republic of Tanzania, for instance. An important question therefore, is to what extent can this be attributed to the role of TFDI?

Figure 2(a): Share of tourism receipts in total export earning, selected countries, 2005 (Per cent)

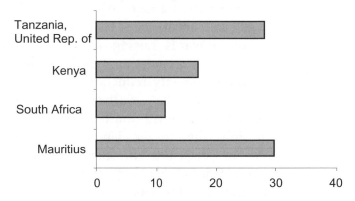

Figure 2(b): Share of tourism in total GDP, selected countries, 2005 (Per cent)

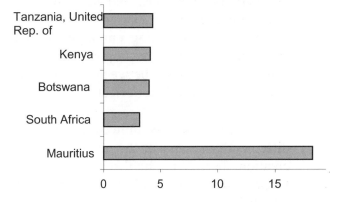

Source: Based on data from the *World Development Indicators* (various years), and from data reported in the case studies of the respective countries. Only those countries are included in the figures for which reliable and comparable data were available.

Although a disaggregation of earnings from tourism by source of investment (foreign or local) could not be undertaken across the six case study countries, it appeared that foreign establishments clearly contributed significantly to revenue creation in the industry. For example, in the United Republic of Tanzania it is estimated that 88 per cent of the total revenue turnover of the surveyed firms for this study came from foreign establishments.

2. Employment and incomes

Job creation is one of the most direct channels through which investors (foreign and local) can be expected to contribute towards raising incomes of a host country's population, and therefore contribute to poverty reduction. Generally, investment in the tourism sector is particularly acclaimed for its potential to create jobs due to the labour- intensive nature of activities in the hospitality industry. One of the key findings from some the country case studies is that, compared to domestic investment, FDI in the tourism industry is more skill and productivity conscious, and may therefore pay more attention to labour market issues, in addition to providing employment. The employment impact is proportional to the strength of linkages between tourism and other sectors (multiplier effect).

Survey results showed considerable differences in terms of the potential for job creation between establishments with a foreign component (joint ventures and wholly foreign- owned) and their local counterparts in individual countries. In Botswana, the survey revealed that joint ventures and foreign-owned establishments in the hospitality sector employed more personnel than did establishments that were wholly locally owned, irrespective of scale of operation (small, medium or large). This is in contrast with the experience in Uganda, where domestically owned hotels seemed to employ more staff than their foreign-owned competitors. Though a straightforward comparison of this kind could not be done for the United Republic of Tanzania, the fact that a disproportionate amount (88 per cent) of revenue turnover of the surveyed firms accrued to firms with a foreign ownership component strongly suggests a similar situation to Botswana's. In Kenya and Mauritius on the other hand, no marked differences were observed in the

number of employees hired by foreign and local firms in the hospitality industry.

For tour operators and travel agents, there appeared to be no differences in number of jobs created by foreign and locally owned firms in countries where foreign entry is permitted (Kenya, Uganda and mainland Tanzania). In Botswana, Mauritius and the islands of Zanzibar (United Republic of Tanzania), these activities are reserved for local firms, which therefore account for all the jobs created in these subsectors.

The findings on employment by gender showed women were highly represented, particularly in the hospitality subsector (hotels, lodges and camps). Mauritius appeared to have the lowest proportion of female employees in the sector (30 per cent) while the United Republic of Tanzania had the highest (51.2 per cent). Except for Uganda where the proportion of female employees was found to be the same in both foreign and local establishments, in other countries foreign firms had a relatively larger proportion of female employees compared to their local competitors. Tour operators and travel agencies employed fewer women in all the countries, compared to hospitality firms (hotels, lodges and camps).

Foreign firms generally were found to pay higher remuneration (salaries and fringe benefits) than their local competitors at the same scale of operation. In Botswana, however, salaries for employees in wholly foreign-owned establishments were perceived to be lower than what was paid to employees with the same skills and similar responsibilities in locally owned firms and joint ventures. A look at job security, (imperfectly proxied by staff turnover), shows that foreign firms were also able to retain their staff for longer periods of time compared to their local counterparts, even where employee salaries were perceived to be lower compared to what local competitors were paying, as in Botswana. Since other benefits in the country, such as pensions and health insurance were similar, this trend could potentially be attributed to non-wage factors, particularly a conducive working environment.

In Kenya, for example, the interviews found that poor organization structures, that limited the movement of employees up the organization ladder, were blamed for a significant employee turnover, especially in locally owned tour operators and travel agencies. Cases were cited of family-owned establishments where the father was the managing director and the son the financial controller, and the other employees remained in junior positions irrespective of length of service. Foreign establishments indicated that they preferred to train their employees on the job so that they moved up the chain (as found in Botswana), which added an element of job security as employees were assured of promotions in the long run (assuming good performance), notwithstanding relatively low pay at the beginning.

3. Technology and skills

The country studies generally found evidence of most locals holding medium- to low- skill jobs, although tourism provided a large employment base in total. With regard to high-level management positions, it was found that firms in the tourism sector (especially foreign establishments) employed more expatriates than local hotels, on the grounds that there was a shortage of high-skilled managers available locally; but some local hotels also employed foreign management staff. Women employees were also found to be underrepresented in managerial positions in both foreign and locally owned firms, perhaps due to their limited skill levels. In Botswana, for example, joint ventures and wholly foreign-owned firms employed an

average of about 4 and 2 expatriates respectively, compared to an average of 2 expatriates employed in locally owned firms. It was also estimated that over 90 per cent of all expatriates employed in the surveyed establishments in Botswana held high-level management positions (as managers and heads of departments).

Employment of a large proportion of expatriate staff in management positions was also found in Uganda, especially in foreign establishments, where the proportion of expatriates in total management personnel was estimated at 50 per cent compared to 36 per cent in locally owned firms. In Kenya, by comparison, expatriates employed in the sector ranged from 0 to a maximum of 3 per firm, with a mean ratio around 1 in the hospitality subsector, and without a significant difference between foreign (more expatriates in managerial positions) and locally owned firms. Among travel agencies and tour operators in Kenya, however, local firms did not employ expatriates, whereas firms with a foreign ownership component did. A high proportion of expatriates in managerial positions was also found in foreign establishments in the United Republic of Tanzania, where they averaged 3 per firm. In Mauritius, hotels had an average of one expatriate for local firms and two for foreign firms/joint ventures.

Knowledge, skills and innovation in the tourism business are key to success. For this reason more than 90 per cent of all firms interviewed in the sector invested in skills development. This was mostly done in-house, but the survey showed that some employees also upgraded their skills in tourism and hospitality training institutes. Foreign establishments appeared to spend consistently more on training and skills development than their local counterparts. In the United Republic of Tanzania, for example, while local firms reported spending on average $4,500 for training, foreign/joint-venture establishments reported spending almost 10 times this amount. In Mauritius the corresponding expenditure on training was around 1 million rupees ($36,000) by local firms and 2 million rupees ($74,000) by foreign establishments.

All the countries were observed to have training institutes for the hospitality and tourism industry. Nonetheless, most employees were recruited without specific skills relevant to the hotel subsector, which meant that training had to be an integral part of these firms' strategy if they were to succeed. In Mauritius, it was found that firms had an additional impetus to invest in training (beyond in-house) since the Government provides incentives to firms that fund their employees' training in nationally recognized institutions in the form of a partial refund of the training costs.

Apart from the direct benefits of training in terms of manpower development, the presence of foreign firms was seen to provide a demonstration effect for improvements by local establishments. It was found that local firms were adopting new ways of doing business, and were seeking to access technologies, marketing channels and management techniques comparable to those demonstrated by their foreign-owned counterparts. This demonstration effect could induce firms in the industry to become more efficient or to raise standards, in order to survive as a profitable business.

In the United Republic of Tanzania in the past, for example, the case study found that when most hotel operators were local, their services were seen as not being customer friendly. More recently, though, local operators had begun to emulate the slogan 'customer is king' and were training their personnel in best practices in customer

care. A manager of a local hotel in Arusha, owned by a religious group, said that after visiting several foreign hotels in Dar es Salaam and Arusha, the group had decided to introduce better customer services in all its hotels. All hotels interviewed (foreign and local) had also modernized their accounting systems. Some local hotels had also started emulating cooking standards and offered menus found largely in foreign hotels in order to enhance their competitiveness and survive in business.

4. Linkages to the local economy

Tourism can make an indirect contribution through its linkages forged with other sectors of the local economy. Indeed, one of the greatest expectations of many host countries in terms of the development impact of tourism is that the benefits may spread to other areas of the economy such as agriculture, construction, manufacturing and infrastructure, through supply chain and multiplier effects (UNCTAD, 2007). Because of the extensive value chain in tourism, the more this industry is linked with other sectors of the economy, the greater is likely to be the effect on, for example, direct and indirect employment and revenue generation.

In the general FDI literature, discussion on these sorts of backward and forward linkages usually focuses on their indirect effects through, for example, inter-industry productivity spillovers to firms. In the tourism literature, however, there tends to be more of a focus on the implications of procurement linkages from the perspective of what it means for tourism-related imports and leakages. Generally, it is seldom possible for any one country to produce all tourism services and goods locally; various activities within the tourism industry may require imports of goods or services that are either not produced locally, or for which local production is not competitive.

The following section focuses on local procurement effects by TNCs and local enterprises to give an idea of their potential linkage and leakage effects. The interviews conducted for the country case studies included questions about the purchasing decisions of hotel and tourism enterprises, including the value and the proportions of goods and services they imported. Questions concerned day-to-day expenditures on items such as food and beverages, as well as occasional expenditures such as those incurred for construction, refurbishment and redecoration. The global studies (UNCTAD, 2007) found that, generally, the level of tourism-related imports appeared to be determined more by the nature of the tourism activity, the level of local supply capacity and the stage of development of the tourism industry, rather than be ownership per se. A similar finding emerged in the East and Southern African studies.

In Kenya, for example, where local supply capacity is well developed and tourism has a long history, the case study found similar procurement patterns between the foreign and local hotels, and hotels and restaurants reported buying about 84 per cent of their food, beverages and cleaning products from local suppliers; and as the suppliers reported importing "only" around 17 per cent of their supplies, the majority of inputs appeared to be sourced locally, with all that this implies for employment and other relevant development indicators. In Mauritius, all hotels reported buying most of their food requirements (90 per cent) locally, (except during cyclone seasons when certain foodstuffs were not available or because of poor quality). They also reported purchasing a major share of their construction materials locally and about 50 per cent of their furniture and fittings. Again, this suggests a significant development impact in terms of job creation and revenue sharing.

Nonetheless, even in Kenya and Mauritius, many hoteliers also expressed concern over the limited availability and quality of some items. For the most part, they blamed this on poor quality and packaging, especially with respect to fresh food products, and on the poor quality of certain manufactured goods, which did not meet the standardization, branding and quality policies of the firms. Limited skills available locally were also reported to be a factor with regard to sourcing local labour inputs.

The limited local availability of needed items was also cited in Uganda, a country that is relatively new to tourism, and where the local supply capacity is also relatively constrained. Of the firms interviewed, 80 per cent reported difficulty in finding some of the items needed for their daily operations (e.g. canned food, wines, cleaning products, equipment and fittings) in the local market. They therefore either imported them directly or bought them from trusted wholesale suppliers/importers.

In the United Republic of Tanzania, more than 90 per cent of the tourism establishments interviewed reported that they sourced their supplies from local wholesalers; in Botswana, all but one bought all their supplies from local wholesalers. On the other hand, the case studies also showed that although tourism firms bought many of their supplies locally, they also imported a substantial amount. For example, one establishment in Botswana reported buying 50 per cent of its requirements from abroad, and in the United Republic of Tanzania, supermarket chains, considered to be among the most trusted local suppliers, may have been sourcing some items locally but many of the products they sold were imported. The Tanzania case study found that foreign hospitality firms had a particularly strong preference for imports, including fresh food products, even though these were available locally. The local produce was not considered to be of a sufficiently good quality, or there were problems with guaranteeing regular supplies in sufficient quantities. Estimates from Tanzanian firms showed that foreign hotels spent about 22 per cent of their turnover directly on the local economy, compared to locally owned firms that spent 64 per cent (excluding labour costs). Data were not available on the absolute values of purchases, and the total value of procurement by foreign hotels may still be significant. Given the relatively low percentage of local purchases, there would seem to be potential for improvement, should local suppliers be able to meet the demand.

The country studies affirmed the argument that strengthening linkages with local suppliers could minimize the leakages from the tourism sector, that is, the part of the tourism dollar that leaves the country to pay for the imports consumed by the tourism sector and for other services. Of course, this does not mean a return to historical policies of import substitution, but rather greater scope for taking advantage of the potential offered by tourism, where the relevant industries exist. This calls for concerted efforts to improve the quality of goods and services in which local producers have a potential comparative advantage and to improve local human entrepreneurial skills. It is also important for achieving overall growth and poverty alleviation.

5. Social impacts: implications for poverty alleviation

In addition to the direct effects of TFDI in terms of employment and technology, there can also be important social impacts. These can be assessed in terms of the nature of the linkages with other players in related sectors and with communities living in close proximity to the firms, who may be serving as labour and suppliers to the firms.

Good linkages imply that more earnings of the firms are spent or reinvested in the local economy, and, through the creation of jobs and supply chains, poverty levels are reduced as the incomes of the local population grow. There can also be important infrastructure effects, if governments improve infrastructure facilities as part of an effort to attract more investors (whether in tourism in particular, or the economy in general). Investment in roads, airports and ports can have important spillover effects on the local communities, in addition to their direct economic effects. And, as mentioned earlier, through demonstration effects, local investors strive to enhance the quality of their own products and services to remain competitive and survive. In doing so, they create more opportunities for spillover effects to reach the micro level. Social impacts can also be looked at from the point of view of cultural influences arising from the proliferation of tourist activities, and how they are contributing to building or eroding traditional cultural values or to the creation of hybrid cultural values.

Experience in the case study countries shows that these kinds of effects are already apparent, but they vary in intensity from one country to another. For example, with regard to supply chain linkages, firms interviewed in all the countries expressed their willingness to work as much as possible with local suppliers and communities. Some direct, and less direct, initiatives by investors and governments to help local suppliers (especially small and medium-scale entrepreneurs) improve the quality of supplies that are produced locally were also cited in all the countries. The survey in the United Republic of Tanzania revealed, for instance, that the Shoprite supermarket chain, which serves many tourism enterprises, had been working with local producers through training and supply contracts to grow and supply fruit and vegetable products of a consistent quality, both for its own business and for other customers, including tourist hotels. Some case studies also showed how investors' unwillingness to compromise on the quality of their purchases had induced local suppliers to strive to improve the quality of their products. Box 1.3 illustrates this with two examples from the Mauritius case-study.

In addition to effects arising from supply chain linkages, the case studies found that some investors also contributed to community development as part of their corporate social responsibility policies. Initiatives of this kind included donations to charity organizations serving disadvantaged communities, direct donations to children's homes, contributions to schools and infrastructure development, famine relief and youth training, and involvement in environmental conservation. Others included promotion of cultural tourism (e.g. allowing local communities to charge for providing entertainment in hotels, and allowing local people to establish handicraft/curio shops in their hotels), and, in some cases, offering preferential treatment to surrounding community suppliers in local procurement of supplies.

Both local and foreign hotels were found to be involved in such community development initiatives. However, perceptions concerning the extent of such involvement by type of ownership varied from country to country. In Uganda, more local tourism establishments appeared to be involved compared to foreign firms, whereas in Mauritius and the United Republic of Tanzania the opposite was perceived. This perception was reinforced by the fact that consistently more foreign hotels had community development programmes formalized in their work

programmes, and spent more on community initiatives as part of their corporate social responsibility policy compared to local hotels.

Box I.3. How investors' procurement standards have helped development of local suppliers

Fruit supplier (Mauritius)

SDL, a fruit supplier, started with a modest distribution chain in the 1980s, supplying mostly to local vendors. With the increasing number of hotels and tourists in the 1990s, it rapidly expanded its activities to become among the largest fruit suppliers on the island catering for the majority of hotels' needs. Since SDL started to concentrate on the hotel market, it was required to supply increasingly higher quality products, particularly by foreign-owned hotels. "International chains, especially, would simply not compromise on the quality…but they are prepared to pay the price and at times we even import the fruits to meet their standards," said a supervisor.

Seafood supplier (Mauritius)

HT is among the largest suppliers of seafood, particularly to the hotel and restaurant industry. Its spokesperson reported that over the past decade it had been obliged to segregate its market and supply the best products to hotels that were placing a growing emphasis on quality. Reputed foreign hotel resort chains with high quality standards and inspection teams tend to be particularly rigid. The spokesperson said, "…we have to supply the very best if we want to remain in the market".

In Kenya, whereas the degree of involvement of local and foreign hospitality firms in community development initiatives appeared not to be markedly different, that of tour operators and travel agents was found to be consistently lower on aggregate compared to the involvement of hotels and restaurants, lodges and camps. Apart from a lack of formalized community initiatives in corporate social responsibility work programmes, this may also be due to the fact that most tour operators and travel agents have their offices in areas far from where local communities live.

Botswana, Mauritius and the United Republic of Tanzania also revealed interesting cases of collaboration between foreign firms and local communities in promoting cultural tourism, with government support. There are formalized programmes to help local communities earn an income from tourism (see box I.4 and I.5 for examples from the Tanzania and Botswana country studies).

Box I.4. Support for cultural tourism in northern Tanzania

With financial and technical assistance from the Government of the Netherlands and a few foreign tourism establishments in Arusha, cultural tourism and development in the United Republic of Tanzania is up and running. Local people are being empowered through financial support and training to provide income-generating services to tourists, such as guiding, preparing meals or providing campsites. In addition, a development fee is charged to all hotel guests, on a per night basis. With this money, primary schools, health services, cattle dips, and small irrigation projects are undertaken and improved. In this way, all the villagers reap the benefits of tourism and this encourages them to participate in government conservation efforts being undertaken by the Tanzania National Parks Authority (TANAPA). The villages benefiting from this support are: Ilkidinga, Longido, Ilkurot, Mkuru, Mto wa Mbu/Engaruka and Ngi'resi. Assistance to these communities in 2005 amounted $115,950 – a relatively small sum of money that has made a big difference in improving the lives of these communities.

The foreign hotels appeared to be more likely to support these cultural tourism initiatives than local tour operators. Asked why, one of the tour operator owners cited low returns from their operations and the possibility of fostering "unnecessary" dependence if a firm

/...

Box I.4 (concluded)

were to support these communities. Another local operator was of the opinion that foreign firms supported these activities partly for their own future gains, because foreign tour operators like to take their customers to visit some of the successful cultural tourism centres and before going on to wildlife parks, while most of the local operators' customers are taken straight to wildlife parks. Another local operator did not even know if cultural tourism existed in Arusha, but was aware of transporting tourists to some cultural centres. A major concern of both foreign and local hotels was the possibility of reduced bed-nights if cultural tour centres began to supply tents and other facilities. Although these present a high security risk for tourists, they are very cheap compared with hotel rooms.

Box I.5. Botswana: Community initiatives in the tourism sector

In Botswana there are controlled hunting areas (CHA) which have been divided into small units and allocated to nearby communities that have formed trusts under the Community-Based Natural Resource Management (CBNRM) programmes. The units can also be used for purposes of both hunting and photographic tourism. Due to the lack of entrepreneurial and managerial skills among these communities, that are allocated a wildlife quota for their respective CHA, these communities are encouraged to form partnerships with the private sector. Most partnerships are formed mainly with foreign firms, which possess the required expertise. In this partnership, communities sell part of or their entire quota to the private firm or lease their land for purposes of photographic tourism. Although the main objective of the community-based projects was purely to achieve conservation objectives, they have come to provide a means of transfer of entrepreneurship and managerial skills, and employment and revenue to the local communities, which in turn contributes to poverty reduction.

---

6. Environmental impacts

Tourism FDI can have an impact on the environment through three main avenues: the environmental performance of TNC affiliates; the environmental implications of economic growth stemming from tourism FDI; and the direct and indirect effects that FDI or TNCs can have on national and global environmental regulations (UNCTAD, 2007). The very existence of a large foreign hotel can, for example, cause direct environmental impacts in terms of its use of water and energy compared to local hotels. On the other hand, many environmental impacts may be more related to tourism in general, rather than to FDI in particular.

The UNCTAD studies did not attempt to replicate specialized environmental research; instead, hotel managers were asked a few simple questions about their environmental strategies. For example, hotels and enterprises were asked whether they had an ISO14000 certificate[5], or whether they were members of the private sector initiative, Green Globe. These two environmental standards are the principle means of ensuring that hotels introduce environmental systems into their operations. Also, interviewees were asked more open questions about the hotels' environmental practices in general.

The East and Southern African country case studies found generally that environmental conservation activities were an important element of tourism firms' activities, particularly hotels, lodges and camps. All the countries have national environmental regulations which firms are required to comply with. Moreover, firms also reported understanding and undertaking environmental protection activities for their own benefit, noting that a clean and well-kept environment in itself attracts customers. Environmental conservation activities conducted regularly by tourism establishments located on coastal areas included: beach clean-up, constructing mudbanks to prevent water overflow inland, and undertaking responsible waste management, reuse and recycling. Other activities included contract pick-up of garbage and use of biodegradable chemicals, installation of incinerators for waste disposal, tree planting and landscaping, installation of energy--saving equipment, water conservation and construction of boreholes. Hotels and lodges also reported having to undergo an environmental impact assessment and periodic audits in all the countries.

These efforts were, perhaps unsurprisingly, mostly conducted by hotels; involvement of tour firms and travel agents in environmental conservation seemed to be fairly limited and virtually absent in some countries. For example, in Kenya they did not seem to undertake any environmental impact assessments, and did not have a regular budget for environmental activities.

Although foreign-owned hotels appeared to engage in environmental conservation activities to the same extent as locally owned hotels, further responses to the case study surveys revealed cases where the entry of foreign firms had induced more commitment and responsiveness of central and local authorities to observance of environmental regulations. In Mauritius for example, 80 per cent of the respondents felt that there was better care for the environment following major hotel developments, particularly when foreign hotel chains were established nearby.

In all the countries, a number of hotels interviewed reported being members of Green Globe 21 – an international certification programme for sustainable travel and tourism – though not many among local establishments were members. In the United Republic of Tanzania, for example, none of the interviewed local establishments were members, though they reported following good environmental practices, whereas five of the interviewed foreign firms were members; in Uganda 10 per cent of the interviewed hotels (both local and foreign) were members; in Kenya, five hotels were members. Some establishments, though relatively few, also reported having received the ISO 14000 certificate for environmental management. Membership of Green Globe 21 entails serious commitment to improving environmental performance. Notwithstanding the efforts being made by tourism businesses, additional efforts are still required from governments and investors, working in partnership, to implement sustainable environmental and conservation measures that go beyond the hotel establishment.

7. Boosting tourism through regional integration

Regional blocs may be an important opportunity to help developing countries secure a larger share of the gains from international tourism andn investment. Studies on effects of regional integration (Tsikata, 1999; Casto, Klaus and de la Rocha, 2004) suggest considerable economic gains for producers and consumers from such cooperation. Through regional groupings such as EAC, COMESA, SADC and the Indian Ocean Rim, member countries could enhance their gains from tourism and reap many other benefits.

For instance, COMESA is one of the largest regional economic groupings in Africa and has agreements to promote the free movement of persons through a common visa arrangement, but this obviously is confined only to COMESA members, including Kenya, and therefore does not include Kenya's neighbours, Botswana or the United Republic of Tanzania. Given that Kenyan investors are a strong presence in the United Republic of Tanzania, this is a missed opportunity to encourage tourism between the two countries. SADC encourages cooperation among its member States in a wide range of sectors including tourism, but this grouping includes the United Republic of Tanzania

though not Kenya. In 2005, EAC members (including Kenya, Uganda and the United Republic of Tanzania) agreed to the creation of a customs union, which would establish a common external tariff and remove all intraregional trade barriers (scheduled to be completed in five years). Establishment of an EAC customs union has necessitated harmonization of customs procedures and domestic regulations that could facilitate trade and encourage tourism FDI and other FDI. Under the EAC arrangements, there are also plans to create a common market, and, in the foreseeable future, a monetary union and political federation.

In all the groupings, a well formulated cooperation and marketing strategy is essential for the members to reap the full benefits of integration, including a greater and positive impact from tourism FDI. In the EAC, for example, the findings suggest that member countries should harmonize their trade and investment policies so as to reduce transaction costs, discourage smuggling and tax evasion, promote further integration and attract more FDI within the bloc, and between it and the rest of the world. Measures to achieve this include ironing out differences between individual countries' customs procedures, removing quantitative restrictions, reviewing each country's competition policy, and reviewing internal tax policies and structures to remove elements that undermine the benefits of a common external tariff.

Regional integration holds promising business opportunities for member countries. For instance, about 22 per cent of the hotels in Kenya do business in the region through hotel chains and branches of tour operating firms based in the United Republic of Tanzania. Evidence from the Kenya study suggest that firms that have some degree of foreign ownership are more likely to be doing business in the region than those that are entirely locally owned. Regional integration appears to have reduced some of the problems that hitherto seriously affected cross-border trade such as customs clearance and cross-border movement of business people. These were perceived to be major problems prior to regional integration. However, other problems persist at the implementation stage. For instance, Kenyan tour firms cannot take tourists across Kenya, the United Republic of Tanzania and Uganda because the labour laws do not allow the exchange of drivers. Also, Kenyan registered vehicles are not allowed to go for game drives into the United Republic of Tanzania, yet those from the United Republic of Tanzania are allowed in Kenya. In Kenyan game parks, vehicles with foreign registration plates are charged special fees that are often high. There is therefore a need for further streamlining of the movement of goods and services in the EAC countries.

The country studies found that the EAC has had some impact on member countries, but there is still some way to go before the full benefits are reaped. Uganda, for example, has made progress in implementing an internationally recognized standardized hotel classification system, and this may help it to take advantage of regional travel. When this is in place, it may encourage tourists staying in a four-star hotel in Kenya to visit a similarly ranked hotel in Uganda. With regard to FDI, Kenya is one of the main sources of FDI in tourism in Uganda. Policies of individual EAC member countries on natural resource management vary

considerably. For example, in the United Republic of Tanzania, big game hunting is still considered a beneficial and profitable form of tourism, while in Kenya there is a total ban on any form of hunting. Immigration procedures also differ considerably, and there are separate visa charges, airport taxes, departure taxes and vehicle permits. This makes a journey between EAC countries unnecessarily expensive, not to mention other complicated procedures. It has been cited as one of the major barriers to an effective regional tourism policy. Members of regional blocs should therefore aim to establish a regional marketing strategy to attract more tourists to their region. Resources in Africa are no doubt limited, but through regional blocs, member countries could pool scarce resources and achieve economies of scale.

Some countries also have a comparative location advantage over others (e.g. Mauritius) and better developed facilities (e.g. South Africa). Still others, such as Kenya, Uganda and the United Republic of Tanzania, have considerable wildlife resources, which give them an advantage over other countries. Regional cooperation therefore could provide a better opportunity not only for South-South tourism FDI to grow, but also for all concerned countries to benefit more effectively from tourism. Regional integration will also increase tourist traffic among member countries if barriers to free movement are removed.

D. Institutional and policy framework

In all the case study countries in East and Southern Africa, researchers found there was recognition of the potential role of FDI in tourism. Almost all countries are taking significant steps to attract FDI flows, although some (Botswana and Kenya) had concerns about its benefits; Botswana, for example is rather taking steps to promote domestic investment. Some countries have introduced and revisited legislation to clarify FDI-related policies and incentives, and others have created institutions to facilitate investment. Legislation also helps to control the quality of investment and the direction investment should take. A summary of the main policies, incentives and institutions operational in five of the six countries are presented in the annex to this chapter.

1. Investment and tourism policy

Botswana introduced its first tourism policy in 1990 (later known as the Tourism Master Plan 2000) with a view to diversifying economic activity and becoming less reliant on natural resources such as diamonds. Tourism was identified as a sector that could be managed sustainably and in a way that would generate income. It was recognized that tourism provided considerable potential for employment and foreign exchange earnings. At first, the Government was very open and welcoming to foreign investment, but more recently it has become more cautious with regard to what FDI can bring to the economy and has departed somewhat from its liberal policies. The country favours FDI that can bring technology, skills and access to foreign markets. Some activities are reserved for nationals only, and FDI, where permitted, is subject to a minimum amount of investment.

In Kenya, the Government is broadly open to FDI in general, including in tourism. At independence, Kenya enacted the Foreign Investment Protection Act to guarantee foreign investors against expropriation and it allowed repatriation of profits. More recently it has established a "one stop shop" for processing and facilitating foreign investment, through the Kenya Investment Authority. However attracting FDI in tourism in particular may have been hindered by the lack (until very recently) of a formal national tourism policy, even though the Government has been working on such a policy to attract FDI since 2002. Historically, Kenya's approach has been described as being inconsistent, poorly coordinated and poorly implemented (Ikiara, 2001a; 2001b). Indeed, research for the country case study found that there was still a lack of integration and consistency between tourism policies, sectoral policies and national development priorities. The current tourism policy stance is to focus on high-spending tourists, although this has not yet been articulated in a comprehensive or formal manner. Most recently, tourism has been brought to the fore in Kenya's latest development strategic plan (2008).

Mauritius and the United Republic of Tanzania emerged in the country case studies as two examples of countries that have general policies designed to boost the tourism industry. The Government of Mauritius, for example, has been emphasizing policies that would render the tourism industry more economically sustainable, socially acceptable and environmentally sound. The Government allows 100 per cent foreign ownership, subject to approval by the Prime Minister's Office, although FDI in tourism was only permitted in hotel development and management, and 100 per cent foreign ownership of new developments was permitted only for hotels of more than 100 rooms. Mauritius has an upmarket image and policies have been aimed at high-spending tourism so as to prevent unacceptable environmental and social pressures, to guard against over-capacity, and to uphold/protect the country's image as a luxury beach holiday destination. The Government has been supporting this sector through policies and strategies such as: (i) improving access by air; (ii) developing Mauritius as a duty-free island; (iii) promoting the island as a centre for meetings, incentives, conferences and exhibitions; and (iv) allowing foreigners to acquire property. These measures are expected to attract further FDI into the country.

In the United Republic of Tanzania, the Tanzania Tourism Master Plan and the Tourism Master Plan for Zanzibar encourage investments in tourism. There is no discrimination between foreign and local investors. Policies recognize the right to private ownership and establishment of business ventures, offer full protection of property rights, a liberalized foreign exchange market, favourable repatriation conditions, a stable and predictable regulatory framework, simplification of investment establishment procedures, and the right to national and international impartial arbitration in the event of an investment dispute. All these are stipulated in the Tanzania Investment Act 1997 and the Zanzibar New Investment Policy enacted in 2001. Other policies that can influence tourism-related investment include the Zanzibar Tourism Policy 2004, which has restrictions on building heights in beach areas (limited to 2-3 storeys), and enforcement and implementation of environmental impact assessments and environmental standards in areas where tourist development takes place, including the creation of a system of zoning in an aim to preserve its special atmosphere. Also, a

specialized trained tourist police unit has been set up to provide security and assistance to tourists and residents.

In Uganda, the Tourism Policy aims to create an enabling environment for growth of the sector, and to ensure that tourism becomes a vehicle for poverty reduction in line with the Government's overall goal of poverty reduction. The tourism policy covers economic development, institutional organization, environmental sustainability and cultural promotion. The Government recognizes the need for stimulating investment in tourism. The policy further notes the importance of marketing the tourism sector and the need to involve all stakeholders in marketing efforts. FDI is handled through the "one-stop shop" established through the Uganda Investment Authority in 1991.

2. Investment regulations

It has been noted in the sample of countries studied that investment policies do not generally discriminate between foreigners and local investors. However, to obtain development certificates in order to start an investment, in several countries foreigners, unlike local investors, are required to put up certain minimum amounts. For example, in Botswana, following the Foreign Investment Code introduced in 2002 the country case study found a decline in FDI flows since a minimum investment of $200,000 was required for foreign companies to invest in that country. This sum can be reduced to $100,000 if invested as a joint venture with local citizens. Under the Botswana Tourism Act of 2006, FDI is not permitted in some activities, which are reserved for locals only or for companies that are wholly owned by citizens of Botswana. These activities are: (i) camping sites including caravan sites, (ii) guesthouses, (iii) *mekoro* operations (i.e. wildlife tours by dugout canoe) (iv) mobile safaris, (v) motorboat safaris, and

(vi) transportation. Until the year 2000, the Government granted tax incentives and financial support for the tourism sector under its Financial Assistance Program, but this was abolished due to substantial fraud. Because Botswana enjoys a high savings rate and has large foreign exchange reserves, FDI is not seen as the only source of capital for investment; rather it is valued for its transfer of skills and technology.

Another example is Kenya's Investment Promotion Act (2004), which introduced a mandatory investment threshold and a restrictive screening procedure for all foreign investments. The Act makes a formal distinction between domestic and foreign investors, and requires the latter to apply to the newly established Kenya Investment Authority (KIA) for an investment certificate. This certificate was initially issued provided the amount invested was at least $500,000, and it was necessary that the proposed investment was deemed by KIA to benefit Kenya, including through employment creation, transfer of new skills or technology to Kenyans, and contribution to taxes or other government revenues. In 2006, however, the Act was amended to lower the minimum requirement for foreign investors to $100,000..

To encourage Kenyans to enter into joint ventures with foreign investors and enhance transfer of technology and management skills, local citizens are required to own at least 51 per cent of the equity in lodges located inside national parks and county council game reserves, and in non-hotel tourist service establishments regardless of their location. Domestic investors are not required to obtain an investment certificate, but they are required to register their investment with KIA. The minimum capital investment for domestic investors seeking such a certificate is $65,000. Once established in the country, foreign investors receive the same treatment as domestic investors.

In the United Republic of Tanzania as well, for foreign investors to benefit from the promotion and facilitation policy implemented through the Tanzania Investment Centre (TIC) on the mainland and the Zanzibar Investment Promotion Agency (ZIPA), the minimum levels of investment are $300,000 for foreign investors and $100,000 for domestic investors. If, however, a foreign firm wants to establish a hotel in Zanzibar, the minimum requirement is $4 million worth of investment. Upon satisfactory completion of the requirements, the investor (foreign or local) is provided with a Certificate of Incentives, which offers certain rights, such as investment guarantees, access to land, the right to transfer funds abroad and employ up to five expatriates. However, if the firm requires additional foreign experts, it has to seek approval from TIC or ZIPA. The approval is fairly automatic if locally qualified experts are in short supply.

In Mauritius, FDI was restricted only to hotel development and hotel management until recently. Although the minimum level of investment was not stipulated, in order to benefit from the Hotel Management Incentive Act 1982, a Hotel Development Certificate was granted. To obtain the certificate, the minimum number of rooms for a foreign-owned company was 100, compared to 60 for a locally owned hotel. There was also a minimum amount stipulated for the construction costs per room, in an effort to keep quality standards high. These conditions have recently been removed and Mauritius has now embarked on a more targeted approach, recognizing for example that there is a new luxury market in very small, rather than large, hotels.

In Uganda, the case study also found that investors have to secure an investment licence to benefit from the taxation and incentive policies under Uganda's Incentive Allowance Scheme. This licence is granted by the Uganda Investment Authority (UIA. To secure the investment licence, foreign investors require a minimum of $100,000, compared to $50,000 for domestic investor. Local investors may proceed with their investments without obtaining a licence from UIA.

3. Legal and institutional framework relating to tourism FDI

a) Oversight of tourism-related FDI issues

Each of the countries studied appeared to have slightly different legal and institutional frameworks relating to tourism FDI. In some countries, the tourism ministry and specialized agencies have the responsibility for the promotion and facilitation of TFDI, as well as managing tourism policy generally, as in Botswana, for example. On the other hand, in Mauritius, Uganda and the United Republic of Tanzania, the tasks of tourism investment and tourism management were seen as being separate, with FDI-related issues being the mandate of "one-stop shops" for investors. In the United Republic of Tanzania, for example, FDI issues are divided between the Tanzania Investment Centre (TIC) and the Zanzibar Investment Promotion Agency (ZIPC), while government tourism offices such as the Tourist Agency Licensing Authority (TALA), Tanzania Tourism Board (TTB) and Ministry of Natural Resources and Tourism (MNRT) focus more on issues relating to tourism policy and tourism management more generally. More details are provided in the individual country case studies.

b) Incentives and taxation policies

Most governments offer incentives in their quest to attract domestic and foreign investment, and investment promotion agencies usually view incentives as an important policy variable in their strategies to attract FDI. Although the evidence on the efficiency of such incentives is still limited, this was also the case in the countries studied.

Basically, FDI incentives may be defined as any measurable advantages accorded to specific enterprises or categories of enterprises by a government in order to encourage them to behave in a certain manner. They include measures specifically designed either to increase the rate of return of a particular FDI undertaking, or to reduce (or redistribute) its costs or risk.

As shown in the annex table, most of the countries sampled (with the exception of Kenya) do provide incentives (financial as well as fiscal) to encourage FDI, in addition to removing barriers or disincentives, such as exchange rate controls or restrictions on the transfer of profits. In Kenya, although the Government has maintained an open door policy for foreign investment in tourism, incentives offered are very limited. Special tax relief is allowed on hotel construction, such as accelerated depreciation on buildings. It is only recently that FDI incentives have been proposed in the Draft National Tourism Policy, but there has been a gradual reduction of policies that could act as barriers. At one time foreign investors in Kenya had difficulties repatriating profits due to foreign exchange controls. There were also restrictions on imported inputs, which affected the quality of services in tourism. In the early 1990s, however, the foreign exchange market was liberalized and import restrictions lifted. Foreign companies can also borrow up to 100 per cent of the funds needed for new investments or for the expansion of existing investments from local institutions, and this was believed to have encouraged foreign investors.

In Mauritius, the policy to attract FDI has been rather more explicit. As shown in the annex to this chapter, Mauritius offers a low tax regime for investors and widespread incentives. It has been one of the more successful African countries in attracting FDI, according to the World Bank survey, *Doing Business in 2006*. To promote tourism, the Government has, since independence accorded numerous special incentives to the private sector, accompanied by legislation to regulate tourism development in accordance with government goals. In July 1974, the Development Incentives Act was passed, which also applies to hotel development, and development certificates were issued to individuals, groups and companies on application to the Ministry. Under this scheme, tax relief is granted to tourism enterprises for a period of 10 years starting from the day a project is launched. To encourage foreign investors in the industry, free repatriation of profits is permitted under the Bank of Mauritius Act and the Income Tax Act. In addition, a Hotel Management Scheme, in accordance with the Hotel Management Incentive Act 1982, was introduced to provide a number of facilities and incentives for hotel development. Like other industries eligible for tax incentives, hotels that are granted a Hotel Development Certificate benefit from a number of incentives. For instance, the company pays a nominal corporate tax of 15 per cent during the lifetime of a project instead of the normal statutory rate of 30 per cent, dividends received by shareholders are exempt from income tax for a period of 10 years from the start of operations of the hotel. In addition, the

company is allowed duty-free import of all items listed in an approved list of equipment, and free repatriation of invested capital, profit and dividends subject to the approval of the Bank of Mauritius. As of 1994, foreign exchange controls were abolished and in 2006, the Hotel Management (Incentive) Act) was repealed so that Mauritius now offers an open and low tax business platform and a competitive business environment with a level playing field for local and foreign investors.

In 2006, the Government of Mauritius announced a series of incentives to attract investments by foreigners and the Mauritian diaspora, including combining residence permits and work permits into an occupation permit for (i) investors generating an annual turnover of more than 3 million rupees; (ii) professionals who offered employment at a salary of more than 30,000 rupees a month; and (iii) self-employed persons who generated an annual income of 600,000 rupees a year.

In the United Republic of Tanzania, once a local or foreign investor in mainland Tanzania completes the minimum requirements, the investor is required to follow normal business codes of conduct. However, for Zanzibar a few extra guidelines have to be followed. The tourism policy and legislation provides various incentives to foreign investors and to TNCs that are approved by the Zanzibar Investment Promotion Agency (ZIPA) or the Tanzania Investment Centre (TIC) (box I.6). For Zanzibar, if the enterprise is a joint venture, only the foreign holder of the certificate can enjoy all exchange control privileges set out in the Investment Act. However, the entire venture can enjoy the tax concessions set out in the Act.

Box I.6. Incentives for local and foreign investors in the United Republic of Tanzania

In order to encourage local and foreign investments, the United Republic of Tanzania provides the following incentives:

- Waiver of land rent during construction period.
- Exemption from customs and import duties and other similar taxes on capital goods such as machinery, equipment, raw materials, fuel, vehicles and other goods necessary and exclusively required during the construction period.
- Exemption from import duties on imported raw materials for trial operations, provided that the quantity of such materials does not exceed 18 months' supply for single-shift production operations.
- Exemption of import duty on goods necessary for use by expatriates.
- Exemption from all export duties payable on finished export goods of approved enterprises.
- Income tax exemption for investors who have made a declaration for reinvestment at the proposed stage up to the first three years.
- Up to 100 per cent repatriation of profits.
- Consideration of tax holidays for approved projects.
- Investment protection and guarantee against confiscation or expropriation. Tanzania maintains linkages with the Multilateral Investment Guarantee Agency (MIGA) and the International Centre for Settlement of Investment Disputes (ICSID) to ensure protection of private investment.

Source: Ministry of Finance and Economic Affairs, Zanzibar, and the Tanzania Investment Centre.

In Uganda, foreign investors who invest more than $500,000 can repatriate their investments and dividends and receive foreign exchange to pay debts incurred in the business. The following are the main tax regulations and incentives: hotels located outside the capital city do not pay the 18 per cent value-added tax; imported hotel materials for construction or renovation are allowed into the country duty free, subject to approval by the Minister of Tourism, Trade and Industry prior to importation; there is a uniform corporate tax of 30 per cent, but special fiscal incentives are provided for the first year of construction; hotel equipment can be imported duty free (provided it is printed or marked by the hotel logo), and there is a tax-free diesel facility for thermal power generation for business operations by hotels.

However, it is important to note that, in terms of attracting FDI, investors surveyed for the country case studies considered the incentives to be secondary to other important determinants, such market opportunities, location, availability of skilled labour and political stability. A similar finding emerged in the interviews associated with the global study (UNCTAD, 2007).

Avoidance of double taxation

Double taxation treaties deal with tax treatment of the income generated abroad. Botswana and Mauritius have a double taxation treaty network. Botswana has concluded such treaties with France, India, Mauritius, Namibia, the Russian Federation, South Africa, Sweden, the United Kingdom and Zimbabwe. Mauritius has several such agreements with both developed and developing countries, mainly in Europe, Africa and Asia. As at 31 July 2006, it had concluded a total of 32 double taxation avoidance treaties.

4. International arrangements.

Commitments under the General Agreement on Trade in Services

International trade agreements on tourism are covered under the General Agreement on Trade in Services (GATS), which came into force in January 1995. GATS incorporates commitments made by

WTO member countries to rationalize market access and national treatment in specific sectors as well as across sectors.

Kenya and Mauritius are two countries in the sample that have made commitments under GATS. (See UNCTAD, 2007, for a global view of countries' GATS commitments). The specific areas covered in Kenya's GATS commitments in tourism made in 1999 were hotels and restaurants, travel agencies, tour operators and tourist guide services. The country also made commitments in three out of the four modes of supply defined by GATS: cross-border movements, consumption abroad and commercial presence. This means that foreigner investors can use these modes to supply tourism services to or in Kenya. The country does not have restrictions on equity holdings, forms of doing business, limitations on purchases and size limitations for establishments.

Mauritius has been complying with the GATS in the design of certain policies on tourism and travel-related services. The specific commitments made by Mauritius in the tourism industry cover hotel operators, restaurant operators, travel agencies, tour operators, tourist guide services, tourist transport operations (car rental), yacht chartering and cruising services, and duty-free shops.

E. Conclusions and recommendations

The objective of this synthesis has been to summarize the main issues and findings arising from the country case studies on East and Southern Africa, and draw broad conclusions that may generally reflect the role and impact of tourism-related FDI on the their economies. FDI in tourism has the potential to create employment, generate incomes, enable transfer of technology and skills and develop talents, as well as improve the standards of living of people in the areas where tourism operations are based. It can also be associated with costs and problems relating to the impact of tourism on the environment and on competition for scarce resources, and its social impact, especially on small and relatively remote populations.

A challenge in the country studies has been to separate out those effects that are related to tourism in general, from impacts that are specifically attributable to the role of FDI in tourism. The negative and positive impacts described above can be associated with both domestic and foreign investment. To the extent possible, however, the studies have attempted to isolate those impacts that are particularly related to foreign participation in the tourism industry, whether through foreign ownership of tourism resources or through foreign management.

The following broad conclusions drawn from the country studies, while made at the risk generalizing, nevertheless provide a snapshot of the key issues that can be addressed by policymakers in Africa in order to sustain/amplify the benefits from both tourism and FDI, and reduce the costs.

(i) ***At the macro level, FDI has significantly increased the scale of the tourism industry in most developing countries, thereby enabling the sector to make a*** ***greater contribution to development.***

The case studies have shown that potentially large benefits from TFDI can accrue to the respective domestic economies. In a number of respects, gains from TFDI may be larger than gains from FDI in other sectors, since some of the features of tourism enable it to respond effectively to local requirements. For instance, apart from gains at the macro level, TFDI is seen to contribute extensively to the welfare of people in host countries through employment creation, linkages with other economic sectors, skills and technology development, fostering efficiency through demonstration effects, improving market access and contribution to community development. Tourism can also have a positive influence on knowledge and culture, and can enable local communities to adopt more efficient ways of producing goods and services, thus reducing their poverty. However, these gains are not automatic; rather, they depend on the existence of a supportive policy and institutional environment and the responsiveness of all parties involved to specific requirements of the industry.

(ii) ***Although the micro-level gains from FDI in tourism are apparent, the evidence on the impact of foreign versus domestic investment is mixed – much depends on country context.***

While positive gains from FDI in tourism clearly exist in the studied countries, assessments of how much these gains differ from gains arising from domestic investments are somewhat mixed. There are some areas where transnational firms seem to offer a clear advantage over domestic firms in terms of their development impact, mostly because of their larger investments and scales of operation compared to local firms. However, in other locations, especially where the tourism industry is well established and has been in place for some time, there appears to be little or no difference in the impact of foreign versus local firms for some variables, because domestic firms are operating at the same level of quality or size as the foreign-owned ones. Instead, there is a more generalized impact of investment as a whole on tourism. For example, in some countries foreign firm have higher employment per scale of operation than local firms, while in others there appears to be little difference. Similarly, in some countries foreign firms are perceived to pay higher salaries than local competitors, while in others the opposite is true.

On the other hand, notwithstanding this observation, the findings support the argument that the presence of foreign establishments leads to improvements in ways of doing business for local firms through their demonstration effect – an important expectation in the general literature on FDI. Furthermore, the entry of foreign establishments appears to have been responsible for inducing greater responsiveness of governments to environmental concerns and to other requirements for the sector's development.

(iii)   *Assessments of the social impacts of FDI in tourism relate more to tourism in general, rather than to the role of foreign direct investment*

The social impacts of FDI in tourism are not as discernible as the economic impacts, and it is even more difficult to disaggregate the impacts that are related to tourism from those that are due to the FDI element. For example, either positive or negative assessments of the impact of tourism FDI may owe much to whether one believes that tourism per se, or exposure to foreign cultures is good (beneficial) or bad (harmful). Certainly, demonstration effects of foreign cultures

through international tourism may have an influence on local cultures, and the impact on society will depend entirely on how that society evaluates local versus foreign culture. Secondly, since tourism has both negative and positive social effects, it is not analytically easy to establish the net effect, let alone isolate that which can be attributed to FDI. At a practical level, it may be more useful simply to identify negative and positive effects so that the negative ones can be eschewed, and the positive ones advocated.

Examples of negative effects include, among others, environmental degradation (e.g. from activity in nature reserves) and prostitution, and the consequent spread of HIV/AIDS. Positive effects may include cultural exchange and exposure, sometimes with economic value (such as the Maasai of East Africa who charge a fee for demonstrating their culture to foreigners), and philanthropic activities or social corporate responsibility towards local communities. While the country case studies found that corporate responsibility effects appeared to be more significant with respect to foreign investors, all of the negative and positive effects described above can be associated with both domestic and foreign investors.

(iv)   *Deeper regional integration may be an effective avenue for realizing the potential of outward FDI*

The impact of outward FDI may differ from that of inward FDI in a number of ways, the most important being that outward FDI augments the linkage effects to the home country as well as within the host economies. However, there are only a few countries in SSA that have the capacity to invest in other countries. In the sample countries, only South Africa and Kenya provide strong evidence of this (although other countries have begun to show potential, such as TFDI from Mauritius to Comoros and Seychelles). The linkage to the home-country economy is not as apparent as that to the host economy; it depends on the strength of the supply capacity of the home economy. The key message from the case studies is that, given the lower transaction costs resulting from regional blocs, these blocs could play an important catalytic role in promoting outward FDI (e.g. Kenya in the EAC and COMESA, and South Africa in SACU and SADC), which in effect may bring be to its situation for the region as a whole.

Some policy recommendations for attracting and benefiting from FDI in tourism

There are two major policy recommendations arising from the case study findings and conclusions. The first and most important one is the need for more proactive promotion of FDI in the tourism industry alongside domestic investment Various countries compete to attract FDI, and many of them offer similar tourism-related characteristics, meaning that global competition is tough. Given that the findings of the country studies suggest that each dollar of FDI in tourism can have a significant development impact compared to other sectors, governments would be well advised to take the tourism industry seriously, and to devote particular policy attention to it.

The second finding is that, since the benefits of FDI are not automatic, and since tourism is a cross-cutting activity, further policies are almost always required for recipient economies to maximize the gains and minimize the detrimental effects from the international tourism industry. These may include deliberate policy initiatives aimed at improving the business operating environment (e.g. licensing, tax regime and factor markets), infrastructure (public utilities and transport) and supply capacity (e.g. entrepreneurship, market development), and reducing transaction costs (e.g. contract enforcement). Evidence from all the case study countries shows that gains from investment in the tourism sector can be enhanced by addressing existing challenges, most of which are structural in nature.

Taking the FDI environment, the East and Southern Africa country studies reinforced trends at the global level. UNCTAD (2007) shows that most countries are becoming increasingly open to FDI and are introducing policy changes that make domestic business conditions more favourable for foreign companies to enter and operate. The types of measures most frequently adopted have been related to sectoral and cross-sectoral liberalization, promotional efforts, operational measures and removal and barriers to FDI admission.

Although there is no "one-size-fits-all" policy for attracting TFDI, lessons can be drawn from the experiences of other countries, but governments need to tailor their approaches to the specific conditions prevailing in their own countries. The country case studies have identified barriers and obstacles that have held back TFDI flows, but also factors that have been responsible for promoting and attracting such flows. From these, the following recommendations can be drawn which may facilitate and attract TFDI and integrate it more effectively into national economies.

- Attractive tax and fiscal incentives, such as lower tax rates on profits, tax holidays and accelerated depreciation, especially in the early stages of tourism development, are frequently used and can be effective in many circumstances. However there is limited information about their relative costs and benefits, and these kinds of incentives are not the main factors that attract foreign investors.

- Financial incentives (e.g. access to capital) or granting exemptions from tariffs and customs duties on the import of inputs, materials and equipment needed for operational purposes are also frequently used; however as above, these are not among the main factors that attract foreign investors.

- Establishing an investment promotion agency to serve as a "one-stop shop" can help to simplify establishment procedures and facilitate investment undertakings; but this will not automatically ensure that tourism is promoted vis-à-vis other economic activities in which FDI is more prevalent.

- Most countries now offer ease of foreign exchange transactions, and free repatriation of invested capital, profits and dividends. It is likely to be very difficult to attract FDI without these minimum requirements.

- Restrictive and uncoordinated civil aviation policies can also be a barrier to FDI in tourism. The case studies show that there is a need to provide international air access and move towards an open skies policies.

- Improving tourism-related infrastructure is essential (e.g. road networks, provision of electricity, water and waste removal facilities). This is the role of government, and it is extremely unlikely that the private sector will undertake the necessary investment.

- A clear policy on access to land is needed (e.g. period of lease should be attractive and long enough; there should be clear indications of how land can be acquired).

- A comprehensive tourism policy (e.g. tourism master plan) and a vision for the tourism sector that fits tourism within the wider development framework is important.

- A regulatory framework/bodies should be established to deal with issues such as labour law, and competition policy needs to be stable, transparent and predictable.

- The government should support the tourism sector, including promoting tourism by actively engaging in marketing the country's tourist attractions.

- Civil and personal security for tourism in particular, but also for the economy more generally, should be improved.

- Good interconnectivity of mobile telephone systems, good Internet connections and telecommunications networks should be developed at a reasonable cost.

- Training institutions need to be created or expanded to improve local skills and develop a competent labour force.

- Limiting bureaucracy and reducing cumbersome procedures, for instance reducing delays in obtaining work and residence permits, creates a more favourable investment environment.

- Incentives can be provided to locate in a particular area that is in need of development.

- Strategies should aim at alleviating poverty through tourism (e.g. through community-based tourism and promotion of indigenous entrepreneurial capacity in tourism).

- Promoting small and medium-sized enterprises to encourage linkages (e.g. for procurement purposes) should be a priority.

- Dispute settlement mechanisms need to be transparent and fair. For example, investors should be assured the right to impartial arbitration in the event of a dispute, including with the government.

- An environment of political, social and economic stability is necessary for attracting FDI.

F. References

Bank of Uganda (2002). *Private Sector Capital Flows Survey 2001 Report,* Lampala: Bank of Uganda.

Castro L, Kraus C and de la Rocha M (2004). Regional trade integration in East Africa: the trade and revenue impacts of the planned East African Community Customs Union. *Africa Region Working Paper Series* No. 72, World Bank, Washington, DC.

Ikiara M (2001a). Policy framework of Kenya's tourism sector since independence and emerging policy concerns. KIPPRA Working Paper WP/02/2001. Nairobi, Kenya Institute for Public Policy Research & Analysis.

Ikiara M (2001b). Vision and long term development strategy for Kenya's tourism industry. KIPPRA Discussion Paper DP/07/2001. Nairobi, Kenya Institute for Public Policy Research & Analysis.

Obwona BM (1998). Determinants of FDI and their impact on economic growth in Uganda, Economic Policy Research Centre, Uganda.

Reinikka R and Collier P (2001). Uganda's recovery: the role of farms, firms and government, Fountain Publishers, Kampala, Uganda.

Tsikata Y (1999). Southern Africa: Trade, liberalisation, and implications for a free trade area. Paper prepared for the Annual Forum of the Trade and Industrial Policy Secretariat, Muldersdrift, South Africa

UNCTAD (2004). Prospects for foreign direct investment and the strategies of transnational corporations, 2004-2007, UNCTAD/ITE/IIT/2004/8.

UNCTAD (2007). *FDI in tourism: the development dimension.* UNCTAD Current Studies on FDI and Development No. 4, New York and Geneva.

Notes

[1]   This chapter is based on a contribution by Ramesh Durbarry, Associate Professor, Head of School, of the University of Technology, Mauritius and Josephat Kweka, Senior Research Fellow at the Economic and Social Research Foundation (ESRF), United Republic of Tanzania.

[2]   Between 1991 and March 1996, 1,788 properties were repossessed and returned to their original Asian owners (Obwona, 1998).

[3]   This is the latest year for which disaggregated data on the market and book value of the contribution of different sectors to total FDEI is available.

[4]   The joint-venture type of ownership is also common in the tourism industry. In some countries, some foreign companies are in joint ventures with the government (especially the previously State-owned enterprises), and others with the domestic private sector. In this context, majority shareholders are key in identifying the ownership category.

[5]   The International Organization for Standardization offers advice on how firms can minimize their negative effects on the environment (e.g. water or air quality).

Annex
Summary of main incentives and policies in five East and Southern African countries

Country	Fiscal Incentives	Financial incentives	Other incentives	Investment policy	Legislative ct(s)	Investment promotion institution(s)
Mauritius	Corporate tax of 15% (instead of 30%) Dividends are exempt from income tax for 10 years from the day the hotel's operations begin. Exemption from payment of customs duty on the importation of an approved list of equipment. Free repatriation of invested capital, profit and dividends	Term loans and overdrafts at preferential rates.	Annual allowances calculated on a reducing balance basis instead of a straight-line basis. The rate for hotel buildings is 30%.	A Hotel Development Certificate or Hotel Management Service Certificate offers specific benefits The main criteria are: missing The minimum number of rooms for a foreign-owned company should be 100. No hotel projects should exceed 200 rooms. Mauritian-owned hotel should have at least 60 rooms In resort hotels, the promoter should have at least 2.5 acres of land. For foreign-owned hotels, the area of land must not be less than 10 acres. The room employment ratio should be about 1:1. The cost of one room should be at least Rs 700, 000 (1990 estimate). For other tourism-related activities, the initial investment should not be less than Rs 10 millions.	Development Incentives Act (1974) Hotel Management Incentive Act (1982) Investment Promotion Act (2000) Business Facilitation Act (2006) The Hotel Management (Incentive) Act was repealed in 2006.	Board of Investment (BOI)

Country	Fiscal incentives	Financial incentives	Other incentives	Investment policy	Legislative Act(s)	Investment promotion institution(s)
Botswana	Businesses are subject to a two-tier income tax system comprising of 15% basic company tax (guaranteed until 2020) and 10% additional company tax. Dividend withholding tax (of 15% for residents and non-residents) can be credited against additional company tax.			Foreign companies' minimum investment should be $200,000. If investing as a joint venture with local citizens, the sum is reduced to $100,000. The number of foreign investors in this arrangement is limited to two. Any additional foreign shareholder will have to invest another $100,000. Certain activities are reserved for citizens only	The Foreign Investment Code (2002)	Botswana Export Development and Investment Authority (BEDIA)
Kenya	Almost standard across all sectors, except in EPZs			Foreigners must invest a minimum of $100,000 (amended in Jan. 2006 from $500,000) Domestic investors seeking an Investment Certificate must invest at least 5 million Kenyan shillings ($65,000)	Investment Promotion Act (2004)	Kenya Investment Authority (KIA)

Country	Fiscal incentives	Financial incentives	Other incentives	Investment policy	Legislative Act(s)	Investment promotion institution(s)
Uganda	• Initial allowances of 50%-70% on plant and machinery depending on location; • Initial 25% per year allowance on start up costs for 4 years • 20% initial allowance on hotel and industrial buildings • 5% depreciation rates for hotels, industrial buildings and hospitals • Zero tax rat on import of plants and machinery • Uniform corporate tax of 30% • Possible VAT (18%) deferral.		Non-citizens can lease land for up to 99 years. No restrictions on the number of expatriates that can be hired by the firm	Foreign investors require a minimum of $100,000 in planned investment in order to secure an investment licence from Uganda Investment Authority. For domestic investors, the minimum requirement is $50,000. Foreign investors who have invested more than $500,000 can repatriate their investments and dividends and receive foreign exchange to pay back debts incurred in the business.	Uganda's Incentive Allowance Scheme (1997) The Investment Code 1991 Tourism Policy (2003)	Uganda Investment Authority

Country	Fiscal incentives	Financial incentives	Other incentives	Investment policy	Legislative Act(s)	Investment promotion institution(s)
Tanzania, United Rep. of	Exemption from customs and import duties and other similar taxes on capital goods such as machinery, equipment, raw materials, fuel, vehicles and other goods necessary and exclusively required during the construction period. Consideration of tax holidays for approved projects Exemption of import duty on goods necessary for use by expatriates Income-tax exemption for investors who have made a declaration for reinvestment at the proposed stage up to the first three years. Up to 100% repatriation of profits Tax holiday until the recovery of capital, which can be written off at the rates of 50% in the first year of operation, and 25% in the second and third years.		Investment guarantees, access to land, the right to transfer funds abroad and employ up to five expatriates Waiver of land rent during construction period	Minimum levels of investment for foreign investors $300,000 and for domestic investors $100,000. If a foreign firm wants To establish a hotel in Zanzibar, the minimum investment requirement for a foreign firm is $4 million.	Tanzania Investment Act 1997 and the Zanzibar New Investment Policy enacted in 2001	Tanzania Investment Centre (TIC) on the mainland, and Zanzibar Investment Promotion Agency (ZIPA)

PART B
COUNTRY CASE STUDIES

II. Botswana country case study[1]

Executive summary

The tourism sector in Botswana has emerged as a major economic activity, and is considered, along with some other sectors, as having the potential to contribute to growth and diversification of the economy and generate socio-economic benefits. For example, within this industry, hotels and restaurants created employment opportunities for 12,729 people out of a total of 449,235 people employed in the formal sector (Household Income Expenditure Survey, 2002/03). The tourism sector has experienced tremendous growth in recent years, with the number of tourist arrivals increasing from 1,396,111 in 1988 to 2,066,599 in 2003. A large proportion of these visitors (72 per cent) were from neighbouring countries (Namibia, South Africa, Zambia and Zimbabwe), their main purpose being to visit friends and relatives. Hence, their expenditure on accommodation, food and drink, transport and recreation was lower than that spent on shopping.

Despite the growth in tourist arrivals, the tourism sector has remained susceptible to international crises. For instance, global events in 2001such as the attack on the World Trade Center in New York (referred to as 9/11), the depreciation of the dollar, the outbreak of severe acute respiratory syndrome (SARS), and political instability in Zimbabwe resulted in a decline in the number of tourist arrivals in Botswana from all its source markets (Africa, North America, Asia and the Pacific, and Europe).

Botswana has been open to foreign direct investment (FDI), including in the tourism industry, recognizing its potential for creating employment and fostering economic growth. The lodges, hotels and camps interviewed in the survey conducted for this study employed a total of 1,765 persons, which is roughly 10 per cent of the total employment in this sector. The largest establishment, which is a joint venture, employed 260 people, while the smallest establishment employed 4. Due to their larger size, foreign-owned establishments and joint ventures employed more personnel (a total of 803 and 605 respectively) than locally owned establishments (a total of 357). Thus developing the tourism sector would be of great benefit to the economy, since the sector has the potential to create further employment at all skill levels. However, the degree to which this potential can be realized depends on the extent to which linkages with the local economy can be promoted. In line with the Government's efforts to empower its citizens, an increasing number of locally owned businesses have been developing over time compared to a declining trend in new foreign-owned and joint-venture investments in the sample analysed. Around 66 per cent of the businesses in the sample that were established after 1998 were domestically owned, signifying that domestic participation in this sector is a relatively new phenomenon.

The survey results also showed signs of linkages between tourism establishments and local wholesalers, retailers and small enterprises. Most of the products used in these establishments (e.g. food, beverages, soaps and furniture) were purchased locally. In addition, there were signs of spillovers to domestic companies such as tour operators.

A. Introduction

1.   Background

Botswana's economy depends mainly on diamonds, which account for 33 per cent of GDP, 80 per cent of government revenue and 80 per cent of export earnings. The Government has recognized the urgent need to diversify the economy away from diamonds. Although diamonds are directly responsible for immense economic success, this industry employs a relatively small proportion of the population, as production is capital-intensive in nature. The need for economic diversification was reflected in the theme of the 8th National Development Plan (NDP) and is also strongly advocated in the 9th NDP.

It is generally believed that Botswana, with its diverse wildlife and still pristine natural environment, has a comparative advantage in tourism. In 2002, tourism accounted for 5 per cent of GDP and 8 per cent of non-mining GDP. The 9th National Development Plan identifies this industry as having the potential to contribute to growth and diversification of the economy and to generate socio-economic benefits. The Household Income Expenditure Survey (HIES) of 2002/03 revealed that hotels and restaurants (a segment of the tourism industry) provided employment for 12,729 people out of a total of 449,235 people employed in the formal sector in the country, or only 3 per cent. Tourism is particularly important as it is labour-intensive and offers job opportunities for both skilled and semi-skilled personnel. Obtaining hospitality skills is not difficult, and people can be easily trained. Moreover, unlike the mineral sector, tourism is likely to have considerable spillover benefits for local communities, contributing thereby to poverty reduction. It is also preferred, because the agricultural sector, on which most Batswana depend, is prone to constant

droughts that adversely affect production. The Government has tried to expand the manufacturing sector, but with only marginal success owing to factors such as the small size of the domestic market, low labour productivity, and high utility and transport costs.

Between 1998 and 2003, the tourism industry experienced tremendous growth, with the number of tourist arrivals increasing from 1,396,111 to 2,066,599, an average growth rate of 6.7 per cent per annum. The Botswana Tourism Master Plan estimated that 4.5 per cent of exports of goods and services were from the tourism industry. Despite this, there was a slight decline in the growth of tourism between 2001 and 2003, due mainly to global events such as the attack on the World Trade Center in New York in September 2001, the depreciation of the dollar and political instability in Zimbabwe. Given the importance of tourism, measures need to be taken to reverse this decline and to exploit the opportunity for increasing tourist numbers to the region, as a result of the 2010 World Cup to be hosted by South Africa. Foreign direct investment (FDI) in tourism is seen as a means of enhancing growth. In general Botswana has been open to FDI and has recognized its ability to contribute to employment and foster economic growth. This study examines the trends, patterns and impacts of FDI in tourism with the view to recommending policies that could foster FDI growth in this industry.

2.   Structure of this case study

This study is structured as follows: section II discusses the tourism profile, section III deals with the role and impact of FDI in tourism, and the last section discusses FDI policies and other relevant policies that affect the tourism sector.

B. Tourism profile

1. Tourism assets

Botswana is richly endowed with outstanding and varied natural features that make it unique in Africa and draw visitors from many parts of the world. Growth of the country's tourism industry has been based on its wildlife and wilderness areas, which constitute outstanding assets. The country's wildlife is regarded as one of the best in Africa, both in terms of variety and numbers (BTDP, 2000). Apart from wildlife, Botswana offers an experience of the wilderness – vast tracts of land untouched by modern developments – which tourists find very attractive. National parks and game reserves cover 17 per cent of Botswan's total land area, and an additional 22 per cent has been designated as wildlife management areas (WMAs) where wildlife conservation is the primary form of land use.

The Okavango Delta is the largest inland wetland habitat of its kind in the world. This unique ecosystem covers 15,000 square kilometres of the African wilderness, where crystalline waters appear to float upon the desert. The Moremi Game Reserve, an African wildlife paradise that covers one third of the Okavango Delta, is the major tourist attraction due to its stunning beauty and abundant wildlife. Another is the Chobe National Park known for its spectacular river setting and large number of elephants (estimated at 60,000), hippos, lions and other species. The Okavango Delta and the Chobe National Park attract a significant number of international tourists. Visits to these destinations are often combined with a visit to Victoria Falls in neighbouring Zimbabwe. In 1998, of the 159,652 visits made to the national parks and game reserves, Chobe National Park attracted 98,045 visitors (61 per cent of the total),

while the Okavango Delta and/or Moremi Game Reserve received 49,556 visitors (31 per cent) (BTDP, 2000). Other national parks and game reserves include the Central Kalahari Game Reserve (CKGR), Khutse Game Reserve, Makgadikgadi and Nxai Pan National Parks, as well as the Kgalagadi Trans Frontier Park. Less known than the Okavango Delta and the Chobe National Park, they received fewer visitors (only 8 per cent) in 1998. Tourist activities in the national parks and game reserves include fishing, hunting, game viewing or game drives, birdwatching, boat cruises and nature walks. These activities have been on the increase and show considerable potential for further growth if appropriate steps are taken to promote them.

There has been a proliferation of camps and/or safari operators and fishing activity in the Okavango Delta, with over 60 camps in the Okavango Delta alone. Unless strict regulations are imposed, this could lead to deterioration and the eventual disappearance of the country's most important tourism product. To prevent this, the Ministry of Tourism has placed considerable emphasis on development strategies for conservation of the country's natural resources. More specifically, the Department of Wildlife and National Parks (DWNP), which is responsible for regulation and management of the wildlife and national parks, has developed measures such as the Controlled Hunting Areas system, Wildlife Management Areas system and the utilization of wildlife within them. These measures are intended to promote sustainable use of these resources and a fair distribution among the users, particularly bearing in mind the needs of the rural people. The large herds of game found in the national parks or game reserves wander into areas where hunting is permitted, thus rendering the resources accessible to hunters.

Apart from the outstanding wildlife and wilderness in the northern part of Botswana, the country offers a limited number of natural tourist attractions such as the Tsodilo Hills, Gcwihaba Cravens and the Aha Hills. Cultural, archaeological and historical attractions, as well as folklore, music, dance, handicrafts and cuisine, are not at present significant components of the tourism product.

2. Seasonality

An examination of monthly data on total arrivals in Botswana in 2003 presents an unclear picture of the seasonality of tourism in the country. Nevertheless, broadly, it seems that the third quarter of the year marks the peak season for holiday/tourist visitors, with the highest number arriving in September (34,762 visitors compared to 22,468 visitors in August) (figure 1). However, this same period showed the lowest number of arrivals for those visiting friends and relatives: these kinds of visitors declined drastically (by 79 per cent) in September 2003 to 9,658 from 45,805 visitors in August before rising more than four times to 45,614 visitors in October. The peak period for business travellers to the country was between June and August.

Figure 1. Seasonality of tourist arrivals in Botswana, by purpose of visit, 2003

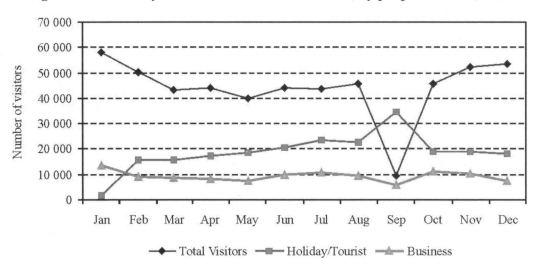

3. Tourists by country of origin and purpose of visit

Tourist arrivals in Botswana more than doubled between 1994 and 2003, rising from 988,657 visitors to 2.1 million. However, in 2001, there was a sharp decline to 1.7 million visitors from 2.2 million in 2000 (a 19 per cent fall). This was largely attributable to the terrorist attacks in the United States in 2001, which resulted in a substantial fall in global travel during the period 2001–2003. In addition, the outbreak of severe acute respiratory syndrome (SARS), which was a major threat worldwide, also had a significant negative impact on the tourism industry as many people cut travelling for fear of contracting the disease. Botswana experienced a decline in visitor numbers from all its source markets (Africa, Europe, America, Asia and the Pacific) in 2001 (figure 2). Subsequently, though, the number of tourist arrivals from these regions increased in 2002 and 2003, except those from North America who continued to stay away.

Figure 2. Tourists arrivals by region of origin, 1994–2003

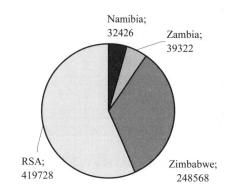

The African region accounted for 88.7 per cent (1.8 million visitors) of the total number of tourist arrivals in Botswana between 1994 and 2003 (figure 2), followed by Europe (3.3 per cent or 68,251 visitors), and the rest were from North America (1.4 per cent, or 28,600 visitors), Asia (0.5 per cent, or 9,854 visitors) and Oceania or the Pacific (0.4 per cent, or 9,067 visitors).

A further distinction by region shows that intraregional arrivals accounted for by far the largest number of visitors to Botswana. In 2003, 72 per cent (1.5 million visitors) of all arrivals were from neighbouring countries, mostly from South Africa and Zimbabwe, followed by Zambia and Namibia. Tourist arrivals from Zimbabwe more than doubled between 1994 and 2003, rising from 248,568 visitors in 1994 to 658,657 in 2003, while those from South Africa grew by 55 per cent, from 419,728 to 648,798 visitors over the same period (figures 3a and 3b).

Regarding visitors from outside Southern Africa, in 2003 the United States led with 24,645 visitors, followed by the United Kingdom (20,626 visitors) and Germany (13,435 visitors). However, Botswana's main source market was Africa.

Figure 3a: Intraregional tourist arrivals, 1994

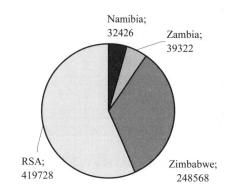

Figure 3b: Intraregional tourist arrivals, 2003

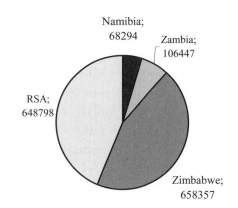

The main purpose was to visit friends and relatives, which in 2003 accounted for 25.6 per cent of total arrivals. A large proportion of such visitors were from Zimbabwe (65.5 per cent) and South Africa (24.6 per cent), while the remaining were from other African countries as well as from other regions of the world. Business visitors accounted for 5.4 per cent, and holidaymakers for 10.9 per cent, while 10.5 per cent were in transit. The remainder were those seeking employment, diplomats and students. South Africans also constituted a large share of holiday and business visitors in 2003 (47.9 per cent and 63.7 per cent respectively), while Zimbabwean holidaymakers and business visitors accounted for 21.1 per cent and 18.1 per cent respectively. European and American visitors were mainly holidaymakers.

Table 1. Tourists arrivals by country of origin and purpose of entry, 2003

	Country of Residence	Returning Resident	Prospective Resident	Seeking Employment	Employment	Visitor	Holiday/ Tourist	Business	In Transit	Diplomat	Student	Other	Unknown	Total
Africa	Zimbabwe	3784	37686	4399	6868	346908	47759	20087	42373	1932	600	106811	39150	**658357**
	South Africa	4746	20933	10880	20078	130081	108351	70730	91645	2746	657	127468	60483	**648798**
	Zambia	780	3139	4046	1101	12976	5508	4276	23752	380	130	34071	16288	**106447**
	Namibia	270	1130	3039	988	6897	3040	1357	36243	181	163	7276	7710	**68294**
	Other Africa	235476	6196	795	16135	7707	5433	3989	3019	1016	1172	34956	34487	**350381**
	Total Africa	245056	69084	23159	45170	504569	170091	100439	197032	6255	2722	310582	158118	**1832277**
Europe	UK	80	464	183	2757	2196	9779	1791	1358	80	134	1295	509	**20626**
	Germany	20	181	354	3736	717	4677	359	1662	22	30	1050	627	**13435**
	Netherlands	40	91	81	2096	464	3303	187	453	22	20	827	539	**8123**
	France	20	70	52	1247	183	2228	181	276	41	0	367	195	**4860**
	Italy	0	42	72	1073	103	1895	54	233	10	10	320	266	**4078**
	Spain	0	0	50	790	30	1835	71	323	0	1	253	316	**3669**
	Other Europe	51	200	175	3294	1000	4933	537	1119	40	50	1437	624	**13460**
	Total Europe	211	1048	967	14993	4693	28650	3180	5424	215	245	5549	3076	**68251**
America	USA	90	493	483	8573	1497	7787	578	1588	250	231	2266	809	**24645**
	Canada	20	110	53	683	223	1,222	93	174	10	-	174	61	**2,823**
	Other America	1	0	10	250	50	420	30	91	0	10	230	40	**1132**
	Total America	111	603	546	9506	1770	9429	701	1853	260	241	2670	910	**28600**
Asia	Japan	10	10	10	880	300	1617	163	121	0	0	270	140	**3521**
	India	110	180	0	261	431	334	180	30	30	0	420	101	**2077**
	China	30	30	10	240	70	351	190	21	50	0	270	70	**1332**
	Other Asia	30	110	20	581	322	1016	121	82	0	0	461	181	**2924**
	Total Asia	180	330	40	1962	1123	3318	654	254	80	0	1421	492	**9854**
	Unknown	4121	5528	1911	5202	16734	10837	5393	12583	434	240	36804	18783	**118570**
	Total	249689	76714	26756	78533	529423	226167	110960	217830	7264	3458	358142	181583	**2066519**

Source: Central Statistics Office, 2003.

Even though most arrivals in 2003 were from African countries, in terms of the share of revenue generated the picture is very different. Overseas tourists spent an average of 350 pula per day while those from African countries spent an average of 100 pula per day, and Zimbabweans, who constituted the largest share of arrivals, spent an average of only 50 pula per day. It follows from this that the sector is more dependent on overseas tourists than African tourists for revenue generation. By purpose of visit, revenue generated from holidaymakers accounted for 49 per cent of the total income generated from tourists, even though they constituted only 23 per cent of the total number of visitors. Since most arrivals from overseas visit for holiday purposes, while those from African countries are either on family visits or on business, it follows that overseas visitors generated most of the revenue from tourism.

Table 2. Purpose of visit and share of revenue by purpose of visit, 2003 (%)

Purpose of visit	Share in total arrivals	Share of tourism-generated revenues
Family visits	66	31
Business	11	20
Holiday	23	49
Total	100	100

4. Arrivals by mode of transport

a. *Entry by road*

Since Botswana is a landlocked country surrounded by South Africa,

Namibia, Zambia and Zimbabwe, access by road is of crucial importance. The available data for the period 1994 to 2003 indicate that Botswana tourism is best served by road transport, followed by air (figure 4). The number of tourist arrivals by road rose from 899,349 visitors in 1994 to 1.9 million in 2003 – a 116 per cent growth. This increase is attributable to an improved road network, especially high-quality, tarred and well-maintained roads that connect major centres in the country and also link Botswana with its neighbouring countries. This has led to an increase in the number of tour operators that operate scheduled services across the borders into South Africa, Zambia and Zimbabwe. Another contributing factor is the improved public transport (bus) services. Unlike in the 1970s and 1980s, public transport now runs on time schedules, which makes it more convenient to use. Moreover, the comfort and additional features (television, radio and refreshments) offered in these buses has led travellers to prefer them to either rail or air services.

The country has more than 20 border crossings connecting it with its neighbours, the most frequently used being Tlokweng, Ramatlabana, Martin's Drift and Pioneer Gate (bordering South Africa), Kazungila Road and Ramokgwebana (bordering Zimbabwe) and Mamuno (bordering Namibia). Most international tourists gain access to Botswana by road through these land border posts.

Figure 4. Tourist arrivals by mode of travel, 1994–2003

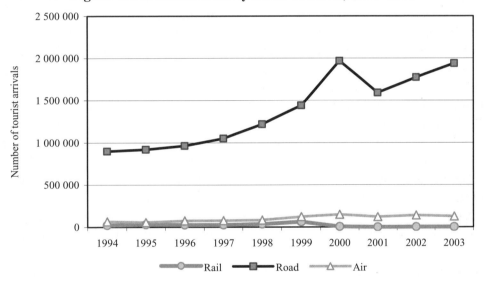

b. *Entry by air*

Air services in Botswana are dominated by Air Botswana, the national airline, which operates international scheduled services to Johannesburg (South Africa), Harare (Zimbabwe) and Windhoek (Namibia). Its current domestic network covers Gaborone, Francistown, Maun (gateway to the Okavango Delta and Moremi Game Reserve), Kasane (gateway to the Chobe National Park and the spectacular natural attractions of Namibia-Windhoek) and Limpopo Valley Airfield (gateway to the Tuli Block bordering South Africa and Zimbabwe).

The most commonly used airports for entry are Sir Seretse Khama Airport in Gaborone (which is the main point of entry), Maun Airport and the Selibe Phikwe and Sowa Airstrips. The principal source and destination of flights to and from Sir Seretse Khama Airport is Johannesburg, but since there is no international airline serving that airport, all overseas visitors are obliged to use other gateways, mainly Johannesburg in South Africa. Sir Seretse Khama Airport also serves domestic flights to other airports in the country, mainly the Francistown, Maun and Kasane airports.

A major development in air travel services by Air Botswana was the introduction of a direct flight between Maun and Cape Town in October 2004, which links the Okavango Delta in northern Botswana to the Cape (in South Africa), two of the premier tourism destinations in Africa. The introduction of this prime route gives tourists a highly attractive option of connecting to the Okavango Delta directly, instead of flying via Johannesburg.

The number of tourist arrivals by air increased by 92 per cent, from 65,478 in 1994 to 126,020 in 2003. Sir Seretse Khama airport received the largest proportion of tourists in 2003 (74,220), followed by Kasane Airport (22,340), Maun (18,660), Sowa Airstrip (8,760), Selibe Phikwe (4,820) and Francistown (1,000). Travelling by air into and within Botswana is considered very expensive compared to other countries, hence most tourists in the region prefer road transport.

The Government of Botswana is faced with the challenge of privatizing Air Botswana, which is expected to improve its operational efficiency and enhance competitiveness in light of the gradually intensifying competition in the aviation market.

c.   Rail transport

Botswana has one main rail track that runs from Lobatse to Francistown. All of its rail services are operated by Botswana Railways. The trains have first and second class accommodation. Although travelling by rail is the cheapest mode of transport in Botswana compared to road and air transport, tourists do not use it much. The number of visitors into the country by rail transport has fallen drastically since 2000, from 62,242 visitors in 1999 to as low as 722 in 2001 before rising slightly to 1,800 visitors in 2003. The decline is attributable to the discontinuing by South African Railways of the transnational train (known as Blue Train) services from Johannesburg (South Africa) to Bulawayo (Zimbabwe) via Botswana. Following this disruption, in early 2000 Zimbabwe constructed a railway line connecting it directly to South Africa. This diverted business away from Botswana Railways. In addition, the improved road network has made road travel more time-efficient than rail travel (with the train usually arriving two to three hours later than buses, especially for long distances), and this, combined with the comfort and additional features introduced in buses, has resulted in travellers preferring them to rail transport. However, the reintroduction of a passenger train between Francistown and Bulawayo in 2006 by Botswana Railways and Zimbabwean Railways is expected to change the situation. Furthermore, other railway links are under negotiation between Botswana and South African railways. In addition to these links, the construction of a railway-line connecting Botswana and Namibia will be of further benefit to Botswana's tourism industry.

C. The role and impact of FDI in tourism

1. FDI trends in the tourism sector

FDI inflows into Botswana increased from 3.5 million pula in 1997 to 10.4 million pula in 2001 followed by a continuous decline that culminated in 4.2 million pula in 2004. However, the trend for FDI in tourism (hospitality) has shown a different pattern. Except for the years 2000 and 2004 tourism-related FDI has generally displayed an upward increase.[2] This seemingly consistent increase notwithstanding, the share of FDI on tourism in the total national FDI stock is only 2 per cent. Given that tourism contributes 3–8 per cent to GDP, this might suggest that a considerable proportion of investment in tourism is funded from internal resources. Trends observed in figure 5 seem to give credence to this hypothesis, which is elaborated on below. However, it would appear that, apart from the outlier year, the rate of growth of FDI in tourism has been solid.

The fact that this industry's share in total inward FDI is almost negligible (figure 5) while the number of tourist enterprises has risen dramatically could be explained partly by the Financial Assistance Policy (FAP) which was implemented by the Botswana Government in the late 1990s and early 2000. This policy, which allowed both foreign and local investors in tourism, among other selected sectors, to receive grants from the Government, clearly gave a boost to investment in tourism (table 3). It must also have given a boost to FDI in general since foreign firms had to bring in some form of equity in order to benefit from the government grant. One noteworthy feature was that between 1998 and 2000 domestic participation in the sector was low compared to participation

by joint ventures and foreign investors. However after 2001 domestic participation shot up and far exceeded these other sources. This was probably a result of the Government's discontinuance of the FAP and the establishment of the Citizen Entrepreneurial Development Agency (CEDA), which discriminated against foreigners. In addition, financial assistance changed from grants to soft loans. It can therefore be concluded that government policy through both FAP and CEDA had a strong impact on the stocks and flows of FDI in tourism.

Table 3. Stock of FDI by industry in Botswana, 1997–2004 (million pula)

Industry	1997	1998	1999	2000	2001	2002	2003	2004
Mining	2 705	4 902	5 524	7 792	8 412	5 615	5 223	2 494
Manufacturing	246	333	273	343	274	280	295	151
Finance	228	226	523	619	729	803	873	931
Retail and wholesale	157	392	670	773	651	756	826	239
Electricity, gas and water	7	8	-	-	-	19	27	39
Real estate and business services	65	112	144	161	115	104	94	93
Transport, storage and communications	31	47	43	105	96	155	154	134
Construction	31	30	8	16	23	13	10	28
Hospitality	44	60	83	17	135	129	154	57
Other	17	50	80	-	1 10	1	1	38
Total	3 529	6 160	7 348	9 826	435	7 876	7 643	4 204

Source: Bank of Botswana, 1998-2005

The share of FDI stock in tourism in total FDI stock ranged mainly between 0.2 per cent and 2 per cent between 1997 and 2004 (figure 5). The lowest figure was recorded in 2000 and the highest in 2003. With the exception of the years 1998 and 2000, the share of FDI in tourism in total FDI generally experienced an upward trend.

Figure 5. Share of FDI in the hospitality industry in total inward FDI, 1997–2004 (%)

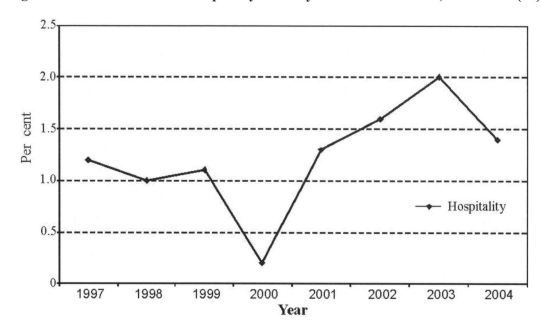

Although the contribution of FDI in tourism remained fairly constant between 1997 and 2004, the growth rates of FDI inflows in the tourism industry fluctuated considerably (table 4), with negative growth rates in 2000, 2002 and 2004.

Table 4. Annual growth rates of FDI in the hospitality industry, 1998–2004

Year	Growth rates
1998	36
1999	38
2000	-80
2001	694
2002	-4
2003	19
2004	-63

As mentioned above, data from the Department of Tourism (table 5), indicate that locally owned establishments have dominated the tourism market since 2002. And while the number of all types of establishments grew each year, the number of locally owned ones increased at a greater rate than joint ventures and foreign-owned establishments.

Table 5. Number of tourist establishments by ownership, 1998–2006

Year	Locally-owned	Joint ventures	Foreign-owned	Total
1998	47	74	81	202
1999	84	99	97	280
2000	102	101	128	331
2001	141	110	140	391
2002	178	116	148	442
2003	202	135	168	505
2004	225	138	179	542
2005	223	129	170	522
2006	247	128	176	551

2. Characteristics of the sample

The tourism industry in Botswana is made up mainly of hotels, lodges and camps that provide accommodation to tourists, and of tour operators that provide organized tours for wildlife experience and similar activities. Table 6 below gives a breakdown of the number and types of tourism establishments and services in the country and those that were interviewed in the survey. Botswana is currently working on its grading system and therefore does not yet have a clear categorization of its hotels. It is however estimated that of the 18 hotels, 7 are equivalent to four stars and above, and 5 of these were included in the survey.

Table 6. Number and sample of tourism services

Type of tourism service	Total number	Survey sample
Hotels	18	8
Lodges	89	11
Guest houses	32	0
Camps	61	5
Safaris	8	8
Motels	9	1
Inns	7	2
Trails & nature reserves	5	0
Other forms of accommodation	25	0
Travel agents and tour operators	109	4
Air charters	12	2
Total	**375**	**42**

Source: *Bajanala*: *A Tourist Guide to Botswana,* Department of Tourism (2004).

For the purpose of the survey, 42 establishments were approached, of which 14 were tour operators and safari organizers and the rest were hotels, lodges and camps. Some types of establishments presented in the table were not included in the survey because their proportion to the entire number was small. Most of the hotels, lodges and camps in the sample were located in Maun (37 per cent), 29.6 per cent in Gaborone, 18.5 per cent in Kasane and 14.8 per cent in Francistown. Also, the sample consisted mainly of upmarket and middle market leisure hotels, which represented 40.7 per cent and 42.1 per cent, respectively, of the total number in the sample. Of the 29 lodges, camps and hotels interviewed, 31.8 per cent were domestic-owned, 36.4 per cent were foreign-owned and 31.8 per cent were joint ventures. Despite the fact that accommodation facilities were predominantly foreign-

owned, spillovers and linkages to other services that are predominantly domestic-owned, such as tour operators, should not be underestimated. A general limitation to the study was the lack of data for the amounts invested within each category. The choice of the sample was mainly influenced by the participation of foreign investors in particular areas. For example, while table 6 shows a significant number of guest houses and lodges, foreign investors are mainly attracted to wildlife areas and hence rarely invest in guest houses. However, they actively participate in camps, which are spread out across the country, but due to budgetary limitations it was difficult to cover most of them. Therefore those areas were sampled where both local and foreign investors operated and that were accessible.

Table 7. Size of establishments by ownership

Size	Locally owned (%)	Foreign-owned (%)	Joint ventures (%)	Total (%)
Small (< 18 rooms)	45	50	0	33
Medium (19 – 51 rooms)	36	25	38	33
Large (> 51 rooms)	18	25	63	33
Total	**100**	**100**	**100**	**100**

For the purposes of this study, large-scale establishments are defined as establishments with more than 51 rooms, medium establishments are those with 19–51 rooms and small establishments have less than 18 rooms. Joint-venture companies own mainly large-scale establishments, while foreign and local establishments are predominantly small scale (table 7). And a greater proportion of foreign-owned establishments are small scale compared to the local establishments. Unlike other countries, in Botswana the Government has never formally owned any hotels; they have always been in the hands of the private sector.

FDI in tourism focuses on high-value tourism and can thus be differentiated from local businesses that tend to provide services to low-value sectors. The data collected indicated that 75 per cent of foreign-owned establishments and 50 per cent of joint ventures targeted the upper segment of the market, compared to only 11.1 per cent of locally owned establishments. On the other hand, 66.7 per cent of local establishments and only 12.5 per cent of foreign ones targeted the middle market segment. Foreign-owned and joint-venture establishments were found predominantly around Maun, catering to high-value, low-volume tourism within the Okavango Delta, where 62.5 per cent of the foreign-owned and 37.5 per cent of joint-venture establishments were located. There was a larger proportion of locally owned establishments in urban areas catering mainly to domestic or regional tourists. Half of all foreign-owned investments were in camps, while 85.7 per cent of local investments were in lodges. Another indicator examined was the average revenue and length of stay in different establishments by ownership. The study revealed that while foreign-owned establishments charged an average of 7,341.64 pula per person and the average length of stay per visitor was 3.8 days, local businesses charged only 1,265 pula and the average length of stay was 3 days. The length of stay of tourists at foreign establishments was longer due to the location of most foreign-owned establishments in destinations like Maun and Kasane, which target holiday tourists, while locally owned establishments seemed to attract mainly business tourists who tend to stay for a shorter period. Also a number of foreign-owned establishments are camps set up for hunting purposes and tourists who come for this activity generally stay longer.

An interesting trend displayed by the data collected is that the number of new locally owned establishments has been increasing over time compared to foreign-owned establishments and joint ventures (table 8). This might reflect a process of "catching-up" of Batswana-owned businesses. About 66 per cent of the establishments that were set up after 1998 are 100 per cent locally owned. The entry of local investors into the industry has increased since 1998, indicating that their interest in the industry has developed only recently. Some interviewees noted that the lack of entrepreneurial skills in operating these establishments partly explained the low number of domestic-owned firms in the early years. A few of the domestic-owned firms surveyed, were operated by locals who had acquired skills by working in other tourism establishments.

Table 8. Year of construction of establishment by ownership

Year of construction	Locally owned (%)	Foreign-owned (%)	Joint venture (%)	Total
Before independence	9	0	29	38
1968–1980	9	38	14	61
1980–1999	36	38	57	131
2000–2004	45	25	0	70

Most of the foreign-owned establishments (75 per cent) operate in the country independently, with no affiliations with establishments in their home country. Chain hotels and lodges operate in Botswana mainly as joint ventures (with 57.1 per cent foreign or domestic ownership). About 86 per cent of chain hotels surveyed, which all happened to be joint ventures, indicated that they operated under a management agreement. Amongst these was the Cresta-Marakanelo Group, a joint venture between Zimbabwean and local shareholders. It manages a number of hotels throughout the country that are owned by Botswana Development Corporations (BDC), which is wholly owned by the Botswana Government. These hotels are the largest chain in the country, with 7 of the 18 hotels being managed under this umbrella.

Another hotel chain interviewed was the Gaborone Sun, which is part of the South African Sun International chain of hotels, which has a number of affiliated hotels and lodges in the region. The Grand Palm, Metcourt Inn and Mondior Summit are also part of a chain owned by the South African Mondior company. The Chobe Marina Lodge in Kasane is a domestically owned lodge that is being operated by a foreign-owned company under a management contract – the only lodge in the sample operating under this kind of an arrangement. The Chobe Game Lodge is an upmarket hotel that belongs to an entity listed on the stock market with two major shareholders – a Motswana (a south African people which makes up a large part of the population of Botswana, also referred to as Tswana) and a local citizen. All local establishments that were interviewed were independent companies.

One of the major assets that FDI brings into Botswana seems to be market access, with 49 per cent of tourists in foreign-owned establishments being booked through foreign tour operators or travel agents, compared with only 12 per cent in local establishments and 18 per cent in joint ventures. Foreign-owned establishments also attract far more visitors for holiday purposes than do domestic-owned enterprises or joint ventures.

Analysing sales and profits of establishments was difficult as more than half of the establishments surveyed did not provide these figures. Table 9 below gives an idea of profits and sales realized by companies that did respond. None of the joint ventures in the sample were able to break down their profits by components such as accommodation, conferences and

restaurants. Conferences normally help augment revenue during the off-peak season, especially for joint ventures located in towns.

Table 9. Average sales and profits by ownership of establishment (in thousand pula)

	Locally owned	Foreign -owned	Joint venture
Total annual sales/turnover	2 417	2 220	7 158
Sales/room ratio	73	43	87
Total profits	405	600	1 469
Profit/room ratio	12	12	18

The survey found that joint ventures realized the largest sales and profits, followed by locally owned and foreign-owned companies. They also had the highest profits/room and sales/room ratios. The occupancy rate was lowest for locally owned establishments, yet their sales/room ratio was greater than that of foreign-owned establishments while their profit/room ratio was similar. However, this could be due to the small size of the sample.

a.   South-South investment

FDI flows into Africa from other developing countries have increased as part of a broader trend, with major sources being Asia and South Africa. This increase has been greater than that of investments from developed countries. Investments from developing countries, especially in tourism in Botswana, has been more resource-seeking than marketing-seeking because of the pristine environment that Botswana offers. South-South investment is said to result in greater benefits for the host country, as it is able to effectively promote more backward and forward linkages within the domestic economy and therefore supports domestic enterprises. Host countries normally have limited absorptive capacities to adopt new technologies and innovation. On the other hand, the smaller technology gap between domestic firms and investors from other developing countries enhances the possibility of technological spillovers through FDI.

The survey indicated that out of the foreign-owned establishments interviewed, 25.9 per cent originated from other developing countries, mostly Zimbabwe (18.5 per cent) and South Africa (7 per cent) (table 10). FDI from Zimbabwe was mainly by the Cresta Marakanelo Group, as mentioned earlier. However, there seemed to be no new establishment owned by investors from other developing countries; almost all the establishments with Zimbabwean and South African ownership had been established before 1995. About 66 per cent of the establishments that began operations after 1998 were wholly domestic owned. Domestic involvement and interest in the industry developed relatively recently, largely after 1998.

Table 10. Proportion of foreign-owned establishments by home country of investors

Home country	Hotels/lodges /camps (%)	Tour operators (%)
United States	25	40
Germany	4	20
South Africa	7	
Portugal	4	
Italy	4	
Zimbabwe	18.5	
United Kingdom	7.5	40
Total	100	100

Establishments with developing-country investment in Botswana appeared to employ, on average, a larger number of employees than those with investment by developed countries. Average employment in South African-owned establishments was the highest, with 142 employees, while those with Zimbabwean ownership/management employed an average of 98 persons. These were followed

by establishments with investments from the United Kingdom (123 employees), the United States (70 employees) and Italy (77 employees).

The survey revealed that while establishments with investments from developing countries also had access to foreign bookings and foreign tourists, they failed to earn significant revenue per tourist, their average revenue being 943 pula per visitor and an average length of stay of 2 days, compared with an average revenue of 8,538.4 in establishments owned by developed-country investors and an average length of stay of 3.83 days (table 11).

Table 11. Employment in different sized establishments by source of investment (averages)

Size of establishment		Type of investment			
		From developing countries	From developed countries	Local	Total
All	No. of full-time employees	110.86	70.22	32	65.37
	Percentage of high-skilled employees	7.29	9.72	8.8	8.71
	Guest/staff ratio	1.2	1.82	12	4.78
	No. of expatriate employees	2.6	3.84	1.31	2.58
	Expenditure on training	37 500	30 000	1 530	14 081
Small	No. of full-time employees	24	26	17	20.6
	Percentage of high-skilled employees	1	10	12	9.94
	No. of expatriate employees	0	1.67	0.4	0.78
Medium	No. of full-time employees	65	88	22	56.11
	Percentage of high-skilled employees	6	11	4	7.4
	No. of expatriate employees	1	5.25	1.58	3.27
Large	No. of full-time employees	137	101	93	119.33
	Percentage of high skilled employees	9	6	14	8.8
	No. of expatriate employees	3.4	4	5.5	3.72

Establishments with investments by developing countries employed, on average, more personnel than those with investments by developed countries. With respect to the size of the establishment, the largest number of employees were found in large establishments owned by investors from developing countries, followed by those from developed countries, with locally-owned hotels having the smallest number of employees on average. In the case of medium-sized category hotels, it was hotels with foreign owners from developed countries that were the largest compared to those from developing countries; and again, the local hotels employed fewer staff (table 11).

3. Contribution of FDI in tourism to the economy

a. *Employment*

It has been acknowledged that tourism has the potential to create employment, especially in the Ngamiland District where tourism activities are predominant. The extent to which tourism can create employment influences the degree of linkages between tourism and other sectors of the economy. Tourism in Botswana has led to the development of camps, lodges, transport, wholesale and retail industries aimed at supplying the tourism industry. The lodges, hotels and camps interviewed for this study employed a total of 1,765 persons. The largest establishment, which is a joint venture, employed 260 people while the smallest employed 8 people. Foreign-owned establishments and joint ventures employed more personnel than domestic-owned establishments, irrespective of the size of the establishment (table 12). Most of the companies (66 per cent) that employed 100 people or more were either 100 per cent foreign-owned or had a percentage of foreign ownership.

Most of the establishments with foreign ownership appeared to employ all staff on a full-time basis, while those with 100 per cent domestic ownership employed

a larger number of casual and part-time staff. Only 2 establishments indicated that they employed some people on a part-time basis and 6 indicated that they employed some casual staff, especially during the peak seasons. On average, joint ventures and foreign-owned establishments employed 100 and 75 persons respectively, whereas domestic-owned hotels employed only 32 persons on average. This analysis shows that joint ventures in Botswana tend to offer more employment opportunities. However, employee/room ratios appeared to be higher in foreign-owned establishments, whether small, medium or large in size (table 12).

Table 12. Average number of employees by ownership of establishment

Size of establishment	Ownership of establishment	Number of employees	Employee/room ratio
All establishments	Local	32.00	0.98
	Foreign	76.00	1.50
	Joint ventures	100.00	1.24
	Overall	65.00	1.28
Small	Local	16.60	1.84
	Foreign	25.75	2.58
	Joint ventures	--	--
	Overall	21.00	2.10
Medium	Local	22.50	0.83
	Foreign	82.50	2.23
	Joint ventures	83.70	2.04
	Overall	56.00	1.65
Large	Local	92.50	1.02
	Foreign	168.50	1.28
	Joint ventures	110.40	1.03
	Overall	119.00	1.09

An examination of the data by gender indicated more female employees in most of the joint ventures and domestic-owned establishments, although most of them were employed in either medium or low skilled positions. On average, in the joint ventures, 51 per cent of employees were women, while in domestic-owned establishments, out of 32 persons employed, 24 were women. However, there were few women employed at the managerial level.

All establishments indicated that the lowest wage offered to employees was equivalent to the minimum wage for the industry. But, surprisingly, foreign-owned establishments paid lower wages than their locally owned counterparts in each of the different categories of staff (table 13).

Table 13. Wages of selected employees by ownership of establishment

Size of establishment	Employee wages	Ownership			
		Local	Foreign	Joint venture	Total
All	Lowest wage	828	717	877	809
	Room cleaner	864	801	1 042	905
	Housekeeper	1 051	826	1 950	1 256
	Front desk manager	1 925	1 417	3 608	2 376
	Total	1 167	940	1 869	1 337
Small	Lowest wage	755	694	-	709
	Room cleaner	833	802	-	815
	Housekeeper	867	845	-	854
	Front desk manager	1 638	1 417	-	1 542
	Total	1 023	940	-	980
Medium	Lowest wage	950	730	781	845
	Room cleaner's wage	925	750	815	849
	A housekeeper's wage	1 300	750	850	1050
	A front desk manager's wage	1 926	950	1 000	1 741
	Total	1 275	558	862	1 121
Large	Lowest wage	790	750	934	861
	Room cleaner'	790	900	1 178	1 047
	Housekeeper	830	900	2 390	1 814
	Front desk manager	2 500	1 550	4 130	3 664
		1 228	638	2 158	1 847

The survey found that the wage of a front desk manager employed in a local establishment was 508.33 pula higher, on average, than that of his/her counterpart in a foreign-owned establishment (table 13). The average front desk manager's wage in a joint venture was roughly twice that of his/her counterpart in a foreign-owned establishment. Joint ventures appeared to

pay higher wages to all categories staff followed by locally owned establishments, except for the front desk manager in medium-sized establishments (table 13).

Staff turnover affected joint ventures more than the locally owned and foreign-owned establishments. On average, joint ventures had an average turnover rate of 15 per cent in 2005, while foreign-owned and locally owned establishments had a turnover rate of 3.6 per cent and 5.6 per cent respectively. However, benefits offered by the employer, such as medical insurance and pensions, were similar across the board. The lower rate of turnover in foreign-owned establishment compared to joint ventures was despite the fact that they offered lower salaries. This could be for reasons such as a more conducive working environment. Foreign establishments also indicated that they preferred to obtain unskilled labour and offer training to enable them to move up the chain. This also provided an element of job security, as employees could expect to be promoted over time.

On the whole, although tourism appeared to provide a large employment base, most locals held jobs that required medium and low skills, while expatriates held management positions. Studies conducted by Mbaiwa (2003) and others strongly support this perception. On the other hand, the survey results indicated that a total of 68 foreigners were employed in all the hotels, lodges and camps that were interviewed, which amounted to 3.85 percent of the total people employed by these establishments. Out of these 68 expatriates, 50 per cent (34 employees) were employed in foreign-owned establishments while 26.4 per cent and 24.6 per cent, respectively, were employed in joint ventures and domestic-owned establishments (table 14). On average each domestic-owned establishment employed 1.71 expatriates, while wholly foreign-owned establishments and joint ventures employed 4.32 and 2.27 expatriates respectively. However, overall, larger establishments tended to employ a larger percentage of expatriates, except foreign-owned medium-sized establishments, which employed, on average, more expatriates than the large establishments. The results also showed that a majority of the expatriate workers (over 90 per cent) were in high-level management positions (i.e. general managers and heads of various departments) and 30 of them were employed in foreign hotels, 17 in joint-venture hotels and 12 in locally owned

hotels. The ratio of expatriates in high-level management to total employment in high level management was highest in the locally owned establishments followed by foreign-owned establishments (table 14). By size of establishment, this ratio was highest for small and large-scale foreign-owned establishments. A few expatriates (only 6) were in middle management positions and three worked in lower positions out of all the establishments surveyed.

Table 14. Employment of expatriates by size and ownership of firm

Size of firm		Local	Foreign	Joint venture	Total
All	Percentage of expatriates in high-level management	24.6	50	26.4	100
	Ratio of expatriates in high-level management to total employment in high-level management	0.68	0.61	0.23	0.38
	Average number of expatriates per establishment	1.71	4.32	2.27	2.58
	Average expatriate/room ratio per establishment	0.05	0.09	0.03	0.05
	Number of expatriates in high-level management	12	30	17	59
Small	Total number of expatriates	2	5	-	7
	Ratio of expatriates in high-level management to total employment in high-level management	0.24	0.53	-	0.38
	Average number of expatriates per establishment	0.5	1.25	-	0.78
Medium	Total number of expatriates	6	16	6	28
	Ratio of expatriates in high-level management to total employment in high-level management	1.5	0.35	0.23	0.62
	Average number of expatriates per establishment	1.58	8	2	3.27
Large	Total number of expatriates	8	13	12	33
	Ratio of expatriates in high-level management to total employment in high-level management	0.19	0.58	0.23	0.32
	Average number of expatriates per establishment	5.5	6.5	2.4	3.72

b.   *Employee training*

Most of the hotels interviewed (24 out of 29) indicated that they conducted on-the-job training to complement the training offered by the Hospitality and Tourism Association of Botswana (HATAB). Many indicated that HATAB training was offered only to employees of lodges and hotels in the north of the country. They also reported that it was much cheaper to fly in a specialist, such as a chef, to train their employees for a period of three months than to send them abroad. Such arrangements

were common mainly among chain hotels, although they are not easy to organize, as trainers require work and resident permits that are difficult to obtain.

In addition to on-the-job training, some employees took some courses locally and a few internationally. Thirteen establishments indicated that their employees attended some courses locally, while three indicated their employees attended courses abroad. All establishments that trained employees reported paying for the training. The training budget varied by establishment, ranging from 450 to 75,000 pula. A number of respondents indicated that they used the Hotel and Tourism Association of Botswana (HATAB) bed levy training programmes to train their employees, and provided only an allowance and transport cost. Most establishments, especially the foreign-owned ones preferred to train employees from scratch, as simple gardeners, for example, and promote them internally, as opposed to employing new staff.

c. Purchases and other linkages

All the hotels, lodges and camps interviewed indicated that they purchased all their food products from wholesalers within the country, although it is possible that these suppliers imported the food items. Only one establishment, a large foreign-owned firm, indicated that it bought 50 per cent of its food items and beverages from outside the country. Almost all establishments in Kasane, both foreign-owned and domestic-owned, reported obtaining their food items from the Chobe farms. About 80 per cent in Kasane indicated that they also bought items such as fish from local small and medium-sized enterprises (SMEs) and street vendors.

Items such as cleaning chemicals were all sourced from local suppliers. Most establishments interviewed (86 per cent) purchased their soaps and shampoos from local wholesalers and SMEs, whereas 25 per cent of foreign-owned establishments and three joint ventures indicated that they obtained these products from South Africa, as the local products were of low quality and not packaged appropriately. Most of the construction materials and labour employed during hotel construction, as well as furniture and fittings, were also sourced locally. Only 16 per cent of both locally owned and foreign-owned firms indicated that they obtained about 20 per cent of their

furniture and fittings, construction labour and materials from either South Africa or Zimbabwe.

Although most items were obtained locally, most respondents, especially in the Maun and Kasane areas, complained of the distance of the source markets. They reported that they had to purchase most of their products from Gaborone and Francistown, which are far from where they operate, resulting in higher transport costs. The domestic sourcing of most inputs by hotels, lodges and camps indicated the existence of linkages (especially backward linkages) between these tourism establishments and their suppliers (e.g. wholesalers, SMEs, retailers and farms), most of which fall under the manufacturing sector (such as those supplying linen, soaps and chemicals) and the agricultural sector (e.g. those supplying fruit and vegetables, meat and meat products), as well as the construction industry. Hence, continued consumption of these products will further stimulate the linkages of the tourism industry to these other sectors of the economy, which will in turn boost domestic production in the supplying industries.

There also seemed to be some significant linkages between tour operators and the safari organizers interviewed. More than 70 per cent of this sample indicated that they served hotels directly, while 50 per cent reported that their main markets were hotels, lodges and camps. Those whose main clients were hotels indicated that these accounted for 53 per cent of their sales, by value. On average, local travel agents and tour operators made 13 per cent and 11 per cent of bookings in locally owned and foreign-owned establishments, respectively, compared to only 1 per cent of bookings in joint-venture establishments. This demonstrates some apparent leakages, as most establishments, especially foreign-owned ones, preferred to use foreign operators located outside the country.

However, this may explain why most international visitors had a preference for foreign-owned establishments. On the other hand, on average, most of the bookings made for local hotels (29 per cent) were made via the internet. The internet thus represents an important means of bridging the gap between domestic-owned establishments and foreign tourists. Access to international tourist markets could be further facilitated through expansion of the official Botswana tourism website (www.botswana-tourism.gov.bw), which could innovatively link domestic businesses with the virtual and global marketplace. This portal could be used to introduce electronic bookings and reservations and to increase linkages between different operators within the tourism industry.

d. Implications for poverty alleviation

Tourism plays a major role in the economy of poor countries such as Botswana, as most tourism facilities and activities are located in rural areas. FDI in tourism in Botswana contributes to poverty alleviation mainly through employment creation, providing a source of livelihood for the local people. A 1995/96 government labour survey (CSO) indicated that the number of formal jobs created by the tourism industry was 9,900, which was about 4.5 per cent of the total employment that year. The 8th National Development Plan (NDP 8) indicated that the total number of people supported financially by the tourism industry was 27,000, which constituted 2.1 per cent of Botswana's population at the time. According to the surveyed sample, joint ventures and foreign-owned firms employed a total of 803 and 605 employees respectively, while local establishments employed only 357 persons.

Community-based activities of the tourism industry are another means by which that industry contributes to poverty reduction. Some tourism activities operate through controlled hunting areas (CHA) that have been divided into small units and allocated to nearby communities that have formed a trust under Community-Based Natural Resource Management (CBNRM) programmes. These units can be used for both hunting and photographic tourism. Due to the lack of entrepreneurial and managerial skills among the communities that are allocated a wildlife quota for their respective CHA, these communities are encouraged to form partnerships with the private sector. Most partnerships are formed mainly with foreign-owned firms that possess the required expertise. In such partnerships, communities sell all or part of their quota to the private partner firms or lease their land for purposes of photographic tourism. Although the main objective of the community-based projects was to achieve conservation objectives, they have become the main source of livelihood for the participating communities, enabling the transfer of entrepreneurship and managerial skills and providing them with employment and revenue, which leads to poverty reduction.

4. Factors affecting FDI in tourism

An administrative and regulatory cost survey undertaken jointly by the Botswana Institute for Development Policy Analysis (BIDPA) and the World Bank's Foreign Investment Advisory Service (FIAS) (2003) showed that different sectors of the economy experienced different obstacles to growth of those sectors. Of the surveyed companies operating in the tourism industry, 70.7 per cent complained that the greatest obstacle they faced was a labour force with inadequate skills and training. Other concerns were low labour productivity (65.9 per cent), high costs of premises (58.5 per cent), crime, theft and disorder (53.7 per cent) and the high cost of telecommunications (51.2 per cent). The survey revealed further, the differences in the ranking of obstacles by foreign-owned firms and domestic-owned firms. Domestic-owned firms were mainly concerned about crime, theft and disorder (67.4 per cent), followed by lack of access to finance and to land (66.3 per cent and 60 per cent respectively). Foreign-owned firms, on the other hand, found the greatest obstacles to be inadequate skills and training of labour (79.4 per cent), low labour productivity (70.6 per cent) and the high cost of premises (70.6 per cent).

The study also indicated that the administrative and regulatory obstacles faced by foreign firms included obtaining work and residence permits, labour regulations and complex procedures for obtaining land. The domestic-owned firms were more concerned about the lengthy and complex procedures required to access land, the Government's regulations relating to tender and the absence of a competition law.

In this present survey, on the other hand, all establishments mentioned the absence of specific incentives to encourage them to locate in the country. Only one domestic-owned company that had access to a loan from the Citizen Entrepreneurial Development Agency (CEDA) indicated that the only incentive offered to it was access to capital. However, this question may not have been answered adequately by others, as most of the respondents were managers and not the owners of the establishment where they worked. Some of the managers had not started working for the establishment at the time of its inception. But even owners who were interviewed stated that there were no significant incentives that attracted them to the country. They reported the greatest benefit from being established in Botswana was being located close to a national park (50 per cent), the Victoria Falls (29 per cent) or the Okavango Delta (21 per cent).

Most of the locally owned companies (43 per cent) and 21 per cent of companies with foreign ownership indicated that being either in or near a town was the greatest benefit of operating in their location, and 13 per cent of foreign-owned businesses further indicated that the low cost of labour was a benefit.

When asked about the best aspects of investing in Botswana, political stability ranked highest for local and foreign investors alike. This was further confirmed by UNCTAD's Investment Policy Review (2003a), which found over 90 per cent of investors citing political and economic stability as important factors influencing their decision to invest in Botswana. All foreign companies that were located in Kasane were concerned about the fact that most of their inputs had to be purchased from Gaborone and Francistown, which were far away, and that suppliers always delivered late, which adversely affected their operations.

With regard to problems encountered in operating in Botswana, 18 per cent of investors cited bad roads and lack of street lighting in their areas of operation (figure 6). Other problems, each cited by 14 per cent of the respondents, were unreliable services by Air Botswana, shortage of skilled labour, and theft and crime. Most of the establishments in Maun and Kasane reported that Air Botswana was unreliable, while those in Francistown stated that inputs had to be sourced from far off places. Also, most establishments in Maun indicated that theft and crime were a problem. Other significant problems faced by investors were insufficient markets, denoted by low arrival figures (7 per cent), high fares charged by Air Botswana (7 per cent), bureaucracy and complex government procedures (7 per cent), Most investors also reported that government officials were unhelpful or very slow to respond to their needs.

Table 15. Problems encountered by ownership of establishment

Locally owned establishments	Percentage of responses	Foreign-owned establishments	Percentage of responses
Shortage of skilled labour	43	Air Botswana is unreliable	21
Bad roads and no street lights	43	Inputs are far from the area of operation	21
Insufficient markets	29	Theft and crime	21
Air Botswana is unreliable	14	Bad roads and no street lights	14
Theft and crime	14	Bureaucracy and complex government procedures	14
Air Botswana is expensive	14	Shortage of skilled labour	7
Border operating hours are too short	14	Air Botswana is expensive	14
Border visas are expensive	14	Difficulty in obtaining a work permit	14
Unproductive labour	14	Power failure and cuts	7
Labour laws favour employees	14	Lack of tourist activities in towns	7

The major concerns of foreign- and domestic-owned establishments differed (table 15). Domestic-owned establishment were mainly concerned about the shortage of skilled labour, the bad state of the infrastructure and insufficient markets. Foreign-owned establishments, on the other hand, tended to worry more about the great distance from which their inputs had to be sourced, the unreliability of Air Botswana, and theft and crime in their area of operation. Interestingly these results are different from those obtained from the BIDPA/FIAS study, at which time most foreign-owned firms cited they were concerned about the shortage of trained and skilled labour. Although locally owned establishments were also concerned about this shortage, only foreign-owned firms indicated that it was difficult to obtain work and residence permits for foreign employees due to the lengthy and demanding process involved. However, this could be explained by the fact that locally owned firms employed fewer expatriates than their foreign-owned counterparts. The unreliability and high costs of Air Botswana were problems cited by both kinds of establishments (table 15)

Figure 6. Greatest problems encountered by investors

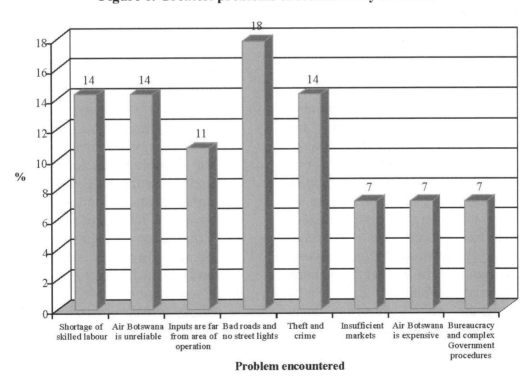

D. FDI policy and related policies

1. Historical overview

a. *General trends in FDI polices*

Botswana historically has been remarkably open to FDI. After independence, FDI primarily provided the country with the scarce capital needed for establishing the first operations in the tourism industry. Subsequently, following successful economic growth, FDI ceased to be the sole source of capital. Today, it plays an important role through its transfer of technology and skills in the tourism industry and its ability to secure access to foreign markets. Policies have been adjusted to target FDI flows that bring these important benefits to the country.

Botswana has somewhat departed from its liberal policies, recently, as it has perceived some foreign investments in tourism to be fraudulent and not filling the skills gap. There are reported cases of economic refugees being able to obtain licences in the tourism industry in order to facilitate entry and obtain resident permits (UNCTAD, 2003a). In 2002, the Government enacted the Foreign Investment Code that stipulates minimum amounts for foreign investments and reserves certain activities for nationals only. Although the Government insists that support for the promotion of domestic-owned businesses is complementary to its desire to promote foreign investment (EIU, 2006a), this has been criticized by foreign investors and the international community. Experts argue that it will reduce much needed foreign investment due to its negative signals without fostering local participation or stopping fraud.

b. *From the first tourism policy in 1990 to the Botswana Tourism Board Act 2003[3]*

Since the first tourism policy in 1990, tourism has played a dominant role in the Government's overall development strategy. Tourism is identified as an economic activity with expanding growth potential that can, when sustainably managed, provide valuable income. There are six major points relating to tourism that have consistently been highlighted in Government policy documents.

(i)   *Diversification of the economy:* In order to reduce the country's reliance on natural resources (particularly diamonds) as the sole source of economic growth, tourism has been identified as a central pillar to diversify the economy. The first tourism policy in 1990 and later the Tourism Master Plan highlighted the industry's great potential for employment creation and foreign exchange earnings. Both of these showed the Government's determination to reap underexploited benefits and revenues through carefully managed growth of tourism assisted by the Government. Whereas the Botswana Export Development and Investment Authority (BEDIA) aims to attract and support foreign investors, the Botswana Development Corporation (BDC) supplies mainly domestic investors with finance, skills and technical expertise.

(ii) *Participation, education and empowerment of Batswana:* All major policy documents relating to tourism give broad attention and priority to the empowerment of local citizens. FDI is not considered an end in itself, but a means for Batswana initially to access scarce capital and subsequently profit from skills and technology transfers. Joint ventures between local businesses and foreigners are highly encouraged (Republic of Botswana, 2003). As of 2002, the entry requirements for foreigners wishing to invest in Botswana have been eased when they collaborate with local citizens. Participation of Batswana in the ownership and management of tourism enterprises is considered a prerequisite for employment creation, skills transfer and active involvement (Republic of Botswana, 2000). Vision 2016 and the National Policy on Culture, 2001, view this as being not only conducive to development but also a means to promoting national heritage and a sense of pride.

(iii) *Regulation of the private sector and establishing of partnerships:* Generally, Botswana follows the principle that tourism should be "Government led and private-sector driven" (Leechor and Fabricius, 2006: 27). The Tourism Master Plan (2000) clearly identifies the need to establish private-public partnerships. Thus, the Hospitality & Tourism Association of Botswana (HATAB) is supported with technical expertise and finance. Furthermore, the regulatory framework has been strengthened considerably since the first Tourism Policy in 1990. Domestic and foreign tourist enterprises are fairly regulated and require licensing. The 1996 Tourism Regulations provide a comprehensive framework of minimal standards for health and safety. The country's development strategy as laid out in Vision 2016 further supports these aspects of the tourism industry.

(iv) *Sustainability:* The Government has long been aware that the conservation of Botswana's main attractions – its wildlife and nature reserves – is of central importance, as reflected in all

relevant policy documents. It has therefore promoted low-volume/high-value tourism, although the Tourism Master Plan (2000) reassessed this policy concluding that high volume/mixed price could also be targeted without "catastrophic costs for the environment". The National Ecotourism Strategy 2002 underscores the importance of sustainable growth of the sector.

(v) *Diversification within the tourism* industry: The industry could achieve greater diversification by promoting sites other than the Okavango Delta and the major national parks, as well as promoting domestic tourism. Economically, this would reduce dependence on volatile and external upmarket tourism flows and could increase the length of stay of tourists in the country. Culturally, it would help foster Batswana's understanding of and pride in the country's heritage and potential.

(vi) *Marketing, promotion and awareness-raising*: The Botswana Tourism Board is the main agency for promoting and marketing tourism abroad and domestically. The branding of Botswana in accordance with the interests of different stakeholders in the industry has been one of the major efforts over the past few years. Integrating foreign investments within general policy guidelines is also the task of the Board. Its stated goal is to "market and promote the establishment of joint tourism business ventures between citizens and foreign investors" (Republic of Botswana, 2003).

Further, raising the level of local hospitality by creating awareness among citizens of the benefits they could derive from tourism is important, as Botswana is not a traditional destination for international travellers. To this end, professional training on the one hand and awareness-raising on the other are important. The Botswana Tourism Board, functions as the main body to implement these policies. It also consults decision-makers on beneficial adjustments.

2. FDI entry and establishment policies

a. *Government policies and targeting of FDI*

As stated above, Botswana has traditionally been open to FDI and was able to reap enormous benefits from it, particularly in the years immediately following independence. In that regard, the country differed decisively from its neighbours that favoured extensive government involvement in industrial policy and adopted infant industry protection or import substitution policies. However, whereas many countries are now attempting increasingly to liberalize their economies, Botswana has been re-evaluating its FDI policy (UNCTAD, 2003a). The Foreign Investment Code introduced in 2002 represented a substantial shift in its former policy stance by discriminating against foreign investors on an unprecedented scale. Until then, Botswana had been known for its non-discriminatory policies, and experts have argued that these changes will result in reduced FDI inflows. FDI has indeed fallen, but due to its volatile nature it is too soon to draw any significant conclusions as to the reasons for this decline. Foreign companies wanting to invest in tourism now face a minimum investment requirement of $200,000, but when investing in a joint venture with local investors the minimum requirement is reduced to $100,000. There are only two foreign investors that have opted for this arrangement so far.

Some of Botswana's laws contain restrictions on the flow of FDI into certain sectors in the economy with the aim of protecting local entrepreneurs. In the past, there had been no restrictions on FDI in tourism, but recent amendments to the regulations have resulted in certain activities being reserved for citizens. According to the amended Botswana Tourism Act (2006), the following tourism-related areas are reserved for citizens of Botswana or for companies that are wholly owned by citizens of Botswana: (i) camping sites, including caravan sites, (ii) guest houses, (iii) *mekoro* (canoe safari operations), (iv) mobile safaris, (v) motorboat safaris, and (vi) transportation. The remaining tourism-related activities are not subject to these restrictions. Other sectors in the economy not subject to FDI restrictions are mining, most manufacturing and financial services. FDI is not permitted in selected, mostly small-scale, businesses in retail trade services and manufacturing.

Until 2000, the Government operated a Financial Assistance Program (FAP) for the tourism industry, which granted tax incentives and financial support for companies investing in non-traditional sectors. However due to substantial fraud by domestic and international investors alike, it was abolished. Fraud ranged from inflating the cost of machinery to pay for a beneficiary's contribution to a small-scale FAP-supported project to falsifying claims for a labour subsidy rebate from multimillion pula projects, which cost the Government hundreds of thousands of pula. The Directorate of Corruption and Economic Crime established a dedicated investigation unit in 1998 to concentrate on fraud relating to the FAP. Approximately a quarter of the 400 to 500 cases under investigation in 2000 involved fraud. At the end of 1999, the Directorate was actively investigating 106 FAP cases involving approximately 27 million pula in potential fraud. A study by the Botswana Institute for Development Policy Analysis concluded that the FAP was no longer achieving its objectives and should be replaced due to corruption. But it also highlighted the need for some form of support to promote the catching up of local businesses (BIDPA, 2000).

The policies regarding tourism, outlined above, have influenced the Government's approach to FDI in tourism as indicated below:

(i) *Diversification of the economy:* The Foreign Investment Code (2002: 6) states that "foreign investors are expected […] to assist in the diversification of the economy". BEDIA is supporting the Government's efforts to position Botswana as a good location for FDI (*Daily News*, 7 April 2004).

(ii) *Participation of Batswana and skills transfer:* Botswana enjoys an unusually high savings rate and vast foreign exchange reserves, which signifies that FDI is no longer the only source of capital for investment. It is now recognized that the main benefits deriving from FDI are through skills and technology transfers. The Foreign Investment Code thus encourages foreign investors to establish joint ventures and has reserved certain activities for Batswana. The Code further requires the foreign investor to "transfer technology" and "transfer skills to Batswana by promoting their involvement and participation in positions as supervisory, middle and senior management levels in the company" (Foreign Investment Code, 2002: 6). The Government insists, however, that support for the promotion of domestic-owned businesses is *complementary* to its desire to promote foreign investment (Economist Intelligence Unit, 2006: 22.

3. Botswana's investment climate: advantages and drawbacks

a. *Comparative advantages of Botswana*

Botswana has overcome its disadvantage of being a landlocked country by creating comparative advantages in other areas. Tourism presents a special category in the export sector, as it is relatively insensitive to distance. Although poor infrastructure can present a significant obstacle, the remoteness of many parts of Botswana is one of the reasons why tourists are visiting the country. In addition to this, the following factors contribute to making Botswana attractive to FDI in tourism.

(i) *Safety and political stability*: A survey of foreign investors in Botswana (UNCTAD, 2003a) confirmed that political and economic stability are two of the most important features that attract FDI to Botswana. The interviewed firms ranked political stability as the strongest element in the country's business environment. Particularly relevant for tourism is the perceived security in Botswana, which clearly distinguishes it from neighbouring countries such as South Africa and Zimbabwe. The World Bank/BIDPA study (2002) on tourism in Botswana identified the reputation as a safe place as one of the main intangible assets adding significant value to the "brand" Botswana. Related to this is the country's low corruption index that is maintained through severe penalties for any illegitimate acts. However, of late crime in Botswana has escalated, and interviewees indicated this to be an area of considerable concern.

(ii) *Repatriation and convertibility:* Botswana does not restrict the transfer of profits or proceeds of disinvestments, and in 1999 it abolished all foreign exchange controls (UNCTAD, 2003a: 28). The national currency is managed by maintaining a stable relationship with the South African rand. The country's long history of convertibility and sound economic management provides a generally good climate for investing in tourism.

b.   *Problem areas*

(i) The Foreign Investment Code 2002: This policy document, which introduced minimum requirements for investment in Botswana, as described above, has substantially changed the former liberal approach to FDI in general and to FDI in tourism in particular. The rationale behind this policy is the empowerment of Batswana who thus far have been unable to realize substantive benefits through FDI in tourism. Further there have been abuses of the legislation by foreign nationals for reasons of economic migration. While the empowerment of Batswana and the creation of linkages with the local economy should be the highest priority, some experts question whether this policy will achieve its stated goals. UNCTAD's Investment Policy Review (2003), in particular, believes the code will send negative signals which far outweigh its positive goal of reducing fraud. The report argues that Botswana has a substantial need for further training and skills transfer, particularly in tourism, and that discouraging FDI in this industry would be counterproductive. It is questionable if the minimum requirements for investment will translate into improved incentives for citizens to invest in small-scale enterprises and

significantly reduce their foreign competition.

(ii) Length of contracts: There has been some discussion about the length of period for which foreigners are granted land rights. Many have complained that the rather short time period of 15 years, reduces the incentive to invest sustainably. While this system has been able to provide the Okavango Delta in particular with high-quality structures, even the Government has identified this as an area of concern. The low-volume, high-value policy has led to significant oligopoly rents for tourist establishments currently operating within the restricted zone. Through the artificial limitation of supply, prices remain exorbitantly high and firms operating within the area can extract a surplus that is not related to their productivity or service delivery, but simply attributable to the fact that they are one of the few providers of that service. Strictly speaking, rent means a financial income which is not matched by corresponding labour or investment in the market sense. This regularly leads to moral hazard behaviour, where businesses find it more cost-effective to lobby the Government for the continuation of their preferential rights rather than investing in enhanced productivity.

As the licensing of new establishments must be limited for environmental reasons, the resulting market distortion is influencing the current debate on FDI in tourism. Whereas foreign expertise was necessary to establish initial operations that catered to the upmarket segment of the industry, domestic firms and the Government are now interested in benefiting from these rents themselves.

Expressions of xenophobia must be seen in this context, reflecting concerns that rents can be sent abroad through the repatriation of funds, rather than recycled within the local economy, thence limiting the production of economic benefits and spillover effects.

(iii) *Xenophobia:* Anecdotal evidence and results from the interviews reflect concerns about increased xenophobia among Batswana with regard to foreign investment. Expatriate managers or owners of establishments expressed concern about this trend, fuelled by developments in neighbouring Zimbabwe and to some extent also in South Africa. Despite the urgent need for greater citizen empowerment, this is an issue that could harm the long-term prospects of the industry as a whole. President Festus Mogae expressed concern about this issue, stating that FDI was crucial to the country's development and that foreign investors had many other options to choose from (*Daily News*, 8 August 2006). The Economist Intelligence Unit (EIU, 2006:22) has noted that expressions of xenophobic sentiments by proponents of citizen empowerment are undermining the country's long-standing reputation for welcoming foreign involvement, and several recent reports have indicated serious deficiencies in the ease of doing business.

(iv) There are efforts to liberalize and privatize parts of the economy. Vision 2016 cites game reserve management as a potential candidate. The underperformance of the national airline, Air Botswana, has had a significant impact on tourism. The airline's monopoly has caused persistently high prices that lower demand even by high-value

customers. The opening up of additional routes and increased efficiency should be addressed as essential aspects of promoting FDI in tourism.

4.   General measures and conditions[4]

a.   Foreign exchange

During the 1990s Botswana progressively eliminated foreign exchange controls, until 1999 when they were entirely abolished. Inflation has been kept at a moderate level and manageable, with the Government maintaining an exchange rate at a stable level with the South African rand. Botswana has a long history of convertibility with the prospect of continued sound economic management, as evidenced by the positive investment grade status awarded to it by international credit rating agencies.

b.   Taxation

Botswana's corporate tax rates are among the lowest in the region and thus provide an incentive for foreign investors. Businesses are subject to a two-tier income tax system that consists of a 15 per cent basic company tax (guaranteed until 2020) and a 10 per cent additional company tax. Dividend withholding tax (which is 15 per cent for residents and non-residents) can be credited against additional company tax. This attractive feature of business taxation leads to a moderate tax on distributed earnings and near neutrality between distribution and retention of earnings for reinvestment. However, annual capital allowances are modest. The usual range of deductions is allowed with adequate provisions to limit transfer pricing. Losses may be carried forward for five years. The International Financial Services Centre (IFSC) provides further incentives, such as exemption from withholding taxes on interest, commercial royalties, management or consultancy fees and dividends paid by an IFSC company to a non-resident, and access to Botswana's expanding double taxation treaty network, at present comprising France, India, Mauritius, Namibia, the Russian Federation, South Africa, Sweden, the United Kingdom and Zimbabwe. The top marginal tax rate for residents and non-residents alike is 25 per cent and value added tax (VAT) is 10 per cent. As part of the Southern African Customs Union (SACU), Botswana is bound by common external tariffs on imports. These have been sharply reduced because of South Africa's membership of the World Trade Organization (WTO).

c.   *Employment*

Botswana generally has had good industrial relations; the labour law is in conformity with international standards and adheres to the conventions of the International Labour Organization (ILO). There is relatively little unionization and collective bargaining. There are minimum wages for roughly a third of business activity, which could pose potential problems for foreign investors. However, in an UNCTAD survey (2003a), employers did not see the minimum wage, currently set at 3.10 pula per hour, as an impediment, although it should be pointed out that employers who had not established businesses because of wage considerations were naturally excluded from this survey. One foreign investor who was interviewed pointed out that Botswana's labour laws tended to favour employees as opposed to employers. Wages for semi-skilled and skilled workers are relatively high due to an overall scarcity of skills. As already mentioned, scarcity of skills is one of the biggest challenges for future development of the economy. However, it is worth noting that this problem arises in some industries because of a mismatch in the

demand and supply of labour. This mismatch has also contributed to the rising unemployment rate among the educated youth..

Due to the lack of skills, employment of expatriates plays a significant role in the whole of the economy. However, many investors expressed frustration with the inappropriate policy and bureaucratic bottlenecks concerning the granting of work permits, which they considered to be slow and inefficient. The trade-off between empowerment of Batswana and sound commercial requirements for the employment of non-citizens needs to be carefully considered. Despite the priority given to vocational training over the past 30 years, there are still gaps in managerial, professional and technical skills for business. Another impediment to the liberalization of the labour market has been the growing concern that foreign investment has become a channel for economic migration, particularly from struggling Zimbabwe. Further, the HIV/AIDS problem has exacerbated the skills shortage making it all the more imperative to establish rapid recruitment procedures. .

d.   *Land*

Land is owned as tribal land, State land or freehold land. The acquisition of land by foreign investors is subject to explicit ministerial approval. The fast growing economy has put pressure on the land allocation system. The main challenge is the conversion of agricultural land to commercial and industrial use and ownership. Many investors have complained that the 15 years for land lease awarded in this sector in the tourism industry is too short to allow meaningful investment.

e.   *Competition Policy*[5]

Botswana's parliament passed a long-awaited Competition Policy in 2005, which aims to provide a coherent framework that integrates privatization, deregulation, and liberalization of trade and investment, into a strategy for promoting a dynamic market-led economy. In addition, the new SACU Agreement (2002) states that the SACU Council established under the agreement "shall develop policies and instruments to address unfair trade practices between Member States." Accordingly, the Agreement states, "Member States agree that there shall be competition policies in each Member State and that Member States shall cooperate with each other with respect to the enforcement of competition laws and regulations". The Competition Policy provides a framework for preventing anti-competitive practices and conduct by firms, and creates a business-friendly environment that encourages competition and efficient resource allocation. This in turn promotes investment and innovation, broadens choices for consumers, reduces monopoly rents and consumer prices, and contributes to improving the quality of goods and services produced.

f.   *Rule of law*

Botswana enjoys high standards of adherence to the rule of law, respect for contracts and protection of property rights. The judicial system is regarded as fair and competent, and court judgements are enforced. Administrative corruption is low and severe criminal penalties are imposed for acts of corruption. Complementary legislation to protect intellectual property rights was completed in 2000.

E. Summary and conclusions

Botswana has a clear vision of what it seeks to achieve when attracting FDI in tourism. As the country embarked fairly early on a strategy that targeted the low-volume, high-value tourist market, FDI was particularly important for gaining market access and for the transfer of skills. More recently, empowerment of Batswana and the creation of economically beneficial linkages has received prominent attention. Given these goals, joint ventures seem to be an appropriate way forward. They combine both market access and skills transfer with the active participation of Batswana nationals to lay the foundations for local ownership of establishments that increasingly cater to the upmarket segment of the industry.

Particularly relevant for other developing countries is the analysis of the determinants and challenges for FDI in Botswana. The politically and economically stable situation in the country – especially in comparison with Botswana's direct neighbours – has been a decisive advantage. Maintaining this stability and vigorously fighting crime and xenophobic tendencies should remain a high priority. Liberalization of air travel should be encouraged in order to lower the high airfares that tourists face when they travel to Botswana. This is not to grant visitors cheap access to the country's natural tourist sites, but rather to make their travel to Botswana more efficient and predictable.

The analysis also shows that FDI in tourism has the potential to create employment as well as improve the standards of living of people in the areas where tourism operations are based. However, the lack of skilled labour represents the biggest obstacle to increasing linkages in the Botswana economy and encouraging diversification. Lack of skilled Batswana, especially for high-level managerial positions in the tourism industry calls for the establishment of a tourism training school which would help bridge the skills gap among the locals as well as reduce the number of expatriates employed in the sector. The survey showed the existence of positive linkages between the tourism industry and other sectors of the economy. To further strengthen these linkages, especially with the agricultural sector, the country should develop its arable areas by making better use of its northern regions, especially the Okavango and Chobe areas that always have sufficient water supply. This will result in increased yields and production of the agricultural sector, and therefore increased supply to the tourism industry and to other sectors of the economy, thus reducing import volumes (especially of fruit and vegetables) which affect domestic prices.

F. References

Botswana Institute for Development Policy Analysis (BIDPA). (2000). Financial Assistance Policy: Fourth Evaluation. Gaborone, May.

BIDPA and FIAS. (2003). "Report of the Botswana administrative and regulatory cost survey" (Gaborone).

Central Statistics Office (1996). Labour Force Survey 1995/96 (Gaborone: CSO)

Central Statistics Office (2004). Household Income Expenditure Survey 2003/4 (Gaborone: CSO)

Chudnovsky D. and Lopez A. (1999). "Globalisation and Developing Countries: FDI and Growth and Sustainable Human Development", Paper prepared for, UNCTAD/UNDP Global Programme on "Globalization, Liberalization and Sustainable Development". Geneva, February.

Economist Intelligence Unit (2006a). Botswana Country Report.

Economist Intelligence Unit (2006b). Botswana Country Profile.

Grant S. (2004). Bajanala: A Tourist Guide to Botswana. Republic of Botswana, Department of Tourism (Gaborone: Government Printers)

International Monetary Fund (2006). International Financial Statistics, Botswana.

Leechor C. and Fabricius M. (2006). "Developing Tourism in Botswana: Progress and Challenges", Background paper, Botswana Export Diversification Study (World Bank/Botswana Institute for Development Policy Analysis).

Mhone G. and Bond P. (2001). "FDI in Zimbabwe and Botswana: Relative success and comparative failure" No. 2001/38 (UNU/WIDER).

Mbaiwa J (2003). "The socio-economic sustainability of tourism development in the Okavango Delta, Botswana" (Maun: Okavango Research Centre, University of Botswana).

Pigato M (2001). "The Foreign Direct Investment Environment in Africa", Africa Region Working Series No.15 (Washington, D.C: World Bank).

Pradeep M (2006). Competition Regimes in the World: A Civil Society Report (Jaipur: Consumer Unity & Trust Society).

Republic of Botswana (1990). Tourism Policy (Gaborone: Government Printers).

Republic of Botswana (1992). Tourism Act (Gaborone: Government Printers).

Republic of Botswana (1996), Botswana Tourism Regulations. Department of Tourism (Gaborone: Government Printers).

Republic of Botswana (2000). Botswana Tourism Master Plan. Botswana Tourism Development Programme, Department of Tourism (Gaborone: Government Printers).

Republic of Botswana (2002a). Botswana National Ecotourism Strategy (Gaborone: Government Printers).

Republic of Botswana (2002b). National Development Plan 8 and 9 (Gaborone: Government Printers).

Republic of Botswana (2003). Botswana Tourism Board Act (Gaborone: Government Printers).

UNCTAD (2003a). Investment Policy Review: Botswana (New York and Geneva: United Nations).

UNCTAD (2003b). *FDI in Landlocked Developing Countries at a Glance* (New York and Geneva: United Nations).

UNECA (2003). *Tourism and Trade in Africa: How can African Countries Benefit from the Doha Round of Multilateral Trade Negotiations – Evidence from Three Countries.* Background paper, Economic and Social Policy Division.

World Bank (2006a). *World Development Indicators* (Washington, DC.).

World Bank (2006b). *Global Development Finance Statistics* (Washington, DC.).

Zhang J and Jensen C (2005). "Comparative advantage in tourism? A supply-side analysis of tourism flows", Paper prepared for, 45th Congress of the European Regional Science Association (ERSA) Vrije University, Amsterdam, August 23rd – 27th.

Notes

[1]   Based on contribution by N.H. Fidzani, A. Okatch, K. Sekolokwane, P. Sewing and Botswana Institute for Development Policy Analysis (BIDPA).

[2]   We are confident that the trend has been upward because an investigation of the 2000 outlier figure revealed that the Bank of Botswana did not receive all data submissions for that year and that its estimate of a decline from 83 million pula to 17 million pula was clearly faulty.

[3]   For a comprehensive overview, see Leechor, Chadand and Fabricius, 2006.

[4]   This section draws on UNCTAD (2003a), except for the discussion on competition policy, which is based on the latest legislation.

[5]   This section is largely taken from INCSOC, 2006.

III. Kenya country case study[1]

Executive summary

Foreign direct investment (FDI) is thought to have played a major role in Kenya's tourism sector. However, neither the economic dynamics of that FDI nor its extent, determinants or impact are well understood. Also, little is known about the linkages between FDI in tourism and the local economy.

This study attempts to build upon the existing work done by UNCTAD on the development trends and impact of FDI in tourism in Kenya. It seeks to investigate the main trends, determinants and impact of FDI in tourism in Kenya, with the general aim of providing information on how Kenya could benefit more in terms of increased competitiveness and growth, and poverty reduction.

Data for the study were obtained from several sources. Secondary data were obtained from the Kenya National Bureau of Statistics, the Kenya Tourism Board, Kenya Wildlife Services (KWS), Kenya Tourist Development Corporation (KTDC) and other published sources. Primary data for the study was obtained during the years 2006-2007, during which time a total of 35 hotels and restaurants, 30 tour operators/travel agents, and 14 suppliers of goods and services to hotels and restaurants were interviewed. Besides this, focused group discussions were held with key stakeholders in the tourism sector.

Even though the sample was small, the survey showed that 57 per cent of the hotels/restaurants and 75 per cent of the tour operators/agencies were locally owned, which belies the perception that Kenya's tourism sector is foreign dominated. Most of the local owners were of Asian and British origin, which could explain this misconception. There was evidence of South-South FDI, though that appeared to be limited. Financing in the sector seemed to be generally through loans (64 per cent) and equity (20 per cent). However, with no long-term credit available to the sector, most of the firms financed expansions and renovations from their own funds, which were rather limited.

There appeared to be no major differences in capacity, turnover, profits and taxes between foreign-owned enterprises and the locally owned ones. However, there was evidence of a marked difference in the amount of purchases by local enterprises and those with foreign ownership: hotels with foreign ownership made much higher purchases. Most of the purchases were from wholesalers/distributors, with little sourced from small and medium-sized enterprises (SMEs). Goods and services consumed in the sector were mainly sourced from within the country with only about 17.3 per cent imported, indicating substantial linkages between the tourism industry and the local economy. The use of the Internet for booking clients for both local and foreign-owned hotels and tour operators has been increasing, which shows the growing importance of technology. The emergence of e-ticketing is likely to affect the role of tour operators and travel agents in the future.

The survey also showed that there were no marked differences between locally owned enterprises and those with some foreign ownership with regard to level of employment and gender distribution. However, and quite surprisingly, hotels with foreign ownership tended to have more low-skilled workers. Training of staff in tourism-related activities is mainly provided at the Utalii College. However, concerns were expressed at the lack of post-graduate training opportunities in the country.

Some of the firms in the tourism sector undertake environmental activities such as tree planting and landscaping, installation of energy saving technologies, borehole construction and water conservation. Most of the hotels undertake an environmental audit mandated by the National Environmental Management Authority. However, compliance with ISO 1400, which is necessary for enhancing international competitiveness, appeared to be limited. The study found no major differences between locally owned enterprises and those with foreign ownership with respect to environmental protection. The same applies to community initiatives that include donations to various charitable organizations, and providing space to souvenir sellers within hotel premises.

Regional integration holds promising business opportunities for Kenya. About 22 per cent of the hotels reported doing business in the region. The proportion was considerably higher for tour operators and travel agents (about 50 per cent). The results did not show marked differences in perceptions of the cross-border trade before and after regional integration for firms that were predominantly locally owned and those with foreign ownership.

Although there has been no comprehensive and consistent tourism policy, Kenya has maintained an open door policy to foreign investment since its independence. However, there are no sector- specific incentives to attract FDI, although the draft tourism policy that is soon to be formalized proposes some incentives that include tax relief on hotel construction, provision of long-term loans and exemptions from value added tax for small hotels and restaurants. While the legal and institutional framework has improved considerably, there are still some bottlenecks, such as a minimum capital investment requirement, multiple licensing requirements and restrictions on work permits.

There appeared to be no marked differences in the business environment faced by the two categories of tourism enterprises: local and foreign. The main challenges the industry faces include high electricity costs, poor road infrastructure, insecurity, a demanding tax regime, and cumbersome licensing requirements among others. These will need to be addressed for tourism to become more attractive to both local and foreign investors.

This study shows that there are considerable data gaps. For example, there is little information on trends in FDI in tourism, and on casinos, souvenirs and car rentals, yet these are important components of tourism infrastructure in the country. Neither is there much information on the perceptions of communities surrounding the tourism establishments.

Five major policy implications emerge. First, there is an urgent need to finalize and formalize the tourism policy. This should go beyond general policy provisions by including proactive policy interventions, designing an elaborate incentive package for tourism investments (both local and foreign), and encouraging competition and technology transfer. These policy interventions should be coherent and in line with the country's long-term development strategy, *Vision 2030*. The strategy views tourism as one of a few selected sectors that will turn Kenya into a middle-income country by 2030. The incentives should direct investments into new tourism circuits (e.g. western circuit) and new tourism products for sustainable tourism development, and should favour joint ventures partnerships with local communities. Second, the business climate should be improved. This will involve improvements in infrastructure (with priority given to roads, railways and energy), seriously tackling corruption, simplifying and reducing licensing requirements, streamlining and harmonizing taxation, and relocating and organizing beach operators, among others. In addition, the legal and regulatory framework should be reviewed to enhance FDI. Third, enhanced regional integration could attract FDI to Kenya. This includes marketing the East Africa region as a single destination, formulation of regional classification and standardization criteria, introduction of a regional tourist visa, and complete removal of cross-border bottlenecks in the movement of tour vehicles. Fourth, domestic tourism should be vigorously promoted through increased budgetary allocations among other interventions.

Finally, further research should be conducted to confirm the findings of this study. This should cover more hotels and tour operators in order to increase the robustness of the results, include other tourism infrastructure about which little is known so far, such as casinos, souvenirs and car rentals, and generally build a reliable database for the sector.

A. Introduction

As in many developing countries, tourism is an important industry in Kenya's economy, accounting for about 13 per cent of GDP. It is not only the country's third largest foreign exchange earner but also an important generator of direct, indirect and induced employment. Its other benefits include contribution to tax revenue, stimulation of demand for local products, and development of remote areas and of entrepreneurial skills.

Foreign direct investment (FDI) is thought to have played a major role in the country's tourism industry. However, the economic dynamics of FDI in tourism are not well understood, particularly its extent, determinants and impact. Information is needed, for example, about the relative impact of different forms of foreign investment on jobs, revenue, the sources and magnitude of value-added and "leakages", and how these can change over time. Little is known about the linkages between FDI in tourism and the local economy, and the extent and impact of South-South FDI in tourism.

1. Objectives

Building upon and extending the existing work by UNCTAD on the determinants, development trends and impact of FDI in tourism in Kenya (UNCTAD, 2006), the general aim of this study is to provide information on how Kenya can benefit more from such FDI in terms of gaining competitiveness, enhancing growth and reducing poverty. The study provides a snapshot of the Kenyan tourism economy and in particular the role played by FDI, during the period 2006 and part of 2007.

The specific objectives of the study are to:
- Determine the extent of foreign ownership of tourism enterprises in Kenya and its implications for development;
- Determine the extent of South-South trade;

- Identify the preferred modes of investment in tourism enterprises;
- Identify potential beneficial linkages that could be made between the activities of transnational corporations (TNCs) and domestic firms, including SMEs.
- Establish the potential role of regional integration, investment and tourism policies in influencing the trends and impacts of FDI in tourism.
- Evaluate the current policy environment, including regional and national policies, and identify critical policy gaps that need to be addressed in order to enable Kenya to benefit more from FDI in tourism.

2. Methodology

This study drew on several sources of data, both secondary and primary. The secondary sources were the Kenya National Bureau of Statistics (CBS), the Kenya Tourism Board (KTB), Kenya Wildlife Services (KWS), the Kenya Tourist Development Corporation (KTDC) and other published sources. With respect to primary data, the study used a more detailed, localized and microeconomic approach compared to the earlier UNCTAD work. A total of 35 hotels and restaurants, 30 tour operators/travel agents, and 14 suppliers of goods and services to hotels and restaurants were interviewed for the study. Efforts were made to select as representative a sample as possible, in terms of surveying an equal number of foreign-owned and domestic firms of comparable size. An attempt was also made to include firms from the coast, within Nairobi, Nakuru and Machakos. Besides this, focused group discussions were held with key stakeholders in the tourism sector (see annex 1 for a list of the participants in the discussions).

Both qualitative and quantitative methods were used in the analysis. Descriptive statistics such as means and frequencies were used to establish whether there are differences in the performance of tourist enterprises on the basis of degree of foreign ownership.

B. Overview of the Kenyan economy and the tourism industry

This section presents a brief overview of the Kenyan economy and the country's tourism industry, thereby providing the background upon which subsequent analysis is based.

1. Kenyan economy

Since independence in 1963, the Kenyan Government has been struggling with development challenges through numerous development plans, sessional papers, fiscal papers and recovery strategy papers[2]. However, the country moved from being among the most promising in Africa in the first decade after independence to having more than half of the population living below the poverty line in the 1990s and early 2000s. During the first decade after independence, Kenya registered real GDP growth of about 7 per cent per annum, while per capita income increased at about 4 per cent per annum. However, although real GDP grew at an annual average rate of about 3.3 per cent between 1972 and 2003, per capita real GDP grew at only about 0.2 per cent per annum. As a result, real per capita income in 2003 ($426) was far below that of the late 1970s and 1990s (KIPPRA, 2005).

Since 2003, however, the economy has been experiencing a gradual economic recovery; it grew by 1.8 per cent in 2003, 4.3 per cent in 2004,[3] 5.8 per cent in 2005 and 6.1 per cent in 2006 in real terms. Despite these gains the country's poverty status remains a problem, with 50 per cent of the population living below the poverty line.

Agriculture and forestry, transport and communications, manufacturing, wholesale and retail trade activities, hotels and restaurants, and building and construction accounted for 55.2 per cent of GDP in 2006. Specifically, hotels and restaurants held the largest share of GDP with 14.9 per cent, followed by wholesale and retail trade's contribution of 10.9 per cent. The share of agriculture and forestry was 5.4 per cent, a decline of 18.4 per cent from its contribution in 2005 of 24.2 per cent (GoK, 2006/7.

2. Kenyan tourism industry

a. Tourism products

Kenya has a lot to offer tourists. Its tourism industry is built around the country's rich wildlife and beautiful coastal beaches. The greatest attraction of Kenya as a tourist destination is that a tourist can enjoy a safari and a beach holiday on the same trip. Thus, even though the coast accounts for about 60 per cent of all bed nights in the country, the prime attraction for 70–80 per cent of all tourists visiting the country is its wildlife (Ikiara and Okech, 2002). The national tourism master plan identified no less than 120 major tourism destinations in the country, including 84 national parks and reserves (GoK, 1995). According to the master plan, Kenya is competitive (or fairly competitive) in such tourist market segments as:

- Mountain and highland resort tourism, with Mt. Kenya and access to the world famous Mt. Kilimanjaro being key attractions. Other geographical/physical features that have great potential for tourism in the country include the Great Rift Valley and its associated spectacular landscape, the world's second largest freshwater lake, Lake Victoria, and the fact that the equator runs through the country.
- Special interest tourism such as archaeology, ethnology, ornithology, botany and zoology.

- Rail safaris, cruises and activity holidays.
- Conference tourism, mainly because Nairobi is a regional air transport hub, and has relatively sophisticated conference facilities with experience hosting international conferences. It is the only city among developing countries that hosts two United Nations bodies: the United Nations Environmental Programme (UNEP) and the United Nations Centre for Human Settlements (UNCHS-Habitat).

Besides these, Kenya boasts of a very diversified culture in its 42 tribes, and rich historical and cultural resources, including museums and historical sites (table 1).

Table 1. Kenya's natural, historical and cultural resources

Nature of resource	Number
National parks	24
Marine parks	4
National reserves	24
Marine reserves	5
National sanctuary	1
Cultural museums	18
Ruins and historical sites	12

Source: Government of Kenya, 1995.

Since the master plan was developed, new forms of tourism have emerged, including promotion of local foods, ecotourism, promotion of Kenyan contemporary arts and culture, private ranches and village tourism.

b. *Performance and contribution of tourism to the economy*

The Kenyan tourism industry has experienced tremendous growth since the country attained independence, except during the period 1995–2002, when unprecedented challenges led to its erratic performance. Tourism arrivals and earnings have been on an upward trend since 2003, generally reflecting the fortunes in the economy. Tourism revenue increased by close to 52 per cent in 2004, from 25.8 billon Kenyan shillings in 2003 to 39.2 billion Kenyan shillings in 2004 and to 48.9 billion Kenyan shillings by 2005 (GoK, 2006), with estimates of a further rise, to 60 billion Kenyan shillings in 2006. Visitor numbers have also risen sharply, from 1.1 million in 2003, to 1.4 million in 2004 (18.7 per cent) and to 1.5 million in 2005. The number of bed nights rose by 46 per cent, from 2.6 million in 2003 to 3.8 million by 2004. This means that not only did more tourists arrive; they also stayed longer, potentially offering more opportunities to buy related local goods and services. Tourism has been a major driver of the country's economic growth contributing to about 13 per cent of the GDP (GoK, 2006), and it is one of the key sectors expected to drive the country into a middle-income economy by 2030.

International tourist arrivals in Kenya grew by an average of 9.8 per cent between 2000 and 2005, which was almost double the average growth of 5.4 per cent for Africa (WTTC). The most recent data available from the Government of Kenya indicates that, in 2006, the number of tourist arrivals remained at around 1.6 million but rose to 1.8 million in 2007. Arrivals in 2008 are likely to decline due to the political upheavals in early 2008.

Foreign exchange earnings from tourism have continued to play a significant role in improving the country's balance-of-payments position. For a long time Kenya relied heavily on agricultural exports, mainly coffee and tea, but after 1987, tourism became the third most important foreign exchange earner after these two commodities, and had overtaken them by 1997(table 2).

Table 2. Foreign exchange earnings from tourism, tea and coffee, 1999–2004 (million Kenyan shillings)

Year	Share of coffee in total exports		Share of coffee in total exports)		Share of coffee in total exports		Total exports
	Coffee	(%)	Tea	(%	Tourism	(%	
1999	12 029	10	33 065	27	21 367	17	122 559
2000	11 707	9	35 150	26	21 553	16	134 527
2001	7 460	5	34 485	23	24 239	16	147 589
2002	6 541	4	34 376	20	21 734	13	169 283
2003	6 286	3	33 005	18	25 768	12	183 153
2004	6 944	3	36 072	17	39 200	18	214 791

Source: GoK, *Statistical Abstracts,* various years.

Tourism is a major source of employment in the country. The sector is becoming increasingly important for employment generation; the latest Kenya data shows that tourism has consistently accounted for about 9 per cent of total formal employment (table 3). A similar picture emerges from the World Travel and Tourism Council's latest data, which shows that the contribution of the travel and tourism economy to employment is expected to rise from 483,000 jobs in 2008, 8.7 per cent of total employment or 1 in every 11.5 jobs, to 623,000 jobs, 9.1 per cent of total employment or 1 in every 11 jobs by 2018 (WTTC, 2008).

With regard to tourist spending, it is estimated that 66 per cent is spent in the Coast Province,[4] 14 per cent in Nairobi and 8 per cent in the Rift Valley Province (TTCI, 1998). This pattern of high concentration indicates that income and employment benefits from tourism are unevenly distributed throughout the country.

Despite the importance of tourism in Kenya's economy, the industry has been facing numerous challenges. These include substantial social and environmental costs, seasonality of employment, stiff competition from other countries, poor road infrastructure, insufficient institutional and regulatory frameworks, vulnerability to changes in the international market, and domestic unrest that gives the country a poor image.

Table 3. Contribution of tourism to wage employment in modern sector, 1999–2004 (thousand)

1999	2000	2001	2002	2003	2004
1 673.5	1 676.8	1 677.1	1 699.7	1 727.6	1 763.3
153.6	155.3	156.9	157.5	162.7	168
9.2	9.3	9.4	9.2	9.4	9.5

Source: GoK, Economic Surveys (various).

c. *Tourism infrastructure*

Hotels and tour operators

Kenya has about 168 classified hotels (table 4) with an estimated total of 29,385 beds. The majority of these hotels are in Nairobi (50), followed by Mombasa (26), Malindi (23), Kwale (11), and Nakuru & Elburgon (9). In addition to the classified hotels, 1,078 unclassified hotels and restaurants are registered with the Ministry of Tourism and Wildlife.

The majority of the hotels in the country are locally owned (63.7 per cent), while 22.6 per cent are jointly owned and 13.7 per cent are foreign-owned (table 4). Regions with a large number of beds among the classified hotels are Nairobi (9,078), Mombasa (5,010), Kwale (4,583) and Malindi (4,519).

Private villas and homes are another category of tourism accommodation, of which only 400 are registered.[5] This is because the Government started the registration process only from mid-2005 to ensure they operated within the law.

Table 4. Number of classified hotels, by class and ownership, by region

Region		1-star	2-star	3-star	4-star	5-star	Total	Local	Joint-venture	Foreign
		Number of hotels by class						Ownership		
Nairobi		5 (435)	12(1506)	21(3 084)	2(230)	10 (3 823)	50(9 078)	39	4	7
Nyeri		-	1(182)	2(190)	2(198)	-	5(570)	3	1	1
Kilifi		1(168)	2(90)	-	1(600)	1(600)	5(1 458)	2	2	1
Kwale		-	6(831)	3(3 132)	2(620)	-	11(4 583)	6	3	2
Lamu		-	2(92)	-	-	-	2(92)	-	-	2
Mombasa		2(182)	13(2 143)	7(1 621)	4(348)	1(716)	27(5 010)	11	13	3
Taveta		-	1(104)	-	-	-	1(104)	1	-	-
Embu		1(85)	-	-	-	-	1(85)	1	-	-
Machakos		1(118)	-	-	-	-	1(118)	1	-	-
Meru		2(114)	-	1(125)	-	-	3(239)	3	-	-
Kisii		1(80)	-	-	-	-	1(80)	1	-	-
Kisumu		2(160)	1(140)	-	-	-	3(300)	3	-	-
Malindi		1(280)	15(2427)	5(1380)	1(278)	1(154)	23(4 519)	10	7	6
Baringo		-	-	1(96)	1	-	2(266)	-	2	-
Kajiado		-	-	-	-	-	-	-	-	-
Kericho		1(130)	1(77)	-	-	-	2(207)	2	-	-
Laikipia		-	1(133)	-	-	-	1(133)	1	-	-
Nakuru & Elburgon		1(120)	6(335)	3(274)	-	-	10(729)	8	1	1
Narok		-	-	1(155)	-	1(168)	2(323)	2	-	-
Samburu		-	-	-	-	-	-	-	-	-
Kitale		1(24)	-	-	-	-	1(24)	1	-	-
Eldoret		1(82)	1(210)	-	-	-	2(292)	2	-	-
Webuye		1(50)	-	-	-	-	1(50)	1	-	-
Kakamega		-	2(159)	-	-	-	2(159)	2	-	-
Nanyuki		-	-	2(165)	-	1(230)	3(395)	1	2	-
Thika		-	1(64)	-	-	-	1(64)	1	-	-
Voi		-	2(88)	1(104)	-	-	3(192)	2	1	-
Naivasha		-	2(151)	3(164)	-	-	5(315)	3	2	-
Total		21 (2 028)	70 (8 732)	50 (10 490)	12 (2 444)	15 (5 691)	168 (29 385)	107 (63.7%)	38 (22.6%)	23 (13.7%)

Key: Numbers in brackets represent the number of beds.
Source: Ministry of Tourism and Wildlife, 2006. The Ministry list was updated with input from the Kenya Association of Hotel Keepers and Caterers (KAHC).

There are 2,075 registered tour operators and travel agents in the country, the majority of them (76 per cent) located in Nairobi and Malindi (table 5). About 74 per cent of these are locally owned, 17 per cent are jointly owned, and 9 per cent are foreign-owned.

Table 5. Registered tour operators and agents by ownership and by region

Region	Local	Joint ownership	Foreign	Total
Nairobi	1 178	101	105	1 384
Malindi	140	20	41	201
Mombasa	3	64	1	68
Kilifi	20	9	-	29
Nyeri	12	-	2	14
Rest of the country	178	155	46	379
Total	**1 531** (73.8%)	**349** (16.8%)	**195** (9.4%)	**2 075** (100%)

Source: Ministry of Tourism and Wildlife, 2005.

Air transport services, casinos and souvenirs

Air transport services are critical for tourism in Kenya, as more than 50 per cent of tourists arrive by air.[6] The major airlines are Kenya Airways (KQ), in partnership with Royal Dutch Airlines (KLM), and Emirates, South African Airways and Ethiopian Airlines. There are domestic flights to Mombasa, Malindi, Lokichogio, Kisumu and Eldoret, which are offered by Kenya Airways, Air Kenya, East African Safari Air, Jetlink, Aero Kenya and Air Leasing Services. Private chartered flights from smaller domestic airports to other areas in the country are also available.

Kenya Airways has been instrumental in ensuring easy and reliable access to Kenya for tourists. Under public management, the airline made perpetual losses but was sustained through government subisidies (Ikiara, 2001a). Following its partnership with KLM, which owns a 26 per cent stake, Kenya Airways has improved its financial base and flies to many locations worldwide. It is one of only three airlines in Africa that have met standards set by the International Air Transport Association (IATA), and it is one of the leading providers of air transport services in the continent. It is also among the most profitable airline companies in East Africa.

Casinos are mainly concentrated in the main tourist zones in Kenya as they are part of the tourism infrastructure. They are concentrated in Malindi, Mombasa and Nairobi. Souvenirs for tourists include handicrafts, curios, wood carvings and cooking pots. They are sold mainly in Nairobi, Nakuru, Wamunyu, Mombasa and Malindi, and provide livelihoods for a substantial number of households. However, there are no estimates for the actual number of people that are dependent on selling souvenirs for a living.

3. Conclusion

Tourism has been a major driver of the country's economic growth, accounting for about 13 per cent of its GDP. Since 1997, tourism has been the leading foreign exchange earner, having overtaken tea and coffee. The Kenyan tourism industry has developed considerable infrastructure with diverse services, including new products such as local foods, arts and culture, and ecotourism. The industry is very competitive, and local investment dominates, particularly in hotels and tour operations.

C. Trends in foreign direct investment and performance

1. FDI trends in Kenya

FDI flows to Kenya have been rather volatile over time (figure 1). Overall, they increased between 1970 and1979 though very slowly (see also annex table 1). In 1988 they fell sharply to as low as $0.39 million, followed by an abrupt rise in 1990, and then another decline to $4.30 million in 1994 followed again by a sharp rise in 2000. New investments by mobile phone companies and financing of electricity generation activities largely explain the post-2000 growth in FDI (Ngugi and Nyangoro, 2005).

Figure 1. FDI flows to Kenya, 1970–2002
($ million)

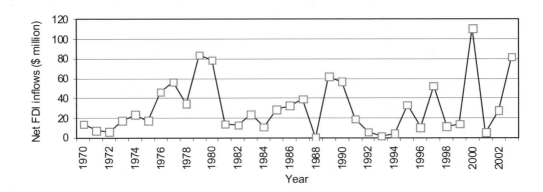

The Investment Policy Review of Kenya undertaken by UNCTAD in 2005 revealed that although Kenya was the lead destination of FDI within the East African Community (EAC) in the 1970s and 1980s, the relative level of inflows was never high by developing-country standards, as illustrated by FDI stock, which was only 7.5 per cent of GDP in 2003, compared with 25.3 per cent for Africa as a whole and 31.5 per cent for developing countries (table 6). In addition, unlike its neighbours, Kenya has benefited little in the global surge in FDI flows that started from the mid-1990s. FDI inflows into Kenya in the period 1996–2003 averaged $39 million a year compared to $280 million going to the United Republic of Tanzania and $220 million to Uganda. The country drew only $1.3 FDI inflows per capita during the period 1996–2003 compared with an average of $41 for developing countries as a whole, thus ranking Kenya 129th out of 140 countries.

Table 6. FDI inflows and stock in Kenya and selected developing countries/regions, 1996–2003

Country/region	Annual FDI inflows ($ million)	FDI stock ($ million)	FDI stock per capita ($)	FDI stock in GDP (%)
Kenya	**39.2**	**1 045.9**	**21.7**	**7.5**
Uganda	220.7	2 042.2	78.5	32.9
Tanzania, United Rep. of	282.2	2 582.5	68.0	26.8
South Africa	1 986.8	30 373.1	675.0	19.5
COMESA	3 656.3	51 900.3	136.7	29.4
Africa	11 513.8	167 111.3	196.5	25.3
Developing countries	197 331.1	2 280 171.3	449.2	31.5

Source: UNCTAD, 2005.

Kenya's poor performance in attracting FDI, especially in the 1970s and 1990s, is attributed to the lack of significant progress in economic reforms and their stop-go nature, corruption, a mediocre growth performance, deterioration in the quality of infrastructure and rising costs of labour services. In addition, Kenya lacked a large-scale privatization programme and has limited mineral resources, which normally also attract FDI in Africa.

2. Trends of FDI in tourism in Kenya

Tourism accounted for 10.7 per cent of the 820 projects with foreign participation registered by the Kenya Investment Authority (KIA) between 1997 and 2004 (table 7). While not all investment projects have to be registered with KIA, this data provides a reasonable estimate of the sectoral distribution of investments during the period. However, it does not capture the stock of FDI existing before 1997 or capital injections in existing enterprises.

Table 7. Registered projects with FDI participation, 1997–2004

Sector or industry	Share of foreign capital (by value) (%)
Manufacturing	23.6
Power	15.4
Tourism	10.7
Agriculture and agro-processing	9.9
Petrol services	4.4
Pharmaceuticals	3.0
Mining	2.5
Garments	2.2
Others	24.2
Total	100.0

Source: UNCTAD, 2005.

The Coast Province accounted for 20.3 per cent of all registered FDI projects in Kenya (table 8). The bulk of the FDI projects in the province are in tourism activities.

Table 8. Regional distribution of registered FDI projects, 2000–2004

	Region	Share in total (%)
1.	Nairobi	55.5
2.	Kisumu	17.6
3.	Mombasa	16.6
4.	Malindi	2.3
5.	Kilifi	1.4
6.	Migori	0.3
7.	Others	6.0
	Total	100.0

Source: UNCTAD, 2005.

The country's diversified tourism sector has long been a magnet for foreign investment. Foreign operators such as United Touring Company (United Kingdom), Express Travel (United States), Abercrombie and Kent (United Kingdom) and Pollmans (Germany) dominate this industry. However, the largest projects are the establishment of hotels and lodges for coastal and safari tourism. A number of the major international hotel chains are present, including Hilton, Intercontinental, Serena Hotels, Block Hotels and Holiday Inn (UNCTAD, 2005).

3. Conclusions

The flow of FDI to Kenya has generally been low and volatile over time. The sharp rise in 2000 has been attributed to new investments by mobile phone companies and the financing of electricity generation activities. Kenya's poor performance in attracting FDI compared to Uganda and the United Republic of Tanzania has been linked to the prevalence of corruption, the poor quality of infrastructure and rising costs of labour services. FDI flows in tourism accounted for about 10.7 per cent of the total flows into the country between 1997 and 2004.

D.   Extent and patterns of FDI in tourism: Survey findings

This section, including the tables and figures, presents the findings of the survey of tourism enterprises conducted during 2006 and 2007. Table 9 presents a summary of the hotels/restaurants and tour operators/agencies interviewed, by ownership. In addition to these, 14 suppliers to hotels and restaurants were also interviewed. Of the hotels/restaurants, about 69 per cent in our sample were locally owned and the remainder had at least 41 per cent foreign ownership. About 63 per cent of the tour operators and travel agencies in our sample were locally owned.[7]

Table 9. Sampled hotels and tour operators, by ownership, size and number of employees

Category	Hotels				Tour operators/travel agencies	
	Number	Average bed capacity	Average number of rooms	Average number of employees	Number	Value of assets (million Kenyan shillings)
100% locally owned	24	229	130	184	19	8.3
1-40% foreign- owned	0	-	-	-	2	2.2
41-80% foreign- owned	2	400	216	183	4	26
81-100% foreign-owned	9	331	180	220	5	23.8
Total	**35**	**265**	**148**	**193**	**30**	**15.1**

The ratio of the number of rooms to beds was about 1:2 for the hotels. Due to the variability of the sample in terms of capacity, hotels with a bed capacity of less than 150 were excluded from the analysis. This left 14 hotels with local ownership and 9 with a foreign presence, and this was the sample used for the subsequent analysis.

1.   Extent and form of FDI in tourism

Ownership of hotels and tour companies is predominantly local (table 10).[2]

a. Hotels and restaurants

Based on the number of rooms, 42.8 per cent of the hotels were foreign-owned, while 57.2 per cent were local. However, in terms of the gross turnover 56.2 per cent of the hotels had foreign ownership while 45.8 were locally owned. The results suggest that hotels with FDI may be performing better than the local ones, at least in terms of turnover.

Table 10: Ownership of hotels and tour operators, by number of rooms, turnover, asset .value and foreign reserves (%)

Category	Ownership	Rooms	Turnover	Asset value	Foreign reserves
Hotels	Local ownership	57.2 (N=23)	45.8 (N=23)		
	Foreign ownership	42.8 (N=23)	56.2 (N=23)		
Tour operators	Local ownership		75 (N=24)	59.5 (N=21)	61.7 (N=16)
	Foreign ownership		25 (N=24)	41 (N=21)	38.3 (N=16)

These findings differ from those of Sinclair (1990) who reported that about 78 per cent of the major coastal hotels, 67 per cent of hotels in Nairobi and 66 per cent in national parks had some foreign investment. Consultations with some stakeholders revealed that a number of local investors of Indian origin had bought hotels from foreigners, particularly after the 1997 Likoni clashes. This may partly explain the apparent reduction in foreign ownership. Indeed, most of the local owners are of Asian and British origin and this has contributed to the widespread perception in the country that the tourism sector is foreign dominated. Many Kenyan investors in this market have historical or current family links with countries such as India and the United Kingdom. As a result, they have many of the advantages that are typically associated with foreign investment, such as access to world markets, access to capital markets, and knowledge of international practices and changing tourism tastes or fashions (UNCTAD, 2006).

b. Tour operations/agencies

Using turnover as the weight, 25 per cent of the tour operators and travel agencies in our sample had some foreign ownership while 75 per cent were locally owned (table 10). The extent of foreign ownership rises to about 40 per cent when value of assets and foreign reserves are used as weights, indicating that the enterprises with foreign ownership had more assets and foreign reserves.

2. Classification

Some of the hotels are classified both locally and internationally to serve the different markets. The majority of the sampled hotels were 4-star (34.8 per cent) and 5-star (34.8 per cent). The 2-star hotels constituted 17.4 per cent of the sample. Hotels with foreign ownership were more likely to be 4 -star and 5-star, while the local ones covered all the categories (table 11).

Since foreign tour companies link local hotels with tourists, it is imperative for tourist hotels to have an international classification that is easily understood. The international rating is based on security and other parameters. Having an international rating for domestic hotels enables international visitors to gauge the kinds of services they are buying in relation to the foreign-owned hotels. Some hoteliers have been lobbying for the process of

classification to be improved, as it currently takes between one and two years. Although the Hotel and Restaurant Authority (HRA) has a criterion for classification, the exercise is complex, as it uses a host of parameters including size of rooms, bedroom fittings, the extent of services, the quality of food, available recreational facilities and the location. However, there have been concerns that more than 40 per cent of hotels and lodges in the country may be offering substandard services, well below the quality expected of their category.[3]

Table 11. Classification of hotels by degree of foreign ownership

Degree of foreign ownership	Classification of hotels				
	1-star	3-star	4-star	5-star Un-classified	Total
100% Local ownership	1			2	14
41–80% foreign ownership	0			0	2
81–100% foreign ownership	0			0	7
	14 (17.4%)	8 (34.8%)	8 (34.8%)	2	23

3. Financing

The survey found that financing of hotels was generally through loans and equity, with about 53 per cent of them financed through loans from commercial banks, 21 per cent through equity, and 16 per cent through a combination of loans and equity (table 12). The rest were financed from own savings and capital. It was not possible to distinguish from the sample whether the loans were from foreign sources or not. However, one hotel in the sample financed renovations from foreign sources. Although the Kenya Tourist Development Cooperation (KTDC) has the mandate to provide funding (in form of loans and/or equity participation) to cover short- and long-term investor needs, the corporation stopped extending loans to hotels in 2001 due to lack of funds.

From our sample, hotels with foreign ownership were more likely to rely on their own resources and equity for financing. However, the option of borrowing locally remained open even for hotels with foreign ownership.

Table 12. Type of financing by ownership

Category of ownership	No. of hotels by type of financing				
	Loans	Own money	Equity	Loans and equity	Total
100% local ownership	10	0	1	0	11
41-80% foreign ownership	0	1	0	1	2
81-100% foreign ownership	0	1	3	2	6
Total	10 (52.6%)	2 (10.5%)	4 (21.1%)	3 (15.8%)	19

4. Chain membership

About 57 per cent of the hotels surveyed were part of a chain or branch (figure 2). The survey results suggest that a foreign owned hotel is more likely than a local one to belong to a chain, as half of the hotels with foreign ownership belonged to a chain compared with only about one-third of the locally owned ones.

Figure 2.   Chain membership by degree of foreign ownership

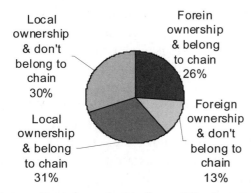

Note: Data shown in this figure differ from those in table 13 since 4 questionnaires had missing values on "type of association if a chain".

There are different types of chains: local chains such as the Sarova and Alliance hotels; international chains, some of which are locally owned, such as the Serena; and foreign-owned chains such as La Mada and Hilton. The relationship within chains is mainly through management contracts (table 13). Only one firm had a franchising agreement. The advantage of being a member of an international chain is that it allows exploitation of a bigger market and enables benchmarking against international standards. There are also sister hotels that are owned by the same group of people, have different names and are managed differently. A good example is the Fairmount chain of hotels, which include the Norfolk and the Ark. This kind of chain may carry fiscal advantages (i.e. tax reduction and tax exemption), as each is taken as a separate entity and therefore is subject to lower taxes than when taken together.

Table 13. Type of association of chain hotels, by ownership

Category of foreign ownership	Type of association of chain hotels		
	Management contract	Franchising agreement	Total
100% local ownership	4	0	4
41-80% foreign ownership	1	0	1
81-100% foreign ownership	3	1	4
Total	8	1	9

5. Extent of South-South FDI

There is some evidence of South-South FDI in the Kenyan tourism industry, although it is very limited. It was found in only two hotels and two tour operators in the sample. Investors from South Korea owned one of the hotels, while those from South Africa owned the other. Investors from China owned one of the tour operators and investors from India owned the other. The turnover of the two hotels and the two tour operators owned by these foreign investors constituted 36.2 per cent of the gross turnover for the sample with a foreign presence. Although the extent of South-South FDI was small, it seems likely to increase. Though not captured in the sample, the South African tour giant *Tourvest Group* acquired a majority stake in Vintage Africa,[4] a travel business with operations in Kenya and the United Republic of Tanzania. As Gelb (2005) and others have noted, there has been a rapid increase in South-South FDI over the past 10 years.

The survey results showed that tour operators and travel agents with foreign ownership tended to have more customers from developing countries than those that were fully locally owned.

6.   Conclusion

Contrary to the widespread perception that Kenyan's tourism industry is foreign dominated, the survey found that there was not a significant amount of FDI in tourism. Most of the local owners were of Asian and British origin and this may have contributed to this perception. The level of FDI in tourism appears to have declined, especially after the 1997 Likoni clashes when local Indians bought hotels from foreigners. The mode of financing in the sector has been mainly through loans and equity. More than half of the sampled hotels were part of a chain or a branch. Although the extent of South-South FDI is small, it is likely to increase.

E. Impact of FDI in tourism

This section consolidates the findings of the survey with respect to the impact of FDI in tourism.

1. Visitors, turnover, profits and reinvestment

Visitors

The number of visitors and bed nights and the occupancy rate for hotels have been on the increase since 2003. This has been attributed to a vigorous promotion campaign by KTB, tsunamis in Asia and the Middle East crises. The promotion campaign has been targeting high- spending rather than mass tourists.[11] The occupancy rate for locally owned hotels and those with foreign ownership was similar, at about 80 per cent in 2005, having risen from about 60 per cent in 2003. The average number of visitors per hotel was 65,800 in 2003, 73,000 in 2004 and 74,400 in 2005 for hotels with foreign ownership. In these hotels, the number of bed nights also increased from 57,500 in 2003 to about 100,000 in 2005. In the case of locally owned hotels, the number of visitors per hotel rose from 37,000 in 2003, to 48,000 in 2004 and to 57,600 in 2005. The average number of bed nights also rose from 75,000 in 2003 to 100,000 in 2005. Thus there appeared to be no major difference in the number of visitors received and the occupancy rates between hotels with foreign ownership and those that were locally owned. Hotels with a foreign presence had a much lower average number of domestic visitors (about 12,000) in 2005 compared to those that were fully local (about 21,000). On the other hand, they had a higher number of international visitors – about 62,400 on average – compared to the locally owned hotels that had an average of 36,600 visitors. The European Union (EU) accounted for the majority of the international visitors, with Germany and the United Kingdom being the main source countries. Regarding the purpose of visits, hotels with foreign ownership had a markedly higher percentage of visitors (87 per cent) arriving for holidays than the fully local hotels (43 per cent). Local hotels received more visitors on business (29 per cent) than hotels with a foreign presence (13 per cent).

The tourism slump in the late 1990s and early 2000s led to the closure of many hotels, and some were transformed into schools and hospitals. According to the Kenya Association of Hotel Keepers and Caterers (KAHC), which had a membership of 78 hotels in 2004, 17 hotels closed. All of these were locally owned, suggesting that local hotels have less resilience than those with foreign ownership. The hotels that survived the slump only did so with the help of domestic tourism, which shows the importance of this market segment.

South-South trade in terms of the number of visitors has generally been on the increase. For instance, from Africa, the number of bed nights increased from 849,600 in 2002 to 1.4 million in 2005, while those from Asia increased from 93,800 in 2003 to 173,800 in 2005. The number of African visitor departures rose from 64,600 in 1980 to 145,100 in 2000 and fell to 69,200 in 2002, while Asian visitor departures were 27,100, 55,600 and 44,700 in the corresponding years respectively (GOK, 2005). These figures indicate the growing significance of south-south tourism. The sample used in this study found that visitors from Asia and Africa as a proportion of international visitors was only about 2 per cent. This proportion is rather small but is likely to increase as a result of regional integration efforts by the Africa Union, the Common

Market for Eastern and Southern Africa (COMESA), the Intergovernmental Authority on Development (IGAD) and the East African Community (EAC).

Turnover

There is evidence of substantial turnover in the tourism industry. The tourism sector received a total of 48.9 billion Kenyan shillings in 2005, 56.2 billion Kenyan shillings in 2006 and 65.4 billion in 2007, which is expected to rise to 60 billion Kenyan shillings in 2006. However, consultations with stakeholders indicated that other countries like Egypt and Mauritius receive much higher tourism revenue. Results of our survey showed that tour operators have a turnover that ranges from 150,000 to 500 million Kenyan shillings, with a mean of 56.25 million Kenyan shillings. Hotels, on the other hand, have a gross annual turnover ranging from 38 million to 960 million Kenyan shillings, with a mean of 343 million Kenyan shillings. A larger proportion of the turnover is from accommodation and restaurant services for both local and foreign-owned hotels (annex table 3).

Table 14 shows the average capacity, gross turnover, profits and taxes by degree of foreign ownership. Although hotels with some foreign ownership had a higher number of beds, profits, taxes and gross turnover relative to those that were

Table 14. Average profits, taxes, and turnover of hotels by category of ownership

Category of ownership	Number of rooms	Profits	Taxes	Gross turnover
100% local ownership	169.4	79.1	100	258
1-100% foreign ownership	219.4	114.4	150	457
41-80% Foreign ownership	216.0	192.5	-	413
81-100% Foreign ownership	220.4	103.2	150	470
Total	**189**	**94.0**	**117**	**343**

Note: Monetary figures are in millions of Kenyan shillings.

fully locally owned, the differences were not significant. This may be attributed to the apparently low level of FDI. Another reason could be that the domestic firms belong to the same networks. Some of the hotels are either chains or members of clubs with better access to information, which narrows potential gaps in technology and management expertise.

In the case of tour operators, firms with foreign ownership had a higher value of assets while locally owned tour firms had a higher level of foreign exchange reserves (table 15), which may be attributed to the repatriation of profits (about 42 per cent) by those with foreign ownership.

Table 15. Average value of assets, gross turnover and foreign exchange reserves of tour operators by ownership (million Kenyan shillings)

Category of ownership	Value of assets	Gross turnover	Foreign exchange reserves
100% local	8.3	43.04	37.1
1-100% foreign	23	72.0	26.0
1-40% foreign	2.2	250.8	-
41-80% foreign	26	36.0	33.9
81-100% foreign	23.8	29.0	20.1
Total	**15.1**	**56.3**	**31.0**

Profits, reinvestment and new products

Most of the hotels and tour operators made profits in 2005. For tour operators with foreign ownership, about 78 per cent of the profits were shared among the owners compared with about 30 per cent for local tour firms. Locally owned tour operators had a significantly higher percentage of profits that were reinvested (90 per cent compared to 22.2 per cent for those with foreign ownership).

Hotels with local ownership also reinvested a higher percentage of profits (71 per cent) as compared to those with foreign ownership (40 per cent). The latter repatriated about 42 per cent of their profits. However, there were no differences in the share of profits distributed among owners.

Hotel reinvestment was mostly for renovations and expansion, which was fuelled by strong growth of the industry since 2003. A good example is the Fairmont chain of hotels (Mount Kenya Safari Club, The Ark, Aberdare country Club, the Norfolk and Mara Safari club), which, at the time of the survey, were undertaking renovations expected to cost 2.6 billion Kenyan shillings.[2] The hotels are owned by Saudia Arabia-based Kingdom Hotel Investments, Kuwait-based IFA Hotels and Resorts and the United States-based Fairmont Hotels and Resorts. They acquired the facilities in 2005 from Lonrho hotels. The Sun N' Sand, a locally owned 5-star hotel located on the coast, also undertook renovations at a cost of 400 million Kenyan shillings. Other hotels that were making additional investments were Sarova Whitesands, Baobab Beach Resort and Neptune Paradise. The latter was adding 40–50 new rooms.

Some hotels were introducing new products into the market. The Fairmont Hotels & Resorts chain was introducing signature restaurants, soft adventure activities, cultural education and experiences, technology and expansion of services.[3]

2. Booking systems, business relationships and kinds of packages

Booking systems and business relationships

Sinclair (1990) found short-term contracts as the main form of contractual arrangement between tour operators and hoteliers. She also found that besides foreign individuals and institutions, a number of foreign tour operators had invested in hotels in Kenya in the form of either total ownership or joint ventures with local investors. However, our survey found practically no permanent or long-term chain agreement with tour operators. Many of the tour firms liked to operate independently, but a few had a common ownership with hotels. For example, the same group owns Pollmans Tours and Travel Ltd and Baobab Beach Resort and Taita Hills Salt Lake Hotel.

From our survey, hotel bookings were mainly made by individuals (79.2 per cent), followed by local tour operators (71 per cent), foreign tour operators (66.7 per cent) and through the Internet (66.7 per cent). Tour operator services were mainly booked by individuals, followed by the Internet and foreign tour operators (table 16).[4] The percentage of bookings made through the Internet is growing, which shows the increasing importance of technology in tourism.

Hotels with foreign ownership had significantly higher level of bookings through the Internet than foreign tour operators, while hotels with 100 per cent local ownership had significantly higher level of bookings through local tour operators. With respect to tour operators, those with 100 per cent local ownership had significantly higher levels of bookings through other local tour operators, local travel agencies, the Internet and individuals.

Table 16. Mode of booking clients by hotels and tour operators

Mode of booking	Hotels Percentage of bookings	Tour operators and travel agents Percentage of bookings
Local tour operators	71.0	23.3
Foreign tour operators	66.7	56.7
Foreign travel agents	45.8	20.0
Local travel agents	45.8	40.0
Internet	66.7	60.0
Individuals	79.2	73.3
Organizations	4.2	0

Reliance on other local tour operators for customers is due to the nature of their relationship with foreign tour operators. The relationship is characterized by unfavourable terms, largely because the local tour companies have low negotiating power compared with foreign tour operators. Consultations indicated that local tour operators received unfavourable terms and rates from the international tour companies, including requirements to employ expatriates from abroad as tour guides. For example, Pollmans Tours and Travel Ltd. (a local firm) is obliged to employ three tour guides from Tui (an international tour operator). While this used to make sense a few years ago due to language barriers, a significant number of Kenyans, who have more information about the country, are now fluent in most of the major foreign languages. Moreover, local tour firms also receive low rates due to lack of adequate information. Foreign tour operators are supposed to transfer money deposited by customers in their accounts to local tour operators less their commissions. However, local tour operators do not know exactly how much the foreign tour firms receive from customers. They find it difficult to compete against the foreign tour operators, many of which are large, with a presence in most European countries.

The use of foreign tour operators leads to a major leakage of tourism revenues: most of the money is paid abroad, and may remain there, as most hotels have offshore accounts. It also constitutes an entry barrier for new tour operators entering the domestic market because without relationships with foreign tour operators it is difficult to compete with those that have such relationships.

Most hotels use their own booking system (table 17). However, about 78 per cent of the tour firms and travel agents use Galileo booking systems for ticketing, 14.3 per cent use their own systems and 7.1 per cent use Amadeus.

Table 17. Types of booking systems used by different ownership categories of hotels

| Category | Booking system used by hotel | | | | |
	Galileo	Gateway	Fidelio	Own system	Total
100% local ownership	3	0	0	5	8
41-80% foreign ownership	0	0	0	1	1
81-100% foreign ownership	0	1	1	4	6
Total	3	1	1	10	15

All-inclusive packages

The survey results showed that tour operators with foreign ownership had significantly fewer individual customers than locally owned tour operators. They were more likely to have customers on all-inclusive packages. With respect to hotels, those with foreign ownership had a much higher number of visitors on tour operators' packages compared with the local hotels. All-inclusive packages benefit international chains at the expense of the local economy. This is because tourists on such packages tend to limit their spending on activities within the chains and very little on goods and services provided by the business clusters that surround the hotel chains. All-inclusive packages also affect the quality of services provided to the tourists, because the huge discounts hotels offer on such packages force them to provide low quality wine, beer and food. This has a negative impact on the image of the destination.

3. Purchases

Spending by hotels on items such as food, beverages and cleaning chemicals range from 1.3 million to 270 million Kenyan shillings per annum, with a mean of 92 million Kenyan shillings. The survey showed that about 84 per cent of these items were purchased locally, of which about 87 per cent were purchased from local distributors/wholesalers and about 12 per cent from local small and medium-sized enterprises (SMEs). This indicates a substantial spillover to the local economy. Most of the local purchases were sourced from local wholesalers, supermarkets (e.g. Nakumat, Uchumi), Kenya Breweries and Kenya Wines Agency. In addition, they outsourced some services such as transport, staff transport, security and laundry services to SMEs. Some of the hotels reported importing about 20 per cent of their purchases, mainly equipment and linen. The hotels did not import any consumables directly; but sourced them from local suppliers, again creating spillover effects. Interviews with suppliers of goods to hotels showed that about 17 per cent of purchases of the suppliers were imported. The reasons given for procuring goods and services abroad included better quality, reasonable prices and unavailability of goods locally.

The survey showed that hotels with foreign ownership had a higher level of total purchases than most of the local hotels. Similar results were obtained with respect to specific commodities such as food, beverages and cleaning materials. Both categories of hotels incurred significant costs of electricity that ranged from 230,000 to 40 million Kenyan shillings with a mean of 11 million Kenyan shillings, but with no significant differences between the two kinds of hotels. Because of power outages and fluctuations, most hotels (foreign-owned and local) had stand-by generators.

About 76 per cent of the hotels had a central procurement policy for goods and services. Of these, about 85 per cent were locally owned hotels and about 63 per cent were foreign-owned hotels (table 18). Thus the results suggest that there is a greater tendency for local hotels to have a central procurement policy compared to hotels with foreign ownership.

Table 18. Central procurement policy by hotel ownership

Category of foreign ownership	Is there a central procurement policy for the hotel/group?		
	Yes	No	Total
100% local ownership	11 (84.6%)	2 (15.4%)	13
41-80% foreign ownership	1	1	2
81-100% foreign ownership	4	2	6
1-100% foreign ownership	5 (62.5%)	3 (37.5%)	8
Total	**16**	**5**	**21**

With respect to tour operators, total annual purchases of goods and services ranged from 30,000 to a maximum of 35 million Kenyan shillings with a mean of 28.12 million Kenyan shillings. The proportion of goods and services imported by locally owned tour operators was 27.5 per cent compared with 26.2 per cent for those with foreign ownership, which is not a statistically significant difference.

4. Employment, wage policy and social policies

Employment

The sampled hotels and restaurants had a total of 5,818 employees, out of which 76.2 per cent were full-time employees followed by part-time workers (8.8 per cent), contract workers (8 per cent) and casual workers (7 per cent). Female employees accounted for 28.5 per cent of the total.

The majority (75 per cent) of full-time employees in the tour operations and travel agencies were men, and they constituted an even higher proportion (79 per cent) when all employees are considered. The survey of tour operators and travel agents showed that the number of women employed in each firm on a full-time basis ranged from 0 to 15 with a mean of 4.1, compared with a range of 0–105 men with a mean of 12.4. Of the total number of employees, the number of men employed ranged from 2 to 124 with a mean of 16.3, while for women they ranged from 0 to 15 with a mean of 4.4.

In the tourism industry in Kenya, there are three seasons in the year based on the number of tourist arrivals: high season, low season and shoulder season. During the low season, most of the employees are laid off leaving a skeleton staff. Some hotels close down and often use that period to undertake renovations. In the high season, hotels use casual and part-time workers, which affects the quality and efficiency of services due to the inexperience of these workers. The need to encourage employers to employ permanent staff as opposed to casual staff has been noted, (e.g.Ministry of Tourism and Wildlife, 2006).

There were no significant differences between locally owned hotels and hotels with foreign ownership in terms of the number of employees they hire (table 19).

Table 19. Average number of employees in hotels and tour operators by ownership

Category of ownership	Men Hotels	Men Tour firms	Women Hotels	Women Tour firms	Total Hotels	Total Tour firms
100% local ownership	189.9	14.6	65.5	4	255.4	18.6
1-100% foreign ownership	166.7	14.9	82.6	3.9	249.2	18.8
1-40% foreign ownership	-	63.5	-	7.5	-	71
41-80% foreign ownership	116.5	4.25	66.5	4.0	183.0	8.3
81-100% foreign ownership	181.0	3.4	87.1	2.6	268.1	6

Similarly, there were no significant differences in employment between local and foreign-owned tour operators and travel agencies, or with respect to gender and distribution of skills among the employees (table 20). Many of the tour operators surveyed were basically family businesses with the father as the managing director and the son as financial controller and the remaining employees were junior staff. The firms were not adequately structured to enable an upward movement of staff. This lack of opportunity to move up the ladder could explain why there was a high turnover of staff in these firms.

The guest-to-staff ratio was extremely high for both types of hotels: 298:1 for hotels with a foreign presence and 226:1 for those that were fully local. This suggests that service quality is an issue of major concern.

Expatriates

The number of expatriates employed in hotels ranged from zero to a maximum of three with a mean of 1.55. There was no marked difference in the number of expatriates employed by the two categories of hotels. However, in the case of tour operators, there was a marked difference: those with foreign ownership had expatriates while local ones had none. As mentioned earlier, this may be linked to the type of contracts they have with overseas tour operators.

Skills composition and salaries

Out of all the employees working in the hotels and restaurants, 36.1 per cent were low-skilled, followed by medium-skilled (33.7 per cent) and high-skilled (30.2 per cent) (table 20). The low-skilled workers were paid an average of 6,102 Kenyan shillings per month as compared to the high-skilled workers who earned an average of 18, 310 Kenyan shillings per month.

Table 20. Number of hotel employees by skill level and gender, and average monthly salary

Skill level	Male	Female	Total	Average monthly salary (Kenyan shillings)
High skills	1 217	538	1 755 (30.2%)	18 310
Medium skills	1 272	688	1 960 (33.7 %)	10 032
Low skills	1 564	539	2 103 (36.1%)	6 102
TOTAL	**4 053**	**1765**	**5 818 (100%)**	

Contrary to expectations, hotels with foreign ownership had a significantly lower number of skilled employees and skilled women employees. The same category of hotels also had a significantly larger number of employees with low skills.[15] By contrast, it was the locally owned tour operators that had a significantly larger number of employees with low skills. (However, the definition of skills levels was qualitative and the study could not check that all interviewees meant the same time when they defined a job as being 'high' or 'low'-skilled.)

Minimum wages ranged from about $31 (2,285 Kenyan shillings for unskilled workers to $97 (7,295 Kenyan shillings) for a higher skilled position (GoK, 2006). [16] Judging by these standards, the wages for those working in hotels appeared to be relatively higher than the minimum wages. With respect to tour operators, the starting wage for a front desk manager was significantly higher in firms with foreign ownership compared with locally owned ones.

Training and mobility

The majority of the members of staff working in hotels (75 per cent) received their training from Utalii College. Staff trained in technical institutes accounted for 16 per cent as compared to 9.3 per cent trained in universities. About 75 per cent of the hotels reported that their local management staff acquired their training within the country and in particular from Utalii College, while 6.3% of the hotels reported sending their local management for further training abroad (India South Africa and the United Kingdom) as compared with only 3.3% for tour operators and travel agents.

All the hotels reported sending their staff for refresher courses to Utalii College, and these courses generally last 2–6 weeks.

Each hotel has an allocation of 10–15 members of staff who can attend those courses every year. A training levy collected from hotels and restaurants meets the cost for the refresher courses, which also are an incentive for staff upgrading. Other training incentives include, for example, a programme sponsored by the Federation of Kenya Employers (FKE), through which member companies are reimbursed some part of the training expenses. In addition to the refresher courses, all hotels had in-house training. About 16 per cent of the hotels had a regular annual training budget of an average of 161, 000 Kenyan shillings. Hotels invest in training and development of staff in order to create a culture of excellence.[17]

This is unlike tour operators, that do not pay any training levy. Even though the training offered at Utalii mainly focuses on accommodation, a majority of the employees working in tour operating firms acquired their training from Utalii before being employed. There are refresher courses being offered in the local universities and middle level technical colleges like Mombasa and Kenya Polytechnic. One firm reported sending its employees to India and the United Kingdom for training.

Utalii College is unable to meet the high demand for training. Training for the hotel industry has been at the certificate and diploma levels and there was felt to be need for post-graduate training in the hospitality industry. There was also a feeling that Utalii offers only traditional courses that are not regularly revised to keep pace with the current changes, and therefore may not be equipping staff with the most up-to-date knowledge and practical training in the rapidly changing industry. Moreover, the college is constrained by limitations in terms of funding, numbers of classes and the capacity of the Utalii Hotel to offer practical training and staff. There was not evidence of differences in training and mobility between those firms that were fully local and those that had some foreign ownership.

Health insurance and HIV/AIDS policy

More hotels with foreign ownership reported providing their staff with health insurance (table 21) than the locally owned hotels. However, there were no marked differences with respect to HIV/AIDS policy.

Table 21. Degree of foreign ownership and health insurance and HIV/AIDS policy among hotels

	Health Insurance		
	Yes	No	Total
Firms with foreign ownership	8 (100%)	0	8
Local firms	12 (92.3%)	1	13
Total	20	1	21
	HIV/AIDS policy		
	Yes	No	Total
Firms with foreign ownership	6 (67%)	3 (33%)	9
Local firms	8 (57%)	6 (43%)	14
			(100%)
Total	14	9	23

Similarly, there were more tour operators and travel agents with foreign ownership who reported providing health insurance to their staff and having an HIV/AIDS policy than the locally owned firms (table 22).

Table 22. Health insurance for staff and HIV/AIDS policy among tour operators, by ownership

	Health Insurance		
	Yes	No	Total
Firms with foreign ownership	10 (91%)	1 (9%)	11
Local firms	3 (43%)	4 (57%)	7
Total	13	5	18
	HIV policy		
	Yes	No	Total
Firms with foreign ownership	4 (57%)	3 (43%)	7
Local firms	2 (15.4%)	11 (84.6%)	13
Total	6	14	20

5. Environmental conservation

Environmental conservation activities commonly undertaken by firms in the tourism industry include tree planting and landscaping, installation of energy-saving technologies (e.g. more efficient electric bulbs), borehole construction, installation of incinerators for waste disposal and water conservation. Of the 23 hotels in the survey sample, 18 reported having an environmental impact assessment or audit undertaken by the National Environmental Management Authority (NEMA), while 5 hotels were members of the Green Globe Movement and 7 had an ISO 14000 Certificate (table 23). However, many others did not seem aware of ISO certification or what it meant. One of the five hotels with Green Globe 21 certification is the Serena chain, which has won numerous awards for its environmental and sustainability approaches. Two hotels, one locally owned and the other foreign-owned, indicated they planned to seek a Green Globe 21 certificate in the future.

Table 23. Environmental conservation by hotels and tour operators

	Hotels		Tour operators	
Conservation methods	Frequency	Percentage of respondents	Frequency	Percentage of respondents
Waste disposal	19	82.6	12	40
Energy saving technology	17	73.9	10	33.3
Water conservation	14	60.9	9	30
Afforestation/reforestation	15	65.2		
Impact assessment audit	17	73.9	-	-
ISO 14000 Certificate	7	30.4	-	-
Membership of Green Globe	5	21.7	-	-

In the draft national tourism policy, the Government undertakes to ensure that the Environmental Co-ordination and Management Act of 1999 (and related regulations) is enforced (MOT&W, 2006). In general, hotels undertake the mandatory annual environmental audits required by NEMA. About 56.3 per cent of the hotels reported that they had not incurred any expenditure on environmental activities in 2005. The other hotels claimed an expenditure ranging from 3,500 to 2.4 million Kenyan shillings. No tour firms and travel agents reported undertaking any environmental impact assessment or environmental audit.

Hotels with foreign ownership appeared to engage in environmental conservation activities to the same extent as locally owned hotels (table 24). In the case of tour firms, very few reported undertaking any environmental activities, a fact associated with their location in towns and cities, and the fact that their activities are not carried out in one location. Tour operators did not have a regular budget on environmental activities.

Table 24. Environmental activities of hotels, by ownership

Energy-saving technologies			
	Yes	No	Total
Firms with foreign ownership	6 (66.7%)	3	9
Local firms	11 (84.6%)	2	13
Total	17	5	22
Water conservation			
	Yes	No	Total
Firms with foreign ownership	6 (66.7%)	3	9
Local firms	8 (66.7%)	4	12
Total	14	7	21
Waste disposal			
	Yes	No	
Firms with foreign ownership	8 (88.9%)	1	9
Local firms	11(91.2%)	1	12
Total	19	2	21
Afforestation/reforestation			
	Yes	No	
Firms with foreign ownership	6(66.7%)	3	9
Local firms	9(69.2%)	4	13
Total	15	7	22

6.   Community initiatives

Some of the community initiatives of hotels and tour operators included donations to schools, the Red Cross, Christian organizations, youth organizations, prisons, churches, children's homes and famine relief organizations, and some stated they provided spaces to curio sellers within the hotel premises (table 25). Of the hotels surveyed, 56.3 per cent reported that they provided donations to

children's homes, 28.1 per cent to schools, 9.4 per cent to famine relief, and 6.3 per cent were involved in training young people.

Table 25.   Community initiatives of hotels and tour operators

	Hotels		Tour operators	
	Number of	Percentage	Number of	Percentage of
Initiative	hotels	of total	hotels	total
1. Youth training	2	6.3	1	3.3
2. Donations to children homes	18	56.3	3	10.0
3. Donations to schools	9	28.1	1	3.3
4. Contributions to famine relief	3	9.4	0	0
5. Others	0	0	6	20

The amount of money spent by hotels on local community initiatives in the year 2005 ranged between 5, 000 and 10 million Kenyan shillings, depending on the size of the hotel. At least 22 per cent of the hotels spent over 500,000 Kenyan shillings on local community initiatives in 2005.

The local communities do not benefit much in terms of employment, except for manual jobs such as gardening.[18] For beach hotels, most of the jobs appeared to be given to people from other regions in Kenya as the local people lacked the required skills and expertise. However, the hotels reported allowing dancers from the local communities to entertain tourists for payment, and local people to sell curios. Another local community initiative is that of giving preferential treatment in the purchase of agricultural commodities. Fairmont Hotels, for instance, reported giving the surrounding farmers first priority for the supply of chickens, eggs and vegetables.[19]

Generally, tour operators appeared to engage in fewer community activities than the hotels (table 25), which may be attributable to the fact that they are not located within areas where communities live. Unlike hotels, tour operators did not seem to have a regular budget for community initiatives. Due to the limited responses, it was not possible to ascertain whether tour operators with foreign ownership were more involved in community initiatives than their locally owned counterparts. In addition, communities were not interviewed to gauge the impact of the initiatives.

7. Conclusions

We did not find consistent evidence of significant differences between the impact of foreign investment and local investment in tourism. This suggests that locally owned tourism enterprises in Kenya have matured and built capacity to the extent that there are only a few aspects of performance in which they differ significantly from enterprises with foreign ownership, and these may be related more to size, scale or market segment than to ownership per se.

F. The role of regional integration

Regional integration holds promising business opportunities for Kenya. About 22 per cent of the hotels and even a larger number of tour operators and travel agents (about 50 per cent) reported having clients from the region or, in the case of chains, having branches in other countries of the region. Some tour operators like Pollmans, for instance, have branches and sister companies in the United Republic of Tanzania, which has many national parks, including the Serengeti, that offer a large diversity of wildlife. While Pollmans is a locally-owned enterprise, the results of the survey suggested that firms with some degree of foreign ownership were more likely to be doing business in the region than the locally owned ones (table 26), although the survey sample was of course limited.

Table 26. Hotels doing business in the region, by ownership

	Category of tourism firms	Yes	No	Total
	Fully local	2	12	14
Hotels	With foreign ownership	3	6	9
	Total	5 (21.7%)	18	23
	Fully local	8	9	17
Tour firms	With foreign ownership	7	4	11
	Total	15 (53%)	11	28

Perceptions of local tourism enterprises and those with foreign ownership about cross-border trade before and after regional integration were not markedly different, perhaps because integration is a relatively recent phenomenon.

Regional integration appears to have reduced some of the major problems that hitherto seriously affected cross-border trade, such as customs clearance and cross-border movement of business people.

However, some teething problems are being experienced especially with regard to implementation. First of all, Kenyan registered vehicles are not allowed across the border for game drives in the neighbouring United Republic of Tanzania, yet those from the United Republic of Tanzania are allowed in Kenya. In Kenyan game parks, vehicles with foreign registration number plates are charged special, often high, fees. There is therefore need for further streamlining of the movement of goods and services in the EAC countries. Some stakeholders consulted also claimed that Kenyans were often treated with suspicion in Uganda and the United Republic of Tanzania. Secondly, tour operators cannot take tourists across the three countries because the labour laws do not permit the exchange of drivers. Thus, Kenyan drivers cannot take over when Tanzanian drivers cross over into Kenya, even though they know their own terrain better.[20] As a result, firms are forced to rely on guides and maps, which costs time. This applies even to firms that have branches in the three countries. In one incident, scores of tourists heading to the United Republic of Tanzania from Kenya were stranded at the Namanga border point after their drivers were denied entry. They were expected to hand over their vehicles and tourists to local drivers.[21] Thirdly, tourists with a visa to one of the countries of the EAC region require visas to enter the other two countries. This is rather expensive and tends to discourage tourists from visiting the three countries as part of a single package.

If these bottlenecks could be addressed under the customs union, which is expected to evolve into a political federation, there is considerable potential for marketing East Africa as a single tourism destination. There are a variety of attractions in the three countries within very short distances. These include coastal beaches and national parks in Kenya and the United Republic of Tanzania, gorillas in the Ruwenzori Mountains in Uganda, and conference facilities in Nairobi. Marketing the region as a joint destination could attract more FDI, and would be particularly beneficial for Kenya. The EAC believes a regional marketing strategy would bring more tourists to the region and give it a competitive advantage.[22] It is expected that a regional approach will enable the pooling of scarce resources and achieve economies of scale. There are currently plans for joint regional marketing of tourism, including formulation of regional classification and standardization criteria for hotels, lodges and restaurants. Creation of a common visa would allow tourists access to all three countries. Other areas where a regional approach could maximize cost effectiveness include joint development of shared facilities and destinations such as Lake Chala, Lake Victoria and Mount Elgon (MOT&W, 2006).

However, given the slow progress in dealing with the various teething problems of regional integration, the findings suggest that Kenya should consider becoming more proactive. For example, the Ministry in charge of regional integration could team up with the one in charge of tourism to encourage the EAC to deal with these problems as matter of priority.

Conclusion

Regional integration is having a positive impact on Kenyan's tourism industry and may attract more FDI in tourism if the teething problems still facing the customs union are addressed. These problems include cumbersome customs clearance procedures, difficulties in cross-border movements of business people, and the requirement of individual tourist visas for each country. To enhance the role of regional integration, the EAC should consider joint tourism promotion, harmonization of classification and standardization criteria for hotels, and a regional tourist visa as a priority.

G.   Policy, regulatory and institutional issues affecting FDI in tourism

1.   Tourism policy

Kenya's tourism policy has in the past been characterized by inconsistency, poor coordination, lack of a vision and overall development strategy and poor implementation (Ikiara, 2001a and b). Moreover, there is inadequate integration and harmonization with related sectoral policies and national development priorities. With the exception of the Sessional Paper No. 8 of 1969 on Development of Tourism in Kenya (GoK, 1969), the country for a long time lacked a specific tourism policy document. It is only very recently that the long-awaited tourism policy has become a concrete tool. This may have affected FDI in tourism, together with other aspects of the industry, in the country.

Since independence, the Government has adopted a generally open door policy for foreign investment in tourism. Liberalization of borrowing regulations in 1977, for example, allowed foreign companies to borrow from local financial institutions up to 100 per cent of the funds necessary for new investments or for increasing existing investments, which encouraged foreign investors (Sinclair, 1990). The main aspects of tourism policy development in the country, which influenced FDI in one way or another, can be summarized as follows:

- At independence, Kenya enacted the Foreign Investments Protection Act and provided special tax relief on hotel construction, such as accelerated depreciation on buildings (GoK, 1970). At the same time, policy focused on a mixture of mass and upmarket tourism. The Foreign Investment Protection Act guaranteed investment against expropriation and allowed repatriation of profits.

- Between 1965 and 1994, the Government's focus on upmarket tourism gave way to an emphasis on mass tourism by allowing uncontrolled development of tourism facilities. As a consequence, the role of "package tourism" and "all-inclusive tours" increased over time. It is estimated that by 1979 about 40 per cent of the tourists came on package arrangements (GOK, 1980).

- There was a requirement that local citizens own at least 51 per cent of the equity in lodges located inside national parks and county council game reserves (GoK, 1974) and in non-hotel tourist service establishments, regardless of their location. Majority foreign ownership was allowed for hotels located outside parks and reserves. This policy provided an opportunity for Kenyans to enter into useful joint ventures with foreign investors, thereby enhancing transfer of technology and management skills.

- The Government established the Investment Advisory Centre as an important institution for promoting private foreign investment. In 2004 the Kenya Investment Authority was established, through the Investment Act 2004, with a mandate to promote private investment from both local and foreign investors.

- Foreign exchange controls were introduced in 1974 to curb the illegal transfer abroad of foreign currency (GoK, 1974). The Central Bank and the Income Tax Department introduced new reporting requirements for tourism firms. The tourism sector was therefore subject to foreign exchange control procedures and penalties, which remained in place until the early 1990s, when the foreign exchange market was liberalized and import restrictions lifted. This served historically as a disincentive to foreign participation in tourism, as foreign investors could not easily repatriate their profits. Moreover, the quality of services in hotels was affected due to difficulty in purchasing imported inputs.

- The Domestic Tourism Council (DTC) that operated between 1984 and 1994 had a considerable impact on the growth of domestic tourism. As pointed out earlier, domestic tourism helped even enterprises with foreign ownership to stay afloat during the period 1995–2002 when the sector experienced unprecedented challenges.

- Kenya made commitments under the General Agreement on Trade in Services (GATS) in October 1999 (Ikiara, 2001a), including in the area of tourism. The specific areas affected were hotels and restaurants, travel agencies, tour operators and tourist guide services. The country also committed to three out of the four modes of supply defined by GATS: cross-border, consumption abroad and commercial presence. This meant that foreigners could use any of these modes to supply tourism services to or in Kenya. The country does not have restrictions on equity holdings, forms of doing business, or limitations on purchase and size of establishments.

- Since the 1990s, there has been considerable public divestment of the sector, as in other sectors of the economy, although the pace has slowed down substantially. This was set to pick up again following the passing by Parliament of the Privatisation Bill in 2005.

- Between 1994 and 2000, Government policy focused again on upmarket tourism although no tangible measures were taken.

- Since 2000, Government policy has reverted to that of the independence period, focusing on a mixture of mass and upmarket tourism. However, even during this period no concrete measures have been taken to improve the country's ability to provide high-value tourist products, even though the policy focus is on high-spending tourists.

- In 2002 the Government found it necessary to develop an elaborate National Tourism Policy (box 1). However, at the time of writing this report the policy was still under preparation and had yet to be finalized. Only very recently, in 2008 did it appear that the policy would be finalised.

- In 2003, a tourist police unit (TPU) was established in response to one of the main bottlenecks to tourism – insecurity. In addition, there is an anti-terrorist police unit.

- The Economic Recovery Strategy for Wealth and Employment Creation (2003/2007) spelt out measures aimed at increasing tourist arrivals and diversifying tourist source markets. The measures included:
  - Aggressive marketing of the country as a major tourist destination, which is being given greater priority than ever before;
  - Introduction of a tourism promotion levy;
  - Exploitation of newly developed niche markets, notably targeting the film industry, conference and sports tourism;
  - Encouragement of domestic tourism;
    - Diversification of tourism products;
    - Reorganization and upgrading of the tourist police force;
    - Review of the legal and regulatory framework on licensing and issuance of permits; and
    - Promotion of investments in the tourism sector through provision of affordable finance.

Box 1. Proposed FDI incentives in the draft national tourism policy

The Government of Kenya recognizes the importance of attracting foreign investment in order to achieve the growth and development objectives of the tourism sector. Foreign investment is expected to increase competition and improve standards, as well as create employment and facilitate economic growth.

The Government aims to establish a climate of political stability, economic growth and profitability, and provide transparent, stable and consistent policies to attract foreign investment, and, through the Kenya Investment Authority, to provide an effective "one-stop shop" for the facilitation and processing of foreign investment.

In order to ensure that the tourist product is both up to standard and offers value for money, the Government shall continue to offer tax and other incentives to investors so as to encourage upgrading of existing tourist accommodation facilities and investment in new facilities. Incentives, whether tax-related or otherwise, shall not be limited to the accommodation sector alone, but shall also include operators of other tourism services. Particular attention shall be given to investment incentives for previously neglected regions and well-organized community-based tourism projects. Tourism incentive schemes shall be in accordance with overall government policy in this regard, and may include special tax relief on hotel construction, provision of long-term and soft loans, VAT exemption for small hotels and restaurants, accelerated depreciation and waiver of import duties for buildings related to hotel services.

Other policy strategies for investment and financing will include:
- Promotion of tourism as a priority sector for domestic and foreign investment;
- Establishment of a favourable fiscal, legal and regulatory framework;
- Dissemination of information about tourism investment opportunities to domestic and international investors and developers, including the streamlining of investment procedures, in order to attract investors;
- Provision of fiscal and non-fiscal incentives to investors;
- Progressive reduction of VAT on tourism as new sources of sustainable funding are identified;
- Duty-free importation of solar energy equipment and other items needed for meeting environmental standards; and
- Promotion of proactive forms of community partnership, especially through joint ventures with the private sector and State conservation agencies.

Source: MOT & W, 2006

Other initiatives to support FDI indirectly include expansion of the Jomo Kenyatta International Airport, revision of the Wildlife Policy & Act and development of Vision 2030. (The vision was launched after the research and writing of this report, and it highlights tourism as being 'a leading sector in achieving the goal' of becoming a newly industrialised middle-income country. (Government of the Republic of Kenya, 2007).

The recent government directive requiring all public institutions to hold seminars, workshops and meetings only in public institutions such as the Kenya School of Monetary Studies and Utalii Hotel is a drawback to the tourism industry, since conferences and seminars had become an important source of revenue for hotels. This is more likely to affect local hotels and tour operators as they often obtained such contracts from government.

2. Legal and institutional framework

The legal framework for FDI is provided by the Companies Ordinance (chapter 486), the Partnership Act (chapters 20 and 30), the Foreign Investment Protection Act (chapter 618) and the Investment Promotion Act, 2004. To attract investment, the Government undertook several reforms, especially in the early and mid-1990s. These included abolishing export and import licensing, except for a few items listed in the Imports, Exports and Essential Supplies Act (chapter 502), rationalizing and reducing import tariffs, revoking all export duties and current account restrictions, freeing exchange rate controls allowing both residents and non-residents to open foreign currency accounts with domestic banks, and removing restrictions on borrowing by foreign as well as domestic companies. The legal framework does not discriminate between the operations of local and foreign-owned businesses. Moreover, there are no sector-specific incentives for attracting FDI.

Investment Promotion Act (2004)

The Investment Promotion Act (2004) introduces a mandatory investment threshold and a restrictive screening procedure for all foreign investments. The Act makes a formal distinction between domestic and foreign investors by stating that "a foreign investor shall not invest in Kenya unless (it) has been issued with an investment certificate", which is issued by the Kenya Investment Authority (KIA). The

KIA is allowed to issue this certificate to a foreign investor on the following conditions:

- The amount invested must be at least $500,000, or the equivalent in another currency.
- The investment must be deemed by KIA to be to the benefit of Kenya, including through employment creation, transfer of new skills or technology to Kenyans, and contribution to tax or other government revenues.

This second requirement is laudable if the historical challenges of policy implementation could be surmounted. However, in addition to this requirement, incentives should be designed that are pegged to how well foreign investments create linkages to the domestic economy.

Domestic investors are not required to obtain an investment certificate, but they are required to register their investment with KIA. The minimum capital investment for domestic investors seeking an investment certificate is lower – 5 million Kenyan shillings ($65,000) – but they too must fulfil the requirements that the investment should benefit the country (UNCTAD, 2005). Once established in the country, foreign investors receive the same treatment as domestic investors.

The minimum capital requirement of $500,000 probably discouraged FDI in tourism, especially because competing investment destinations such as Ethiopia, Uganda and the United Republic of Tanzania had very low, if any, minimum capital requirements (UNCTAD, 2005). Consequently, the Investment Promotion Act 2004 was amended in January 2006 to lower the minimum requirement by foreign investors to $100,000, and made it optional for them to hold an investment certificate. The Act also provided for the establishment of a National Investment Council (NIC) to advise the Government on ways of increasing investment.

Although the legal and regulatory framework has considerably improved, some issues remain. As mentioned earlier, there are no sector-specific incentives for attracting FDI: different sectors require different incentives. While the reduction of the capital requirement to $100,000 is commendable, there should be a provision to make this requirement a prerequisite for an investor to enjoy the various investment incentives. Other constraints include cumbersome processing of work permits, delays in VAT refunds by the Kenya Revenue Authority, delays in obtaining a duty waiver for capital goods from the Ministry of Finance, delays in obtaining the requisite licences, and lack of investor tracking. Moreover, the Kenya Investment Authority is not yet a one-stop shop, and is facing funding problems for its operations.

Tourist Industry Licensing Act and the Hotels and Restaurants Act

The Ministry of Tourism and Wildlife regulates the industry through two main acts:

- The Tourist Industry Licensing Act (CAP 381) of 1970 (revised in 1990), which issues licences to tourism enterprises and generally regulates the private sector (tour operators, travel agents, tour guides, curio dealers and charter planes, among others).
- The Hotels and Restaurants Act (CAP 494) of 1972 (revised in 1986), that provides for the licensing of hotels, lodges and restaurants, classification of hotels and restaurants, collection of a training levy from hotels, lodges and restaurants, and the establishment of Utalii College. Hotel managers are also licensed under this legislation and foreign

managers first need to acquire a work permit before they are licensed. The Hotel and Restaurants Authority (HRA), established by this Act within the Department of Tourism, thus issues three kinds of licences: a hotel licence, restaurant licence and hotel manager's licence.

The numerous delays and cumbersome procedures in licensing of tourism enterprises make the country less attractive to FDI. Moreover, the HRA Act does not provide for licensing of private home stays, private sanctuaries and hotels with less than five beds. Yet these facilities account for a significant, albeit unknown proportion, of tourism business, thereby giving the licensed businesses an unfair advantage. On the other hand, in general, informal business, including beach operators who sell safaris to tourists and freelance tour guides, have an unfair advantage over formal businesses that have overhead costs and pay taxes, and this contributes to a negative image of the sector. The draft tourism policy recognizes this shortcoming and provides for the revision of the HRA and TILA acts to include regulation of these facilities. Indeed, as of 2006 private villas needed to obtain a licence.

Work permits for foreign workers

Those involved in the tourism industry, especially tour operators with foreign ownership, have complained of delays in obtaining work permits for foreign workers. However, the ministry argues that, according to the law, expatriates can be employed only if the talents/skills required cannot be sourced locally. The Work Permits Committee of the Ministry of Tourism and Wildlife has discretionary powers to make recommendations on such applications to the Immigration Work Permit Committee that has the final authority. In the case of intra-corporate transfers, the applicant must have worked with the parent company for not less than two years.

The time it takes to obtain a work permit and the lack of transparency of the process are obstacles cited by the tourism industry. This is largely due to weak capacity in the Government in terms of personnel, training and funding, and poor governance (Ikiara, Chemengich and Okatch, 2005). Moreover, the requirement that a company seeking a work permit must place an advertisement in the print media to ascertain lack of qualified Kenyans for the job imposes high costs on the company. Also, the lack of locally available requisite skills, corruption and dishonesty have affected the issuance of work permits. Thus, for example, more than 50 per cent of the work permit applications for tourist guides are under intra-corporate transfers. The applicants often claim to be tour leaders with special foreign linguistic skills while others claim to represent investor interests. The Ministry lacks the capacity to verify such claims.

3. Investment climate

The country survey found that a number of businesses are relocating to Uganda and the United Republic of Tanzania because of their more favourable policies, legal, regulatory and institutional set-ups. Industry stakeholders surveyed believed that the investment climate in the United Republic of Tanzania was good and its open door policy enabled investors to obtain licences in a very short time with little corruption experienced. Duty on imported vehicles and parts is higher in Kenya than in the United Republic of Tanzania, thereby making Kenya less competitive for tourism investments. Research by the Kenya Investment Authority (KIA) showed that Kenya was no longer the preferred destination for FDI and that Uganda and the United Republic of

Tanzania had overtaken it.[23] At the same time, Kenyans also are increasingly taking advantage of the better investment environment in these neighbouring countries, making Kenya the top source of FDI flows into Uganda, and the third biggest source of foreign investments in the United Republic of Tanzania.

A study by the World Bank (2006) confirms the extent to which the Kenyan investment environment is uncompetitive. It shows that it takes an average of 54 days to set up a business in Kenya, while it takes 30 and 16 days in Uganda and the United Republic of Tanzania respectively. According to the report, it costs $917 to import one container into the United Republic of Tanzania compared to $2,235 for Kenya. It also takes 39 days to import a container into the United Republic of Tanzania, while the same takes 45, 67 and 95 days to import into Kenya, Uganda and Rwanda respectively.[24] Ethiopia has relatively good roads and better security than Kenya and offers a longer tax holiday of 10 years. In recent years, a number of African countries have put in place various incentives to make them more competitive locations for FDI.

Poor infrastructure

The quality of infrastructure in a country is an important factor affecting the investment climate, both directly with regard to the ease of establishment and operation of business and indirectly by influencing operational costs vis-à-vis other regions. Balasubramanyam (2001) defines infrastructure to include transport and communications, but also a favourable environment for work and leisure. Biswas (2002) asserts that the marginal effect of infrastructure on investment is positive and significant at a 1 per cent level, indicating that investors are attracted to a country with better infrastructure.

In Kenya, most of the roads to national parks, game reserves and even along the coast for beach tourism are dilapidated. This not only increases the cost of doing business but also discourages visits to some of the game parks, and reduces the attractiveness of tourism to investors. There is need to revive railway transport to ease congestion on and destruction of the roads by large trucks. Some efforts are being undertaken in this regard with the concession of Kenya Railways to a consortium of investors from South Africa. This is also expected to boost domestic tourism. The ongoing expansion of Jomo Kenyatta International Airport, as mentioned earlier, is also a step in the right direction. In addition, the Government is looking into the potential for public-private partnerships in the development and management of other international airports in the country (GoK, Budget speech 2005/2006). (This was cited again in the Vision 2030, released after work has been conducted for this report.)

High cost of energy

Unreliable supplies and the high cost of electricity are also a major hindrance to tourism in Kenya. Most hotels pay an annual electricity bill of between 230,000 and 40 million Kenyan shillings, which represents about 3 per cent of gross turnover, even after installing energy-saving bulbs. Electricity costs about 9 cents per Kwh in Kenya compared to 4 cents/kWh in Egypt, 2 cents/kWh in South Africa, and 3.9 cents/kWh in Ethiopia (Kamfor, 2002). Stakeholders suggest that this should be cut to at least 6 cents/Kwh. Moreover, there are frequent power outages and fluctuations that add considerable costs to business operations. To cope with this, hotels are forced to buy and maintain generators (table 27). As the table shows, there are no marked differences in ownership and use of power generators

between locally owned hotels and those with foreign ownership.

The rising cost of fuel is also having a negative impact on the tourism industry, in particular on tour operators.

Table 27. Use of electricity generators by hotels

Category	Do you have an electricity generator			Frequency of use of generator in 2005		
	Yes	No	Total	Very frequently	Less frequently	Total
100% local ownership	14	0	14	3	11	14
41-80% foreign ownership	2	0	2	2	0	2
81-100% foreign ownership	7	0	7	4	3	7
1-100% foreign ownership	9	0	9	6	3	9
Total	**23**	**0**	**23**	9	14	23

Insecurity

Although the Government has been addressing this issue through the establishment of a tourist police force, insecurity remains one of the major hindrances to tourism in Kenya. A study on security and growth (Ngugi et al., 2004) indicated that insecurity was hindering the growth of business in the country.

High taxation

Most of the stakeholders consulted decried the high level of taxation in Kenya. They attributed relocation of business to the United Republic of Tanzania and Uganda to the high tax rates in the country. In addition, the United Republic of Tanzania and Ethiopia offer tax holidays for longer periods than those offered in Kenya.

Moreover, the Kenya Revenue Authority (KRA) has stated that it can only remit tax refunds to businesses that attach receipts from electronic tax register (ETR) machines. This has meant that hotels prefer to source goods from those suppliers that have installed such machines. Since many small and medium-sized enterprises cannot afford ETRs, they are unable to do business with these hotels.

Inadequate destination marketing

Government budgetary allocation to the Kenya Tourist Board (KTB) for destination marketing is very low relative to those of competing destinations such as Egypt, Mauritius and South Africa. During the 2006/07 financial year, for instance, KTB was allocated only 750 million Kenyan shillings compared to stakeholders' belief that 2 billion Kenyan shillings was required. Due to its limited resources, KTB often holds trade fairs in Europe and contracts a foreign organization based in Europe to market the destination. Besides inadequacy of resources, KTB's marketing efforts appear to have been concentrated on coastal beaches and game parks/reserves, leaving out other regions including some with classified hotels. Moreover, KTB does not include low-cost hotels in its overseas promotion efforts.[25]

High air transport costs

Due to the general increase in the price of petroleum products and threats of terrorism, air transport costs have risen. Besides, there are capacity problems associated with the high cost of aircraft, low use of information and communication technologies (ICTs), and management weaknesses. There is also a problem with the number and current state of airports and air navigation facilities in the country. [26] Kenya requires more international airports and surface transport connecting the airports and major urban centres, as well as more airport hotels.

Lack of incentives for FDI in tourism

The draft national tourism policy does not contain specific and adequate incentives for supporting FDI in tourism.

Others

Other factors that affect the business environment include weak industry organizations, absence of long-term credit, reliance on traditional tourism, corruption in government, low promotion of South-South tourism, poor public transport, problems associated with increasing numbers of street children, water rationing and inadequate parking space for hotels located in towns.

4. Conclusion

Kenya's tourism policy has been characterized in the past by inconsistency, poor coordination, lack of a vision and overall development strategy and poor implementation. Moreover, the tourism policy has not been harmonized with related sectoral policies and national development priorities. Although Kenya has maintained an open door policy for FDI, there has been no clear and specific incentive package to attract tourism-related FDI. Neither has there been any proactive policy to attract and direct tourism-related FDI to meet desired outcomes. Despite concerted efforts to improve the investment climate in Kenya, bottlenecks still remain. These include the high cost of energy, insecurity, high taxes, inadequate destination marketing, poor infrastructure and high air transport costs.

H. Conclusions and policy implications

1. Conclusions

As noted earlier, Kenya is lagging behind its neighbours in the region in attracting FDI. The tourism sector accounted for 10.7 per cent of the foreign investment registered with the Kenya Investment Authority in 2004, which is a fairly good indication of this industry's role in attracting FDI.

A number of conclusions emerge from this study. First, it was found that local investors dominated the tourism industry (about 57 per cent in hotels and restaurants, and 75 per cent in tour operators), contrary to perceptions that foreign investors were dominant. Most of the local owners are of Asian and British origin, which perhaps explains this perception. These investors have historical or family links with the United Kingdom and India. There was also evidence of South-South FDI and South-South trade becoming increasingly important.

Second, financing in the sector was found to be generally through loans (64 per cent) and equity (20 per cent). However, given the lack of long-term credit, most of the firms had to finance expansions and renovations from their own funds, which were limited.

Third, there appeared to be no major differences between firms that were entirely locally owned and those with foreign ownership in terms of capacity, turnover, profits and taxes paid.

Fourth, there was evidence of a marked difference in the size of purchases between the two categories of hotels. Hotels with foreign ownership made much higher purchases, and most of these were from wholesalers/distributors, with little

purchased from small and medium-sized enterprises. Goods and services consumed were mainly sourced in the country with only 17.3 per cent imported. This is an indication that there is a substantial linkage between the tourism industry and the local economy.

Fifth, the use of the Internet is becoming an important mode of booking clients for both local and foreign-owned hotels and tour operators, underlining the increasing importance of technology in the sector. The emergence of e-ticketing is likely to affect the role of tour operators and travel agents in the future.

Sixth, there seemed to be no marked differences between locally owned and foreign-owned enterprises with respect to the level of employment and gender balance. However, hotels with foreign ownership appeared to have more low-skilled workers. Training of staff in the sector was mainly done locally, particularly at Utalii College. However, there were concerns at the lack of postgraduate training opportunities in the country.

Seventh, the environmental activities commonly undertaken by firms in the tourism industry are tree planting and landscaping; installation of energy-saving technologies (such as energy-saving bulbs), borehole construction, and installation of incinerators for waste disposal. Most of the hotels reported undertaking environmental audits mandated by the National Environmental Management Authority. However, compliance with ISO 14000 was limited, yet such compliance is necessary for enhancing international competitiveness. There appeared to be no major differences between locally owned enterprises and those with foreign ownership with respect to environmental protection. The same result was found for community initiatives such as donations to schools, the Red Cross, Christian organizations, youth organizations, prisons, churches, children's homes, famine relief efforts and giving spaces to curio sellers within hotel premises.

Eighth, regional integration holds promising business opportunities for Kenya, especially if East Africa can be jointly marketed as a single destination. About 22 per cent of the hotels surveyed did business in the region. The figure was considerably higher for tour operators and travel agents (about 50 per cent). Our survey found that doing business in the East African region is an important determinant of an enterprise's turnover. With regard to the perception of cross-border trade before and after the regional integration, the results did not show marked differences between locally owned enterprises and enterprises with foreign ownership.

Ninth, even though there has been no comprehensive tourism policy document, the country has largely maintained an open door policy to foreign investment since independence. Nevertheless, there are policy and regulatory issues that continue to affect FDI in tourism. These include the recently set minimum capital investment, multiple licence requirements, and restrictions on the number of work permits and the process for acquiring the permits. Moreover, there are no sector-specific incentives to attract FDI in Kenya.

Tenth, there seemed to be no marked differences in the business environment faced by the two categories of tourism enterprises. There is no coherent integration and harmonization of tourism policy with related sectoral policies and national development priorities. Government policy, as well as the legal, regulatory and institutional environment,

make for a sub-optimal business environment in the country. It is characterized by, among others, high electricity costs, poor road conditions, insecurity, a high and demanding tax regime and cumbersome licensing requirements and procedures. These need to be addressed for tourism to become more attractive to both local and foreign investors.

Eleventh, there are considerable data gaps. There is little information on trends of FDI in tourism. Information on casinos, souvenirs and car rentals is scanty, yet these are important components of the tourism infrastructure in the country. In addition, little information is available on the perception of communities surrounding the tourism establishments.

2. Policy implications

Given that FDI in tourism is small and is not having a significant differential impact on Kenya's tourism industry, several policy interventions are necessary.

Finalization of a tourism policy

The tourism policy should be finalized and formalized as a matter of urgency, and that policy should be consistent, coherent and in line with related sectoral policies and national development priorities. It is also necessary to go beyond general policy provisions and design an elaborate incentive package for tourism investments – both local and foreign – to encourage competition and technology transfer. Similarly, proactive policy interventions are necessary. The incentives should direct investments into new circuits (e.g. western circuit) and into new tourism products for sustainable tourism development – away from overcrowded areas like the coast, Maasai Mara and Amboseli – and they should also favour joint ventures with communities.

Improvement of the business climate

In order to attract FDI and local investment into the tourism industry, the infrastructure should be improved considerably, with priority given to improving roads, railways and energy. Consideration should be given to involving the private sector in infrastructure development through tax rebates. Serious efforts should also be made to improve the business climate, such as tackling corruption, simplifying and reducing licensing requirements, streamlining and harmonizing the tax regime, making available long-term credit on competitive terms for expansion, and relocating and organizing beach operators. In addition, the legal and regulatory framework should be reviewed. Further, there is need to improve security by strengthening the tourist police unit. Incentives should be designed in a way that they are pegged to how well foreign investments creates linkages to the domestic economy.

Deepening regional integration

Regional integration should be deepened so as to promote greater South-South cooperation in tourism, and the East African region jointly marketed as a single destination. Efforts being made to this end, such as the formulation of regional classification and standardization criteria for hotels, lodges and restaurants, should be increased. This may require introduction of a regional tourist visa modelled along the lines of the Schengen visa in Europe, promotion of regional insurance coverage, removal of bottlenecks in the movement of vehicles carrying tourists within the region, and joint tourism promotion. Kenya should consider becoming proactive in speeding up these interventions.

Promoting and strengthening domestic tourism

Domestic tourism was instrumental in the survival of many tourism enterprises during the crisis period of 1995–2002. It should therefore be developed further, including through awareness campaigns among hotel staff to change their negative attitude towards domestic tourists, development of appropriate products for domestic tourists, and introduction of incentives such as differential pricing.

Need for further research

While this survey represents one of the first attempts to quantify the absolute and relative contribution made by FDI in tourism in Kenya, its results are likely to be sensitive to the small sample size. As the omission or inclusion of even a few hotels can alter the overall findings when sample size is small, it is recommended that further research be undertaken with a view to increasing the sample size. Besides, there is need to build a reliable database for the tourism industry. Research should also be conducted on critical tourism infrastructure such as car rental services, casinos and souvenirs as little is known about them.

I. References

Aykut A.D and Ratha D (2004). "South-South FDI flows: How big are they?", *Transnational Corporation*, 13(1).

Baer GD (2001). "Risk and capital flows to the emerging markets", paper presented at the seminar on Current Issues in Emerging Market Economics, organized by the Croatian National Bank, Dubrovnik, 28th-30th June 2001, (draft).

Balasubramanyam VN (2001). "Foreign direct investment in developing countries: Determinants and impact", paper presented at the OECD Global Forum on International Investment, New Horizons and Policy Challenges for Foreign Direct Investment in the 21st Century, Mexico City, 26–27 November 2001.

Biswas R (2002). "Determinants of foreign direct investment", *Review of Development Economics*, 6 (3): 492–504.

Blomstrom M and Kokko A (2003). "The economics of foreign direct investment incentives", *NBER Working Paper* No. 9489. February.

Calhoun K, Yearwood S and Willis A (2002). "The effect of wage rate on foreign direct investment flows to individual developing countries", *Puget Sound Journal of Economics*, November.

Christie I and Crompton D (2001). "Tourism in Africa" (Washington DC: World Bank).

Cross Border Initiative (1999). "Road Map for Investor Facilitation", paper prepared by the co-sponsors (AFDB, EU, IMF, WB) of the Fourth Ministerial Meeting in Mauritius, October 1999.

Dunning JH (1993). *The Globalization of Business*. (London: Routledge).

Gelb S (2005). "South–South investment: The case of Africa", in *Africa in the World Economy: The National, Regional and International Challenges*, Teunissen J. and Akkerman A., editors (The Hague: Fondad).

Globerman S and Shapiro D (2002). "National political infrastructure and foreign direct investment", Industry Canada Research Publications Program working paper No.37.

Feenstra R C and Hanson GH (1997). "Foreign direct investment and relative wages: Evidence from Mexico's maquiladoras", *Journal of International Economics*, 42 (3-4): 371-393.

Fung KC et al. (2000). "Determinants of US and Japanese foreign investment in China" (Manila: Asian Development Bank Institute).

GOK (Government of Kenya). (1969). Sessional Paper No.8 of 1969 on Development of Tourism in Kenya. (Nairobi: Government Printer).

GOK (Government of Kenya) (1970). Development Plan 1970-1974 (Nairobi: Government Printer).

GOK (Government of Kenya) (1974). Development Plan 1974-1978 (Nairobi: Government Printer). GOK (Government of Kenya) (1984-1988). Development Plan 1984-1988 (Nairobi: Government Printer).

GOK (Government of Kenya). 1980. Development Plan 1980-1984. Nairobi: Government Printer.

GOK (Government of Kenya) (1995). The study on the National Tourism Master Plan in the Republic of Kenya, Volume 1 (Nairobi: Government Printer).

GOK (Government of Kenya) (2005). Statistical Abstract 2005. Central Bureau of statistics, Ministry of Planning and National Development (Nairobi: Government Printer).

GOK (Government of Kenya) (2006/7). Economic Survey 2006/7. Central Bureau of statistics, Ministry of Planning and National Development (Nairobi: Government Printer).

Government of the Republic of Kenya (2007). Kenya Vision 2030. Nairobi: Government Printer.

Ikiara M (2001a). "Policy framework of Kenya's tourism sector since independence and emerging policy concerns", *KIPPRA Working Paper* WP/02/2001 (Nairobi: Kenya Institute for Public Policy Research & Analysis).

Ikiara M (2001b). Vision and long term development strategy for Kenya's tourism industry. *KIPPRA Discussion Paper* DP/07/2001 (Nairobi: Kenya Institute for Public Policy Research & Analysis).

Ikiara M, Chemengich MK and Okatch FO (2005). "Services trade-related development strategies in tourism, telecommunication and banking services in Kenya" (Revised draft) (Geneva: UNCTAD)

Ikiara M and Oketch C (2002). "Impact of tourism on environment in Kenya: Status and policy", *KIPPRA Discussion Paper* DP/19/2002 (Nairobi: Kenya Institute for Public Policy Research & Analysis).

Ikiara M and Nyangito HO (2001c). "Effects of visa waiver and increase in airport tax on Kenya's tourism industry", *KIPPRA Policy Paper* PP/03/2001 (Nairobi: Kenya Institute for Public Policy Research & Analysis).

Jacobs S (2003). "The importance of institutions in determining the investment Environment", keynote address 1 of South Asia FDI Roundtable in Maldives, 9–10 April 2003, Foreign Investment Advisory Service (FIAS) (discussion draft).

Kamfor Company (2002). "Study on Kenya's energy demand, supply and policy strategy for households, small-scale industries, and service establishments", *Kamfor Final Report* (Nairobi: Ministry of Energy).

KIPPRA (2005). "Improving the enabling environment in Kenya". Intercontinental Hotel, Nairobi.

Loungani P, Mody A and Razin A (2002). "What drives FDI? The role of gravity and other forces", *Notes* (Tel Aviv: Tel Aviv University).

McGee RW (2003). "Foreign direct investment in Southeastern Europe", *Andreas School of Business Working Paper Series* (Miami Shores, Florida: Barry University).

McLure C (1999). "Tax holidays and investment: a comparative analysis", *Bulletin for International Fiscal Documentation*, November.

Ministry of Tourism and Wildlife (MOT&W) (2006). Draft National Tourism Policy (Nairobi: Ministry of Tourism and Wildlife).

Ngow HP (2001). "Can Africa increase its global share of foreign direct investment (FDI)?" *West African Economic Review*, 1525–4488.

Ngugi, R.W., Kimenyi, M.S., K. Nyangoro, Muriu, P., Nderitu, P., Kariuki,E., Kimilu, G., Bikuri, K., and Njuguna, S. (2004). "Security risk and private sector growth in Kenya: A survey report", *KIPPRA Special Report* No.6. Nairobi: Kenya Institute for Public Policy Research & Analysis.

Ngugi RW and Nyangoro O (2005). "Institutional factors and foreign direct investment flows: Implications for Kenya", *KIPPRA Discussion Paper* DP/48/2005 (Nairobi: Kenya Institute for Public Policy Research & Analysis)

Nunnenkamp P (2002). "Determinants of FDI in developing countries: Has globalization changed the rules of the game?", *Kiel Working Paper No.*1122 (Kiel: Kiel Institute of World Economics).

Phillips LC, et al. (2001). "Does it pay to court foreign investment?" Policy Brief Number 48, January (Arlington, Virginia: International Business Initiatives).

Ritchie JRB and Crouch GI (2003). *The Competitive Destination: A Sustainable Tourism Perspective* (Wallingford: CABI International).

Rogoff K and Reinhart C (2002). "The role of price stability and currency instability", *IMF Working Paper* No. 03/10. Paper prepared for the Annual World Bank Conference on Development Economics, Washington DC, April 29-30, 2002

Shah A. (1995). *Fiscal Incentives for Investment and Innovation.* (Oxford: Oxford University Press).

Sinclair,T. (1990). "Tourism Development in Kenya" A Consultancy Report (World Bank).

Smarzynska BK and Shang-Jin Wei (2000). "Corruption and composition of foreign direct investment: Firm-level evidence" *NBER Working Paper* No.7969, October.

Touche Ross Management Consultants (1995). Identification mission in the tourism sector. in Kenya. Final Report.

TTCI (Tourism & Transport Consult International) (1998). Impact of tourism on the economy of Kenya 1996, *Final Report.*

UNCTAD (2003). The development dimension of FDI: Policy and rule-making perspectives.Proceedings of an expert meeting held in Geneva, 6– 8 November 2002. (New York and Geneva: United Nations).

UNCTAD (2005). *Investment Policy Review: Kenya* (New York and Geneva: United Nations).

UNCTAD (2006). "Foreign direct investment and TNSs in tourism in Kenya: the development dimension", Working draft, 21 April (New York and Geneva: United Nations).

Wheeler D and Mody A. (1992). "International direct investment location decisions: The case of US firms", *Journal of International Economics*, 33 (1-2), August: 57-76.

World Bank (2006). "Doing business in Kenya" (Washington, DC: World Bank).

World Travel and Tourism Council (2008). *The 2008 Travel & Tourism Economic Research: Kenya* (Oxford Economics: Oxford, UK)

Notes

[1]   Based on contribution by Moses Ikiara, Samuel Mwakubo, Robert Gichira, Peter Njiraini, Kenya Institute for Public Policy Research and Analysis (KIPPRA).

[2]   Some of the key blueprints in the country's history include Sessional Paper no. 10 of 1965 on African Socialism and its application in Planning and Management, Sessional Paper no. 1 of 1986 on Economic Management for Renewed Growth, Sessional Paper no. 1 of 1994 on Recovery and Sustainable Development to the year 2010, the Poverty Reduction Strategy Paper (PRSP) of 2002, and the Economic Recovery Strategy for Wealth and Employment Creation (ERS) of 2003, and Vision 2030 of 2008.

[3]   The large increase in the growth rate in 2004 is, however, partly attributable to the adoption of a new data system, the SNA 1993, which included hitherto neglected, or poorly captured, economic sectors such as the micro, small and medium enterprises and horticulture.

[4]   The coastal areas of Kenya are administratively governed together as the Coast Province. It has 12 districts namely, Mombasa, Kilindini, Kilifi, Kaloleni, Kwale, Msambweni, Kinango, Tana-River, Malindi, Taveta, Taita and Lamu.

[5]   Peter Musa, Tourism boom exposes Kenya's lack of beds, *East African,* 16-22, 2006.

[6]   In fact 63 per cent in 1995 and 2000.

[7]   Of the 42 members of the Kenya Association of Tour Operators (KATO) for Mombasa, only one is locally owned. KATO has a membership of 206 tour operators in the country.

[8]   See also annex table 2 for ownership of some of the beach hotels.

[9]   Thoya, F, "State to crack whip on hotel standards", *Sunday Nation*, August 27, 2006: 23.

[10]   Michael Wakabi, " SA firm wins concession in Serengeti", *The East African*, August 28-September 3, 2006, page 22.

[11]   John Kariuki of Budget hotels said he wanted the Tourism Board to include them in overseas promotions, *The East African*, October 9-15, 2006: 24.

[12]   The *East African Standard*, Tuesday 1 August 2006.

[13]   The *East African Standard*, 9-15October 2006: 15.

[14]   The percentages do not add up to 100 per cent since hotels use more than one type of booking.

[15]   Information gathered in our survey was not sufficient to establish whether skilled workers in locally owned firms were originally in foreign firms and to determine the degree of mobility by skill levels.

[16]   The survey showed that minimum wages differed by level of skills and sector.

[17]   The *East African Standard*, 9-15 October 2006: 15

[18]   However, the country as a whole benefits, since most employees in the sector are nationals.

[19]   The *East African Standard*, Tuesday 1st August 2006.

[20]   Anthony Omuya, "Tour firm expands its operations", Smart Company, The *Daily Nation* Business Magazine, Tuesday 22 August 2006: 7.

[21]   Correspondent, " Tour drivers denied entry into Tanzania", *Saturday Nation*, 2 September 2006: 36.

[22]   Jeff Otieno, *Sunday Nation*, 23 July 2006.

[23]   Tom Moguso, " Kenya lags in FDI flows", *The East African Standard*, 23 August 2006: 18.

[24]   Kimathi Njoka, "Graft, high business costs stain Kenya's rating grades", The *East African Standard*, 12 September 2006: 4.

[25]   John Kariuki, "Budget hotels want Tourism Board to include them in overseas promotions", The *East African*, 9-15 October 2006: 24.

[26]   The Kenya Airports Authority, through a Chinese company, is undertaking a three-year expansion and renovation of Jomo Kenyatta International Airport.

Annex table 1. FDI inflows to Kenya, 1970–2003

Year	Net inflows ($ million)	Share of net inflows in GDP (%)	Share of net inflows in gross capital formation (%)
1970	13.80	0.86	4.37
1971	7.40	0.42	1.83
1972	6.30	0.30	1.36
1973	17.26	0.69	3.32
1974	23.42	0.79	4.10
1975	17.16	0.53	2.61
1976	46.37	1.33	6.68
1977	56.55	1.26	6.00
1978	34.41	0.65	2.59
1979	84.01	1.38	5.81
1980	78.97	1.09	4.71
1981	14.15	0.21	0.88
1982	13.00	0.20	1.06
1983	23.74	0.40	2.20
1984	10.75	0.17	0.96
1985	28.75	0.47	2.69
1986	32.73	0.45	2.30
1987	39.38	0.49	2.52
1988	0.39	0.00	0.02
1989	62.19	0.75	3.86
1990	57.10	0.67	3.23
1991	18.80	0.23	1.21
1992	6.00	0.07	0.44
1993	2.00	0.04	0.21
1994	4.30	0.06	0.32
1995	33.00	0.36	1.71
1996	10.55	0.11	0.58
1997	52.52	0.49	2.81
1998	11.41	0.10	0.60
1999	13.82	0.13	0.86
2000	110.90	1.06	7.26
2001	5.31	0.05	0.34
2002	27.63	0.22	1.71
2003	81.75	0.59	5.21

Source: UNCTAD, 2005.

Annex table 2.   Ownership of selected beach hotels

North coast		
Hotel	**Main owner**	**Nationality**
1. UTC	Ketan Somaia	Kenyan
2. Voyager	Mama Ngina	Kenyan
3. Bahari beach	Mahihu	Kenyan
4. Mombasa beach	Semi-government	-
5. Reef	Sodhi	Kenyan
6. Bamburi beach	Merali	Kenyan
7. Sarova Whitesands	Sarova family	Kenyan
8. Boabarb Holiday Resort	-	Chinese, Kenyan
9. Severin Sea lodge	Severin	German
10. African Safari Club	Dr. Rundel	Swiss
11. Serena Mombasa	Aga Khan	Kenyan
12. Sun n' Sand	-	Kenyan
South coast		
1. Indian Ocean Beach	Karume	Kenyan
2. Southern Palm	-	Kenyan
3. Leisure Lodge	Kantaria	Kenyan
4. Leopard Beach Hotel	Singh	Kenyan
5. Diani Sea Resort	-	German
6. Diani Sea Lodge	-	German
7. LTI Kazi Kaz	-	German
8. Two fishes	-	Kenyan
9. Alliance Hotels	Matiba	Kenyan
10. Lagoon Reef	-	British
11. Boabab beach	-	TUI/Kenyan
12. Neptune	Merali	Kenyan

Mr. Sondhi, Chairman, Mombasa and Coast Tourist Association (MCTA)

Annex table 3. Summary of gross turnover (million Kenyan shillings)

	Fully loca	With foreign ownership		
Average gross turnover	258	Share in total (%)	457	Share in total (%)
Accommodation	122.9	47.6	241.7	52.9
Restaurants	95.6	37.1	216.6	47.4
Conferences	29.1	11.3	138.3	30.3
Bars	49.4	19.1	-	-
Other	15.3	5.9	24.8	5.4
Gross profit	79.1	30.7	114.4	25.0
Gross tax	100.0	38.8	150.0	32.8

Source:

IV. Mauritius country case study[1]

Executive summary

This country case-study on the experience of Mauritius is part of a wider UNCTAD research and policy analysis project on the role and impact of TNCs in global tourism (Box 1, Overview). Mauritius was chosen for the study because it is widely perceived to be a development success story, and because of the significant role that both tourism and FDI have played in this success. A country once considered doomed, with a high rate of population growth and dependent on the production of sugar, it has been successful in diversifying its economic base to manufacturing, tourism and financial services.

Mauritius is well known for being a high quality tourist destination. This has not been a natural, chance occurrence but the result of deliberate efforts. The Government has been very supportive to investors – local and foreign – by setting clear policies, eliminating bureaucratic procedures (although there is still room for improvement), offering incentives and creating an environment conducive to investment.

Tourism in 2007 accounted for about 8 per cent of gross domestic product (GDP). Tourist arrivals in 2007 have reached around 907,000 and tourism receipts were about 40 billion Mauritian rupees (about $1,297 million). There were 94 hotels that were operational when the fieldwork for this study was conducted, in 2006-2007: 22 foreign owned and 72 domestic owned. More than 90 per cent of tourists visited for holiday purposes, while the remainder arrived for business/conferences (4 per cent), were in transit or visiting friends and relatives (3 per cent).

The Government of Mauritius conducts its marketing activities through the Mauritius Tourism Promotion Authority.

Hotels also do their own marketing and deal mainly with foreign tour operators.

Foreign direct investment (FDI) has been important for Mauritius. Originally, FDI policies towards tourism were quite restrictive as there were fears that this might lead to an overcapacity of hotel rooms. Full foreign ownership was only permitted for hotels of more than 100 rooms. However, foreign investment is now permitted in restaurants, yachts and travel agencies among others. It has brought not only the needed capital for further investment, but also the necessary technological know-how and skills, and has led to the construction of world-class hotels and villas. Local ownership has also however been very significant, particularly compared to the experience of some other developing countries where domestic investment has been much less prevalent. With the introduction of the Integrated Resort Scheme in 2005, which primarily is the acquisition of villas for residential purposes only by foreigners, foreign direct investment has increased significantly in recent years. As from 2006, a substantial number of villas have been built. Also, in 2008 the government has announced that there are more than 25 new hotels projects underway (many of which are transnational companies) to increase capacity so as to accommodate the target set by the government to have 2 million tourists by the year 2015.

Although significant amounts of foreign exchange are flowing in the country, it is still not clear how much leaks out in terms of imports for example as many products consumed by the hotel industry are imported. Also, there exist no such studies to assess the multiplier effect of the revenue generated by the industry in the economy. In terms of investment, contrary to some expectations that FDI would crowd out local investment, there was no evidence found of such negative impacts. This is due to the expansion of the sector where opportunities exist and also the expertise and know-how of the local investors in the field.

Highlights of hotels surveyed

From the surveyed hotels, there did not seem to be a wide disparity between foreign-owned and domestic-owned hotels in terms of turnover, employment, visitors' composition, marketing and involvement with the community. Only the wage level and turnover of employees seemed to differ between the foreign-owned and domestic-owned hotels. The wage level was higher in foreign-owned hotels, especially for high-skill jobs, while labour turnover was higher in domestic-owned ones. The hotels, both foreign- and domestic-owned, tended to recruit people from the local community as workers.

In terms of businesses with local enterprises, the hotels purchased most of their food items locally, although many hotel managers complained about the quality. Many SMEs expect better linkages and at times they find that opportunities are limited. They would have liked a better communication with hotels to sell their products and services. They find that hotels tend to favour some 'big' companies only.

There were significant differences between hotels and tour operating firms in terms of linkages with the community. Many hotels reported sponsoring social events and activities, such as funding football teams and various clubs in the region, as well as hosting village committees and helping the elderly. Some hotels reported assisting people in the local community to better market their products and providing space on their premises to display their products. The tour operating firms, on the other hand, had few if any such linkages.

The survey revealed that hotels made significant contributions towards improving the environment through wastewater management, recycling of water and waste, recycling of plastics and using environmentally friendly products. Many of them were also involved in measures to improve the environment and educating staff about environmental conservation.

Highlights of tour operators surveyed

- Tour operating firms generated sales ranging from $66,700 to $3.3 million.
- They employed around 15 to 70 employees and almost all the firms were local.
- The firms reported benefiting significantly from hotels, which recommend certain services such as car rental agencies, leisure parks, catamaran cruises and taxis.
- The firms' main customers were from France followed by visitors from the United Kingdom, Italy and Germany.

Impact on livelihoods

- Employment creation is one of the obvious benefits from the tourism industry, especially in hotels. Indirect employment has also been substantial in many tourist areas.
- Some residents surveyed were concerned about the price inflation resulting from tourism, and the limited availability of quality items such as vegetables, fruit and seafood, as most of these are sold to the hotels.
- Most inhabitants appeared to welcome tourism development for bringing improvements to the infrastructure and amenities in their areas. Local inhabitants and businesses benefited from better road conditions, sewage systems, communication infrastructure and also new or better police and fire services.

- Most local residents surveyed believed that hotels have been doing enough to preserve the environment, although fishermen complained of no longer having access to the sea with their boats at certain sites.
- On the cultural front, there has been a renewed interest in traditional and other folk songs and dances of the region, which are well appreciated by tourists.
- Increased employment opportunities in hotels and in the region have meant that more women are directly or indirectly engaged in paid jobs. While there has been a positive gain in terms of increased income, some family tensions have arisen when women work odd hours in hotels.

Challenges ahead

Major stakeholders were interviewed, including officials from various ministries, public officers, hotel managers, firms operating in the sector, non-governmental organizations (NGOs) and the wider community. The following are the main points highlighted by the respondents:

- Significantly more investment is required over the next 10–15 years to give tourism the boost that the government vision requires. This will involve a major input from both local and international investment.
- The boost in investment in tourism is needed in part because other sectors, such as agriculture and manufacturing, are not able to absorb the increasing number of unemployed. There will also be a challenge to ensure that the jobs that are created are sustainable, involve skills transfer and sustainable livelihoods, etc
- The air access policy is being reviewed to increase the number of tourist arrivals by increasing the number of flights from new markets.

Some new carriers have started operating, such as Corsair.
- Many stakeholders in the tourism sector considered airfares between major destinations to be too high. Given the increasing competition from destinations that are closer to Mauritius' major tourism markets, it will be a challenge to meet the targeted number of tourist arrivals of 2 million by 2015 coupled with soaring oil prices.
- The Meeting, Incentives, Conference and Exhibition (MICE) market represents another area where the Mauritian Government is giving its full support in marketing the destination. Challenges include availability of conference centres, necessary technology, skilled personnel to cater for such events and issues related to the obtention of visa at immigration, which have been a problem.
- Security of tourists is becoming an important issue for all destinations and the Government has made firm commitments to make Mauritius a safe destination.
- Many stakeholders said they favoured the "stopover' and "shopping" tourism concept in addition to encouraging multi-destination holiday packages involving a number of other destinations in the region. Challenges with this include ensuring that tourists have sufficient time exploring the island, that there are regular flights to regional destinations, there is harmonisation of visa entry clearance and so on.

A. Introduction

1. Purpose of the study

Mauritius is well known in the African region for having a buoyant and successful tourism industry. The country has been able to reduce its economic dependence on sugar by promoting manufacturing and tourism. Investment in the tourism sector was initially mainly by local investors who reinvested their profits from the sugar industry into tourism, but then foreign investment became increasingly important. The Government has also created generous incentives to attract FDI to further boost the sector.

This study looks at the success of the tourism sector by first providing a historical background of Mauritius and highlighting the main landmarks in its development It examines the various incentives offered by the Government and policies, often reviewed, to make the sector more attractive for investors. .

This study is organized as follows. Section I provides an overview of the Mauritian economy and describes the evolution of the tourism industry in terms of tourist arrivals and receipts, and the composition and contribution of the industry. Section II looks at the importance and trends of FDI in tourism in Mauritius. A broad definition of FDI is used, that includes the activities of TNCs as well as more traditional definitions based around capital inflows only (Box 2 Overview). The policies that have been developed to attract FDI in tourism are highlighted. Section III presents the new policies introduced, particularly liberalization of the investment regime, while section IV discusses policies specifically aimed at attracting FDI in tourism, as well as new schemes to further boost investment in the sector. Section V makes an assessment of

the impacts of FDI based on the survey of hotels, firms operating in the tourism sector and the community. Results of the survey are discussed and a comparison is made between foreign- and domestic-owned hotels, including the linkages between hotels, firms and the community. Section VI highlights the challenges that lie ahead as perceived by various stakeholders.

2. Overview of the Mauritian economy

Mauritius is a small island in the Indian Ocean covering an area of about 1,860 square kilometres, with approximately 1.2 million people from different cultural and ethnic backgrounds. The capital city is Port Louis. Strategically located at the crossroads of Africa and Asia, Mauritius is reputed for its beautiful scenery and its 150 kilometres of white sandy beaches and transparent lagoons. Mauritius enjoys a maritime, subtropical climate and is therefore a year-round holiday destination. It is a stable democracy with regular, free elections and a good human rights record. It has attracted considerable foreign investment and has one of the highest per capita incomes in Africa. Average real annual growth has been 4-5 per cent over the period 1997-2006. This remarkable achievement is reflected in higher life expectancy, lower infant mortality, and a much improved infrastructure. The living standard in Mauritius is among the highest in the African region.

Mauritius has undergone significant transformations since independence, with the economy achieving sustained growth over the past three decades. As a result, it has developed from a low-income, agriculture-based economy to a middle-income, diversified economy with increasing emphasis on financial services and tourism. Tourism has evolved to become a reliable growth industry, even outperforming the traditional sectors. Numerous and generous incentives have been provided by the authorities to deepen this industry. However, the phasing out of preferential markets, contraction in the manufacturing sector, mainly in the Export Processing Zone (EPZ), rising unemployment and fiercer competition from the fast growing East Asian economies present some challenges to the economy.

The 1970s were marked by a strong government commitment to diversifying the economy and providing more high-paying jobs to the population. The promotion of tourism and the creation of the EPZ contributed much to the realization of these goals. In the 1980s, with a general political consensus on broad policy measures, the economy experienced steady growth, declining inflation, high employment and increased domestic savings. The EPZ came into its own, surpassing sugar as the principal export earner and employing more workers than the sugar industry and the Government combined. However, the economy slowed down in the late 1980s

and early 1990s, mainly due to new challenges facing the two main engines of growth, the sugar and textile industries. These included the erosion of preferential trade arrangements stemming from the proposed reforms of the European Union (EU) sugar regime, the phasing out of the Multi-Fibre Arrangement (MFA) and the increasing trend towards the globalization of world trade. The prospects of intensified global competition from low-wage countries (particularly China and India) and limited opportunities for preferential trade arrangements in the future represent serious constraints on future growth.

The economy is now facing some serious challenges, including a decline in the rate of economic growth, rising unemployment, a huge public sector deficit and an increasing domestic debt. The unemployment rate, for instance, rose constantly between 2000 and 2005, from 7.7 per cent to 9.6 per cent, indicating stagnation in few sectors (table 1). Real GDP growth rate fell from 9.7 per cent in 2000 to 4.8 per cent in 2004 and to 2.3 per cent in 2005.

Table 1. Mauritius: Selected economic indicators, 1976–2005

Year	1976	1980	1990	2000	2004	2005
GDP at basic prices (million rupees)	4 165	8 697	33 415	105 206	152 638	163 860
Real GDP growth rate (%)	16.2	-10.1	7.3	9.7	4.8	2.3
Real GDP per capita ($)	186	180	296	4 430	4,452[a]	4,461[a]
Inflation rate (%)	13.4	42	13.5	4.2	4.7	4.9
Unemployment rate (%)	--	--	6.7	7.7	8.5	9.6
Gross Domestic Fixed Capital Formation/GDP (%)	30.9	27.5	36.4	22.9	21.6	21.2
Gross domestic savings /GDP (%)	25.6	10.3	26.0	26.3	22.7	17.4
Net exports/GDP (%)	-6.9	-10.3	-7.2	-0.6	-2.4	-6.2
FDI inflows (million rupees)	--	--	609	7,265	1,796	2,368
Population (mid-year)	903 610	966 039	1 058 775	1 186 873	1 233 386	1 243 253
Infant mortality rate	40.2	32.9	20.4	23.5	21.8	19.0

Source: Central Statistical Office, *Annual Digest of Statistics*. [a] computed.

The situation in 2005 deteriorated further owing to lower projected revenue collections associated with lacklustre activity and the widening deficit of a state-owned enterprise related to the suspension of adjustments of retail petroleum prices in early 2005 to reflect import costs. In addition, the sugar sector began experiencing difficulties because of the planned reduction of sugar prices in the EU. The recent surge in world oil prices has had a further adverse effect on the economy, leading to a worsening of the external current account, loss of reserves and a depreciation of the exchange rate, and a slowdown of economic activity. It is believed that the economy will continue to be adversely affected over the next few years. The negative impact on real GDP growth is projected to average 1.2 percentage points over the next five years (assuming that competitiveness in the textile and sugar sectors is restored).

Today, Mauritius stands at the crossroads of its future development. Given the decline in performance of the traditional sectors, new sources of growth have had to be identified, such as financial intermediation and tourism. In recent years, tourism has outperformed the traditional sectors and its contribution to GDP is projected to grow to 7.9 per cent in 2006 from 7.6 per cent in 2005 (table 2).

Table 2. Sectoral contribution to GDP, 2002-2006

Year	1976	1980	1990	2000	2004	2005	2006[a]
Agriculture, hunting, forestry and fisheries	19.9	10.5	12.9	7.0	6.3	5.8	5.4
Manufacturing	13.4	13.0	24.4	23.5	20.8	19.6	19.0
Construction	7.1	6.5	6.7	5.6	5.8	5.5	5.6
Transport, storage and communications	7.6	9.6	10.4	13.0	13.1	13.5	13.7
Financial intermediation	5.0	4.3	4.9	9.7	9.8	10.3	10.6
Tourism	1.6	2.0	3.9	7.4	7.4	7.6	7.9

Source: Central Statistical Office, *Annual Digest of Statistics*. [a]Estimates for 2006.

Apart from an emphasis on tourism, Mauritius has embarked on an ambitious development strategy to identify other new drivers of economic growth, including the development of information and communication technologies (ICT) and the promotion of Mauritius as a seafood hub in the region, using existing facilities in the free trade zones at the port and airport. Measures are also being taken to modernize and restructure the sugar and textile industries through better technologies and greater capitalization.

B. Tourism in Mauritius

1. Introduction

Tourism in Mauritius has developed gradually since the early 1970s to become one of the main growth industries of the country. It is considered the third pillar of the Mauritian economy. Whilst most of the discussion of Mauritius's miracle has focused on the EPZ and the impressive expansion of the textile industry, the performance of the tourism industry has enjoyed less attention, even though it has been truly remarkable (Sacerdoti et al., 2005). It has been a reliable growth engine for the nation's economy, eclipsed only by the EPZ during the early 1980s. And while the EPZ showed signs of contraction at the turn of the century, tourism continued to grow at a steady pace. The objective of the Government is to maintain, if not improve, the standards of tourism.

2. Tourist arrivals

The tourism industry in Mauritius has recorded a consistently robust performance over the past five years. Tourist arrivals increased nine fold between 1975 and 2002, and rose from 681,648 to 761,063 between 2002 and 2005, representing an increase of more than 11 per cent (figure 1). In 2006, although there were significant cancellations registered (mainly by French tourists) particularly in March 2006 because of the spread of *Chikungunya* (an infectious disease spread by mosquito bites), the number of arrivals increased to 788,276. In 2007, arrivals have been more promising, 906,971 tourists visited the island, representing an increase of around 15 per cent over 2006.

Figure 1. Tourist arrivals in Mauritius, 1972–2007

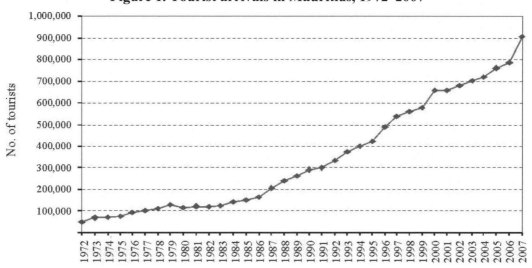

Source: Central Statistical Office.

3. Tourist arrivals by source region/country

Mauritius has received a substantial proportion of its visitors from Europe since the 1980s, with a rapidly increasing share since the early 1990s. This share grew to

more than 50 per cent in 1993, to 60.9 per cent in 1997 and to 65.7 per cent in 2007. The total number of visitor arrivals from Europe in 2007 was 595,653 against 439,889 in 2000 (table 3). The main European markets are France, the United Kingdom, Germany and Italy. France represents the main source of tourist arrivals; in 1995 it accounted for 17 per cent of total arrivals and 48 per cent of total European arrivals, and in 2007, France accounted 28 per cent of total arrivals and 45 per cent of total European arrivals. As noted earlier, in 2006 arrivals from France and Reunion Island were affected due to the fear of *Chikungunya* and many cancellations were registered. *Chikungunya* was more alarming in Reunion Island and as many French tourists stopover in Reunion for a couple of days before coming to Mauritius this affected the arrivals in Mauritius. The United Kingdom is becoming an important source market in relation to the increase of arrivals over recent years. This can be explained due to the increase in the number of flights to the UK. The UK, which was positioned fourth in 1995, has now overtaken Reunion Island (which has traditionally being the second origin market) to become the second important source market as from 2006.

Table 3. Tourist arrivals by source regions/countries, 1995–2007

	1995	2000	2005	2006	2007
Total tourist arrivals	681 648	702 081	761 063	788 276	906 971
Europe	244 070	439 889	502 715	510 479	595 653
France	116 701	198 423	220 421	182 295	240 028
United Kingdom	31 324	74 488	94 407	102 333	107 297
Germany	41 637	52 869	55 981	57 251	65 165
Italy	17 834	39 000	43 458	69 407	69 510
Africa	143 586	163 921	185 208	189 458	210 952
Reunion Island	78 431	86 945	99 036	89 127	95 823
South Africa	42 653	48 683	58 446	70 796	81 733
Seychelles	7116	9229	10,084	12 023	14 275
Madagascar	6 885	7 075	7 397	7239	8 842
Asia	24 386	39 407	49 202	60 121	68 449
India	11225	17 241	29 755	37 498	42 974
China	1918	2 459	5 526	4 875	7 739
Oceania	5902	9 460	14 424	17 704	20 656
Australia	5 558	8 772	13 486	16 660	19 635
America	3 617	7 680	8 850	9 787	10 473
United States	2 093	3 704	4 890	5 220	5 451
Other and not stated	902	496	664	727	788

Source: Central Statistical Office.

Tourist arrivals from Africa have constantly increased over the years, for instance, from 143,586 in 2005 to 210,952 in 2007 (table 3). Arrivals from Reunion, the major market of the African region,

contracted by 6.9 per cent, while those from South Africa increased by 11.2 per cent from 2004 to 2005. Seychelles and Madagascar also accounted for a major share of total tourist arrivals in Mauritius from the African region. Those from the Asian market rose significantly in recent years, with a large proportion coming from India. In 2006, tourists from Asia rose by 22.2 per cent to reach 60,121 and in 2007, arrivals rose by 13.9 per cent to reach 68,449. Tourists from the Oceania region account for around 2 per cent of total and arrivals are primarily from Australia.

The good performance in tourist arrivals can partly be attributed to the perception that Mauritius is a secure destination, as well as to the promotional efforts of the Mauritius Tourism Promotion Authority (MTPA) in Europe and India. Recent opening up of the access is another major factor contributing to the recent growth. Moreover, there are a growing number of visitors from Australia, Austria and Spain.

4. Purpose of visit

Since Mauritius is seen as a holiday destination, more than 85 per cent of tourists visit the country for leisure and recreational purposes. In 1994, almost 86 per cent of visitors came for holidays, that rose to almost 91 per cent in 2005 tourists (table 4). The number of tourists visiting Mauritius for holidays remains the main motive of visitors.

Table 4. Percentage arrivals by main purpose of visit, 1994–2007

Purpose of visit	1994	2000	2004	2006	2007 [a]
Holidays	85.8	85.0	91.0	90.4	90.3
Business/conferences/official mission	8.5	9.2	4.2	3.4	3.3
Transit	--	--	3.5	3.8	3.9
Visiting friends/relatives	2.7	3.6	--	0.7	0.5
Sports	--	--	0.2	0.3	0.1
Other and not stated	3.0	2.2	1.1	1.4	1.9

Source: Central Statistical Office. [a] Figures for 2007 are provisional

5. Receipts from tourism

In the early 1970s, earnings from the tourism sector were very low, amounting to only 52 million rupees in 1972 (US $9.7m). Gross receipts from tourism grew more than 30-fold in 1987 (in rupee terms) to reach 1,786 million rupees (US $139m), and have since then been on the rise. Figure 2 illustrates tourist receipts in rupees and US dollar terms. Tourism earnings in 2006 were 31,942 million rupees and in 2007 an increase of 27.4% was achieved to reach 40,687 million rupees (around US $ 1,297m). This is attributable to Mauritius' success in attracting tourists at the high end of the market.

Figure 2. Tourism receipts, 1972–2007: Rs million and in US $ million

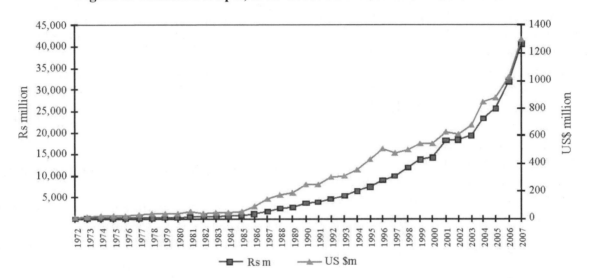

6. Tourism expenditure

Total expenditure increased by 30 per cent from 2002 to 2004, with the share for accommodation, which is the largest item of tourists' spending, rising by 34 per cent, from 9,155 million rupees to 12,231 million rupees (table 5). Expenditure on accommodation is likely to be high essentially in the best hotels, though those for food and beverages and shopping are also among major items of expenditure. Expenditure on shopping has increased significantly in the space of 10 years. For instance, in 1994 expenditure on shopping was 945 million rupees and in 2004 this has increased to more than 3000 million rupees. This increase can be attributed to the duty free concept brought in by the government in the early 2000 and also in the increase of the number of shops around the island.

Table 5. Types of tourist expenditures, 1994–2004

Type of expenditure	Expenditure (million rupees)				
	1994	1998	2000	2002	2004
Accommodation	3 405	6 415	7 479	9 155	12 231
Meals and beverages	997	1 818	2 470	3 327	4 203
Transport	583	804	941	1 232	1 339
Entertainment	214	685	839	986	1 353
Shopping	945	1 691	2 002	2 450	3 010
Other	330	351	457	624	981
Total	**6 472**	**11 764**	**14 187**	**17 775**	**23 117**

Source: Central Statistical Office, *Annual Digest of Statistics*, various years.

7. The tourism industry in the economy

For the period 2002 to 2007, the average contribution of the tourism sector to GDP, as measured by the industry group Hotels and Restaurants in the national accounts, was 7.8 per cent (table 6). A higher than average contribution of 9.5 per cent is forecast for 2008. Further, the real growth rate in the tourism sector has nearly doubled in recent years, from 3.1 per cent in 2002 to 5.6 per cent in 2005. The year 2007 was an excellent year for the tourism industry where a growth rate of 14.0 per cent has been achieved, however, in 2008, it is expected to grow by 7.1 per cent.

At the end of 2007, 97 registered hotels were in operation. The room occupancy rate for all hotels in 2006 averaged 66 per cent, while the bed occupancy rate was 59 per cent. Large hotels (i.e. well-established beach hotels with more than 80 rooms) represent 42 per cent of all registered hotels. The average room occupancy rate for these hotels in 2006 was 69 per cent, while their bed occupancy rate averaged 62 per cent. In 2007, the room occupancy rate was 76 per cent, while bed occupancy rate was 68 per cent. For large hotels the room and bed occupancy rates were 78 and 70 per cent respectively. Tourists also appear to have spent more nights in 2007, with a rise of 18 per cent in 2007 relative to 2006.

Table 6. Main indicators for the tourism industry, 2002–2008

	2002	2003	2004	2005	2006[1]	2007[1]	2008[2]
Tourism earnings (Rs m)	18 328	19 415	23 448	25 704	31 942	40 687	
Contribution to GDP (%)	7.1	6.9	7.4	7.7	8.5	9.4	9.5
Real growth rate in tourism (%)	3.1	3.0	2.4	5.6	3.5	14.0	7.1
Number of hotels	95	97	103	99	98	97	96
Room occupancy rate (%)	--	63	63	63	66	76	
Bed occupancy rate (%)	--	55	56	57	59	68	
Average tourist nights ('000)	6 769	6 952	7 119	7 537	7 761	9 160	
Employment creation[3]	20 729	21 860	22 613	25 377	25 798	26 322	

Source: Central Statistical Office, *Annual Digest of Statistics*, various years.
Note: [1]Revised   [2] Forecast
[3]Figures are as at end March (Central Statistical Office, *Survey of Employment and Earnings in Large Establishments*. Large establishments are those employing 10 or more persons).

8. Employment in tourism

Direct employment in the tourism sector in establishments employing 10

persons or more stood at 26,233 at the end of March 2007, which is 2 per cent more than the previous year (table 7). This represents 5 per cent of the labour force in the economy. Hotels employ the majority of workers in the tourism industry (around 77 per cent in 2007).

Table 7. Employment in tourism, 2002–2007

Establishments	2002	2003	2004	2005	2006	2007
Restaurants	1 252	1 719	1 623	1 809	1 805	1 793
Hotels	15 503	16 069	16 853	19 226	19 536	20 233
Travel and tourism [1]	3 974	4 045	4 137	4 342	4 457	4 296
Total	20 729	21 860	22 613	25 377	25 798	26 322

Source: Central Statistical Office, *Survey of Employment and Earnings in Large Establishments*, various years.
Note: [1] including employment in travel agent and tour operators.

9. Marketing by Mauritian Authorities

The Government of Mauritius established the Mauritius Promotion Tourism Authority (MTPA) in 1996, with a mandate to:

- "promote Mauritius abroad as a tourist destination by conducting advertising campaigns, participating in tourism fairs and organising, in collaboration with the local tourism industry, promotional campaign and activities in Mauritius and abroad.

- provide information to tourists on facilities, infrastructures and services available to them in Mauritius; initiate such action as may be necessary to promote cooperation with other tourism agencies;

- conduct research into market trends and market opportunities and disseminate such information and other relevant statistical data on Mauritius;

- and advise the Minister on all matters relating to the promotion of tourism" (http://www.gov.mu/portal/site/tourist).

The Ministry of Tourism, Leisure and External Communications participates annually in major tourism fairs that are organised in the main countries of tourism origin which also helps to get closer to the customers.

10. The Integrated Resort Scheme

The Government of Mauritius has launched a project for the construction and sale of luxury villas to foreigners near the coastal region of Mauritius: The Integrated Resort Scheme (IRS). Under the IRS, the acquisition of a villa for residential purposes only by foreigners will allow foreigners and their families to reside in Mauritius as long as they hold the property. Villas sold under the scheme will form part of a complex of luxury villas of international standing with facilities including a golf course, marina and individual swimming pools, nautical and other sports facilities, a health centre and catering. Maintenance, waste disposal, gardening, security and other household services will also be included. The area of land for each villa shall not exceed 1.25 arpents (0.5276 hectares). It will be possible to acquire the villa on the basis of a plan or during the construction phase. The acquisition of a villa under the Scheme shall grant resident status to the investor, the spouse and dependants.

A minimum investment of $500,000 is required in the investment of a luxury villa, of which $70,000 will be paid as a fixed duty (Land Registration Duty) to the Government of Mauritius. Persons eligible to apply for IRS are:

- Non-citizens of Mauritius (including the spouse and dependants);
- A foreign company under the Companies Act (of Mauritius) 2001;
- A citizen of Mauritius;
- A company incorporated under the Companies Act 2001.

The selling back of immovable property requires notice to be given to the Board of Investment 30 days prior to the sale, and will result in the loss of residence status. No authorization from the Prime Minister's Office is required for acquisition of immovable property by non-citizens or foreign companies. This scheme is expected to increase the number of tourists, foreign exchange and the level of employment, among many others benefits. The IRS is expected to boost the flows of foreign direct investment in the country.

11. Regional flows of tourists

Mauritius has been benefiting from a significant inflow of regional tourists since the 1990s (table 9). In general, the largest number of tourists has come from the islands of Reunion and Rodrigues, which are the closest origins to Mauritius. The Mauritius Shipping Corporation, through Coraline Ltd, operates a frequent maritime shuttle service to and from these islands, and on a less frequent basis, to Madagascar. This relatively low-fare service is believed to have contributed to increasing tourism from the region. Another sizeable regional market is that of South Africa, which accounts for an average of about 8 per cent of total tourist arrivals.

The other regional sources of tourists to Mauritius (e.g. Comores, Kenya, Seychelles and Zimbabwe) have not contributed significantly in terms of arrivals.

Table 8. Tourist arrivals in Mauritius from the region, 1990–2004

Year	Reunion	Madagascar	Comoros	Seychelles	Zimbabwe	Kenya	Zambia	South Africa
1990	73 310	6 550	700	3 500	3 670	1 440	1 490	41 860
1991	77 840	6 010	990	3 420	3 580	1 240	890	43 020
1992	81 260	7 260	1 010	4 710	2 990	1 720	310	39 790
1993	84 960	7 740	930	5 420	3 460	1 070	340	42 350
1994	77 035	6 849	1 148	5 650	3 539	1 278	337	39 762
1995	78 431	6 885	1 348	7 116	2 965	1 158	443	42 653
1996	82 272	11 401	1 223	9 325	3 402	1 170	391	50 361
1997	82 628	10 143	969	8 995	4 248	1 230	340	51 249
1998	83 966	9 213	907	8 529	3 796	1 684	330	49 676
1999	83 749	7 880	728	7 893	2 606	1 655	350	46 583
2000	86 945	7 057	945	9 229	3 435	1 801	460	48 683
2001	91 140	6 674	860	10 687	3 860	1 734	500	47 882
2002	96 276	7 417	945	13 368	3 185	1 507	523	42 685
2003	95 679	11 044	1 437	9 869	2 343	1 510	490	45 756
2004	73 310	6 550	700	3 500	3 670	1 440	1 490	41 860

Source: Ministry of Tourism, Leisure and External Communications, *Annual Handbook of Tourist Statistics,* various years.

In terms of departures, Mauritians travel mostly to Rodrigues, Reunion and South Africa within the region for tourism purposes as illustrated in Table 10.

Table 9. Tourist departures from Mauritius to selected destinations, 2003–2005

Year	Rodrigues	Reunion	South Africa
2003	63 649	33 980	14 010
2004	60 862	32 274	13 128
2005	53 534	29 994	13 384

Source: Ministry of Tourism, Leisure and External Communications, *Annual Handbook of Tourism Statistics*, various issues.

C. FDI in tourism in Mauritius

1. Contribution of FDI to the economy

Foreign Direct Investment (FDI) has contributed significantly to the diversification of the Mauritian economy. In 1970, the Government enacted an Export Processing Zone Act to attract small Asian investors to locate textile and garment manufacturing operations and benefit from preferential access to the European and United States markets. But it was only in the mid-1980s that FDI started entering Mauritius, mostly in the EPZ and the tourism industry. It played an important role at the time more because of the technological know-how it brought rather than because of the capital inflows per se (UNCTAD, 2001). This transformed the EPZ and tourism into leading sectors of the economy. However, FDI in Mauritius has been highly concentrated in terms of industries, skills and capabilities, therefore limiting the capacity to rapidly upgrade and diversify production (UNCTAD, 2001). As Mauritius shifts increasingly into higher value added activities, FDI will be critical for boosting growth and international competitiveness.

Mauritius is among the few sub-Saharan African countries to have successfully competed with other countries for FDI. Its open door policy and integration into the globalization process has attracted significant export-oriented FDI, which now plays a pivotal role in the development of the country's economy. Figure 3 shows the trend in FDI inflows into Mauritius over the period 1990–2005.

Figure 3. FDI inflows into Mauritius, 1990–2005

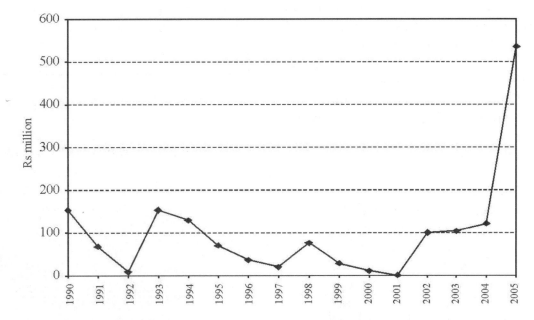

Note: In 2000, France Telecom invested 7,204 million rupees in Mauritius Telecom, but this investment has not been included in the data for this figure. For more details see table 11.

Before independence, the Mauritian economy was almost entirely dependent on sugar production as it was guaranteed a certain quota of sugar exports to the EU. After independence in 1968, export-oriented manufacturing was seen as a potential source of growth along the same lines as some small Asian economies such as Singapore, Taiwan Province of China and Hong Kong (China).

The EPZ Act of 1970, which aimed to attract domestic and foreign investors in export processing enhanced export-oriented FDI. The establishment of an EPZ and the strategy of export-oriented manufacturing proved a resounding success and transformed the Mauritian economy as a result of increasing FDI inflows. From 1970 to 1980, FDI grew at an average annual rate of 12.5 per cent after the setting up of the EPZ, which attracted two thirds of all FDI inflows, mainly from Asia. These were concentrated in knitwear and garments manufacture. From 1985 to 1990, FDI increased further, at an average annual rate of 49.5 per cent, going not only to the EPZ but also to other sectors of the economy. In the early 1990s, however, foreign capital flows started to decline, recording an average annual growth rate of 13.9 per cent due to a slowdown of FDI in the EPZ. Then in the late 1990s, inward FDI nearly doubled, with considerable investment in banking (table 11). In 2000, telecommunications received a boost as a result of France Telecom investing in Mauritius Telecom through a direct sell-off of shares. This one-off form of investment has been common in sub-Saharan Africa, in particular through a wave of privatizations of large enterprises, principally utilities and public infrastructure, such as power, railways, electricity, water and, especially, telecommunications.

The setting up of the EPZ induced mainly export-oriented FDI, but other industries also benefited from these inflows. Dominated by textiles and garments, the EPZ attracted a steadily growing share of foreign capital. It accounted for more than 40 per cent of total inward FDI in 1991 while the tourism sector accounted for 23 percent (figure 4). Over a period of 15 years or so, EPZ exports grew more than six fold in terms of foreign exchange earnings to reach $900 million in 1995. More than 90 per cent of

EPZ exports are destined to Europe. During the period 1997–1998, EPZ merchandise exports amounted to more than 68 per cent of total exports. From 1983 to 1999, total factor productivity of the EPZ averaged about 3.5 per cent per annum compared with 1.4 per cent for the economy as a whole, while average annual productivity growth was 5.4 per cent.

Table 10. FDI in the EPZ and in major industries, 1990–2005 (million rupees)

Year	EPZ	Tourism	Banking	Telecom-munications	Other	Total
1990	270	152	–	–	187	609
1991	130	68	51	–	48	297
1992	203	8	3	–	16	230
1993	92	152	–	–	27	271
1994	41	129	–	–	190	360
1995	245	70	–	–	10	325
1996	51	35	55	–	517	658
1997	–	20	1 122	–	22	1 164
1998	27	75	117	–	73	292
1999	300	27	215	–	701	1 243
2000	8	10	–	7 204	43	7 265
2001	3	–	600	–	333	936
2002	41	100	316	–	522	979
2003	77	103	1 301	–	485	1 966
2004	248	121	310	38	1 079	1 796
2005	106	365	454	175	1 268	2 368

Source: Bank of Mauritius, Monthly Statistical Bulletin Issues.

Figure 4. FDI in Mauritius by sector, 1991

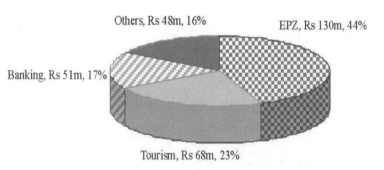

The success of the EPZ lies in the provision of a variety of incentives such as exemptions from import duty, zero tax on

dividends for foreign subsidiaries located in Mauritius, provision for infrastructure and possibility to have joint ventures with the Mauritian counterparts. Incentives as well as preferential access to the EU and United States markets under the MFA proved to be beneficial for export-oriented FDI. However the phasing out of the MFA over the period 1995 to 2005 has presented a new challenge for export-oriented FDI. The complete removal of exchange controls and further trade liberalization have facilitated FDI inflows into the economy and have even encouraged outward investment from Mauritius to other African countries including Mozambique and Seychelles.

FDI in the manufacturing sector flows essentially into labour-intensive industries, as Mauritius presents itself as a low-cost location with cheap labour. The garment and textile industries employ a disproportionate number of women. The minimum wage for women was lower than for men in the early 1990s and the conditions of overtime work were very flexible. However, rapid development, rising labour costs and the presence of active trade unions have led to a decline in Mauritian EPZ exports, and foreign investors have moved to other, lower cost locations in sub-Saharan Africa, such as Kenya, Madagascar and Zimbabwe.

The decline in the competitiveness of EPZ exports has led to a slowdown in FDI, not only in the traditional industries but also in new, high-skill and technology-intensive ones. The proportion of FDI in the EPZ sector has been declining steadily, from more than 72 per cent in 1995 to 24 per cent in 1999. Although reasonably efficient infrastructure and domestic institutions are among the main factors that have attracted FDI into the economy, bureaucratic and structural bottlenecks, limited supply of skilled labour and technological infrastructure, as well as low

local demand for high-technology products have inhibited the spread and quality of inward FDI.

In addition to attracting FDI into export-oriented manufacturing in the EPZ, the authorities have also been seeking to encourage FDI inflows into other sectors of the economy, especially the services sector. Indeed, the Government's diversification strategy aims to establish the services sector as the fourth pillar of the economy. In 1997, banking registered more than 90 per cent of total FDI inflows, and in 2000, as noted earlier, a large amount of foreign capital was secured in telecommunications as a result of the purchase of a 40 per cent equity stake in Mauritius Telecom by France Telecom for 7.4 billion rupees.

Mauritius has been successful in attracting significant export-oriented FDI due to its low-cost labour, efficient infrastructure, preferential access to large markets, sound legal system, political stability, government policies favourable to foreign investors and a strong business environment with a vibrant entrepreneurial culture. Despite this achievement, one major challenge for Mauritius is to develop comparative advantages in established industries and competitive advantages in emerging ones. Investment in relevant education and skills development needs to be made a priority to promote technological upgrading and facilitate research and development.

2. FDI in tourism

In the early 1990s, average FDI inflows in tourism were around 29 per cent over the period 1990-1994 (table 11). As explained earlier, most of the FDI since 1970s was in manufacturing, particularly in EPZ. Over the period 1995-1999, most of the FDI inflows were in banking, FDI in tourism averaged around 11 per cent of the total. In the early 2000, FDI in tourism was very low, in fact, in the year 2000 and 2001 combined a total of only 10 million rupees were invested. It was only as from 2002 that the tourism industry started to attract considerable amount of FDI, particularly in the construction of world-class hotels. This period was also characterised by stagnation in the tourism industry according to the final report on the Master Plan for Air Transport in Mauritius 2004. This raised the question as to whether there is sufficient competition among hotels. The report suggested that the Government should help make the hotel industry more competitive vis-à-vis other destinations such as Dubai and Seychelles. There is also limited competition among the other contributors to the tourism product, such as the airlines. The report recommended that the air access policy be liberalised in a step-by-step manner. At present, the Government of Mauritius is the major shareholder of Air Mauritius Company Ltd; other shareholders are private and foreign companies. Local private firms include Rogers Company Ltd and the employees of Air Mauritius. Foreign shareholders include British Airways, Air France and Air India. The company is also quoted on the official market of the Stock Exchange.

With the focus of the government towards a more targeted approach, the investment strategy is geared to attract international brand names. In 2005, with the introduction of Integrated Resort Scheme (IRS) scheme, which primarily is the acquisition of villa for residential purposes by foreigners only, FDI has risen significantly. Investment under this scheme has driven FDI inflows upward in the Hotel and Restaurant sector. This is expected to grow further in the years to come. Using the International Standard of Industrial Classification Rev 3.1, table 12 illustrates Foreign Direct Investment in Mauritius by sector since the year 2000. It can be noted that in the year 2006 there has been a marked increase of more than 380 per cent

to reach 2,610 million rupees (US $ 84 million) and in 2007 FDI in tourism reached 5,979 million rupees (US $ 191 million). These last two years alone far exceed the total amount of FDI that has flown in over the period 1990 to 2005.

Table 11. Foreign Direct Investment in Mauritius by Sector, 2002-2007 (Rs million)

Sector	2002	2003	2004	2005	2006	2007[1]
Agriculture, hunting and forestry	-	-	484	19	26	12
Fishing	-	1	-	-	-	-
Manufacturing	65	127	387	263	181	271
Electricity, gas and water supply	-	25			17	
Construction	-	1	14	46	11	45
Wholesale and retail trade	386	288	123	510	198	38
Hotels and Restaurants	99	103	121	536	2,610	5,979
Transport, storage and communications	13	1	47	191	56	18
Financial Intermediation	316	1,311	392	481	3,593	4,056
Real Estate, renting and business activities	100	109	228	759	473	1,030
Education	-	-	-	2	55	30
Health and Social Work	-	-	-	-	2	29
Total	**979**	**1,966**	**1,797**	**2,807**	**7,222**	**11,514**

Source: Bank of Mauritius, Monthly Statistical Bulletin Issues. [1]Provisional

With liberalisation of FDI, two sectors that have attracted significant amount of FDI are Hotels and Restaurants (tourism) and Financial Intermediation (banking). In fact, FDI policy towards the tourism sector has evolved from being quite restrictive in the past to almost full liberalisation. At one time, the Government was concerned that overcapacity in hotel rooms was developing, which prompted its introduction of restrictions on new investments though these applied more to foreign than to national investors. Full foreign ownership of new developments was permitted only for hotels of more than 100 rooms, while foreign participation in smaller hotels was restricted to 49 per cent. There was no restriction on foreign hotel management companies. The remainder of the tourism industry was almost entirely reserved for national investors. Foreign participation in restaurant operations was limited to 49 per cent, and only where investment exceeded 10 million rupees ($400,000) which was rare. No foreign investment was permitted in travel agencies, tour operators, tourist guides, car rentals, yacht charters and duty free shops. Despite fears of overcapacity the tourist market has grown rapidly, and there has been significant investment in new hotels by both national and foreign investors. Approximately 40 per cent of the 25 larger hotels (with more than 100 rooms) are partly foreign owned. Restrictions on foreign investment have been removed, however, access to land still remains an issue as it is subject to the approval by the Prime Minister's Office.

3. FDI outflows

Mauritius imposes no restrictions on capital outflows; indeed, it encourages them by granting tax incentives to Mauritian companies (under the Regional Development Certificate). As a result it emerged as an outward investor in the 1990s, with annual outflows of FDI averaging US $18 million in 1990–1994, and around US $6 million in 1995–1999 (UNCTAD, 2001). There was a significant increase in outward investment, from US $9 million in 2002 to US $66 million in 2005 and to US $ 58 million in 2007.

In the early 2000, the bulk of outward FDI went into agriculture, hunting and forestry. However, Mauritian entrepreneurs have significantly invested in Hotels and Restaurants in recent years (table 13), particularly in acquisition and construction of hotels in the region. In fact,

the significant increase in outward investment in tourism is possibly due to the development of core competencies and know-how in hotel management by Mauritian companies (UNCTAD, 2001).

Table 12. Outward FDI in selected Sectors, 2002-2007 (Rs million)

Sector	2002	2003	2004	2005	2006	2007[1]
Agriculture, hunting and forestry	-	523	250	532	271	113
Manufacturing	245	41	210	317	335	235
Hotels and Restaurants	-	137	422	967	391	1,068
Financial Intermediation	-	440	11	14	12	112
Other	-	-	-	-	-	-
Total	**278**	**1,156**	**970**	**1,942**	**1,134**	**1,826**

Source: Bank of Mauritius, Monthly Statistical Bulletin Issues. [1]Provisional

Most of the Mauritian outward investment in tourism has gone to Reunion, Comoros, Maldives and Seychelles. The main investors include Mauritian hotel chains such as Beachcomber Group (Sainte Anne Resorts in Seychelles and a new resort in Morocco), Constance Limited (Lemuria Resorts and Spa in Seychelles) and Naide Resorts (Deroches in Seychelles and White Sand Spa and Resorts in Maldives), and also long-established conglomerates such as Rogers Group, IBL Group, Currimjee Group and the Food and Allied Industries Group. According to these investors reasons for investing abroad were because of the following : i) to expand and diversify existing businesses, ii) to secure better access to a booming and high-spending tourist market, iii) to facilitate group-island (Indian ocean) vacation tours, and iv) to benefit from recipient countries' favourable fiscal and land incentives.

D. FDI policy and operational framework

1. Liberalization of FDI, including in tourism

Mauritius is among the most successful African countries in attracting FDI according to the World Bank survey, *Doing Business in 2006*. In particular, the survey revealed that Mauritius occupies 23rd position out of 155 countries, and is the only African country among the top 25. Over the years, different governments have pursued policies geared towards increasing FDI. The marked success of fiscal incentives (mainly a 10-year tax holiday) in attracting FDI into the EPZ at the early stage of the country's industrialization encouraged the adoption of a variety of other fiscal incentive measures (e.g. duty-free imports, an investment allowance, depreciation allowance and low registration fees for the acquisition of land and building) targeting investment in tourism, agriculture, construction, financial services, ICTs, seafood production, knowledge-based activities, high-tech medical services and the pharmaceutical industry.

The growing importance of tourism and tourism-related activities has caused the Government to undertake various initiatives to promote the industry. For instance, the Tourism Act of 2004 created the Tourism Authority to optimize the social, economic and environmental benefits for Mauritius from tourism, and to promote a sustainable tourism industry. The definition of a tourist enterprise has been broadened under the Tourism Act (2004) to include: hotels, tourist residences, bungalows or villas, guest houses, any accommodation that may be offered for rent to tourists, restaurants, cafes, piano bars, *table d'hote*[2], and pubs. Furthermore, tourism activities have been classified as tourist guides, karting, golf, ecotourism, vehicle rental agencies, water sports, helmet diving, scuba-diving,

parasailing, canoeing, big game fishing, regattas, undersea walks, hawking on beaches facing hotels, travel agents and tour operators. FDI in the above-listed tourist enterprises and tourism activities in Mauritius is governed by provisions of the General Agreement on Trade in Services (GATS) of the World Trade Organization (WTO), which entered into force in January 1995.

As a WTO member, Mauritius has been complying with GATS in its design of certain policies in tourism and travel-related services. The GATS relates to commitments by WTO member countries to rationalize market access and national treatment in specific sectors as well as across sectors. The specific commitments made by Mauritius in the tourism sector extend to areas such as: (i) hotel operations, (ii) restaurant operations, (iii) travel agencies, (iv) tour operators, (v) tourist guide services, (vi) tourist transport operation (car rental), (vii) yacht chartering and cruising services, and (viii) tourist duty-free shops.

As an established pillar of the Mauritian economy and given the difficulties faced by the sugar and textile industries, the tourism industry is expected to play a more important role. In this context, the Government has broadened the scope of tourism by redefining it as the Hospitality and Property Development Sector. Moreover, the Government has been providing proactive support to this sector through strategies such as: (i) having an open skies policy, (ii) developing Mauritius as a duty-free island, (iii) promoting the country as a centre for meetings, incentives, conferences and exhibitions (MICE), and (iv) allowing foreigners to acquire property.
(i) Hotel   development   comprises
       development   of   beach-resorts,

business hotels and upmarket boutique hotels;

(ii) Leisure activities include water-based projects, ecotourism, golf courses, entertainment parks, and heritage and cultural tourism;

(iii) Real estate property development includes development of luxury villas and related projects under the Integrated Resort Scheme (IRS), and construction of shopping malls; and

(iv) MICE encourages activities related to meetings, incentives, conferences and exhibitions.

2. The entry process

Generally, policies do not discriminate against foreign investors. Full foreign ownership is allowed subject to approval by the Prime Minister's Office. In order to encourage investment in prioritised industry clusters, 100 per cent foreign ownership is permitted in export-oriented activities and also where a significant amount of technology transfer is involved. On the other hand, for domestic-market-oriented business activities, a maximum of 50 per cent foreign ownership is allowed, and it is particularly encouraged where technology and knowledge can be imparted. Moreover, for projects involving technology transfer the Government may, on a case-by-case basis, relax some restrictions.

With the abolition of foreign exchange controls in 1994, approval is no longer required for repatriation of profits, dividends and capital gains earned by a foreign investor in Mauritius. In general, businesses have no difficulty obtaining foreign exchange. However, local banks sometimes experience foreign exchange shortages, which can delay transfers.

Regarding expropriation and compensation, legislative regulations against nationalization exist and are respected. Furthermore, the Government has not nationalized any industry so far, and there is no precedent of expropriation in Mauritius.

In 2000, the Board of Investment (BOI) was set up to promote, facilitate and improve the investment climate in Mauritius, and it runs representative offices in Paris and Mumbai to market Mauritius as an investment destination. Under the Investment Promotion Act (2000), it serves as a one-stop-agency to assist local and foreign investors free of charge. In particular, the Investment Facilitation Division of the BOI ensures that all necessary licences, permits and clearances (e.g. development permit, trade licence, work and residence permits) are obtained from relevant ministries in a timely manner. All approved projects are granted an investment certificate, which relates to the incentives offered under a particular scheme. Normally, the time frame for project approval is within four weeks from submission of a business plan. However, for particular industrial activities, complex projects and/or projects requiring an environmental impact assessment or a development permit the time frame is around eight weeks. In October 2006 the Business Facilitation Act revised the regulatory framework to increase opportunity for people to participate in business related activity and to create a climate of greater competitiveness for both foreign and local investors. Notably, the Act has enabled investors to start operation within only three working days.

3. Double taxation avoidance treaties and other agreements

Mauritius has entered into several double taxation avoidance treaties with both developed and developing countries, mainly in Europe, Africa and Asia. As at 31 July 2006, a total of 32 such treaties had been signed. In addition, Mauritius is a member of major multilateral conventions and agreements, including:

- The Multilateral Investment Guarantee Agency (MIGA)
- The International Court of Justice
- The International Center for Settlement of Investment Dispute
- The 1958 New York Convention on the Recognition and Enforcement of Foreign Arbitral Awards.

Mauritius has also signed bilateral investment promotion and protection agreements (IPPAs) with 31 countries.

4. Institutional set-ups in the tourism industry

The Ministry of Tourism, Leisure and External Communication is the apex body responsible for the promotion and development of the island as a prime holiday destination. The mission of the Ministry is to make Mauritius the best island tourism destination in the world as well as to champion leisure, entertainment and recreational activities with a view to enhancing the coexistence and welfare of the locals and tourists.

The Tourism Authority was established under the Tourism Act of 2004 with a view to promoting social, economic and environmental benefits to Mauritius from tourism. It is responsible for the formulation of policy and nationally integrated planning for the tourism industry, for coordination of the activities of the various organizations in the tourism industry and for the issuing and/or renewing of tourist enterprise licences according to a specified fee structure.

5. Incentives

To promote tourism, since independence the Government has accorded numerous special incentives to the private sector, along with the introduction of legislation to ensure that the industry's activities are in line with the Government's overall development objectives. The incentive packages have evolved over time in Mauritius starting by providing fiscal and financial incentives to encourage investment, incentives to increase investment, incentives to regulate and to consolidate the tourism industry.

In July 1974 the Development Incentives Act, which also applies to hotel development, was passed and development certificates were issued to individuals, groups and companies on application to the Ministry. Under this scheme, tax relief was granted for a period of 10 years starting from the commencement of a project. There was also a list of categories of items that were exempt from customs duty (85 per cent duty exemption at first importation and for projects where extensions were approved, and 50 per cent for renovation). Recently, with liberalisation, most items are now totally exempted from customs duty. To encourage foreign investors in the industry, they are allowed free repatriation of profits under the Bank of Mauritius Act and Income Tax Act.

Moreover, the Hotel Management Scheme, in accordance with the Hotel Management Incentive Act 1982, was promulgated to provide additional facilities and incentives for hotel development. Like other industries eligible for tax incentives, hotels that obtain a Hotel Development Certificate benefit from a number of incentives. These can be summarized as follows:

(a) The company pays a nominal corporate tax of 15 per cent during the lifetime of the project instead of the normal statutory rate of 30 per cent.

(b) Dividends received by shareholders are exempt from income tax in Mauritius for a period of 10 years starting from the date the hotel begins operations.

(c) Exemption from payment of customs duty on the import of an approved list of equipment.

(d) Free repatriation of invested capital, profit and dividends subject to the original investment obtaining approved (A) status from the Bank of Mauritius.

(e) Term loans and overdrafts at preferential rates.

In September 1998, the Government made some adjustments to the hotel and restaurant tax (HRT) so that the indirect tax burden would not increase with the introduction of the value-added tax. To this end, the tax rate for hotels and restaurants was reduced from 10 per cent to 4 per cent and, from 1 July 1999, to 2 per cent. In July 2002 the HRT was replaced by a value-added tax, which presently stands at 15 per cent.

First-class restaurants benefit from 50 per cent duty exemption on imported kitchen equipment. They also enjoy free repatriation of profits under the Bank of Mauritius Act and Income Tax Act. Tour operators and car rental agencies benefit from a 60 per cent rebate on duties payable for the import of registered air-conditioned buses and vehicles to encourage tour operators to invest in quality vehicles.

Policymakers are acutely aware of the need to compete for foreign capital to ensure continuous injections of funds into the Mauritian economy. In this context, the 2006/07 national budget reiterated the need to reduce bureaucracy and improve the investment climate in Mauritius, with particular attention to fiscal incentives for foreign investors. In July 2006 the Minister of Finance in his national budget speech proposed harmonizing the cost of doing business across all sectors and business activities, through the following measures:

(a) Corporate tax rates to be harmonized at 15 per cent for all activities;

(b) Annual allowances (depreciation) to be calculated on a reducing balance basis instead of the existing straight-line basis. The rates would be 30 per cent for hotel buildings, 50 per cent for electronic and computer equipment and 35 per cent for plant and machinery;

(c) Industrial buildings and commercial premises, including shops and shopping malls, offices, showrooms, restaurants, other entertainment premises and clinics, to benefit from a 5 per cent annual allowance on a straight-line basis;

(d) Assets costing up to 30,000 rupees each would qualify for a 100 per cent annual allowance;

(e) Tax losses, other than losses arising out of the new regime for capital allowances may be carried forward up to five years;

(f) The rate of an alternative minimum tax would be at 7.5 per cent;

(g) Registration duty on transfer of immovable property would be reduced from 10 per cent to 5 per cent;

(h) Charges on registration of loan agreements to be fixed in five bands ranging from 1,000 rupees on loans of less than 300,000 rupees to 50,000 rupees for loans of over 5 million rupees;

(i) Introduction of a temporary solidarity levy of 0.85 per cent on turnover of profitable hotels, destination management companies and tour operators for four years;

(j) Other fiscal duties under the Registration Act, the Stamp Duty Act and the Transcription and Mortgage Act would range between 50 and 2,000 rupees;

(k) Elimination of customs duties on all inputs for both EPZ and non-EPZ industries.

6. Tourism legislation and regulations

Between 1972 and 1982, the number of hotels doubled from 25 to 51. The government at that time was concerned about the growing number of hotels that would add pressure on existing infrastructure and environment. The Mauritian tourism policy has been since to target the upper segment of the market. Together with concern about the environmental and infrastructural impact of the growing influx of tourists, these have prompted the Government to limit the construction of new hotels. Generally, there is a ban on direct charter flights, and the maximum number of rooms per hotel since 1989 is 200. However, the Ministry of Tourism and Leisure and External Communication may, at its discretion, allow hotels to exceed the ceiling of 200 rooms.

In the 1980s, the government has come up with some criteria to better regulate investment in the tourism industry. For sound management and control of the tourism industry, the Government has set some criteria of eligibility for a Hotel Development Certificate. The main criteria are:

(a) Number of rooms: a Mauritian-controlled company must build a hotel of at least 60 rooms, whereas the minimum number of rooms for a foreign-owned company is 100. No hotel projects should exceed 200 rooms.

(b) The company must be incorporated with the Registrar of Companies in Mauritius.

(c) The project should be financed by at least 40 per cent of equity.

(d) In case of resort hotels, the promoter should have at least 2.5 acres of land. For foreign-owned hotels, the area of land must not be less than 10 acres. This parameter does not apply to inland hotels.

(e) The room-to-employment ratio should be in the region of 1:1.

(f) The cost of one room should be at least 700,000 rupees (1990 estimate).

(g) For large hotels, the promoters should either show evidence of experience in the management and marketing of hotels or give the management of the hotel to a specialised management company.

To manage and market hotel complexes, the Ministry grants Hotel Management Service Certificates so as to guarantee a high occupancy rate in hotels and to ensure that the establishments are run efficiently. The issuance of this certificate is governed by the Hotel Management (Incentives) Act 1982.

Since January 1995, investment in a first-class restaurant requires an initial capital of at least 10 million rupees and foreign participation is allowed for restaurant projects exceeding 10 million rupees.

For other tourism-related activities, the following are some of the main requirements:

(i). The project should be a tourist attraction, such as the development of new, or the substantial extension of existing, nature parks, tourist gardens and aquariums. Excluded are car hire, bus hire, duty-free shops or any other trading activity.

(ii). The company must be incorporated with the Registrar of Companies.

(iii). The project should be financed by at least 40 per cent of equity (value of only freehold land will be considered as part of equity).

(iv). The initial investment should not be less than the 10 millions rupees.

(v). Proof of successful implementation of similar projects elsewhere must be provided as far as possible.

The 2006/07 national budget made it simpler to start a business in all sectors with the abolition of the screening and approval policy, which was previously based on the above-mentioned criteria for investment in the tourism sector such as those listed from (a) to (g) for hotel development and (i) to (v) for other tourism-related activities. As from October 2006, the following categories of foreign investors and foreign talent are allowed to work and reside in Mauritius:

(a) Investors generating an annual turnover of more than 3 million rupees,

(b) Professionals who are offered employment at a monthly salary of more than 30,000 rupees, and

(c) Self-employed persons earning an annual income of at least 600,000 rupees.

The current investment schemes offer a wide range of incentives and facilities to attract FDI and institutional investors. The industry sectors that qualify for government incentive programmes include ICTs, manufacturing, tourism, agro-based industries, fisheries and marine resources, integrated resort projects, education, construction, agriculture, health care, infrastructure, leisure, power industry, freeport (free trade zone) activities, and offshore businesses. Generally, incentive packages include a lower corporate tax rate of 15 per cent (instead of the normal rate of 25 per cent), exemption from customs and excise duties on imports of equipment and raw materials, exemption from tax on dividends, free repatriation of profits, dividends, and capital, loans at preferential rates, and reduced tariffs for electricity and water. In addition, foreigners investing a minimum of $500,000 in the qualifying sectors are eligible for permanent resident status.

E. The role and impact of FDI in Mauritius

To assess the role and impact of FDI in tourism, a series of interviews were conducted with hotels, firms and the wider community. Officials from various ministries, agencies and other sectors were also interviewed to assess the role and impact of FDI in tourism on the economy.

1.   Survey of hotels

There were 94 hotels in operation when the interviews were carried out. Information was obtained from 15 of the 22 foreign-owned hotels and from 33 of the 72 domestic-owned hotels that were operational. The hotels are classified by the following main star ratings: 3-star, 3-star plus, 4-star and 5-star. Table 14 provides a summary of the profile of the hotels surveyed by type of ownership.

Table 13. Profile of hotels in the sample

	Foreign-owned hotels	Domestic-owned hotels
Total number of hotels surveyed	22	72
Sample selected (% of total)	68%	46%
Average number of rooms	180	153
Average number of beds	350	300
Hotel category:		
Upmarket business and/or leisure	75% [a]	56% [a]
Mid-market leisure	38% [a]	63% [a]
Occupancy rate (yearly average)	64%	66%

The average number of rooms of foreign-owned hotels was139 in 5-star hotels, 197 in the 4-star hotels and 260 in three-star and three-star-plus hotels. In the case of domestic-owned hotels, the opposite was observed, the average number of rooms being 130 in 3-star and 3-star plus hotel categories, 165 in four-star hotels and 205 in 5-star hotels. The number of beds was similar for both types of hotels, with a ratio of room to beds of around 1:2.

More foreign-owned hotels were found to be oriented towards upmarket tourists than the domestic-owned hotels: 75 per cent of the foreign-owned hotels compared to 56 per cent of the domestic owned ones. The domestic-owned hotels appeared to cater more for the mid-market type of tourists (mainly tourists from France and Reunion). The occupancy rate for the both types of hotels was similar, averaging around 65 per cent over the whole year. The number of visitors (bed nights) for both types of hotels seemed to be around 11,000, on average, and more than 90 per cent of the visitors were international tourists.

Locally owned hotels generally did not have a management contract agreement; they were primarily own and managed either individually or as part of a group such NAIDE Resorts and Constance Group. Only one domestic-owned hotel in the sample had a partnership agreement. Of the foreign-owned hotels around 25 per cent had a management contract. Both managers of domestic-owned and foreign-owned hotels mentioned that they adopted best practices and know-how and that their activities were standardised.

Foreign ownership varied, but the majority of owners were from Dubai, France (Reunion), India and South Africa. In nearly all cases, they brought equity from their home country, thus providing an injection of foreign currency. However, some of them had recourse to domestic finance for extension and renovation of their business.

Many hotels managers pointed out that the location of their hotel on the island was a major asset, not only in terms of being near a beach but also because of factors such as safety, lack of pollution and a friendly neighbourhood. Some of the reasons cited by foreign-owned hotels for their choice of Mauritius included the low corporate tax rate and tax concessions on equipment, access to land and infrastructure, political stability, guarantee against expropriation, good beaches, a booming industry, availability of skilled labour and the Government's vision.

a.   Hotel revenue

Hotels were somewhat reluctant to provide information about their annual turnover. However, a few hotels surveyed reported sales ranging from 240 million to 300 million rupees ($8 million to $10 million) for both foreign- and domestic-owned hotels (table 15)

Table 14. Summary of revenue

	Foreign-owned hotels	Domestic-owned hotels
Annual sales per hotel (average)	$9 million	$10 million
of which: Accommodation (%)	61	57
Restaurant (%)	34	34
Conferences (%)	4	7
Other (%)	1	2
Profitability: Gross profit	33	30
of which: Accommodation (%)	56	48
Restaurants (%)	33	32
Conferences (%)	3	13
Other (%)	8	7
Average revenue per visitor per day:		
3-star (rupees)	4 000 –6 000	3 000–6 000
3-star plus (rupees)	8 000–10 000	7 000–7 500
4-star (rupees)	8 000–12 000	10 000–20 000
5-star (rupees)	18 000–40 000	2 000–4 000
Average length of stay per visitor	6 days	8 days

For some domestic-owned groups of hotels, total sales were about 1.4 billion rupees (around $46.7 million) for the group. Not surprisingly, for both types of hotels, accommodation generated most of the turnover followed by restaurants and bar activities. Similarly, where hotels were willing to provide information on profitability, gross profits seemed to be about 30 per cent. The hotels did not reveal the amount or percentage of their profits that were shared with the owners or reinvested. A few hotels declared that part of their profits were also shared among employees in terms of productivity and bonus payments. About 45 per cent of domestic-owned hotels and 80 per cent of foreign-owned hotels reported reinvesting their profits.[3] Of the reinvestment, some goes to renovation and a few hotels are investing in the region, for example, acquiring and constructing hotels in Seychelles. Foreign-owned hotels reported repatriating part of their profits.

As far as average revenue per visitor per day is concerned, there seemed to be little difference between foreign-owned and domestic-owned hotels by star rating categories (table 15). Regarding visitors' countries of origin, both types of hotels had a similar composition of tourists from France and Reunion (table 16). However, a higher proportion of tourists from the United Kingdom seemed to stay in foreign-owned hotels, while more tourists from Italy stayed in the locally owned hotels. Both categories of hotels received very few tourists from developing countries: around 5 per cent of their total visitors.

Table 15. Visitors by country of origin, reasons for visit and mode (%)

Country of origin	Foreign-owned hotels	Domestic-owned hotels
France	27	27
Reunion	33	28
United Kingdom	24	12
Germany	13	11
Italy	2	10
Spain	1	9
India	7	3
Visitors from developing countries	4	5
Reason for visit:		
Holiday	91	80
Business	8	19
Other	1	1
Mode:		
Tour operators' packages	86	82
Individual tourists	14	18

The survey revealed that locally owned hotels catered more for businesses and conferences than their foreign counterparts (19 per cent compared to 8 per cent respectively), while there was a higher percentage of visitors for holiday purposes at the foreign-owned hotels (91 per cent) than at the locally owned ones (80 per cent). Also, most of the bookings were made through foreign tour operators (around 84 per cent) and the rest were by Internet or individually (table 17).

Table 16. Booking methods

Booking method	Foreign-owned hotels (%)	Domestic-owned hotels (%)
Foreign tour operators	87	81
Foreign travel agencies	2	5
Local travel agencies	3	6
Internet	5	2
Individually by tourists	3	6

Two foreign-owned hotels that are part of a chain in the region said they allowed their clients to move from one hotel to the other within the region, but that few visitors availed of that opportunity. Some domestic-owned hotels had started planning a similar arrangement, and had adopted strategies to encourage it, including working with other hotels in the region to enable such a movement of visitors. This was considered important so as not to lose customers. As one manager stated, "Long-term visitors tend to get bored, so instead of losing them, it is better to allow movement."

In terms of payments, international visitors tend to pay in foreign currencies such as euros and dollars, while local visitors pay in local currency. Almost all the hotels reported accepting major credit cards.

b. Purchases by hotels

All the hotels surveyed indicated that they purchased more than 90 per cent of food items locally, except for certain types of foods that are not available during a particular season. Other items such as beverages, toiletries and linen were also purchased from local dealers. Some respondents stressed the fact that they gave priority to local merchants and suppliers as part of their programme of corporate social responsibility. However, raw materials were primarily imported from abroad as Mauritius does not have the required natural resources. Services such as cleaning, laundry and security were mostly carried out in-house. However, maintenance of equipment, vehicles and fridges was mostly contracted out to local firms. Concerning purchases during hotel construction, most managers indicated that the construction materials and labour were mainly local, but that some furniture and fittings were imported (50 per cent). All the hotels were equipped with power generators but rarely used them, since the supply of electricity in Mauritius is very good.

Many hotels expressed some concern over the very limited availability of some items on the local market such as good quality vegetables, fruit (which are seasonal), seafood, good furniture, sun beds and cutlery. They also mentioned a shortage of good cooks and architects. The manager of a large international chain mentioned that for his hotel he procured "mostly what is needed in normal times, but at other times, especially during cyclonic season, the quality of vegetables and seafood suffers and this is when we are in trouble." Another manager added, "we are happy to work with the local community as far as possible for the supply of food products, but we need to look beyond them during peak season when they cannot simply supply the amount, or do so at the expense of quality." Some foreign-owned hotels, particularly international chains, reported that they procured items such as cutlery, sun beds and furniture, from abroad because their group had a standardization, branding and quality policy. However, local suppliers appeared to do their utmost to satisfy the needs of the hotel sector (box 1).

Box 1. Procurement of supplies
Fruit supplier

SDL, a fruit supplier, started with a modest distribution chain in the 1980s, supplying mostly to local vendors. With the increasing number of hotels and tourists in the 1990s, it rapidly expanded activities to become among the largest fruit suppliers on the island, catering for the majority of hotels' needs and standards. The hotels, particularly foreign-owned hotels, require higher quality products. "International chains, especially, would simply not compromise on the quality...but they are prepared to pay the price and at times we even import the fruits to meet their standards," said a supervisor at SDL.

Seafood supplier

HT is among the biggest suppliers of seafood, particularly to the hotel and restaurant industry. Over the past decade they have been obliged to segregate their market and supply the best products to hotels, which are increasingly emphasizing quality. Reputed foreign chain resorts with high standards and inspection teams tend to be particularly strict with regard to quality. As their spokesperson said, "We have to supply the very best if we want to remain in the market."

c.   Hotel employees

The hotels employ a sizeable number of staff, ranging from 230 to 600 in foreign-owned hotels and 100 to 800 in domestic-owned hotels (table 18). In domestic-owned 3-star hotels, the average number of employees is around 140 and in the categories, 3-star plus and higher, it is 338. On average, 5-star hotels employ about 490 staff. The majority of employees work full time. Only a few hotels reported employing their staff on contracts.

In terms of skills composition, a similar pattern of composition emerged in both categories of hotels: 6 per cent in high-skill jobs and around 60 per cent in medium-skill jobs. There seemed to be a higher percentage of female workers in the hotel

sector compared to other African countries: about 30 per cent of women worked in all the skill categories in both the foreign-owned and domestic-owned hotels. The guest/staff ratio on average is 2:1, though in 3-star and 3-star plus domestic-owned hotels the guest/staff ratio was seen to be 1.5:1, and in the 4- and 5-star hotels it was 2:1 and 3:1 respectively for both types of hotels.

Table 17. Number of hotel employees, and distribution by skills and gender

	Foreign-owned hotels	Domestic-owned hotels
Total numbers of employees	230 to 600	100 to 800
Proportion of female employees (%)	30–35	20–40
Skills composition:		
High skills (e.g. managerial) (%)	6	6
Medium skills (e.g. catering) (%)	62	54
Low skills (e.g. cleaning/gardening) (%)	32	40
Proportion of female employees:		
High skills (e.g. managerial) (%)	31	28
Medium skills (e.g. catering) (%)	37	39
Low skills (e.g. cleaning/garden) (%)	33	36
Guest/staff ratio	2:1	2:1

d.   Wage levels in hotels

Hotels in Mauritius have traditionally offered higher wages than manufacturing and agriculture, except recently when a shortage of manpower in the agricultural sector has put some pressure on wages (table 19).

Table 18. Average monthly earnings by industrial group, March 2000–2004

Industrial group	2000	2001	2002	2003	2004
Agriculture, forestry and fisheries	6 602	7 581	7 959	8 734	9 334
Manufacturing	5 544	5 856	6 155	6 668	7 299
Construction	8 746	8 972	9 280	10 147	11 465
Hotels and restaurants	7 401	7 799	8 034	8 402	8 947
Transport, storage and communications	11 502	12 000	12 788	13 830	15 189
Financial intermediation	14 814	16 538	17 179	17 734	20 225
Education	11 280	11 299	11 728	12 524	13 993
All sectors	8 178	8 701	9 159	9 826	11 103

Source: Central Statistical Office, *Survey of Employment and Earnings in Large Establishments.*

In most categories of hotels, our survey found that foreign-owned hotels paid slightly higher wages than domestic-owned ones (table 20), but, overall, hotel managers interviewed believed that the same level of wages was offered to their employees by both types of hotels. The turnover of employees appeared to be slightly higher for domestic-owned hotels than foreign-owned ones, ranging from 3 to 15 per cent in domestic-owned ones and from 2 to 10 per cent in foreign-owned hotels. Employees left mainly for better job conditions, higher pay and for promotion. Box 4 takes the examples of two employees who have worked in hotels for more than 20 years.

Table 19. Wage levels of workers by hotel ownership

Job categories	Wages in foreign-owned hotels (rupees)	Wages in domestic-owned hotels (rupees)
Lowest	5 083	5 233
Room cleaner.	5 375	5 235
Front desk manager	32 500	24 000
Executive housekeeper	27 500	20 925

Most hotels have medical and insurance schemes for their staff and they also have provisions for pensions for permanent staff. There appeared to be no specific HIV/AIDS policy in hotels in Mauritius with the exception of one hotel, but the staff were consistently informed and briefed about HIV/AIDS.

Hotels employ very few expatriates: on average one in domestic-owned hotels and about two in the foreign-owned ones. Education and experience of local management were acquired both locally and overseas. One foreign-based hotel mentioned that the local managers acquired education and training from the Hotel School in Mauritius and gained practical experience in-house.

Box 2. Promotion prospects

Case 1:

GA started his career in the 1980s as a hotel restaurant steward in a foreign chain. At that time he was simultaneously pursing his part-time academic studies in hotel management and very soon got promoted to the status of food and beverages assistant. He was subsequently rewarded for his diligent work by being further promoted to manager in the same division. Moreover, after being sponsored by the hotel for a postgraduate course in management, which he successfully completed, he was appointed resident manager in 2006. This is an example of promotion prospects for local residents in foreign-owned hotels, and is particularly true for the food and beverages department as observed from the hotel survey. However, directors of foreign hotels remain expatriates, though they are not necessarily from the owner's home country.

Case 2:

SK has been working in the hotel industry since 1984, when he joined a locally owned hotel as a waiter. After three years' experience he was promoted to the position of floor supervisor and five years later he moved up the ladder to the post of minibar supervisor. In 1997, after 13 years of continuous service in the hotel he became head housekeeper, a position he occupied for another three years. After 16 years of service at that particular hotel he left to join another group of hotels (again locally-owned) as executive housekeeper in 2000. He worked in this capacity for four successive years in two different hotels within the same group/chain. Finally, in 2004 he joined a foreign-owned hotel as executive housekeeper, and in January 2006 he was promoted to room division manager (a middle management position). He believes it takes a lot to become a line manager in the hotel industry: a minimum of 10 years' work experience combined with at least one diploma. However, he also points out that constant on-the-job training is required, though at middle management level such training is more in terms of knowledge about the company's culture and especially the company's standard operating procedure. His perception about the difference between a locally owned and foreign-owned hotel is that international chains tend to offer training very often across borders and countries, whereas locally owned hotels tend to offer training within the country. Similarly, he believes that foreign-owned hotels offer career opportunities in other countries.

All hotel staff in Mauritius receive some form of training, whether on the job, or through seminars, formal training sessions at the Industrial and Vocational Training Board (IVTB), the two universities (box 3), workshops and/or e-learning. Some hotel groups even have their own training academy, for example, Naide Resorts and the Beachcomber Group. The length of the training varies from 2 to 3 days, a week or up to two years. Domestic-owned hotels reported budgeting up to 1 million rupees for training purposes while the foreign-based hotels appeared to spend up to double that amount. The Government of Mauritius has a scheme whereby hotels get a 60 per cent refund of the expenses for training that is approved by the IVTB through the Hotel School of Mauritius and the Mauritius Qualifications Authority. However, many hotels indicated that the procedure to get the refund was slow and very bureaucratic.

Box 3. Tourism and hospitality training institutions

The Hotel School of Mauritius was set up to prepare potential employees for the tourism sector, particularly for work in hotels. Courses offered encompass restaurant and bar service, food and pastry preparation, housekeeping, front office, leisure and entertainment and hospitality management. Courses generally include both academic and on-the-job training and aim at excellence in service delivery. The school has an annual student output of around 250 per year. The University of Technology, Mauritius, and to a lesser degree the University of Mauritius complement the hotel school in offering academic courses leading to undergraduate and postgraduate degrees in tourism, marketing and hospitality management. Around 100 students graduate each year in these fields from these institutions.

---

e. Environment conservation initiatives

All the hotels surveyed were involved in contributing towards improving or conserving the environment. For instance, most hotels were engaged in wastewater management, recycling of water and waste, plastics management, using environmentally friendly products, undertaking environment landscaping and educating staff about environmental conservation. A few hotels had even organised environment days in the region to sensitize the community at large. Recently, in 2006, because of the spread of *Chikungunya*, many hotels were involved in fogging to eradicate mosquitoes, cleaning areas in the vicinity and educating the local community. Hotel managers interviewed believed that they were putting in as much efforts in environmental conservation as the other hotels, and indeed, there seemed little difference between locally owned and foreign-owned hotels in this respect. Only one foreign-owned hotel reported being a member of Green Globe 21, and is in fact one of the founding members; none of the domestic owned hotels were members so far. Also, none of the hotels surveyed had an ISO 14000 certificate, but two hotels did mention that they were in the process of getting one.

f. Hotel linkages with the community

All the hotels surveyed stated that they were highly involved with not only the local community but also with other communities. Many hotels reported sponsoring social events and sports activities (including funding football teams and various clubs in the region), hosting village committees and helping the elderly. The amount spent appeared to be on an ad hoc basis and requests were usually considered and debated at board meetings. Only one hotel reported earmarking a budget of 1 per cent of its profits for community activities. Some also reported providing books to local schools and cleaning the environment in partnership with the community. Others teamed up with NGOs to organize blood donation days. One hotel said it was engaged in helping the handicapped to sell souvenirs in the hotel, including training and assisting them to better market their products by providing finishing touches.

The hotels tended to recruit people from the local community as workers (and also said they helped provide placements and training for their children during school vacations). In addition, they reported purchasing products such as fruit, vegetables and fish from the local community, thereby providing more employment opportunities. A few hotels mentioned having a corporate social responsibility programme, though some acknowledged that although not formalized in hotel policy, they nevertheless engaged in such programmes. In fact, those having a formal corporate social responsibility programme were mostly foreign-owned international chains that were implementing their group's CSR policy. Livelihood surveys (discussed later) have generally confirmed that foreign-owned hotels are slightly more caring towards the society.

The hotels were asked whether they were satisfied with the current level of linkages and relations with the local economy, and if not, what were their top priority for changing it and how. Most of the hotels, whether domestically owned or foreign-owned, were very satisfied with their current level of linkages. They mostly agreed that the community was well integrated and that they helped, for example, in terms of hiring local people.

They cited examples of hiring local taxis, catamarans, purchasing local handicrafts and sourcing small and medium-sized enterprises. A few hotels mentioned that there was a need for the community to supply better quality products such as vegetables, fruit and seafood. They tried to get their hotels more involved with the community and at times even got represented on village councils.

2. Firms operating in the tourism industry

In addition to hotels, the survey covered a sample of 20 firms operating in a wide range of tourism activities such as travel tours, car rental, leisure parks, safaris, nightclubs and restaurants. About 98 per cent of these firms that were observed to have linkages with the tourism sector were locally owned and managed. Most of the firms reported that they had invested in these activities first because of the many incentives offered by the Government, such as tax concessions, in order to promote the tourism industry in line with its vision of making it the first pillar of the economy. Second, because the industry is flourishing, and third, because tour operators are able to get easy access to capital through preferential rates.

a. Activities, employment and revenue

The annual sales of these firms range from 20 million rupees ($66,700) to 100 million rupees ($3.33 million). The average revenue for firms operating in leisure activities ranged from 1,250 rupees per visitor per day for restaurants to about 2,200 rupees per visitor for tour operators (table 21).

Table 20. Profile of selected firms operating in the tourism sector

Category	No. of customers	Average revenue per customer (Rs per day)	Average no. of employees	Basic pay to employees (Rs per month)
Car rental	100 to 200	1 200	30-50	7200
Tour operators	200	2 200	70	7000
Restaurants	70 to 200	1 250	15 to 20	6 500
Other leisure operators	25 to 50	600–2 000	20	6 000–7 000

The majority of the firms partly reinvested and partly shared their profits with the owners. Employment in these types of activities ranged from 20 to 120 persons, implying that the firms tend to vary in size. The basic pay falls in the range of 6,700–9,000 rupees. Employee turnover appeared to be quite low, at about 2–3 per cent, and all the employees were local (no expatriates were employed). Only 5–10 per cent of the workers were highly skilled. In most cases workers would undergo on-the-job training, conducted in-house.

b.   Customer profiles

The firms' main customers are from France followed by the United Kingdom, Italy and Germany. They stay at both domestically owned as well as foreign-owned hotels. Most of the firms work in collaboration with the hotels (e.g. Avis Car Rental works in close association with Sun Resorts). Some of them, such as Mauritours, even have foreign agents for promoting them. Leisure parks and restaurants are mostly recommended to tourists by taxi drivers although they also disseminate information in various forms (leaflets in hotels, advertisements in tourist information brochures and on the Internet). Firms hiring out boats and catamarans generally get their customers through the hotels.

The majority of their customers are Europeans, with a very low proportion from developing countries. Most of the firms

surveyed reported that customers learned of their existence mainly through hotels, either foreign-owned or domestic-owned, and to some extent through the Internet. Most visitors made payments in local currency and by credit card.

c.   Linkages with hotels

In terms of linkages with hotels, the firms surveyed did not make any distinction between domestic-owned and foreign-owned hotels. Many firms would have liked to have closer collaboration with the hotels in order to market their products and services, and see themselves as complementing, rather than competing with hotels. In fact, some respondents suggested that hotels should advise and encourage more tourists to venture out and experience a number of proposed activities since the hotels were often the first contact point for the tourists and could advise them. Most of the firms interviewed said they took initiatives to create or extend linkages with hotels, though the extent of linkages created differed on a case-by-case basis. For example, the car rental companies organized regular meetings and cocktails in order to strengthen their existing linkages with the hotels. Some reported having kiosks in hotel compounds where they distributed brochures to clients and promoted their firms. Hotels generally appeared to have few linkages with restaurants and shops selling t-shirts or souvenirs. However, there was an indication that they were beginning to collaborate.

Many SME firms have indicated that they face many difficulties in selling their products and services to hotels as they rely more on the so-called 'big' firms especially for laundry services, frozen products, poultry products, security and fruits and vegetables. The SMEs believe that hotels could start giving local entrepreneurs a chance to market their goods and services. The main concerns for hotels were in terms of the consistency the SMEs would deliver their goods and services and also the quality. A few hotel managers (especially the foreign-owned ones) have expressed their concerns that many small entrepreneurs do not have quality control system in place due to the small nature of their business and also do not have the ability and capability for processing many products to meet the standards required before delivering them, for example, the farmers.

As far as environmental and social welfare initiatives are concerned, 60 per cent of the firms surveyed tended to believe that hotels owned by foreigners placed more emphasis on such initiatives than locally owned firms.. However, the other 40 per cent were of the view that both types of hotels gave the same importance to environmental and social welfare activities or that neither type really cared much about such issues. Most of the firms interviewed reported that they helped the local communities, though not as much as hotels did. These initiatives were in the form of sponsorship of social events and regional sensitization campaigns, discriminatory pricing, with lower charges for local residents, and also patronage of schools, the elderly and sports clubs among others.

3. Impact of the tourism industry on livelihoods

Investment in more hotels, will result in more tourists in the region, and could have a significant economic impact on the island, particularly in terms of direct and indirect employment creation and the subsequent consolidation and proliferation of many firms operating in the industry. There has already been important and significant impacts on local businesses and inhabitants. The study conducted a livelihood impact survey and carried out

site visits in an attempt to establish the linkages between hotels, tourists and the local community. Face-to-face interviews were conducted with 50 people, consisting of inhabitants, hotel employees, taxi drivers, vegetable and fruit growers, fishermen, handicraft sellers, restaurants, fast food shops and other shops. These were selected across different tourist sites around the island (beaches and tourist attraction sites). The criteria chosen to gauge livelihood impacts generally included effects on living standards, business and employment, local prices, culture, access to education, local amenities and infrastructure, security the environment and social responsibility. Table 22 provides a summary of the main impacts as revealed by the survey.

a. Impact on employment, incomes and standards of living

The overwhelming majority of interviewees were unanimous that more tourists, as a result of more hotels, improved the living standards of the inhabitants and businesses in their vicinity. This was because they tended to purchase more from local suppliers (e.g. fishermen, vegetable and fruit suppliers), and contributed to the creation of full-time and part-time direct employment (mostly in hotels and other firms operating in the tourism industry such as boat operators, tour operators and taxi drivers among others), as well as to indirect full-time and part-time employment (such as beach hawkers, handicraft shops, local dancers, tourist guides, ice cream sellers, local restaurants and fast food sellers). Furthermore, some local residents had seen an increase in the value of their property as a result of hotel construction and infrastructure development in the region.

Table 21. Impacts of the tourism industry on livelihoods

	Positive effects	Negative effects
Employment, income and standard of living	▪ More employment within the region, including indirect employment (e.g. fishermen, vegetable and fruit suppliers). ▪ More part-time opportunities created. ▪ Slightly higher wages offered by foreign-owned hotels. ▪ Increase in property values within the region. ▪ Overall increase in standard of living.	▪ Seasonality of employment and higher risk of losing a job due to poor performance. ▪ Price inflation. ▪ Restricted access for the local population to quality products (vegetables, fruit and fish).
Local amenities and infrastructure	▪ Improvement in tourism infrastructure as well as public infrastructure and other amenities (e.g. roads, sewerage systems, communications and security). ▪ Provision of entertainment facilities to the benefits of the local population.	▪ Available leisure facilities are not always affordable (tourist price charge) though some firms do discriminate between the local population and tourists.
Environment	▪ Local and central authorities and the hotels themselves take better care of the environment. ▪ Foreign hotels tend to care slightly more about the environment. ▪ Spillover of environmental awareness to the local community.	▪ Larger number of hotels has led to more pollution. ▪ Increased congestion in certain areas. ▪ Restricted fishing areas have deprived local fishermen of their traditional sites. ▪ Locals feel the public beaches are being given away.
Cultural and social values	▪ Sense of social responsibility of hotels, particularly foreign-owned ones. ▪ Support to social activities through, for example, sponsorship, sensitization programmes, and educational and professional scholarships),. ▪ Revival of interest in traditional and folk songs. ▪ Higher employment, incomes and standards of living	▪ Westernized culture is taking over ▪ Odd working hours and tourists' lifestyles may cause family tensions among the local communities. ▪ Increased prostitution and reduced security in certain places.
Skills development	▪ Continuous efforts of hotels to invest in skills and academic development. ▪ Setting up of own training facilities. ▪ Authorities have more incentive to provide better educational facilities in general.	▪ Few employees reported some form of discrimination. ▪ Foreign firms, however, seemed to be fairer.

Source: Field Survey

However, as pointed out by about 30 per cent of the respondents, tourism had also caused price inflation in the region as suppliers have artificially been increasing prices of certain commodities. About 10 per cent of the respondents stated that they now lack access to quality products, especially to vegetables, fruit and fish, as these are supplied exclusively to hotels and restaurants. Nevertheless, about 25 per cent of these respondents admitted that on average they were better off in terms of their standards of living compared if tourism activities would have been absent. Some people interviewed also pointed out that the seasonality and risk factor associated with the industry should not be overlooked.

b. Local amenities and infrastructure

Most inhabitants and local businesses in particular, confirmed that the development of tourism in the region had been accompanied by an improvement in tourism infrastructure as well as public infrastructure and other amenities in general. There are an increasing number of tourist shops (selling, for example, brand named shirts, souvenirs and ship models), other shops (such as supermarkets) and leisure facilities, such as water theme parks and botanical gardens, which also benefit the local community at large. But more importantly, the accompanying development of public infrastructure to support the tourism infrastructure and hotels has helped the region. The local inhabitants and businesses have benefited from better road conditions, sewage system, communications infrastructure and new or better services from the police and fire services.

c. Impact on the environment

More than 80 per cent of the respondents to the survey felt that the environment was better taken care of following the establishment of a major hotel in their region, especially if it was part of a large international chain. Many respondents said that the local and central authorities were more environmentally aware so as not to give the tourists a bad impression of the island. Moreover, hotels themselves very often helped to make their immediate and nearby areas environmentally friendly. Inhabitants and businesses had also quickly followed their good example, reporting that they all cared, as a community, about the environment. This was apparent following site visits. However, a minority of respondents believed that more hotels and tourists had led to more noise and air pollution, mainly following increased traffic in the region, though all of them were convinced that hotels were very responsible institutions that undertook waste and plastics management. Fishermen in general were very annoyed with the continued restrictions imposed by the authorities on their fishing space and judged the compensation granted to them as insufficient. Nevertheless, the majority of them, when asked to weigh the overall effects of more hotels in the region, admitted that increased business and better prices were good motivation for them.

d. Cultural and social values

The sense of social responsibility of hotels, especially foreign-owned ones, was well acknowledged and welcomed by nearly all the respondents to the survey. Assistance to local society took a variety of forms, including financial help wtih social activities, association with local NGOs, cleaning up of the environment, sensitization programmes, educational and professional scholarships and giving priority to local communities when recruiting workers. Businesses and other local tourist operators also reported valuable help from certain hotels in allowing them space inside their compounds for marketing and even allowing "open days"[4] at times.

There was also a revival of interest in the traditional and folk songs and dances of the region. Some foreign hotels had even sent local singers and dancers abroad to entertain in their other hotels within the chain. But some of the interviewees deplored the "deculturization" of the region (although they acknowledged the opportunity of sharing host and foreign cultures), as they noted that many young people imitated the so-called Westernized lifestyles of the tourists. Increased work opportunities in the region, meant that more women were directly or indirectly engaged in jobs, mainly in hotels. While there had been a positive economic impact in terms of increased income for the family, some respondents pointed out that the odd working hours in the tourism industry sometimes created tensions within the family. Others, though not many, mentioned an increase in prostitution and drug-dealing in the region, as more tourists were seen to represent a potential market.

e. Skills development

Most of the hotel employees interviewed lauded the continuous effort of hotels to invest in skills and other academic development, giving them an opportunity to upgrade their skills and qualifications. Apart from on-the-job training, courses which the employees have followed included those conducted by local and overseas resource persons in seminars, through their respective hotel training institution and also through approved short courses by the Mauritius Qualification Authority (MQA). Many employees and the skilled level have followed diploma and degree programmes which are offered at the Hotel School of Mauritius and the two Universities which have full time and part time programmes in tourism. Those working in international chains are often given the opportunity to participate in formal and on-the-job sessions abroad thus acquiring international exposure. Employees believed that foreign-owned hotels tended to be fairer in their selection process of candidates for high-level training and even promotion. Overall, they believed the training essential for better service delivery as well as for promotion and mobility in the industry. Moreover, with more hotels and tourists, inhabitants unanimously reported that the authorities had provided better education infrastructure and means to prepare youth for employment in the industry.

F. Conclusion: challenges for the tourism industry

1. The main challenges

For Mauritius to consolidate tourism as an important pillar of the economy and envisaging making it become the first pillar, several challenges need to be addressed. From the interviews conducted, there was a consensus on the major challenges, notably increasing competition from many other destinations, soaring oil prices, disease, and terrorist threats. Stakeholders in the industry are conscious of these problems and aware of the need for appropriate actions for tourism to flourish. In this chapter we outline the major challenges as seen by various ministries, public officers, hotel managers, firms operating in the sector, NGOs and the wider community.

It is widely accepted that in recent years the Government seems to have a clear vision for the tourism industry, however, still more consultation is required with stakeholders to develop a strategic plan. For example, the Government has stated on several occasions that by 2015 the target for tourist arrivals should reach 2 million tourists. This has led many to start thinking about the future and what can be done to achieve this target. It is believed at least 1,800 additional rooms would be needed to accommodate that many visitors. This, in turn, would require a further investment of 9 billion rupees, assuming an investment of 5 million rupees per room. Also, this would necessitate more hotels to be built in the coastal region. Indeed, as at July 2008, 27 new hotel projects have been announced (e.g. Intercontinental, Le Ritz Carlton, Four Seasons, Sheraton/Starwood among others) 5 of which are expected to be in operation before 2010. In addition, with existing hotels undertaking expansion and renovation, the number of rooms is expected to increase by 5000 in 2010 and add to the 10, 857 figure of 2007. It is

estimated that 29 billion rupees (US $ 1,075 million) will be invested in the sector.

With new hotels under construction and other hotel projects in the pipeline, many people, especially local residents, called into question the allocation of land, which is limiting the availability of public beaches, and local fishermen are being denied some access to the sea. Also constructing more hotels is raising environmental concerns by some NGOs and other groups, given that Mauritius is a small island. It should be noted that with every new hotel project, the promoter has to contribute 25 million rupees (about US $925, 000) to the Tourism Fund, which finances infrastructural works, social amenities for the benefit of the inhabitants of the areas where the tourism project is undertaken and maintenance of sites and attractions. The new hotel promoters (mentioned above) have already planned to contribute to social projects in the region as part of their CSR programme, for instance, adult education, school for handicapped children, financing examination fees for children of poor households and also to collaborate with NGOs on the dangers of drugs, alcohol and prostitution. The Intercontinental group of hotels is planning to invest around 4.4 million rupees to improve land productivity of small farmers and finance deep sea fishing activities.

When asked about the current investment climate in the country, hotels managers found it reasonably good and believed there were still many opportunities in the tourism industry. On a scale of 1 to 10 (1 being very bad and 10 very good), their average rating about the investment climate was 7. Some, however, felt that the industry was overtaxed and that the Government should not impose additional taxes.

A major issue raised by investors is the lack of clarity on land policy, as reported in UNCTAD (2001). The Government has been revisiting the Non-citizens (Property Restriction) Act of 1975, and working on other land policy issues to clarify matters relating to land access.. Another closely associated element concerns work permits and other related permits and this is also been addressed by the Government, in line with its firm intention to act as a facilitator in attracting investment, particularly in tourism.

2.   Air access policy

Since August 2005, the air access policy has been reviewed to boost and revitalize the tourism industry and to encourage tourism throughout the year. The Government is adopting a flexible and gradual opening up within the framework of bilateral air services agreements whilst maintaining basic principles of fair and equal opportunity. It has decided to enhance air passenger capacity and competition in all markets with high growth potential, and to encourage and facilitate special flights at any time during the year from the specific markets of Central and Eastern Europe which are not serviced by scheduled flights. Also the Government is allowing special flights during peak periods when existing scheduled carriers cannot cope with demand. Exploration of new markets such as China, Spain and the Russian Federation is also being encouraged.

There have been some recent developments in air access by some airlines such as the French carrier Corsair, and Comair from South Africa, which are expected to bring more tourists to Mauritius.

On the domestic front, only one private company, Ireland Blyth Ltd, had started operations with an airline called Catovair, which was serving only the island of Rodrigues. However, the company had faced many difficulties and has stopped its operations.

There are concerns, however, that total liberalization of air access could undermine the image of Mauritius. Mauritius is against policies that would favour mass tourism and low-spending tourists, as it is believed the costs would outweigh any economic, social and environmental benefits.

Some hotels managers surveyed expressed concern at the high airfares to Mauritius from Europe compared with those from Europe to East and South East Asia or the Caribbean. The surging oil prices are also putting pressure on the profitability of airlines. For instance, Air Mauritius has cut down the number of flights on some European routes.

3.   New markets

Some managers who were interviewed were of the opinion that all the hotels should benefit from more marketing campaigns by the Government, they reckoned that the Mauritius Tourism Promotion Authority was doing a good job in promoting Mauritius. They also felt that the Government should place more emphasis on the MICE market and explore new markets such as China and the Scandinavian countries. A few interviewees also stressed the fact that the Government should aim at creating a more holistic brand identity for Mauritius and believed through more aggressive marketing (through advertising and the Internet) and public relations, and also by consolidating and building more goodwill.

A number of respondents from both the public and private sector also believed that the "triangular travel package" (a combined holiday package covering surrounding islands) could be a fruitful strategy. In addition, some stakeholders were convinced that the Government initiative of making the island duty-free was an important element in the tourism equation, and that this process should be accelerated. This was seen as very important in order to promote Mauritius as a shopping paradise and attract stopover tourists (thus also targeting a new market), particularly given the strategic locational advantage of the island.

Strategic partnerships to include hotels, carriers and major tour operators need to be encouraged. For example, the recent partnership agreement between TUI and some hotels has led airlines such as Corsair, EuroFly and Britannia Scandinavia to land in Mauritius. These will bring more tourists from new source countries.

4. Regional integration

More efforts should be concentrated on deriving greater benefits from regional integration as evident from other regional blocs such as the Association of South-East Asian Nations (ASEAN) and the Southern Common Market (MERCOSUR), comprising Argentina, Brazil, Paraguay and Uruguay, with Chile as an associate member. Mauritius could reap many benefits and increase tourism activities through a number of African regional blocs, such as the Common Market for Eastern and Southern Africa (COMESA), the Southern African Development Community (SADC) and the Indian Ocean Rim. For instance, COMESA is one of the largest regional economic groupings in Africa and has agreements to promote free movement of persons through the adoption of a common visa arrangement. SADC encourages cooperation among member States in a wide range of sectors, including

tourism. Mauritius can position itself as a regional hub, although South Africa is already leading in the area. With new investment incentives and facilitation offered, investment in tourism from the region should be encouraged. Some hotels managers as well as some tourism-related firms were very positive about regional integration. They saw this as an opportunity to increase the business and conference markets.

5. More investment needed

Managers of hotels and tourism-related firms interviewed believed the Government should promote Mauritius as more than a beach tourism destination by highlighting other attractions such as its historical assets, fauna and flora (e.g. birdwatching), its cultural aspects, green tourism and shopping facilities. They also felt that the Government should reassure tourists about safety for night outings to nightclubs, pubs and bars, for example. Managers of tour operations suggested that hotels could and should play a more important role to promote cultural and green tourism through more canvassing, marketing and encouragement by the hotel's public relations officers. As one tour operation manager said, "Hotels, particularly guest relation officers and other frontline officers, are the first contact points of tourists, and moreover, seem good advisers to them." In addition, operators would welcome more space in hotel areas to erect information and booking kiosks. Many stakeholders also raised the problem of congestion, and suggested that the Government should invest more in developing supportive infrastructure (both public and tourism infrastructure) to make tourism an important pillar of the economy.

G. References

Bank of Mauritius (various years) *Monthly Statistical Bulletin Issues*. Government Printing Department. Port Louis.

Central Statistical Office (various years). *Annual Digest of Statistics*. Ministry of Economic Planning and Development. Government Printing Department. Port Louis.

Ministry of Tourism, Leisure and External Communications (various years). *Annual Digest/Handbook of Tourism Statistics*. Government Printing Department. Port Louis.

Sacerdoti, E., G. El-Masry, P. Khandelwal, and Y. Yao, (2005) *Mauritius: Challenges of Sustained Growth*. International Monetary Fund. Washington.

UNCTAD (2001). Investment Policy Review Mauritius. UNCTAD/ITE/IPC/Misc. New York and Geneva, United Nations.

Notes

[1] Based on contribution by Associate Professor Ramesh Durbarry, with research assistance from B. Seetanah, B. Nowbutsingh, V. Tandrayen and S. Ramessur-Seenarain. The author is also thankful to D. Padachi and R. Chintaram in conducting interviews.

[2] "Table d'hote" is a concept where multi-course meals are served with limited choices charged at a fixed price. Local residents have been encouraged to cater for tourists, however, these have to be registered with the Tourism Authority.

[3] One reputed international chain reported that about 4 per cent of its annual turnover was reinvested for refurbishment, maintenance and acquisition of technologically better equipment, and for general renovation.

[4] These are days where businesses would have a booth to display their products and services on the hotel premises.

V. United Republic of Tanzania country case study[1]

A. Introduction

Tourism is an increasingly important sector of economic activity worldwide, and is becoming one of the most promising sources of economic growth and human development in the United Republic of Tanzania.[2] Indeed, tourism already contributes more to foreign exchange earnings in that country than traditional commodity-based or manufactured exports. According to the latest estimates from the World Travel and Tourism Council, it accounted for around $1,000 million in 2008, or 32% of total exports (WTTC, 2008). It can add to the country's gross capital formation with benefits such as transfer of technology and managerial expertise, improving the quality of human resources, creating jobs, boosting overall productivity and enhancing competitiveness and entrepreneurship, as well as increasing knowledge and access to global markets. In this context, therefore, foreign direct investment (FDI) in tourism can contribute towards sustained economic growth over the long term, which is important for poverty reduction and for raising the living standards of the people.

This study is part of a larger UNCTAD project that addresses the complexities relating to FDI in tourism in developing countries. Attracting FDI in tourism is less straightforward than it is in some other sectors of the economy. While countries recognize that it enables them to gain sufficient capital, expertise and access to international travel networks and to potential markets, they fear its impact on their economic and cultural dependence, and its potential damage to their communities and environment (UNCTAD 2005). There have been few studies in this area, particularly with regard to impacts and linkages between FDI in tourism and the local economy (Mitchell and Ashley, 2006). This study seeks to fill this gap by attempting to address some of the main issues related to FDI in tourism in Tanzania.

1. Objectives

The general objective of this study is to deepen understanding of the characteristics and impacts of FDI in tourism at the micro level. To this end, it analyses information and basic data relating to the tourism industry in general, and examines the microeconomic impact of FDI in tourism in particular. Second, it identifies the national policy and institutional framework related to FDI in tourism in order to promote an understanding of its implications, particularly for development. Finally, given the growing significance of regional integration in East Africa, the study provides an overview of the implications of the East African Community's (EAC) integration agenda for tourism development in Tanzania.

2. Methodology

The study builds upon and extends existing work by UNCTAD on the development trends and impacts of FDI in Tanzania (UNCTAD, 2005a), adding a more detailed microeconomic approach. In the general tourism literature, this paper and the UNCTAD pilot study are the only studies that specifically distinguish between foreign and domestic investment in tourism in the country. Our literature review shows that so far the impact of tourism investment at the micro level has not been studied to an extent proportional to the significant growth in size and importance that this sector has experienced in the last two decades (Mitchell and Ashley, 2006). The key argument is that, by its nature, in addition to its economy-wide impact, tourism has much more potential for boosting peoples' welfare and reducing poverty directly in localities where tourism establishments are located. Moreover, FDI in tourism can amplify these effects even further. But this is not automatic, as there must be a supportive policy and institutional environment in place that is not only favourable for investment but also makes specific demands on the industry.

Information to enable such analysis is absent in Tanzania, thus necessitating the collection of primary information from investors and beneficiaries. A case study approach was adopted. Researchers interviewed a sample of respondents to gather more detailed micro-level information to supplement the available national macro-level data, policy documents and other literature. The key aim of the analysis was to distinguish the relative impact of foreign versus domestic tourism establishments in selected areas such as employment, income, skills and technology and entrepreneurship, and to examine this in the context of existing policy and institutional frameworks.

This country case-study was conducted in 2006 and finalised through 2007. The sample size included 31 tourism establishments, of which 18 hotels[3] were on the mainland and 5 in Zanzibar (comprising local and foreign establishments), and 10 tour operators of which 7 were from the mainland and 3 from Zanzibar (all local). Interviews were also carried out with managers and owners of 5 enterprises that supply to tourism establishments, and with a total of 96 employees randomly selected

from the sampled tourism (foreign-owned and domestic) establishments. In addition, some relevant government officials, non-governmental organizations (NGOs) and other social groups were consulted. The data collected through the structured interviews was supplemented by macro and sectoral statistics and other existing information (annex table 3).

3.   Structure of the report

The report is organized in six sections as follows. Section II provides background information on the tourism sector in Tanzania, outlining the special characteristics and history of Tanzania's tourism industry. Section III presents an analysis of selected aspects of the impact of tourism-related FDI in Tanzania based on information collected from the rapid survey of a few tourism establishment and beneficiaries. To deepen our understanding of the context in which the impact of tourism-related FDI occurs, section IV identifies the policy and institutional framework governing the development of investment (foreign and domestic) in tourism for both mainland Tanzania and Zanzibar. Section V discusses the implications of the regional integration agenda of the East African Community (EAC) for the tourism industry in Tanzania. Key aspects include the proposed EAC investment code, the intention to market the region as a single destination and prospects for intraregional FDI in tourism. Finally, section VI concludes and offers some policy recommendations.

B. Tourism Profile of the United Republic of Tanzania

1. Background information

The United Republic of Tanzania (mainland and Zanzibar), only began to develop international tourism in earnest over the past 10 years. After independence and the subsequent establishment of a union between Tanganyika and Zanzibar in 1964 to become the United Republic of Tanzania, the country adopted socialist policies that created a highly protective economic regime, with the Government adopting a command-type approach to economic management and creating a number of State-owned enterprises. Foreign investment was not encouraged and international tourism was not promoted. Between 1985 and 1990, a new government began to reform the economy, liberalizing economic activity, allowing private businesses and privatizing State enterprises (including the large hotel sector). The socio-economic reforms were consolidated between 1990 and 2000, with a major focus on private-sector management of economic activity, including liberalization of the airline industry. Tanzania also adopted a more open foreign investment policy, allowing foreign ownership and according full protection of property rights, thereby creating a favourable environment for attracting foreign direct investment (FDI). Among the initiatives taken to attract FDI was the establishment of the Tanzania Investment Centre (TIC). A new focus on tourism promotion and facilitation included the development of tourism policies and master plans. As a result, FDI in tourism began to grow, including the establishment of foreign-owned and operated hotels and tour operators, and the industry became a leading recipient of FDI.

Tanzania has a limited tourism product range that is based largely on wildlife. There is a high concentration of activity in the northern circuit,[4] though other spectacular wildlife areas in the southern circuit[5] have been poorly advertised and given low priority in terms of infrastructure investment. In addition, coastal tourism is becoming increasingly important along Tanzania's mainland coast (especially Bagamoyo and Dar es Salaam) and in Zanzibar, famed for its Stone Town, dolphin tourism, beaches and spice tours. The Government's focus is on international tourism, and so far there has been little focus on developing local participation and ecotourism in Tanzania.

The policy shift from socialism to market-based, private-sector-led growth since 1986 has led to impressive growth in FDI (figure 2). If this figure is cited first, it should be figure 1 and the subsequent figures renumbered and repositioned. Mining and tourism have been the leading FDI recipients, their share in total FDI averaging 30 and 14 per cent respectively. By contrast, the share of agriculture has averaged only 7 per cent. Earnings from tourism have increased, from an annual average of $14.8 million between 1980 and 1985, to over $44.6 million between 1986 and 1994, and surging thereafter from $95 million (with 50,000 jobs) in 1995 to over $ 746 million (198,500 jobs) in 2004. This surge was largely the result of an improved investment climate. In recent years, both domestic investment and FDI have moved positively with GDP growth (figure 1). Over 2,076 investments were voluntarily registered with the Tanzania Investment Centre (TIC) between 1995 and 2004 (55.3 of which were foreign investments). Total FDI inflows exceeded $2.4 billion during the period 1995–2004, compared with a total of only $90 million in the period 1990–1995 (figure 2). The high growth of

FDI was concentrated in 5 out of 23 regions: Dar es Salaam (tourism, manufacturing), Mwanza (mining), Arusha (tourism), Shinyanga (mining) and Morogoro (agriculture and tourism), and was largely in mining and tourism.

Figure 1. Rates of domestic and foreign investment growth and economic growth, 1990–2004

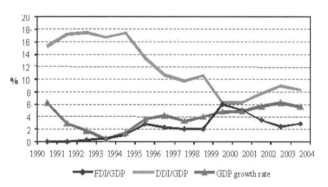

Source: Based on data from the Tanzania Investment Centre and National Bureau of Statistics Any publication(s)/website(s)? This query applies to all the tables and figures that cite a source without indicating the publication.

Figure 2. Trends in FDI inflows into Tanzania, 1990–2004 ($ million)

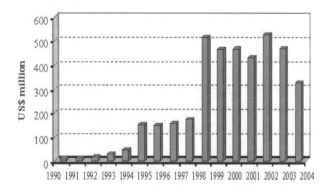

Source: Based on data from the Tanzania Investment Centre and National Bureau of Statistics.

Tanzania is primarily an upmarket tourism destination. The country is endowed with a variety of tourism assets, including six World Heritage sites, numerous wildlife parks, beach resorts, coral reefs and spectacular mountain views.

A total of 28 per cent of Tanzania is protected area, consisting of 15 national parks, the Ngorongoro Conservation Area, 31 game reserves and 38 game controlled areas. Wildlife is the main tourist attraction. The northern circuit, which includes the Ngorongoro crater, Serengeti, and Mount Kilimanjaro, is still the principal destination for wildlife viewing safaris. However, the Government is encouraging the development of the southern circuit, which includes the Selous Reserve (amongst the world's largest nature reserves), to prevent overexploitation of the north and bring more tourism to the south. Other principal tourist destinations include the beach resorts, mainly on the island of Zanzibar. Wildlife safaris and beach resorts are offered both as single destination attractions and as combination packages.

Since the early 1990s, there has been a shift from government-led to private-sector-led commercial development of the tourism industry. The Government formulates policies, regulates and promotes investment services and facilitates development of the supporting infrastructure. The success of this approach is evident. Tourism in recent years has become the largest foreign exchange earner for Tanzania, exceeding even gold exports, which is the top merchandise export item. However, despite much success to date, this industry's potential is yet to be fully exploited, and the benefits associated with high linkages of this sector to other sectors of the economy are low (Kweka, Morrisey and Blake, 2003). Therefore the country has considerable scope for increasing the benefits from tourism through greater promotion of its tourist products, improving the quality of services and infrastructure and adopting a pro-poor tourism strategy.

2. Overall economic contribution of tourism

The Tanzanian Government regards tourism as a priority sector. The contribution of the tourism industry to GDP rose from 1.5 per cent in 1990 to 7.1 per cent in 2004 (annex 1, table 2A). Throughout the 1990s the tourism sector performed very well and showed high growth rates. From 1990 to 1999, tourist arrivals and foreign exchange earnings from tourism increased by an average annual rate of 15 per cent and 27 per cent respectively (table 1 and figure 3). This in turn increased the share of earnings from tourism in total exports from 12.1 per cent in 1990 to 38.5 per cent in 2004 (annex 1, table 2A).

Table 1. Tourist arrivals and earnings from tourism, 1990–2004

Year	Number of tourists	Percentage change (%)	Earnings ($ million)	Percentage change (%)
1990	153 000		65	
1991	186 800	22.1	95	46.2
1992	201 744	8.0	120	26.3
1993	230 166	14.1	147	22.5
1994	261 595	13.7	192	30.6
1995	295 312	12.9	259	34.9
1996	326 188	10.5	322	24.3
1997	359 096	10.1	392	21.7
1998	482 331	34.3	570	45.4
1999	627 325	30.1	733	28.6
2000	501 669	-20.0	739	0.8
2001	525,000	4.7	725	-1.9
2002	575 000	9.5	730	0.7
2003	576 000	0.2	731	0.1
2004	582 807	1.0	746	2.1
Average	392 215	10.1	438	18.8

Source: Based on data from the Ministry of Natural Resources and Tourism and National Bureau of Statistics.

Figure 3. Trend in earnings from tourism services, 1988–2004 ($ million)

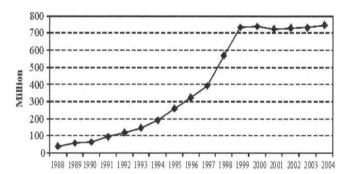

Source: Based on data from the Ministry of Natural Resources and Tourism and National Bureau of Statistics.

There was some fluctuation in the number of tourist arrivals and earnings between 1990 and 2004 (table 1). For example, in 2000 the rate of tourist arrivals fell sharply , partly as a result of a terrorist attack in Dar es Salaam in August 1998. Since 2000, arrivals and foreign exchange earnings have been stagnating, achieving average annual growth rates of only 1.49 per cent and 0.09 per cent respectively.

The share of tourism earnings in total export earnings increased consistently throughout the 1990s to reach about 64 per cent in 1999 (figure 4). Thereafter, its share fell significantly, to 40 per cent in 2004 and about 30 per cent in 2005. As a share of GDP, foreign exchange earnings from tourism declined from about 10 per cent in 1995 to 8 per cent in 2000 and to about 7 per cent in 2005. The decline was due not only to a general depression in the tourism sector, but also to a rise in mineral exports, particularly gold, which reduced the relative importance of tourism in exports. However, tourism remains the second highest earner of foreign exchange after mining. The value of tourism to the national economy is also significant. It has been estimated that its contribution to GDP was about 7.5 per cent in 1995, and since the turn of the century, this has increased to over 10 per cent.[6] This section is a little confusing – it starts off in the first para with the share of tourism in GDP, and comes back to it again in this para. Similarly, the share of tourism earnings in total exports needs to be consolidated in one place.

With regard to Zanzibar, tourism contributes the largest share of export earnings of all the sectors. Estimates from the Bank of Tanzania and the Zanzibar Commission of Tourism indicate that its average share during the period 2001–2005 was between $63 million and $94 million annually, or about 60 per cent of the island's total foreign exchange earnings.

Tourism not only contributes directly to growth, but also indirectly through the linkages it has with other sectors of the economy. A study by Kweka et al. (2003) established that the output multiplier for tourism in Tanzania is 1.8, which is higher than the output multipliers for agriculture, manufacturing and other services. Tourism also requires 44 per cent of its inputs from other sectors, a rate that is above the average for all sectors. The most important inputs for tourism in Tanzania are agriculture, livestock, poultry, fisheries, dairy, manufacturing, non-perishable foods and dry goods, ground transport and handicrafts. Many of the products are sourced locally, but are not necessarily produced in Tanzania.

Figure 4. Proportion of tourism earnings to total exports, 1990 – 2004

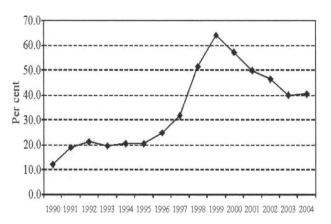

Source: Based on data provided by the Ministry of Natural Resources and Tourism.

3.   Accommodation

FDI in mainland Tanzania's accommodation base increased by 85 per cent, from $280 million in 1999 to $518 million in 2004.[7] According to the National Bureau of Statistics, the investment facilitated an increase of 32.5 per cent in tourist hotels, from 321 in 1999 to 476 in 2004. In terms of ownership, about 71 per cent were locally owned, 22 per cent were foreign-owned and 7 per cent were joint ventures.

With regard to the islands of Zanzibar,[8] according to projects approved by the Zanzibar Investment Promotion Agency (ZIPA), proposed capital investment had reached $818 million by June 2005, of which 71 per cent, or $580 million, went to tourism-related projects. However, actual capital invested by that date was only $188 million, of which 55 per cent was tourism-related. Overall, most tourist hotels in Zanzibar are foreign-owned.

There were 128 investment projects in accommodation (new and expansionary), including hotels, lodges, resorts and camping facilities, registered by the Tanzania Investment Centre (TIC) between 2002 and end September 2004, valued at over $200 million (figure 5).

Figure 5. Mainland Tanzania registered investments in accommodation, 2002–2004

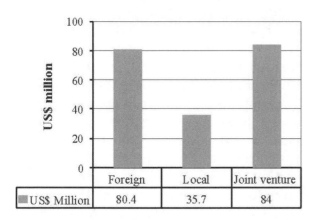

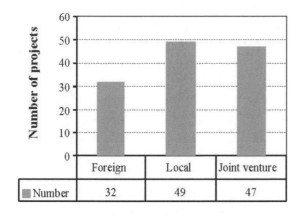

Source: Tanzania Investment Centre.

Further, the data in figure 5 show that about 32 projects or 25 per cent were wholly foreign-owned with investments totalling over $80 million or 40 per cent of total investments. The share of joint ventures between foreign and local firms (by value) was a little higher, at 41 per cent, while that of local firms was 18 per cent. The value of investments made by foreign firms (including in joint ventures) during this period averaged 64 per cent of total investments in accommodation.

In terms of types of investments, about 71 per cent of all investments made were in hotel construction or expansion/renovation, of which 64.8 per cent of the capital contribution, or $92.5 million, was by foreign firms (figure 6).

Figure 6. Mainland Tanzania registered investments in accommodation by type and value, 2002-2004

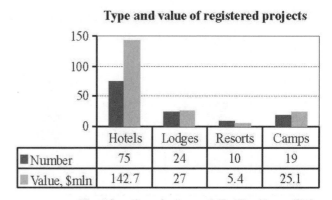

Source: Tanzania Investment Centre.

4.   Tour operations

According to data from the Ministry of Natural Resources and Tourism, there were 179 licensed tour operators in mainland Tanzania as on June 2005. Most of these operators (about 128) were located in Arusha, close to the northern circuit wildlife attractions, and 36 of the 43 travel agencies were located in the capital city, Dar es Salaam. Figure 7 provides a summary of the number and value of investments made by tour operators in mainland Tanzania between 2002 and 2004.The value of investments in the 75 registered tour operation projects was $59 million of which foreign projects accounted for 38 per cent or $ 22.5 million during this period.

Figure 7. Mainland Tanzania registered investment projects in tour operations, 2002–2004

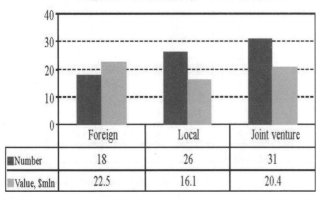

Source: Based on data provided by the Tanzania Investment Centre.

In Zanzibar tour operations are reserved for local firms under ZIPA rules and regulations, which is why all the 159 tour operators that were registered by 2005 were locally owned and operated. However, there were 41 licensed foreign-owned diving companies that invested a total of $1.5 million in equipment and other facilities in 2005.

5.   Employment

The number of employees in the tourism sector has been increasing consistently since 1991, following a similar trend in the number of international visitors and earnings. Direct employment increased nearly fourfold, from about 45,000 in 1991 to over 198,557 in 2004 (figure 8).

Although the level of employment appears to have been increasing over time, it has fluctuated markedly between the high

and low seasons, particularly for casual or temporary employees.

The tourism sector is believed to have significant direct and indirect employment effects because of its extensive linkages with other sectors. The stronger the backward and forward linkages the more significant are the employment (and income) effects. Using an employment multiplier effect for tourism of 5.4 (based on Kweka et al., 2003), employment generated by the tourism industry may have been as high as 868,050 in 2004.[9] Since 1999, employment has been further boosted by an increasing number of people engaged in the production of goods and services such as the Maasai Boma (traditional settlement), curio shops, wood carvings, fishing, and production of vegetables and fruit for the tourist market (Kulindwa, Sosovele and Mashindano, 2001). According to the survey conducted for this study, foreign investment projects in tourism are a larger source of jobs than those with domestic investment. Between 2001and 2004, tourism-related investments approved by TIC created over 10,800 jobs. In Zanzibar during the same period about 9,158 jobs were created in tourism-related investments.

A study of northern circuit hotels and lodges conducted in 2002 by the Multilateral Investment Guarantee Agency (MIGA, 2002) estimated that each room created two jobs directly. Moreover, visitor expenditures created an estimated 64 per cent of gross value added. In addition, according to the findings obtained during the survey for this country-study, it is estimated that 28 per cent of the revenue from tourism goes into imports, 38 per cent into expenditures on goods and services produced in Tanzania, 16 per cent to wages and 22 per cent to government taxes. The average daily expenditure per tourist was $135 in 1996, which rose steadily to $307 in 2004 (annex 1, table 1A). Our survey also found that the average expenditure per tourist in 2005 was $355, about 13.5 per cent higher than the previous year.

Figure 8. Number of employees in the tourism sector, 1991-2004

Source: Based on data from the Ministry of Natural Resources and Tourism.

6. Investment measures and conditions affecting FDI in tourism

Inadequate physical infrastructure for FDI tourism. Tanzania's physical infrastructure is inadequate to support the rapidly growing FDI in tourism. Both the Zanzibar Investment Report of December 2004 and the Tanzania Tourism Master Plan acknowledged the problems related to poor infrastructure (e.g. roads and rail network, and electricity and water supply), including the airport infrastructure, such as the lack of an instrument landing system at Zanzibar airport. In Tanzania's mainland?, improvement of the physical infrastructure is the Government's top priority for resource allocation.

High utility costs and value-added tax (VAT). Surveyed firms observed that telecommunication costs and electricity and water tariffs were very high compared with other countries in the region. The VAT rate of 20 per cent was also perceived as being too high. Tanzania is taking measures to rectify the situation by reducing import tariffs on information and telecommunication equipment to facilitate

access and maximize the advantages of information and communication technologies (ICT) in economic development. Other taxes have been rationalized or removed.

Inadequately trained labour. Labour factors, including an inadequately trained labour force, and an increasing incidence of HIV/AIDS were considered major constraints that discouraged investors in the tourism sector. Some surveyed tourist operators cited inadequately trained and skilled manpower and unsatisfactory work ethics as undermining the efficiency of their services. In order to ameliorate the problems of manpower, the Zanzibar Hotel and Tourism Institute is being revamped and aims at admitting a larger number of students. Similarly, the Tanzania Tourism Institute in Dar es Salaam is being upgraded to college status to train an increasing number of staff. Further, some tourism staff are receiving training at the Utalli College in Nairobi to enhance their skills. With regard to HIV/AIDS, the Zanzibar Aids Commission (ZAC) and its counterpart in the mainland facilitate and coordinate measures aimed at combating this deadly epidemic in all sectors of the economy, not only in tourism.

7. Summary

Box 1 below presents the main statistical data relating to tourism in mainland Tanzania and Zanzibar (see annexes 1 and 2 for additional data).

Box 1. Main statistical data on the impact of tourism in the United Republic of Tanzania, 2004

- Number of international arrivals was 582,807.

- Contribution of tourism to GDP was roughly 7 per cent

- Export earnings from tourism amounted to $746 million or 38 per cent of total exports of goods and services;

- National parks attracted more than 500,266 international visitors, implying that visitors for wildlife viewing accounted for more than 85.8 per cent of all arrivals.

- The number of tourists entering Zanzibar increased by more than 60 per cent between 1995 and 2004.

- Tourism accounted for 80 per cent of all service earnings in Zanzibar.

- The number of hotels increased by over 100 per cent between 1996 and 2006 (212 and 476 respectively), of which about 71 per cent were locally owned, 22 per cent were foreign-owned and 7 per cent were joint ventures.

- The number of employees increased by nearly 100 per cent, from 100,000 in 1996 to 198,557 in 2004. On average, more women (over 60 per cent) were employed in hotels, but fewer in tour operations (18 per cent on the mainland and 38 per cent in Zanzibar). Only about 14 per cent of the women employed in hotels were in the high-skills management level. The majority (61 per cent) were employed in the medium skills category – largely in the catering function.

- Worker remunerations differed by a factor of 2.5 to 3.0 between local and foreign-owned establishments. On average, the minimum monthly basic pay in local firms was $50 and $60 for hotel and tour operations respectively. There were no differences by gender with regard to pay for similar positions. The minimum monthly pay in foreign firms was $120 and $150 for hotel and tour operations respectively.

- All the firms surveyed during this case-study made a profit in 2005. For hotels, conference activities were the most profitable, contributing about 29 per cent of the profits for both local and foreign-owned firms. Accommodation was next (21 per cent), followed by restaurants (7 per cent). Tour operations earned an average of 17 per cent profit on their operations. Profits were largely used for reinvestment (35 per cent) to expand or acquire new ventures, followed by share distribution (13 per cent). None of the sampled foreign-owned firms were willing to indicate what percentage of their earnings was repatriated in 2005.

- The extent of leakage was difficult to establish, but the interviews revealed that foreign-owned hotels spend an average of $20 a day on locally produced items for every hotel room they sell. With a hotel room selling for an average of $120 that means only 17 per cent of the sales are spent directly in the local economy. The equivalent expenditure by a locally owned hotel was over 64 per cent (on average $45 spent in the local economy for every room sold at an average rate of $70). This implies much greater scope for foreign-owned hotels to increase their linkage effects with the local economy, if greater efforts are made to improve the quality and quantity of locally produced supplies.

Source: Secondary data and field interviews for this study (June 2006; annexes 1 and 2).

C. The Impact of Foreign Direct Investment in Tourism

Most of the impacts discussed in this section are microeconomic, but an effort is made to report impacts at macro and industry level as well. The restoration of the Kilimanjaro Hotel, now known as Kilimanjaro Kempinski Hotel (KKH) since 2003, which started operations in late 2005 after its successful privatization, took the tourism industry in Tanzania to another level by offering a 5-star international hotel experience. However, given its exceptional character and newness, the extent of its impact was not yet evident at the time of this survey (see annex 3 for information about this hotel).

1. Investments in tourism

The 31 tourism firms surveyed for this study invested a total of $138.0 million in 2005 (table 2). This includes investment in the only 5-star hotel in Tanzania (Kilimanjaro Kempinski Hotel) that was renovated at a cost of $40 million. None of the other hotels surveyed were constructed in 2005. About 67.9 per cent of investment went into extension or restoration of hotel buildings, 15 per cent into purchases of machinery and equipment and 17.1 per cent into transport and other items. On average, 72.6 per cent of the total investments were made by foreign firms, equivalent to $100.2 million.[10]

Table 2. Survey results on tourism investments ($ thousand)

Investment category	Local firms	Foreign firms	Total	Share of foreign investment in total (%)
Construction/building	23 569	70 131	93 700	74.8
Machinery/equipment	3 450	17 230	20 680	83.3
Transport	6 750	5 990	12 740	47.0
Other investments	3 999	6 881	10 880	63.2
Total	37 768	100 232	138 000	72.6

Source: Field interviews, June 2006.

2. Earnings of tourist establishments

In 2005, the total earnings of all 31 establishments surveyed amounted to $6.36 million, 88 per cent of which were earned by wholly foreign-owned firms (table 3). Activities related to conferences (often funded by donors) were the most profitable, averaging 33 per cent , followed by accommodation (27 per cent on average). Over 72 per cent of the surveyed firms reported that the restaurant component of their business was the least profitable, showing an average profitability of 9 per cent.

Table 3. Earnings by type of establishment ($ thousand)

Establishment Type	Local	Foreign	Total	Share of earnings of foreign-owned firms in total earnings (%)	Average profits (%)
Accommodation	378	3 472	3 850	90.1	27
Restaurant	92	848	940	90.2	9
Conferences	58	379	437	86.7	33
Tour operations	206	683	889	76.8	17
Other	25	218	243	89.7	5
Total	758	5 602	6 360	88.0	18.2

Source: Field interviews, June 2006.

3. Tax revenue

Wholly foreign-owned hotels and tour operators accounted for over 71 per cent of the total tax revenue from tourism (table 4). Overall, firms (local or foreign) did not consider tax rates to be excessively high.[11] Rather, it was the administrative bureaucracy and tax collection that was viewed negatively, especially by foreign enterprises.

Table 4. Tax revenue of the 31 surveyed firms (US$)

Type of establishment	Local	Foreign	Total	Share of tax revenue from foreign-owned firms in total tourism revenue? (%)
Hotels	163 800	427 200	591 000	72.3
Tour operators	93 896	232 434	326 330	71.2
Total	257 696	659 634	917 330	71.9

Source: Based on data provided by the Ministry of Natural Resources and Tourism.

4. Employment and income

The hotels and tour operators surveyed had a combined employment level of 2,461, of which 1,259 (or 51.2 per cent) were women. Table 5 shows how employment varied according to the scale of ownership of an enterprise.

Table 5. Employment of tourism establishments by gender

	Mainland				Zanzibar			
Establishment	Total	Male	Female	Share of women in total (%)	Total	Male	Female	Share of women in total (%)
Hotels	1 568	662	906	57.8	410	148	262	63.9
Tour operations	457	376	81	17.7	26	16	10	38.5
Total (average)	2 025	1 038	987	48.7	436	164	272	51.2

Source: Field interviews, June 2006.

Hotel establishments employed almost an equal number of women and men (49 per cent and 51 per cent respectively, while tour operators tended to employ more men (81 per cent) (figure 9). Annex 2 table 10B provides a breakdown by the mainland and Zanzibar, which indicates that, overall, in Zanzibar more women than men were employed in tourism operations. Also, women tended to be employed more in the medium-skills and low-skills categories (figure 10). Annex 2 Table 11B shows the employee skill composition by gender.) On average, only 17.6 per cent of women

employees were employed in the managerial and high-skills category. Women managers who were interviewed attributed the gender imbalance partly to a shortage of highly skilled women who are

Figure 9. Employment of selected tourism establishments, by gender

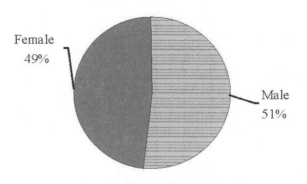

Hotel Establishments

Female 49%
Male 51%

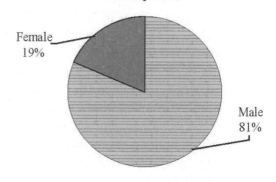

Tour operations

Female 19%
Male 81%

Source: Field interviews, June 2006.

Figure 10. Employment by skill levels and gender

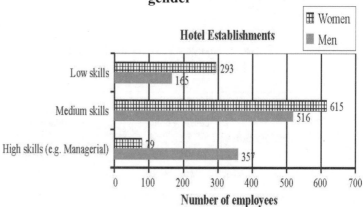

Hotel Establishments

Women | Men

Low skills: 293 / 165
Medium skills: 615 / 516
High skills (e.g. Managerial): 79 / 357

Source: Field interviews, June 2006.

able to compete effectively with men, rather than to discrimination by gender. There was very little distinction between foreign-owned and local operations. Fewer women were employed in tour operations. Only one hotel in the sample (in Bagamoyo) was owned by a local woman entrepreneur. With regard to basic pay, foreign establishments offered better remuneration, paying two to three times more than local firms (table 6).

Table 6. Basic monthly salary, by type of work, (survey respondents) ($)

	Domes tic	Foreign	Ratio of foreign to domestic		Domes tic	Foreign	Ratio of foreign to domestic
	Hotels				Tour operators		
Lowest wage	50	120	2.4:1	Lowest wage	60	150	2.5:1
Room cleaner/ gardener	50	150	3.0:1	Driver	80	180	2.3:1
House-keeper	110	300	2.7:1	Tour guide	85	210	2.5:1
Desk manager	300	420	1.4:1	Manager	215	450	2.1:1

Source: Field interviews, June 2006.

The survey showed that tour operators, both local and foreign, tended to pay better salaries than hotel establishments. However, employees interviewed believed their salaries were low, though they admitted they were a little higher than those received by government employees with similar levels of education. Apart from basic pay, workers in the tourism establishments received several employment benefits, including health care (largely for the worker but not the whole family), bonuses for exemplary work, training, motivational awards and family support to defray funeral expenses. Other benefits included free meals, free transport to and from work and uniforms, and some offered free accommodation or housing allowance that averaged 15 per cent of the basic pay. Some workers interviewed estimated that extra benefits amounted to more than 50 per cent of their basic pay. This partly explains the low turnover in tourism establishments (local and foreign),

apart from the lack of alternative employment opportunities (given Tanzania's high rate of unemployment).

All tourism establishments provided training to their workers to improve skills and customer service. While most tourism businesses had no formalized HIV/AIDS programmes, sensitization seminars and meetings were held, and in some firms, NGOs such as Angaza and Ishi were invited to discuss the HIV/AIDS pandemic. Overall, there was negligible upward movement within the hotel chain or firm, in part because each level requires different skills that have to be learned for an employee to move from one level to another. Training was largely concentrated in enhancing the skills required at that level rather than shifting employees from one skill level to a higher skill level. This explains why over 90 per cent of the employees interviewed had been working in the same job at the same level since they began working there. The only difference was that their remuneration had been adjusted upwards over time. Most firms cherished workers who had stayed with them for a long time and paid them extra remuneration to reflect the length of experience. Firing an employee without cause was uncommon, although renewal of employment tended to be based on performance, especially in foreign-owned establishments. The number of expatriate employees in both local and foreign-owned firms was negligible compared with the total number of employees. The average number of expatriates in most foreign-owned establishments was three, all in managerial positions. Only one local hotel in the sample (located in Zanzibar) had employed an expatriate manager from Kenya, otherwise all other local hotels interviewed employed local staff at all levels of hotel operations.

5. Technology and skills

The application of knowledge, skills and innovation in tourism businesses is key to success. All hotels and tour operators interviewed reported that they provided intensive training to all their staff – skilled and unskilled. Three reasons were cited. First, tourism-related skills of the local staff were inadequate and needed upgrading. Second, each firm had goals, plans and strategies that each staff member needed to know about and understand so that all personnel worked as a team for realizing objectives. Third, few workers had received the necessary training in customer service and knew the business code of conduct.

Most training provided by both local and foreign-owned establishments was in-house. The management would conduct the training or contract an expert from outside the firm to provide specific, tailor-made training. The duration varied considerably, from two days to three weeks, depending on the nature of the training. In all foreign-owned tour operators, over 70 per cent of the staff (excluding drivers and tour guides) had to learn computer skills and new software – taught in-house over a period ranging from six months to one year. Three foreign-owned hotel establishments and two foreign-owned tour operators sent some local employees, including senior level staff, for on-the-job training to foreign hotels or tourism establishments to acquire extra skills and familiarize themselves with the parent establishment.

Staff could also be sent to tourism training institutes for periods ranging from three months to two years, depending on the course. Most hotel and tour operators in Zanzibar trained their staff through Zanzibar's Tourism Training Institute. On the mainland, staff were trained through the Hotel and Tourism Institute in Dar es Salaam. About 40 per cent of the tourism establishments interviewed also sent their staff for training to Utalii College in Nairobi, Kenya. All interviewees believed that this College could become the regional centre of excellence for middle and senior tourism management training. In addition, some 17 employees from three tourism establishments had been awarded scholarships through Irish Aid to study about tourism management training and related services abroad.

The following are the main areas and staff levels for which training is provided:
- Training and retraining of existing managerial staff
- Training of middle management in supervisory skills for the different hotel services such as culinary, restaurant, housekeeping and front office
- Retraining of existing staff to improve attitudes, customer relations, and services
- Skills development for line staff, such as front office, kitchen, waiters, housekeeping, bar, guides and the travel trade
- Tour and safari guide training
- Marketing techniques
- Language training, especially French, Spanish and English
- Computer training and software applications
- Train-the-trainer programmes for increased efficiency and productivity. The trained staff would then be expected to impart the knowledge and skills acquired to co-workers through in-house programmes.

The cost of training differed considerably by business establishment, and by the nature and duration of training. Overall, locally owned firms spent an average of $4,500 per annum for in-house and short duration training. Foreign-owned establishments spent about 11 time more, or an average of $49,500 per annum, which made their local staff more technologically skilled than locally owned hotels.

The major impact of this training has been to create relatively skilled local manpower that can use skills and knowledge creatively to achieve the objectives of the tourism business. This has also made Tanzania more competitive in the tourism industry, thus rendering it more attractive to tourism-related FDI. Additionally, the locally owned tourism operators benefit from the demonstration effects of foreign investors as they copy or adapt new technologies, marketing channels and management techniques. This is creating a more level playing field between local and foreign establishments, thus forcing all firms in the industry to become more efficient in order to survive as profitable businesses. For example in the past, when most hotel operators were local, working styles generally were not customer-friendly. Now local operators have emulated the slogan "customer is king". For example, a manager of a local hotel in Arusha owned by a religious group observed that after visiting several foreign hotels in Dar es Salaam and Arusha, it was decided to introduce better customer services in the hotel. As a result, the staff there had learned to greet customers with a smile, attend to their requests promptly, and say "thank you" as they received payment – courtesies they had not shown previously. Others offered customers a free soft drink while they waited for service. All hotels interviewed (foreign and local) had modernized their accounting systems. Some local hotels had even emulated cooking standards and menus that were offered mainly in foreign-owned hotels to enhance competitiveness and survive as a business.

Another area of impact relates to value addition. All hotels, locally owned and foreign-owned, revealed that an average of 15–25 per cent of the food items (e.g. fruit and vegetables, meats, fish) were not usable because of low local quality controls. As a consequence, all hotels had to clean, sort, grade, process and repack items purchased locally. These processes added value to the products, but also entailed extra costs by hotels. Some hotels had therefore started training local suppliers in the areas of food hygiene, quality control, cleaning, processing and packaging. Two hotels even provided some small and medium-sized enterprises (SMEs) with refrigerated containers for delivery of the agreed supplies. One hotel in Zanzibar reported that it provided refrigerated containers for its fresh fish suppliers without charging for the containers. The idea was to get the fish to the hotel as fresh as possible. Another hotel in Dar es Salaam mentioned providing milk containers to its SME supplier from Tanga along with strict cleaning instructions and delivery timetables to ensure the milk arrived in Dar es Salaam as fresh as possible. Other areas of value added cited by tour operators included introduction of new ways of doing business to the local staff, such as use of new computer software in business accounting and financial control and Internet access to process information and communicate effectively, as well as inculcating the practice of working hard.

6. Linkages to the local economy

The contribution of tourism to economic growth and poverty reduction comes not just from the tourism industry itself, but also from its linkages to other sectors of the economy. Strengthening these linkages would be important for achieving overall growth and poverty alleviation. The survey clearly showed a high proportion of imports by the tourism sector. This points to the need for concerted efforts to increase the value-added of supplies from the local economy to replace or reduce those imports. Strengthening linkages also addresses the concern of "leakages" from tourism (that is, the part of the revenue from tourism that leaves the country to pay for the imports consumed by the tourist sector).

Backward linkages from tourism in Tanzania are spread over many activities, particularly in the agricultural sector, thus providing market opportunities for local produce.[12] The most important include: fruit and vegetables, livestock (beef, lamb, and pork), poultry (chicken and eggs), fisheries (fish and sea food) and dairy. In the manufacturing sector, they include equipment, furniture and building materials, non-perishable foods and dry goods (e.g. flour, rice and sugar), while in services, they include ground transport (e.g. tour operator transfers and packages and local taxis), handicrafts and labour. Annex 2, table 14B provides a summary of selected products used by the tourism industry.

a. Sources of tourism supplies

The survey showed that, overall, local tourism firms tended to source locally for over 90 per cent of their supply requirements. Foreign-owned tourism establishments were more selective, depending on perceived quality and regularity of available local supply. With regard to insurance, all the firms interviewed on the mainland and in Zanzibar sourced locally, although foreign firms also had insurance cover from their countries of origin. Similarly, telecommunication services were sourced locally, although all equipment was imported. Over 90 per cent of the firms surveyed, local and foreign-owned, used local firms to provide security services, although the equipment used for the security systems was imported. Utilities (e.g. water and electricity) were sourced locally by all firms. However, all firms (local and foreign-owned) had stand-by electricity generators because of frequent power outages. Since Tanzania's current power supply is rationed, generators are used frequently and are very costly per unit of energy supplied. According to interviews conducted for the UNCTAD (2005) pilot study for this project, the CCA lodge in

Serengeti provides energy for a number of SMEs nearby as well as for the village. The generators were sourced locally but imported into the country. Also, most hotels, especially in Dar es Salaam, extracted deep groundwater to ameliorate the problem of frequent water shortages. Cleaning and laundry services were sourced entirely locally by local and foreign-owned establishments.

With regard to materials for construction, most firms (local and foreign-owned) sourced locally. However, while locally owned firms sourced over 97 per cent (mainland) and 80 per cent (Zanzibar) locally, foreign-owned firms tended to source a little less locally (85 per cent on the mainland and 75 per cent in Zanzibar). Imports by local and foreign-owned firms were highest for furniture, fixtures, fittings and equipment. Foreign-owned establishments imported, on average, over 80 per cent of their furniture, equipment, fittings and linen, while locally owned firms sourced more than 85 per cent of these items locally. In terms of dollar value, foreign firms' imports were considerably higher because of the large scale of their business. For example, the UNCTAD pilot study (2005) found that a single foreign 5-star hotel in Dar es Salaam was renovated using largely imported materials at a cost of $35 million, whereas most local hotels imported much less than $1 million worth of materials for construction or renovation.

The most selective sourcing was for food items. Local firms sourced nearly 100 per cent of their supplies from the local market, while foreign-owned establishments were more selective. For example, foreign-owned firms sourced more than 82 per cent of their fish and seafood requirements locally, and imported more than 70 per cent (Zanzibar) and 30 per cent (mainland) of their beef requirements. Zanzibar imports most of its beef from the mainland. Presumably, Tanzanian fish and seafood products are certified as conforming to the European Union's (EU) quality standards, which enables them to be exported to the EU. This gives enterprises additional confidence in the quality of these products, as opposed to beef products that do not appear to be certified for any existing international standards. Establishments in Zanzibar tended to import more food items (from the mainland and Kenya) than mainland Tanzania.

Most of the tourist firms interviewed for this survey said that they purchased their supplies from local sources (Annex 2, table 14B). However, many of the products are not produced in Tanzania. Foreign-owned establishments that most often purchase their food items from Shoprite – the South-African-owned supermarket chain that has outlets in Arusha and Dar es Salaam – may believe they are sourcing locally, but most of the items in that shop are imported, particularly from South Africa. Similarly, furniture, and dry and non-perishable foods (e.g. sugar, coffee packets, sauces, plastic plates and spoons) are mostly imported, from China, Dubai, Kenya, South Africa and Europe. Although chicken is sourced mostly from local suppliers, foreign firms import other meats such as beef and lamb from Kenya and South Africa. Almost all machinery and vehicles are imported, including refrigerators, cooking ranges, air conditioners and tour vehicles.

b. Linkages of tourism to key sectors

An observation made by this survey was the low linkage between the tourism industry and local agriculture and manufacturing. Even where local supplies are abundant, tourism firms (both local and foreign-owned), tend to import them because of the limited variety and quantity available locally, as well as the relatively low quality.[13] For example, construction materials, tiles, paint, ketchup, baked beans, and tomato puree are all produced locally, but tourism businesses, especially foreign-owned, tend to import them. Most of the construction materials are imported, including glass (from Dubai and Spain), card locks (from Sweden) and even doors (from Kenya). Some locally produced agricultural products are not of uniform quality and this is a big problem, especially for large hotels, although some small hotels and small enterprises, do not seem as concerned. For example, some beans are uneven in size, canned products have low-quality packing that does not guarantee a long shelf life, and sometimes the same product has a variable taste. To ameliorate this problem, the supermarket, Shoprite, in Dar es Salaam is helping local producers in the Mbagala area, through training and supply contracts, to grow and supply uniform quality fruit and vegetable products for its business as well as for other customers, including tourist hotels.

c. Spending in the local economy by foreign-owned hotels

Clearly, substantial opportunities exist for increasing the linkage effects of FDI in tourism to the local economy. On average, an international hotel in mainland Tanzania spends $46 on locally produced items for every hotel room it sells (table 7). This figure excludes labour costs, and varies considerably depending on the size of the hotel. In a hotel room that charges an average room rate of $210, only about 22 per cent of the sales are spent directly on the local economy. The equivalent data for a locally owned hotel is about 64 per cent, which means that on average $45 are spent on the local economy for every room sold at an average of room rate of $70 (excluding labour costs). Again, this spending varies depending on the size of the local hotel, as shown in table 7.

In Zanzibar, a foreign-owned hotel spends an average of $65 on locally supplied items for every hotel room it sells at an average room rate of $180 (table 8). That means 36 per cent of the sales are spent directly in the local economy, which is higher than on the mainland, partly because most Zanzibar establishments are beach hotels that try to blend local and foreign attractions, both in construction and food items. The equivalent data for a locally owned hotel is about 65 per cent spent on local procurement, which translates into an average of $33 spent in the local economy for every room sold at an average rate of $50 (excluding labour costs).

As discussed in section IV, tourism does not fall under the union Government. The mainland and Zanzibar each have a different institutional framework that facilitates and promotes tourism. It is also worth mentioning that although different categories of hotels serve different markets, and the higher rates charged by foreign-owned hotels may reflect better amenities, there is little scope for increasing local purchases unless improvements are made in the quality of local goods. Supporting local processing of agricultural products and improving transport and packaging, along with greater efforts to improve the quality and quantity of locally produced supplies, could increase the scope for foreign-owned hotels to increase their linkages to the local economy. Indeed the foreign hotels surveyed were of the opinion that it would be cheaper for them to source all their requirements locally if quality and consistency of supply could be assured.

d. Reducing leakages

Several other issues were observed during the survey. First, tourism firms were resolute about sourcing locally. To them, importing entailed extra costs because most large operators have to hire clearing agents, which increases the cost of imports. However, some products imported from China, Dubai, Indonesia and Thailand are still cheaper than those produced locally. This implies that some of Tanzania's products are not competitive, in part due to relatively high utility costs and taxes. Therefore efforts should be made to improve Tanzania's competitiveness in the global market, without, however, resorting to an import substitution policy that causes other inefficiencies. There is need to focus on what could be feasibly and economically achieved.

Another challenge relates to the inability of local suppliers to deliver on time. This is an important consideration for hotels, restaurants and tour operators who have little room for delays in providing services to their customers. The delays are partly a result of economy-wide structural and economic rigidities, including poor transport and communication systems and cultural attitudes that do not take time seriously. Further, there is almost no merchandising of products, which makes the purchasing process inconvenient for tourism businesses. Some of the hotels interviewed said they needed a central bulk purchasing market such as exists for hotels in other countries - there is a gap in the market here which an entrepreneur could potentially fill. The other alternative is for hotels to set up their own contracting arrangements directly with suppliers, but this takes time and is expensive. Moreover, such a system would work to the disadvantage of local suppliers because they may be unable to market and sell high margin items profitably. In addition, efforts by tourism businesses to establish links with medium, small and microenterprises are hampered by lack of information. For example, there are no avenues for local suppliers to know the demand from foreign hotels, and door-to-door solicitation of information is cumbersome and at times considered "unethical". Lack of information on markets and supply/demand reduces possibilities of fostering greater linkages between the local economy and foreign-owned businesses. Domestically owned hotels link up fairly easily with local suppliers because they generally purchase most of their supplies from the local market.

Strengthening information flows between SMEs and tourism businesses should facilitate identification of opportunities and potential suppliers of particular tourist items. Location matters a lot in fostering those linkages. Hotels located in small towns like Arusha should be able to identify potential suppliers fairly quickly, and are less likely to import items such as fresh fruit and vegetables. In a big city such as Dar es Salaam, on the other hand, information on supply and demand is critical and the linkages may not be as easy as in small localities. As for wildlife lodges, supply contracts are a necessity because these are located in areas without nearby suppliers. In all cases, however, the Tanzania Tourist Board could play a more proactive role by providing linkages between SME suppliers and hotel requirements through bulletin boards and other information-sharing facilities.

Overall, the backward and forward linkages with the tourism industry (hotels, restaurants and tour operators) are extensive. Kweka et al. (2003) carried out a linkage analysis to examine the interdependence between tourism and other sectors in Tanzania using input-output (IO) analysis. The results showed that the tourism sector had an important role, not only as an earner of foreign exchange, but also in terms of generating demand for the output of other sectors. They estimated that the total output impact associated with international tourism in 1992 was equivalent to 5.8 per cent of GDP, and about 1.6 per cent of the labour force. In addition, spending by the tourism industry generated labour income worth 1.3 per cent of GDP, it provided 4.1 per cent of indirect revenue and accounted for 2.1 per cent of

imports. The paper recommended improving the infrastructure and government investment policy so as to enhance the linkage effects of tourism.

7. Social impacts

Based on the interviews, there were found to be both positive and negative social impacts of tourism-related FDI. With regard to positive social impacts, a number of establishments gave direct financial support to improve local social and economic services. There were many examples of such interventions, but, overall, they had certain common characteristics. First, such support was given more by foreign-owned enterprises then locally owned ones. Domestic enterprises considered themselves as operating at "home" and some even said they paid taxes that the Government should plough back to the community. On the other hand, most foreign-owned firms, which also paid taxes, were of the opinion that they had a social responsibility to contribute towards alleviating poverty in the communities surrounding their businesses. Secondly, they differed widely in size: from a small contribution in support of a local football team to constructing schools, for example. These contributions depended very much on management policy, because the size of the contribution was not related to the size or type of business (small or large, domestic or foreign). Thirdly, recipients were from a variety of sectors, but most were in social services, infrastructure development and sustainable tourism development. One foreign-owned hotel collaborated with particular development partners to support a cultural tourism programme (box 2). Such interventions are more to do with corporate social responsibility (CSR) than with philanthropy. A recent study (Mlulla, 2006) concluded that, although most foreign-owned establishments have been giving and are still willing to give to the local community (out of a sense of corporate social responsibility) such donations (mostly in health, education and water) have not been efficiently coordinated by the responsible authorities.

The following are a few examples of support to local communities gathered from the interviews conducted in Zanzibar:

- A foreign-owned hotel in Ras Nungwi (on the northern tip of Zanzibar beach) donated $32,000 in 2005 to the local community to improve local schools and their earth road. The same hotel organizes beach clean-ups using local people who are paid for participation, thus improving their income.
- An international hotel in Zanzibar donates $900 annually to sports clubs.
- A hotel in Mazizini donates $800 annually to local events.

Examples from Arusha included the following:

- Two local tour operators contribute about $22,450 annually in support of community cultural tourism at Sakisi and Singisi villages. The proceeds from the cultural tour activities are used to improve primary education and health services.
- Three foreign-owned tourism businesses spend about $42,000 annually on the Ng'iresi Cultural Tourism Programme under the aegis of the Netherlands Development Programme,. The programme helps the village, which is situated along the slopes of Mount Meru, to improve primary education, and to carry out soil conservation, small-scale irrigation and cross-breeding of traditional livestock to improve yields.
- Another foreign-owned tourist firm spent about $35,000 to support development in Ilkidinga village (7 kilometres north of Arusha) and improve its cultural tourism activities. The proceeds from the cultural activities were used to improve health facilities and primary education.

Box 2. Support for cultural tourism in northern Tanzania

With financial and technical assistance from the Government of the Netherlands and a few tourism establishments in Arusha, Tanzania's cultural tourism and development is up and running. Local people are being empowered through financial and training support to provide services to tourists, such as guiding, preparing meals or providing campsites. These activities earn them income. In addition, a development fee is charged. With this money, primary schools, health services, cattle dips and small irrigation systems projects are undertaken and improved. In this way, all the villagers see the benefit of tourism and this encourages them to participate in government conservation efforts being undertaken by the Tanzania National Parks Authority (TANAPA). The villages benefiting from this support include: Ilkidinga, Longido, Ilkurot, Mkuru, Mto wa Mbu/Engaruka, and Ngi'resi. The combined assistance to these communities in 2005 amounted to $115,950 – a small sum of money that has made a big difference in improving the lives of these communities.

None of the local tourism operators were found to support cultural tourism. Asked why, one of the tour operator owners cited low returns from their operations and possibilities of fostering "unnecessary" dependence if a firm begins to support these communities. Another local operator was of the opinion that the foreign firms supported these activities partly for their own future gains if such support turned out to be successful. To illustrate, the respondent claimed that foreign tour operators liked to take their customers to visit some of the successful cultural tourism centres and then to wildlife parks while most of the respondent's customers were taken straight to wildlife parks. Another local operator did not even know that cultural tourism existed in Arusha, but was aware of transporting tourists to some of those cultural centres. A major concern of both foreign-owned and local hotels was the possibility of reduced bed nights if cultural tour centres began to supply tents and other facilities that were a high security risk for tourists but very cheap compared to a hotel room.

- Another international tourist firm spends about $16,500 per annum to support the Ilkurot Masai Cultural Tourism Programme. The village, which is located 20 kilometres from Arusha town, uses the proceeds from its cultural activities to improve community schools and provide assistance to HIV/AIDS widows and orphans.

This kind of support for community tourism enables local people to benefit from the income generated from tourism, albeit in a small way. The local people interviewed greatly appreciated the assistance being given because they believed it had improved their livelihoods and family income. A summary of the impact on livelihoods is presented in box 3. The Zanzibar Commissioner of Tourism acknowledged other social benefits included fostering a sense of national identity and pride, peace and respect for human rights and freedom.

However, beyond the benefits that are trickling to the local communities, are concerns about negative social effects. These include, for instance, changes in family structures and transformation of local values. The demonstration effect is considerable, particularly with young men and women adopting Western styles/fashions and consumerism. To echo this, the Zanzibar Director of Tourism noted, "Rich Western tourists mixing with the less well-off host population has led to a number of concerns, including undesirable effects such as an increase in alcoholism, drug addiction and, in some few cases, prostitution. Although these social problems have no direct relationship with tourism, the industry has the potential for contributing to those social ills unless action is taken to curb them…" This is a concern of tourism in general, although according to some observers it is the large, foreign-owned hotels catering to international tourists that are more likely to have such an impact, than the small local hotels. On the other hand, this could be location-specific and moreover, not all tourists are culturally insensitive; many have a very positive appreciation of other people's culture and may not behave in a manner that has an adverse social impact.

Another issue of concern is a loss of cultural identity. One clear reason why FDI is more likely to erode cultural identity is that foreign-owned hotels are more compelled to abide by the set global standards of their respective parent company (e.g. hotel chain). Thus in tourism destinations where foreign organizations have control over the tourist product, resorts/hotels may be designed with Western preferences in mind, with little attention to indigenous designs, materials and customs. Although this may not always be the case, it is of concern. Since the demand for tourism in a developing country like Tanzania is driven largely by natural endowments, any loss of cultural identity diminishes the comparative advantage of many tourist attractions. Therefore, tourism destinations need to be protected against undue exploitation and modification.

Finally, one of the most important issues in assessing the impact of tourism-related FDI is its direct link with poverty reduction. One of the most significant ways in which tourism can reduce poverty in developing countries is by employing local people in tourism establishments (Mitchell and Ashley, 2006). A detailed analysis of this question is beyond the scope of this study, which focused in particular on the topic of FDI[14]. Although these questions are beyond the scope of this report, we can make a few generalizations on the basis of the findings of the survey and interviews, which indicate that there are plausible reasons to believe there might be some link between FDI in tourism and poverty reduction.

Clearly, as discussed above, the economy-wide multiplier effects are strong for the tourism industry. This implies that there could be considerable potential for FDI in tourism to enhance economic growth and contribute to poverty reduction. Also as noted earlier, even if a foreign-owned hotel that charges an average of $120 for its rooms spends an average of only $20 on locally produced items, for the local community this is a substantial injection of funds, which if tapped well could be used to improve social services and generate further growth. Casual earnings from the sale of crafts or the supply by SMEs of inputs to foreign-owned tourism establishments (hence positive income effect) through small contracts can have a considerable impact, although they are difficult to quantify due to lack of data. In general, however, it would appear that the potential contribution of FDI in tourism to poverty reduction is weakened by the poor supply capacity of the local economy.

While the negative social impacts of tourism-related FDI cannot be dismissed, there is no reliable information to be able analyse and corroborate such effects. Or rather, it seems to be that the negative effects are associated with tourism in general, rather than with FDI in tourism, as compared to domestic investment in tourism. Most of the arguments in box 3 are merely opinions. Furthermore, these issues have yet to feature significantly in the policy debate, although it is still important to analyse them in order to advocate a more balanced policy intervention that does not undermine the widely accepted contribution of tourism-related FDI to development.

8. Impact on the environment

All tourism businesses, local and foreign-owned, maintain high environmental standards. Flowers and well-tended gardens make hotels attractive to customers. Interviewed managers were of the opinion that good rooms without an attractive environment would not be likely to attract tourists. Environmental activities conducted regularly by tourism establishments located along coastal areas included: beach clean-up, constructing banks to prevent water overflow inland, and undertaking responsible waste management, reuse and recycling. Wastewater management, reuse and recycling, where feasible, were also undertaken. Other activities included contract pick-up of garbage and use of biodegradable chemicals.

Five foreign-owned tourist operators (three on the mainland and two in Zanzibar) reported being members of Green Globe 21 and two had ISO 14000 certification. Interviewed officials from one of these operations noted that membership of Green Globe entails a serious commitment to improving environmental performance. None of the local operators were members of Green Globe 21, but said they followed good environmental practices. One foreign-owned hotel in Zanzibar (Zanzibar Serena Inn) had received an environmental award for exemplary work in environmental care and conservation. Overall, foreign hotels appeared to be more aware of environmental good practices. However, all interviewed hotels (local and foreign) were found to be environmentally sensitive and maintained relatively high environmental standards. Despite good efforts by the tourism businesses, additional efforts are needed by the Government and investors working in partnership to implement sustainable environmental and conservation measures that go beyond the hotel establishment.

Table 7. Mainland: Spending in the local economy by foreign-owned versus locally-owned hotels[a]

Quality of hotel	Average size		Price of room[b] ($)	Average spending (excluding labour) (%)		Average spending in the local economy per room (excl. labour costs) ($)
	Number of rooms	Average number of employees		Local supplies	Imported supplies	
1. Foreign-owned hotels						
5 stars (sample of 1 hotel)[c]	159	350	$175–$540 (average of $300)	15	85	45
3-4 stars (sample of 5 hotels)	142	192	$140 – $450 (average of $220)	23	77	51
1–3 stars (sample of 5 hotels)	74	99	$45 – $240 (average of $110)	30	70	33
FDI average	125	213	$210	22	78	46
2. Locally owned hotels						
5 stars (None)						
3–4 stars (sample of 3)	107	150	$78– $210 (Averaged of $115)	55	45	63
1–3 stars (sample of 6 hotels	74	73	$35 –$120 (Average of $70)	63	37	44
No stars (sample of 3)	31	50	$20–$60 (average of $35)	74	26	26
Local average	71	91	$70	64	36	45

Source: Field interviews, June 2006

[a]   Ranking provided in this report is based on responses from management of the sampled hotels, as Tanzania does not yet have its own hotel rankings. The ministry responsible for tourism is in the preliminary stages of the hotel ranking exercise.

[b]   Price of rooms excludes royal and presidential suites, which range between $1,500 and $2,000.

[c]   Only one of the sampled hotels – a recently renovated hotel in Dar es Salaam overlooking the Indian Ocean – claimed to be in the 5-star category.

Table 8. Zanzibar: Spending in the local economy by foreign-owned versus locally owned hotels

Quality of hotel	Average size		Price of room[a] ($)	Average spending (excluding labour costs) (%)		Average spending in the local economy per room (excl. labour costs) ($)
	No. of rooms	Average no. of employees		Local supplies	Imported supplies	
1. Foreign-owned hotels						
5 stars (none)						
3-4 stars (sample 1)[b]	51	72	$140 – $540 (average of $240)	30	70	72
1-3 stars (sample of 2 hotels)[c]	42	64	$42– $230 (average of $120)	41	59	49
FDI average	46	68	$180	36	64	65
2. Locally owned hotels						
5 stars (none)						
3-4 stars (none)[d]						
1-3 stars (sample of 2 hotels)	35	46	$20 -$110 (average of $50)	65	35	33

Source: Field interviews, June 2006

[a]   Price of room excludes royal and presidential suites, which range between $1,500 –2,000.

[b]   According to officials of the Zanzibar Commission for Tourism, there are only two hotels that can be ranked as 3 or 4 stars: Serena hotel and Zamani Zanzibar Kempinski.

[c]   The sample was 40 per cent of the foreign-owned hotels in this category.

[d]   None of the local hotels could be ranked as 3-4 star. A few were considered 1-3 stars and most would not qualify for any stars. Over 85 per cent of the hotels in Zanzibar (foreign-owned and local) had fewer than 50 rooms.

Box 3. Assessment of the impact of FDI in tourism on livelihoods in Tanzania		
	Positive effects	**Negative effects**
Jobs/employment/skills/education	▪ Compared to local firms, foreign-owned firms offer higher wages (2-3 times), more jobs per room (1 1/2 times), higher training expenditure per employee (11 times) and impart higher levels of skills and innovation ▪ There may be a positive effect of job retention being dependent on performance (for employers). In most cases it should provide a good incentive for workers to improve performance.	▪ Seasonality of employment and higher risk of losing a job due to low performance. Although neither foreign-owned hotels nor local ones are more seasonal or less, local hotels retain most of their employees regardless of the seasonal nature of the tourism industry. ▪ .There may be a negative positive effect of job retention being dependent on performance, from the perspective of employees. Highly competitive employment conditions and skill requirements may disqualify many local job-seekers, as there appears to be insufficient skills training for locals.
Livelihood activities such as farming, crafts and cultural tourism	▪ Income that improves quality of life; ▪ Capacity-building by increasing awareness of income-generating opportunities; ▪ Giving economic value to the popular (e.g. Maasai) culture; ▪ Value addition for local products.	▪ "Commoditization" of traditional cultures, although this can apply to local as well as foreign-owned businesses.
Markets, market opportunities	▪ Business opportunities for SMEs; ▪ Learning marketing and negotiating skills; ▪ Improving value added through training.	▪ Likely vulnerability when opportunities diminish due to seasonality of the industry.
Opportunities for informal sector and small businesses	▪ High, but meeting quality, quantity and reliability of supply is a constraint. Therefore low levels of supply to foreign-owned firms ▪ Training and skills enhancement	
Casual labour opportunities	▪ High casual labour employment due to seasonality of the industry, hence more income opportunities; ▪ Possibilities for full-time employment	▪ Consistently low pay due to high unemployment; ▪ Seasonal effects are higher and more likely to affect unskilled labour.
Infrastructure: water and energy supply, roads and ICT services.	▪ Infrastructure improvement and access to utility services (e.g. telephone, water and electricity) in remote areas (e.g. Nungwi in Zanzibar, some local communities in Arusha).	▪ Pressure on government to undertake large investment in infrastructure when resources are limited, thereby disrupting planned priorities (i.e. biased provisions)
Access to natural resources	▪ Value added to unexploited resources; ▪ Direct income for local communities from natural resources, through jobs, business and taxation opportunities	▪ Overexploitation of natural resources may lead to depletion or/and environmental degradation; ▪ Overactivity in national parks could disrupt wildlife and reduce this resource.
Access to investment funds, loans	▪ Improved access to financial resources for employees/SMEs involved with the foreign-owned firms; ▪ Presence of foreign-owned firms enhances donor interest in supporting local communities.	▪ Lack of development finance institutions in rural areas reduces access to the tourism value chain, for the wider community This is a problem of both foreign-owned and local hotels.
Local culture	▪ Adoption of more efficient work ethics; ▪ Possibilities for improving local culture through a mix of good aspects of each culture (e.g. greater civil liberties).	▪ Remoulding of traditional institutions and growing concern over Western lifestyles; ▪ Loss of authentic local cultural identity due to emphasis on Western cultures as best.
Community organization, cohesion, pride	▪ Foreign-owned firms are keen to engage local community by funding sustainable tourism development for improving livelihoods; ▪ Institutional community-building awareness	▪ Being wholly dependent on donors is not sustainable, and may restrict the freedom of the community to pursue other opportunities with other players

Box 3. Assessment of the impact of FDI in tourism on livelihoods in Tanzania		
	Positive effects	**Negative effects**
Political voice: policy environment and influence over policymakers	▪ Fostering a policy and business environment favourable to FDI and building competitiveness (e.g. by improving the infrastructure); ▪ Increased support of home-country donors	▪ Risk of terrorist attack if the foreign investment is sourced from high-risk Western powers.
Overall impact on households	▪ Increased income through the channels discussed above	▪ Overdependence on the tourism establishment could make households vulnerable to the sensitivity of the industry to external shocks, thus compromising sustainability of household income, savings and livelihood. This relates to tourism in general. The lesson is that the sector is a vulnerable one, which makes it important to develop policies that will reduce that vulnerability (e.g. adding value, making the industry less seasonal, and having many source markets rather than just one or two).

Source: Field interviews, June 2006

D. Policy and Institutional Framework

1. Investment policy

Tanzania's investment policy provides for openness to domestic and foreign investment, the right to private ownership and establishment of business ventures, full protection of property rights, a liberalized foreign exchange market, favourable repatriation conditions, a stable and predictable regulatory framework, simplification of investment establishment procedures, and the right to national and international impartial arbitration in the event of an investment dispute. This policy stance is enshrined in the Tanzania Investment Act 1997 and the Zanzibar New Investment Policy enacted in 2001. The main thrust of the policy is to promote FDI as part of the overall strategy for economic growth and development. Implementation of the policy is vested in the Tanzania Investment Centre (TIC) on the mainland, and in the Zanzibar Investment Promotion Agency (ZIPA).

2. Investment regulations and incentives

The investment promotion agencies, TIC and ZIPA, provide one-stop investment facilitation. Except for a few small businesses (such as hairdressers, taxis, car hire firms and guest houses), their policies and promotion activities do not distinguish between domestic and foreign investors. However, in order to benefit and be registered under TIC or ZIPA, minimum levels of investment are required: $300,000 for foreign investors and $100,000 for domestic investors. If, however, a foreign firm wants to establish a hotel in Zanzibar, the minimum requirement is $4 million worth of investment. Upon satisfactory completion of the requirements, the investor (foreign or local) is provided with a Certificate of Incentives, which gives access to certain rights, such as investment guarantees, access to land, the right to transfer funds abroad and to employ up to five expatriates. However, if the firm requires extra foreign experts, a justification has to be submitted to TIC or ZIPA for approval. The approval is fairly automatic where local qualified experts are in short supply. Apart from the incentives illustrated in box 4 below, there is also a tax holiday until the recovery of capital, which can be written off at the rates of 50 per cent in the first year of operation, and at 25 per cent in the second and third years.

Once a local or foreign investor in mainland Tanzania completes the minimum requirements, the investor is required to follow normal business codes of conduct. However, for Zanzibar there are a few extra guidelines that have to be followed. The Guidelines for Investors and Private Zanzibaris intending to Invest in Zanzibar states clearly that "foreign investors in Zanzibar will be given the option to decide whether to operate as exclusive owners of their investment project or as majority or minority partners in joint ventures with local interests, private or public". There are no requirements specific to foreign investors. The tourism policy and legislation provides various incentives for FDI and TNCs approved by the Zanzibar Investment Promotion Agency (ZIPA) or the Tanzania Investment Centre (TIC) (box 4). For Zanzibar, if the enterprise is a joint venture, only the foreign holder of the certificate can enjoy all exchange control privileges set out in the Investment Act. However, the entire venture is entitled to the tax concessions set out in the Act.

Box 4. Incentives for local and foreign investors in Tanzania

In order to encourage local and foreign investments, Tanzania provides the following incentives:

- Waiver of land rent during the construction period.
- Exemption from customs and import duties and other similar taxes on capital goods such as machinery, equipment, raw materials, fuel, vehicles and other goods necessary and required exclusively during the construction period.
- Exemption from import duties on imported raw materials for trial operations, provided that the quantity of such materials does not exceed 18 months' supply for one-shift production operations.
- Exemption of import duty on goods for necessary use of expatriates.
- Exemption from all export duties payable on finished export goods of approved enterprises.
- Income tax exemption for investors who have made a declaration for reinvestment at the proposed stage, up to the first three years.
- Up to 100 per cent repatriation of profits.
- Consideration of tax holidays for approved projects.
- Investment protection and guarantee against confiscation or expropriation. The United Republic of Tanzania maintains linkages with the Multilateral Investment Guarantee Agency (MIGA) and the International Centre for Settlement of Investment Disputes (ICSID) to ensure protection of private investments.

Source: Ministry of Finance and Economic Affairs, Zanzibar, and the Tanzania Investment Centre (TIC)

a. Policy guidelines

In addition to the general investment incentives outlined in box 4, the Zanzibar Tourism Policy of January 2004 provides several guidelines that have a bearing on investment. These include:

- Encouraging eco-lodge development designed to attract and serve a broader ecotourism market.
- Restricting building heights in the beach area to a limit of 2 to 3 storeys.
- Encouraging use of indigenous architecture in order to maintain an aesthetic appearance, and building styles and materials should reflect the characteristics of the site and the environment and social context of the setting.
- Enforcing and implementing environmental impact assessment (EIA) and environmental statements (ES) where tourism development takes place.
- Creating zoning systems to encourage the establishment of marine parks for better management and sustainable tourism development.
- Setting up a specialized trained tourist police unit to provide security and assistance to tourists and residents.

b. Tourism activities

The policy and legislation encourages both foreign and local private investment to engage in:

- Constructing and operating tourist class hotels,
- Providing tourist-related services such as restaurants and photographic services,
- Developing tourist sites,
- Providing game fishing facilities, and
- Tour operations (with the exception of ground handling which is reserved for local investors).

Thus, for the development of Tanzania's tourism sector, there is little if any discrimination between foreign and local investors. However, policy guidelines for the mainland are different from those for Zanzibar, given the specific conditions in Zanzibar as an island economy.

Both the Tanzania Tourism Master Plan and the Tourism Master Plan for Zanzibar encourage investment in tourism that is "culturally and environmentally sensitive and based on a 'low volume high price' policy that intends to attract high-spending tourists" (CHL, 2003). However, as the expenditure per tourist shows, Tanzania is far from achieving this objective, in part because the country is still in the initial stages of developing world-class tourism accommodation and tour operation services that are sufficiently competitive and offer the value for money necessary to enforce such a policy.

c.   Labour

Tanzania's labour laws are undergoing review in collaboration with the International Labour Organization (ILO). The main thrust is to ensure that labour laws support the promotion of accelerated development, decent work and good governance that is consistent with international standards. With regard to investments, the Investment Act stipulates that every investor shall, in respect of employment, give priority to Tanzanians unless it is necessary to employ foreign experts. The Zanzibar act is more specific and states:

> "Without prejudice to the rights of investors, the investor may, if so wishes appoint and retain key personnel such as the posts of General Manager or Managing Director, financial controller or chief accountant, chief maintenance engineer and or any other person who shall be approved by the Government from time to time."

Apart from those stipulations, there are no additional restrictions on employment of non-citizens. The survey conducted for this study revealed that approval of employment for non-citizens was fairly automatic. There

are no bureaucratic restrictions on employing foreign experts. However, hotels and tour operators interviewed were resolute about replacing foreign staff with skilled local staff when available in order to reduce the operational costs of their businesses.

d.   Promotion of FDI in tourism

There is close collaboration between TIC and ZIPA in promoting FDI in tourism activities. They also work closely with the World Association of Investment Promotion Agencies (WAIPA), which provides networking opportunities and facilities, and enables the exchange of best practices in investment promotion. The various strategies they use to promote tourism, include a website, editorial coverage in appropriate media (such as travel magazines), production of specialized publications (such as the Tanzania Travel and Tourism Directory, Dar es Salaam Tourism Guide, Tanzania: Authentic Africa), and investment promotion tours abroad. Based on the increasing number of tourists to Tanzania in recent years, these promotional activities can be rated a success. However, much remains to be done both in terms of advertising Tanzania's tourism products more and improving the quality of tourism services, including infrastructure.

3.   Other initiatives related to tourism development

Reducing leakages in tourism income and protecting the environment. In a bid to support the long-term welfare of Zanzibar's tourism industry, the Ministry of Finance and Economic Affairs (MOFEA) has introduced fiscal reforms and coordinates cross-departmental projects that aim at: plugging leakages in income from tourism, linking tourism with the poverty reduction strategy, securing existing government revenues, improving sociocultural understanding between investors and local communities and protecting the island's fragile environment, culture and heritage.

Establishment of a Tourism Development Fund (STDF). The rapid development of the Zanzibar tourism industry, coupled with the increasing volume of tourist arrivals, is leading to increasing pressure on the environment and infrastructure. In order to maintain healthy, long-term growth prospects for Zanzibar as a prime tourism destination, a sustainable tourism levy, of $2 per visitor/per night has been introduced to augment the STDF. The STDF's resources are used for the following activities: environmental protection, village community tourism-related activities, improvement of tourism infrastructure, regeneration of public areas (particularly parks and open spaces), tourism promotion, and training in tourism-related occupations and skills.

4. Institutional and regulatory framework

a. Mainland Tanzania

The Ministry of Natural Resources and Tourism (MNRT) is responsible for managing Tanzania's tourism industry. Its work is organized in five divisions: tourism, wildlife, forestry & beekeeping, fisheries and antiquities, each headed by a director. The combining of the tourism department with the above departments reflects the fact that the Tanzanian tourism product is primarily natural resource (wildlife) based. Below we describe only the departments that are key to the functioning of the tourism industry.

Tourism Division

The Tourism Division within MNRT is responsible for sectoral policy and planning, manpower training and classification and licensing of hotels and travel agencies. The division is also responsible for the Hotel and Tourism Training Institute (HTTI) and more generally for the State's public regulatory and promotional organization, the Tanzania Tourist Board (TTB). Other institutions under its authority are the Tourism Training Unit, which coordinates tourism staff training, the Tourist Agency Licensing Authority (TALA), which is responsible for issuing licences to tourism establishments/businesses, and for inspecting travel agencies and tour operators to ensure that they conform with regulations. However, at present not all tour operators or travel agencies are licensed. The Hotels Board is responsible for classification and licensing of hotels and for inspection and monitoring of their standards. Standards are yet to be benchmarked in a region-wide initiative under the auspices of the East African Community (EAC), which aims at establishing grading of standards for the hotel and accommodation segment of the industry in East Africa. The division also deals with research and statistics.

Tanzania Tourist Board

The Tanzania Tourist Board was established in 1992 by an Act of Parliament to oversee and coordinate the marketing and promoting of Tanzanian tourism. Since its establishment in 1992, the Board has been involved in a number of awareness-raising and promotional initiatives through brochures, and organizing and participating in trade fairs and tours. Although it has achieved tremendous results over the past 10 years, it is still acutely underfunded (by the Government), and, as a result, understaffed. These problems have prevented it from realizing its full potential, but they are likely to be addressed in the short run as they have been given top priority in its second strategic plan that is currently being finalized for implementation.

Wildlife Division

The Wildlife Division has responsibility for wildlife management. It is split between the Wildlife Division and five government agencies: the Tanzania National Parks Authority (TANAPA), which manages the wildlife tourism component; the Ngorongoro Conservation Area Authority (NCAA), which is responsible for conserving this World Heritage site; the College of African Wildlife Management (CAWM) at Mweka, that provides training on issues related to wildlife management; and the Tanzania Wildlife Research Institute (TAWIRI), responsible for the research needs of the entire wildlife sector. The Wildlife Division is responsible for all wildlife management outside the national parks and the Ngorongoro Conservation Area, and issues hunting concessions and licences, including to TAWICO and Mweka College, for wildlife utilization. These organizations report back to the Ministry individually through the Permanent Secretary. The Marine Parks and Reserves Board that manages marine and coastal tourism resources is also part of the MNRT.

Antiquities Division

Antiquities have been transferred from the Ministry of Education to the Ministry of Natural Resources and Tourism. The Division is responsible for national museums.

b. Zanzibar

Zanzibar, like mainland Tanzania, considers tourism to be multi-sectoral, requiring various institutional arrangements for effective implementation. Just as the Tourism Directorate is responsible for all tourism activities in mainland Tanzania, in Zanzibar responsibility for these activities is vested in the Commission for Tourism. The commission is legally mandated to perform the following functions: development, planning, investment guidance, policy promulgation, product inventory and enhancement of regulation and control, marketing and promotion, information services, research and statistics, human resources and public awareness-raising.

Other institutions or government departments in Zanzibar that are involved in activities related to tourism include the Zanzibar Ministry of Finance, Zanzibar Investments Promotion Agency (ZIPA), Department of Land and Registration, and the Environment Department.

c. Improvements needed in the policy and institutional framework

All firms interviewed, both local and foreign-owned, believed there was a need for improvements in the tax regime. In particular, they mentioned the need for eliminating the multiplicity of taxes and reducing investors' transaction costs and costs of doing business. Local firms also pointed to the need for a review of business licensing to eliminate unnecessary licences. In addition, both foreign-owned and local firms wanted a review of labour laws to enable them to attract and retain skilled labour, whether foreign or local. Foreign-owned firms, in particular, wanted greater flexibility in hiring workers.

Most local firms suggested that further efforts were needed for improving access to long-tem credit, particularly for small and medium hotels and tour operators. In addition, both local and foreign-owned firms suggested that the government should continue to undertake improvements in the physical infrastructure, especially electricity and water supply, roads, harbours, and transport and communications.

E. Implications of Regional Integration for Tourism Development

1. Introduction

Tourism has always been one of the world's largest industries. In 2003, for example, the industry recorded $563 billion in sales (excluding air travel), of which Africa alone received over $22.5 billion (World Bank, 2005). These receipts, compare favourably with other international financial transfers to Africa in 2003, such as official aid ($26 billiion) and workers' remittances ($20.5 billion) (World Bank, 2005). However, although these contributions from tourism appear to be large, they represent only 4 per cent of the total tourism receipts worldwide. Africa could increase its share of tourism receipts through regional integration.

As figure 11 shows, tourism is making a significant contribution to the economies of East and Southern Africa. Tourism earnings as a percentage of export earnings are significant for Mauritius (29.8 per cent), Tanzania (28.1 per cent), Kenya (17.1 per cent), and South Africa (11.5 per cent). This implies that the region as a whole has a variety of tourism attractions.

Successful marketing of a tourism destination is a formidable challenge, and one of its key ingredients is product diversification. This entails being able to offer a rich variety of products within a single destination. Cultural and historical attractions have become a part of the itineraries of tourists in Kenya, in addition to wildlife and beaches, for example. Niche tourism has become popular in the global market. Specialized adventure tourism, ecotourism, agro-tourism, incentive and business tourism and many more have also become thriving industries. It is for this reason that major benefits can accrue to East and Southern African countries if they join forces to market the region (or

subregions) as a single destination offering a variety of tourist products that would attract a greater share of international tourist spending. It would allow each country to reap the benefits of its neighbour's unique attractions.

Figure 11. Tourism receipts in selected countries of East and Southern Africa, 2003 ($ million)

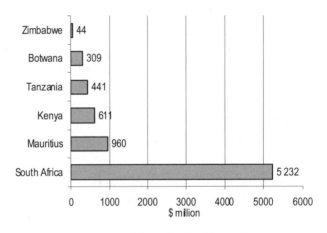

Source: Based on World Bank, *World Development Indicators 2005.*

Taking East Africa as an example, promotional activities could adopt a regional strategy. Uganda could take advantage of the wildlife and coastline attractions offered by Kenya and Tanzania, while also attracting guests with its own unique tourist activities that include gorilla and primate viewing and birdwatching. The migration of millions of wildebeest from Tanzania to Kenya has been billed as one of the world's greatest wildlife spectacles and attracts visitors from all over the globe. Yet this event remains divided into two separate camps – those viewing the migration from the Serengeti in Tanzania and those watching the approach of the herds from neighbouring Maasai Mara in Kenya. Current marketing campaigns insist that each side offers a better experience than the other. The wildebeest know better: to them the border is just an invisible line to be crossed in search of fresh green grass. Marketing East Africa, as a single destination would allow tourists free passage throughout the area in order to follow the migration and witness the full natural cycle in its entirety. Efforts to realize this objective are under way in the EAC development strategy. Similar objectives are being pursued in Southern Africa, where efforts are under way to establish "mega-parks" combining national parks that share common borders with a unified park administration, management and pricing. South Africa, Namibia, Botswana and Mozambique have taken the first steps towards marketing Southern Africa as a single regional destination. For FDI, such initiatives can significantly reduce the transaction costs of establishment in the region as investment procedures/policies become harmonized.

2. Implications of regional trade and investment policies for FDI in tourism

East Africa has a long history of regional integration, dating back to 1917 when it formed a customs union. Subsequent regional arrangements included the East African High Commission (1948–1961), the East African Common Services Organisation (1961–1967), the East African Community (1967–1977), and East African Co-operation (1993–1999). In July 2000 the three East African countries Tanzania, Kenya and Uganda re-established the East African Community (EAC), signed the EAC Trade Protocol in March 2004 and launched a customs union in January 2005. The latter established a common external tariff and aimed to remove all intraregional trade barriers to be completed over a five-year transition period. Plans are also under way to create a common market, and, later, a monetary and political union. These integration steps augur well for EAC efforts

directed at attracting increasing FDI for tourism in the region.

The establishment of an EAC customs union has necessitated harmonization of customs procedures and domestic regulations that can help facilitate trade and encourage tourism and FDI. An analysis conducted by Castro, Kraus and de La Rocha (2004) using a partial equilibrium model that took into account the responses of producers and consumers to tariff and price changes following the formation of the customs union, suggested that trade between Tanzania and EAC partners would grow by 3.1 per cent over the 2000 levels, while their trade with third countries would increase by 16.3 per cent. This implies, in part, that trade growth between the EAC partners is largely a result of regional tariff preferences rather than any comparative advantage between the countries.

Another way to evaluate the economic impacts of regional integration, including those of tourism-related FDI, is to assess the complementarities of the member countries' trade structures using a bilateral product complementarity index (the higher the index, the greater the product complementarity) (Tsikata, 1999). Using that analysis, the bilateral complementary index for Tanzania's exports and Kenya's imports is 52.8 and for Tanzania's imports and Kenya's exports it is 42. The corresponding values for Tanzania's trade with Uganda are 49.7 and 31. The indices for other regional trade agreements (RTAs) are: EU 53.4, North American Free Trade Agreement (NAFTA) 56.3, Latin American Free Trade Association (LAFTA) 22.2 and the Andean Pact 7.4. What these indices tell us is that despite the low EAC intraregional trade intensity, each partner country stands to benefit from enhanced regional integration. This implies that adequate potential exists for fostering regional FDI in the tourism sector.

In order to reap full benefits of integration and attract more benefits from FDI in tourism several actions need to be taken by all three EAC member States. In particular, they need to iron out differences between their customs procedures and remove further quantitative restrictions, as well as reviewing each country's competitive policy and internal tax policies and structures to remove elements that undermine the effectiveness of a common external tariff (CET). Thus, harmonization of trade and investment policies should reduce transaction costs, discourage smuggling and tax evasion, promote further integration and attract more FDI within the EAC and between it and the rest of the world.

With regard to FDI in tourism, EAC member countries' policies on management of natural resources vary considerably. For example, in Tanzania, big game hunting is still considered a beneficial and profitable form of tourism, while Kenya firmly maintains a total ban on any form of hunting. Immigration procedures also differ considerably, with separate visa charges, airport taxes, departure taxes and vehicle permits. A journey between EAC countries can become unnecessarily expensive given these differences and the inherent multiple charges, not to mention other complicated procedures. This is a barrier to an effective regional tourism policy. Few visitors would agree to pay for three separate visas in a single trip to East Africa. Perhaps the EAC countries should consider emulating some countries of the European Community that have agreed to issue a single Schengen visa for all tourists visiting those countries that are party to the agreement.

3. Other obstacles and constraints on regional tourism

The following are some of the obstacles and constraints documented in the literature and cited from the interviews conducted for this study, from the Tanzanian perspective on regional integration prospects in the EAC.

a. Access and inter-country travel

- Constrained international access, including difficulties in travelling between the member countries (e.g. cumbersome and time-consuming customs and immigration procedures).,
- Inadequate transport infrastructure; and
- Restrictive and uncoordinated civil aviation policies that prevent the full use of the countries' airports and airstrips to fly tourists to and between key sites of tourist interest.

b. Inadequate support for and facilitation of tourism

- Inadequate government support for the tourism sector, which is not in line with their stated prioritization of the sector in their economies;
- Weak institutional capacity at provincial and local levels; and
- Low public-sector investment for improving tourism-related infrastructure.

c. Other issues

- In all the East African countries, levels of violence and armed robbery require action to increase civil and personal security;
- Airport taxes and other multiple charges and obstacles are deterrents to intraregional tourism;
- Poor infrastructure (e.g. dilapidated roads) connecting the tourism centres of the three countries;
- Poor interconnectivity of mobile telephone systems of the three countries; and
- Inadequate product, marketing and operations to enhance regional tourism development.

4. Towards joint promotion of tourism in the East African Community

Following the establishment of the EAC customs union in January 2005, joint development of the tourism sector is under way. Preparations include a commissioned study that will outline an overall tourism marketing plan and strategy, and development of a joint export and investment promotion strategy and a private-sector development strategy. According to interviews conducted with EAC Secretariat officials in Arusha, regionally coordinated action on tourism should include: involvement of communities in wildlife conservation and management; encouragement of wildlife farming; development of infrastructure such as roads and power in national parks and game reserves; arranging access to soft loan facilities to be provided by the East African Development Bank (EADB); a co-operative approach to control poaching; and much greater cooperation between the member States in developing and marketing an integrated East African circuit.

Thus the focus of cooperation in the tourism sector should be to develop a collective and coordinated approach to the promotion and marketing of quality tourism into and within the Community. Other measures that are being contemplated for inclusion in the strategy include:

- Creating a regional approach to the development of regional tourism and promotion of East Africa as a single destination;
- Harmonization of the member States' tax regimes, immigration (especially facilitation of free movement across the region) and tax procedures;
- Establishment of a regional marketing body and a regional tourism master plan on the basis of which the region will be marketed and coordinated as a single tourist destination;
- Emphasizing exploitation while ensuring environmental sustainability;
- Achieving a regional open skies policy;
- Joint training of tourism staff, including for example at Kenya's Utalii College, given its proficiency and comparative advantage;
- Involvement of local populations in tourism development, and coordinated programmes of community-based tourism; and
- Promotion of indigenous entrepreneurial capacity in tourism.

Within the above-proposed framework, an East African Investment Code is under preparation that will provide for the following:

- Openness to foreign investment;
- Right to private ownership and establishment;
- Full protection of property rights;
- Liberalized foreign exchange markets;
- Conducive repatriation conditions;
- A stable, transparent and predictable regulatory framework;
- Simplification of establishment procedures for foreign investors so as to replace the regulatory role of investment screening and approvals with promotional assistance and facilitation;
- National treatment status; and
- The right to national and international impartial arbitration in the event of a dispute with the government.

In addition, the ambitious steps towards joint development of tourism resources in the region should be matched by resolute action to harmonize partner States' investment laws and tourism policies, as a systematic way of moving towards achieving the goals of regional integration and development.

F. Conclusions and Recommendations

1. Conclusions

Tourism has become one of the largest industries worldwide, and an important source of growth for many developing (especially African) countries. In the United Republic of Tanzania, the sector is the second largest contributor to foreign exchange and the second largest recipient of FDI after (mainly gold) mining. While the importance of FDI in tourism at the macro level is adequately documented, there is little information about its actual scale and scope, and little, if any, evidence of its impact at the micro level. FDI has been the single most important source of dynamism in the tourism industry in many parts of the developing world, including Tanzania. This study has presented key data on the tourism industry trends in Tanzania, the impact of foreign versus domestic investment in tourism and the implications of regional integration for tourism development in the member countries and for attracting more FDI into this industry. In-depth interviews were conducted with tourist establishments (both foreign and local), suppliers of these establishments and some representative institutions to complement existing secondary data and literature.

Following Tanzania's transition from socialist to market-based economic management of economic activity in the mid-1980s, concerted efforts have been made to attract and promote FDI, especially in tourism. Investor-friendly policies, rules and regulations have been put in place that guarantee protection of private property rights, repatriation of profits and impartial arbitration in case of disputes. Success is evident. More than 2,076 investments were registered in Tanzania between 1995 and 2004, 55.3 per cent of which were FDI inflows. These inflows exceeded $2.4 billion during that period, compared with only $90 million between 1990 and 1995. In tandem, earnings from tourism increased from $95 million in 1995 to over $746 million in 2004, making this industry the second highest foreign exchange earner.

The impact of FDI in tourism has been mixed. For example, with regard to labour issues, this study found that foreign-owned hotels had higher employment per room, but largely of workers in the middle- and low-skills categories. Foreign-owned establishments paid their employees higher wages than did their local counterparts – some of them two to three times higher. However, despite this higher pay, the monthly wages were still low: $120–$150 for the majority of their employees. Foreign-owned firms provided employees with more training, incurring about 11 times higher costs on training than local firms. Transfer of skills and knowledge was also higher than that of local firms, particularly with regard to the use of computer-related technology, customer service and work ethics.

Although revenue per visitor was higher in foreign-owned firms (typically more than twice their local counterparts), little was retained in the local economy and there is significant potential to increase this. A foreign-owned hotel spent an average of $46 on locally produced items for every hotel room it sold (not including wages and salaries). With a hotel room selling for an average of $210, that means only 22 per cent of the sales were spent directly on non-employment goods and services provided by the local economy. The equivalent data for a locally owned hotel was over 64 per cent (on average $45 spent on the local economy for every room sold at an average room rate of $70). Also corporate responsibility of foreign-owned hotels was low: although they did support a few community-wide social and economic services that have made a difference to the lives of the beneficiaries, the levels of support were too small (relative to their profits) to have a significant countrywide impact in terms of reducing widespread poverty. However, some firms may argue that their corporate social responsibility also includes efforts to source locally and to strengthen local supply networks that are weak, in addition to donations. In terms of their public contribution, the direct effect of the involvement is of course through taxes, which, as shown, are high. The high propensity of foreign-owned establishments to import rather than source locally, in part due to the low capacity of the local economy to supply adequate quality and quantities of goods, reduces the impact of foreign-owned establishments through linkages with the local economy.

Overall, however, FDI in tourism in Tanzania is having some impact, and with increased assistance to local entrepreneurs to supply more and better quality goods and services, its impact could be greater in the foreseeable future. Policy measures are needed to protect the economy (and particularly local communities) from the shortcomings of the industry, especially its sensitivity to seasonality and to external shocks, by promoting growth of domestic investment in tourism and domestic tourists to boost it to levels similar to the levels of FDI and international tourists respectively. Regional tourism could also be beneficial, in addition to expanding the use of tourist circuits within the country, an area in which hotel chains could potentially help.

With regard to regional integration, there are clear steps being taken by the East African Community secretariat to market and promote the region as a single tourism destination. A study of potential EAC

tourism products and development of a tourism master plan are under way, an investment code is under preparation and strategies for private sector participation are being devised following the establishment of a customs union in January 2005. However, these good intentions are not being matched with resolute action to harmonize member States' investment laws and tourism policies, which is necessary for effective regional integration of the tourism industry. Nevertheless, Tanzania has already benefited from greater integration by attracting a number of FDI projects in tourism from the two regional blocs, the Southern African Development Community (SADC) and the EAC, in particular from South Africa and Kenya. However, the establishments owned by these foreign investors prefer to import their supplies from their home countries, particularly products that are not produced locally or are of lower quality.

2. Recommendations

a. Strengthening linkages with the local economy

There are significant opportunities for strengthening the forward and backward linkages of foreign-owned tourist establishments with the local economy in order to enhance their impact. Most importantly this can be done by assisting local entrepreneurs to:

- Increase the value of agriculture production through improved techniques for processing (along the supply chain) and enforcement of quality standards for fruit and vegetables, meat (including poultry) and other food products;
- Improve local supply capacity of food products through better monitoring of the supply chain, packaging and storage to increase shelf life and hygiene;

- Improve the value of locally made furniture by helping to increase capacity and train employees;
- Improve importing procedures to cut down costs of the imported products that are needed by tourist establishments;
- Improve information and physical infrastructure to enhance communication between buyers and sellers for timely provision and delivery of required quantity and quality of products; and
- Establishing central, wholesale markets for hoteliers.

b.   Improving infrastructure

Major efforts are required to improve infrastructure, particularly roads (including those at destination points), airports (including small inland airstrips), the rail network and telecommunications, in order to enhance sustainability. Utilities such as water and electricity require improvement, both in terms of regularity and stability of supply. Due to their inadequate provision, investors have had to install their own facilities, such as back-up generators, which is costly both from a capital perspective as well as operationally, as it increases the cost of doing business. Foreign investors can assist the Government in addressing these problems through support to infrastructure development in partnership with the Government and the local private sector.

c.   Providing training for capacity-building

A lack of adequately skilled manpower hampers efficient business performance and necessitates undue and costly employment of foreign experts in the tourism industry. There is a need to improve tourism training institutes through curriculum reform and better training techniques, and to foster on-the-job training by foreign-owned establishments. Foreign-owned hotels could support upgrading of the Zanzibar Tourism Training Institute and the Hotel and Tourism Institute in Dar es Salaam, as well as facilitating greater linkages with the more experienced Utalii College in Nairobi Kenya. These hotels themselves are also a good source of training and could be encouraged to accept internship trainees from the tourism institutes for an agreed period of time.

d.   Developing the southern circuit and other tourism products

The northern circuit is becoming overexploited and there is a growing concern over the environmental effects. In order to relieve the pressure on the northern circuit, it is necessary to develop the southern circuit (e.g. Selous, Ruaha and Udzungwa national parks) as well as promoting coastal tourism products. The construction of accommodation and other facilities and infrastructure could degrade the landscape or sites where the style and architecture is not in harmony with the environment. Therefore, planning and coordination are needed to ensure tourism development achieves a balance between the tourist activity and its scale in relation to the absorptive capacity of different ecosystems, local cultures and sustainable exploitation. This may require the Tanzania Investment Centre to be more proactive in soliciting and promoting TNCs to invest in diversification of Tanzania's tourism products.

e.   Strengthening pro-poor tourism linkages and programmes

Owing to its large contribution to GDP, employment and foreign exchange earnings, tourism has the potential to serve as an engine of sustained growth of the economy. Maximizing the pro-poor impact of tourism would require more than supporting small community-run activities. It will also require foreign-owned as well as local tourism establishments to change their business practices, adopt new ways of destination management, provide greater support for infrastructure development and change their procurement patterns. Better regulation of the industry is also needed. In addition, the Government should be more proactive in promoting the growth of small and medium-sized enterprises and in encouraging greater community participation in tourism activities.

G. References

Bank of Tanzania (BOT) (2005). *Monthly Economic Review*, May. Dar es Salaam.

Bird RM (1992). Taxing tourism in developing countries. *World Development*, 20 (8): 1145-1158.

Ashley, C, Roe D and Goodwin H (2001). Pro-poor tourism strategies: Making tourism work for the poor. London, Overseas Development Institute.

Castro L, Kraus C and de la Rocha M (2004). *Regional trade integration in East Africa: the trade and revenue impacts of the planned East African Community customs union. Africa Region Working Paper Series* no. 72. World Bank, Washington, DC.

CHL Consulting Group (2003). Indicative Tourism Master Plan for Zanzibar and Pemba. Final Report. Dublin.

Kulindwa K, Sosovele H and Mashindano O (2001). *Tourism Growth for Sustainable Development.* Dar es Salaam University Press.

Kweka J (2004). Tourism and the economy of Tanzania: A CGE analysis. Paper presented at the CSAE Conference on Growth, Poverty reduction and Human Development in Africa, in Oxford, United Kingdom, 21-22 March 2004, .

Kweka J, Morrisey O and Blake A. (2003). The economic potential of tourism in Tanzania. *Journal of International Development*, 15: 335-351, Willey International Science.

Mitchell J and Ashley C (2006). Can tourism help reduce poverty in Africa? Briefing Paper. London, Overseas Development Institute.

MIGA (2002). Tourism in Tanzania: Investment for growth and diversification, September. Washington: the World Bank Group.

MIGA (2006), Attracting investment in tourism, Tanzania's investor outreach programme, Investing in Development Series, Washington: the World Bank Group.

Mlulla A Globalisation and rural transformation in Tanzania. Globalisation working paper (May 2006). Dar es Salaam, Economic and Social Research Foundation (ESRF).

Tsikata Y (1999). Southern Africa: Trade, liberalisation, and implications for a free trade area. Paper prepared for the Annual Forum of the Trade and Industrial Policy Secretariat, Muldersdrift, South Africa?. Dates of the meeting?

UNCTAD (2005a). FDI in tourism: the development dimension. Methodological issues note. Geneva, United Nations.

UNCTAD (2005b). The role of FDI in Tanzania tourism. Working paper. Investment Issues Analysis Branch, UNCTAD, Geneva.

United Republic of Tanzania (2002). *Tourism Sector Policy.* Government Printers, Dar es Salaam.

United Republic of Tanzania (various years), *Economic Survey*s, Ministry of Planning and Economy and Empowerment (MPEE), Dar es Salaam.

Wangwe S et al. (2005). Evaluation of growth and impact of investment in Tanzania. Dar es Salaam, The Tanzania Investment Centre (TIC).

World Travel and Tourism Council (WTTC), (2008), Tourism Satellite Account, Tanzania.

World Bank (2005). *World Development Indicators 2005.* Washington, DC, World Bank.

Notes

[1]   Based on contribution by Josaphat Kweka and Daniel Ngowi, Economic and Social Research Foundation, United Republic of Tanzania.

[2]   The World Travel and Tourism Council (WTTC) estimates that the travel and tourism economy currently contributes over 8% to total employment and that this will rise to 9% by 2018 (WTTC, 2008). Export earnings by international tourists are forecast to account for 11% of total exports in 2008.   Ttourism is the largest single   foreign exchange earner in one third of all developing countries, and among the top five earners in four out of five developing countries.

[3]   Although Tanzania has not ranked hotels by standards (in terms of "stars"), we requested the managers of the interviewed hotels to rate their hotels. Based on this rating, the number of hotels for a corresponding grade or "stars" are as follows. For FDI owned hotels, 5 stars (1), 3-4 stars (5), 1-3 (5), no stars (none). For locally owned hotels, 5 stars (none), 3-4 stars (3), 1-3 stars (6), no stars (3). Most local hotels could not rank their standard, presumably indicating that their quality is less than a 1-star ranking. About 70 per cent of the 1-4 star hotels were interviewed.

[4]   The tourism attractions in the northern circuit include: the Ngorongoro crater, the Serengeti, Manyara, Tarangire and Arusha national parks and the Mkomazi game reserve, and Mount Kilimanjaro and Meru. In addition, Olduvai gorge is an important historical site.

[5]   Tourism attractions in the southern circuit are mainly national parks (each with their own unique features) such as: the Mikumi, Ruaha and Udzungwa mountains as well as the famous Selous game reserve.

[6]   Note that the tourism sector is defined in the national accounts as hotels, restaurants and retail trading. Thus in 2005, the sector's contribution to GDP was over 10 per cent, inclusive of retail trading, and about 7 per cent, excluding retail trade.

[7]   Major investments in hotel accommodation took place in Dar es Salaam, Arusha and Zanzibar.

[8]   Zanzibar comprises the two main islands of Zanzibar and Pemba.

[9]   That is, for every person directly employed in the sector, five more jobs were created indirectly, so that total employment in 2004 may have been as high as 160,750 x 5.4. The input-output values used were for 1992, implying that the linkage and multiplier effects are presumably much higher today.

[10]   Tour operators, both local and foreign account for over 85% of the total invested in transport.

[11]   Employing computer generated equilibrium analysis, Kweka (2004) found that a reasonable increase in tax rates (say by 10 per cent) on tourism-related activities was not harmful to the industry or economy, yet this increased tax revenue significantly. This is consistent with the findings by Bird (1992), that an increase in taxes on tourism establishments/activities is the most effective way for LDCs to benefit from growth in tourism.

[12]   See Kweka et al. (2003) for a more detailed discussion on aggregate linkage effects of the sector.

[13]   Preferences for imported varieties may also have been enhanced by a more liberalized trade policy regime, both through unilateral liberalization and greater regional integration, which has resulted in a further opening up of the borders. Nevertheless, it is clear that importing involves additional costs (e.g. for meeting sanitary and phytosanitary requirements, transport and handling costs) even when trade policy is favourable, since the types of products imported by tourism establishments are subject to relatively higher (protective) tariffs. Thus it is most likely that reasons for increased imports of food products go beyond trade policy considerations.

[14]   The current survey did not lend itself to obtaining substantive information on poverty reduction issues. Not least, the focus on foreign owned hotels meant a focus on city centres, where hotels have little or no direct interactions with rural areas where the poor are typically located. (For those foreign hotels located in some rural areas, they may of course however be the only source of formal employment.) Also, the assistance given to the local communities needs to be evaluated in terms of establishing a link between the good intentions of the "donor" with actual reductions in poverty of the "recipient". This raises questions for a future study, such as: are the donations targeted, how efficient is the targeting mechanism, and is the "recipient" actually poor?

Annexes

Annex 1. Basic data on tourism in the United Republic of Tanzania

Table 1A. Tourism business trends in the United Republic of Tanzania, 1996–2004

Year	1996	1997	1998	1999	2000	2001	2002	2003	2004
Number of international tourists in the country	326 188	360 000	482 331	627 325	501 669	525 122	575 296	576 198	582 807
Number of international tourists in hotels	296 193	345 000	457 331	564 593	479 652	501 081	550 000	552 000	562 332
Earnings ($ million)	322.37	392.41	570.00	733.28	739.06	725.00	730.00	731.00	746.14
Average number of days per tourist	7.30	7.50	7.60	7.70	8.00	8.00	11	11	11
Average expenditure per tourist per day ($)	135.00	145.00	155.50	152.00	162.8	172.58	153[1] 82[2]	153[1] 82[2]	188[1] 119[2]
Number of hotels	212	213	215	321	326	329	465[a]	469[a]	476[a]
Number of rooms	6 970	7 470	7 500	9 575	10 025	10 325	25 300[a]	30 600[a]	30 950[a]
Number of beds	12 348	13 248	13 400	17 235	17 303	18 284	45 500[a]	55 500[a]	56 200[a]
Total tourist bed nights (thousand)	880	1 479	1 695	2 534	1 888	1 955	2 146	2 153	2 193
Average room occupancy per year (%)	56.40	56.30	59.90	63.7	54.02	58.6	51	47	53
Number of employees in tourism industries	100 000	110 000	132 000	148 000	156 050	156 500	160 200	198 000	198 557

Source: National Bureau of Statistics, and Tourism Department

[1] Package tour.

[2] Non-tackage tour.

Table 2A. Share of tourism earnings in total export earnings and in GDP, 1990–2004

Year	Tourism earnings ($ million)	Total exports earnings ($ million)	GDP ($ million)	Share of tourism earnings in GDP (%)	Share of tourism earnings in total export earnings (%)
1990	65	538	4 250	1.5	12.1
1991	95	504	4 378	2.2	18.8
1992	120	565	4 509	2.7	21.3
1993	147	750	4 644	3.2	19.6
1994	192	938	4 783	4.0	20.5
1995	258	1266	5 217	4.9	20.4
1996	322	1299	5 426	5.9	24.8
1997	392	1235	5 643	7.0	31.8
1998	570	1110	5 868	9.7	51.4
1999	733	1144	6 103	12.0	64.1
2000	739	1291	9 092	8.1	57.3
2001	725	1456	9 443	7.7	49.8
2002	730	1568	9 807	7.4	46.5
2003	731	1828	10 297	7.1	40.0
2004	746	1938	10 460	7.1	38.5

Sources: Based on data provided by the Ministry of Natural Resources and Tourism and the Bank of Tanzania

Table 3A. International visitor arrivals and receipts in Tanzania, 1995–2004

Year	Number of visitor arrivals	Annual change (%)	Receipts ($ million)	Receipts (million Tanzanian shillings)
1995	295 312	12.89	259.44	155 663.00
1996	326 188	10.46	322.37	194 220.00
1997	359 096	10.09	392.39	235 446.00
1998	482 331	34.32	570.00	370 500.00
1999	627 325	30.06	733.28	586 624.00
2000	501 669	-20.03	739.06	628 201.00
2001	525 000	4.65	725.00	665 115.00[15]
2002	575 000	9.52	730.00	705 618.00[2]
2003	576 000	0.17	731.00	759 070.40[3]
2004	582 807	1.18	746.02	812 676.89[4]

Source: Ministry of Natural Resources and Tourism, Tourism Department.

Table 4A. Visitor arrivals by month, 1996–2004

Year	1996	1997	1998	1999	2000	2001	2002	2003	2004
TOTAL	**326188**	**360 000**	**482 331**	**627 325**	**501 669**	**525 122**	**575 296**	**576 198**	**582 802**
January	24 483	22 370	23 000	24 611	35 066	34 701	51 785	48 480	45 658
February	22 886	22 890	23 400	27 200	35 529	35 186	42 673	42 893	42 176
March	20 177	23 640	23600	28 302	36 549	36 254	44 427	39 842	42 176
1st quarter	**67 546**	**68 900**	**70 000**	**80 113**	**107 144**	**106 141**	**138 885**	**131 215**	**130 010**
April	17 673	20 890	25 500	29 101	82 048	56 826	37 370	38 260	36 324
May	16 568	22 144	26 500	30 100	22 722	27 792	35 897	36 469	37 579
June	20 460	23 400	28 000	32 000	26 970	50 275	43 855	43 499	48 157
2nd quarter	**54 701**	**66 434**	**80 000**	**91 201**	**131 740**	**134 893**	**117 122**	**118 228**	**122 060**
July	27 614	38 400	46 500	48 524	34 638	63 311	54 304	54 895	61 968
August	37 401	43 700	68 500	56 117	40 821	53 751	64 471	64 436	58 164
September	45 325	47 700	70 931	95 041	35 074	37 716	55 998	51 720	56 237
3rd quarter	**110 340**	**129 800**	**185 931**	**199 682**	**110 533**	**154 778**	**174 773**	**171 051**	**176 369**
October	41 346	32 400	58 700	52 099	31 504	32 977	51 146	49 145	47 046
November	26 634	31 786	48 300	64 211	64 201	49 167	41 136	45 050	53 426
December	25 621	31 180	39 400	140 019	56 547	47 167	52 160	61 509	53 896
4th quarter	**93 601**	**95 366**	**146 400**	**256 329**	**152 252**	**129 311**	**144 442**	**155 704**	**154 368**

Source: Ministry of Natural Resource and Tourism, Tourism Department Based on data from Immigration.

Table 5A. Visitor arrivals by mode of transport, 1996–2004

Mode of transport	1996	1997	1998	1999	2000	2001	2002	2003	2004
Total	326 188	359 096	482 331	627 325	501 669	525 122	575 296	576 198	582 807
Air	145 866	160 000	311 406	364 575	311 612	315 073	316 000	320 000	257 195
Sea	21 600	35 000	7 995	6 442	15 081	21 005	20 000	25 000	23 681
Road	149 218	149 996	152 251	220 300	155 116	173 290	214 000	215 000	297 302
Rail	9 504	14 100	10 679	36 008	19 860	15 754	25 000	16 000	4 629

Source: Ministry of Natural Resources and Tourism, Tourism Department Basis data from Immigration

Table 6A. Visitor arrivals by purpose of visit, 1996–2004

Purpose of visit	1996	1997	1998	1999	2000	2001	2002	2003	2004
TOTAL	326 188	360 000	482 331	627 325	501 669	525 122	575 296	576 198	582 807
Leisure, recreation and holidays	219 282	246 000	299 946	383 155	339 596	341 329	358 000	337 000	458 679
Business and professional	64 505	80 982	127 994	132 802	130 201	152 285	115 000	133 000	83 415
Other	42 401	33 018	54 391	111 368	31 872	31 507	102 000	106 000	40 713

Source: Ministry of Natural Resources and Tourism, Tourism Department Based on data from Immigration

Table 7A. Visitor arrivals, by major regions, 1996-2004

Year	Region			
	Africa	North America?	Europe	Asia
1996	141 069	32 184	96 861	56 309
1997	155 909	35 570	107 051	62 230
1998	208 599	47 594	143 229	83 256
1999	271 345	61 908	186 311	10 305
2000	208 959	49 001	157 470	86 601
2001	219 516	45 544	162 225	99 356
2002	252 845	59 077	191 982	73 347
2003	269 922	49 781	191 025	66 144
2004	257 778	53 424	221 865	50 302

Source: Ministry of Natural Resource and Tourism, Tourism Department Based on data from Immigration.

Table 8A: Number of visitors to the main national parks, 1999–2004

National Park	1999	2000	2001	2002	2003	2004
SERENGETI	198 934	113 867	124 553	149 498	152 544	199 302
L/MANYARA	67805	67 935	70 273	71 168	81 285	107 578
TARANGIRE	41 147	48 499	56 871	68 076	61 077	85 791
ARUSHA	19 137	21 731	21 930	25 372	22 338	36 929
KILIMANJARO	21 940	21 025	24 775	25 250	29 523	34 530
MIKUMI	10 986	12 347	11 352	15 766	15 696	19 287
RUAHA	5 274	5 646	6 088	13 094	6 984	11 482
UDZUNGWA	483	751	1 027	1 455	1 569	1 983
KATAVI	368	325	325	1 574	671	1 247
GOMBE	401	361	688	858	667	859
MAHALE	217	196	271	916	586	820
RUBONDO	330	354	266	573	824	458
TOTAL	367 022	293 037	318 419	373 600	373 764	500 266

Source: Ministry of Natural Resource and Tourism

Table 9A. Mainland: Registered investment projects in accommodation, 2002—2004 ($ million)

Ownership	Number	Project value $ million)		Total
		Foreign	Local	
Hotels	75	92.5	50.2	142.7
Lodges	24	19.3	7.7	27
Resorts	10	1.6	3.7	5.4
Camps	19	15.3	9.8	25.1
Total	128	128.7	71.4	200.2

Source: Tanzania Investment Centre

Table 10A. Mainland: Registered investment projects in tour operations, 2002–2004 ($ million)

Ownership	Number	Project value ($ million)		Total
		Foreign	Local	
Foreign	18	22.5		22.5
Local	26		16.1	16.1
Joint venture	31	12.9	7.5	20.4
Total	75	35.6	23.6	59

Source: Tanzania Investment Centre

Table 11A. Mainland: Registered investment projects in restaurants, 2002–2004 ($ million)

Ownership	Number	Project value ($ million)		Total
		Foreign	Local	
Foreign	8	7.4		7.4
Local	6		1.9	1.9
Joint venture[a]	6	2.4	1.7	4.1
Total	20	9.9	3.6	13.4

Source: Tanzania Investment Centre
[a] For purposes of this study any joint venture where the majority shareholding is contributed by a foreign investor was considered as FDI. There were only 2 firms in the sample.

Annex 2. Survey results

The survey was conducted in June 2006 and findings were subsequently analysed and verified at a number of regional meetings through 2007 and 2008. The sample size of tourism establishments interviewed was 31, of which 18 hotels were on the mainland and 5 in Zanzibar, comprising local and foreign-owned establishments. The ranking of the hotels in terms of "stars" is shown in tables 7 and 8 in the main text. Of the tour operator, 10 were interviewed, of which 7 were from the mainland and 3 from Zanzibar.

Table 1B. Annual Accommodation Capacity

Location	Number of rooms	Number of beds	Room occupancy rate (%)	Bed occupancy rate (%)
Arusha	157	440	41.2	28.5
Dar es Salaam	1 123	2 268	53.9	38.6
Zanzibar	244	411	52.2	38.2
Total /average	1 524	3 119	49.1	35.1

Table 2B. Category of tourism market

Location	Upmarket/leisure (%)	Mid-market leisure (%)	Other (%)
Arusha	62.5	30.5	7
Dar es Salaam	55	41	4
Zanzibar	65	30	5
Average	60.83	33.83	5.33

Table 3B. International visitors by purpose of visit

	Number of visitors	Percent
Holiday	39 990	81
Business	4 195	8.5
Others	5 165	10.5
Total	49 350	100

Table 4B. International visitors by nights spent

	Nights Spent	Number of Visitors	Per cent
1	1–3 nights	3 210	6.5
2	4–7 nights	16 840	34.1
3	8 –28 nights	28 100	57
4	29+	1 200	2.4
Total		49 350	100

Table 5B. Proportion of international visitors by travel arrangements and purpose

Travel arrangement	Purpose of visit	
	Holiday	Business
Package tour (%)	71.5	7.4
Non-package (%)	28.5	92.6
Total visitors	39 990	4 195

Table 6B. Main countries of origin of international visitors[a]

	Country	Mainland		Zanzibar	
		Number of tourists	Per cent	Number of tourists	Per cent
1	United Kingdom	4 517	14.5	3 895	21.4
2	Netherlands	4 236	13.6	3 185	17.5
3	Germany	3 022	9.7	1 110	6.1
4	United States	2 928	9.4	1 037	5.7
5	South Africa	2 087	6.7	1 001	5.5
6	Spain	1 838	5.9	855	4.7
7	France	1 589	5.1	819	4.5
8	Australia	1 464	4.7	710	3.9
9	Norway	1 028	3.3	655	3.6
10	Belgium	997	3.2	437	2.4
11	Canada	903	2.9	400	2.2
12	Switzerland	685	2.2	382	2.1
13	Italy	654	2.1	309	1.7
14	Sweden	561	1.8	273	1.5
15	Austria	467	1.5	218	1.2
	Other	4 174	13.4	2 912	16
	Total	31 150		18 200	

[a] Visitors from developing countries were mainly from South Africa

Table 7B. Earnings by type of establishment ($ thousand)

Establishment type	Local	Foreign	Total	Foreign as % of total	Average profitability (%)
Accommodation	378	3 472	3 850	90.1	27
Restaurant	92	848	940	90.2	9
Conferences	58	379	437	86.7	33
Tour operations	206	683	889	76.8	17
Other	25	218	243	89.7	5
Total	758	5 602	6 360	88.0	18.2

Table 8B. Booking arrangements

How bookings were made (%)		
	Foreign-owned firms	Locally owned firms
Using foreign tour operators	43	7
Using foreign travel agencies	15	4
Using local agencies	4	68
Through Internet	23	16
Individually by tour	15	5

Table 9B. Employment

Establishment	Mainland				Zanzibar			
	Total	Men	Women	Share of women in total (%)	Total	Men	Women	Share of women in total (%)
Hotels	1 568	662	906	57.8	410	148	262	63.9
Tour operators	457	376	81	17.7	26	16	10	38.5
Total/average	2 025	1 038	987	48.7	436	164	272	51.2

Table 10B. Employees by skill composition and gender

	High skills (e.g. managerial)				Medium skills (e.g. catering)			Low skills (e.g. cleaning)		
	Total	Men	Women	Share of women in total (%)	Men	Women	Share of women in total (%)	Men	Women	Share of women in total (%)
Hotel	1 393	230	45	16.3	237	584	71.1	87	210	70.7
Tourism	622	127	34	21.1	279	31	10.0	68	83	54.9
Total/average	2 015	357	79	18.1	516	615	54.3	165	293	63.9

Table 11B. Basic monthly pay ($)

	Domestic	Foreign	Ratio of foreign to domestic		Domestic	Foreign	Ration of foreign to domestic
	Hotels				Tour operators		
Lowest wage	50	120	2.4:1	Lowest wage	60	150	2.5:1
Room cleaner/gardener	50	150	3.0:1	Driver	80	180	2.3:1
Housekeeper	110	300	2.7:1	Tour guide	85	210	2.5:1
Desk manager	300	420	1.4:1	Manager	215	450	2.1:1

Table 12B. Average revenue per visitor ($)

Establishment	Mainland			Zanzibar			Tanzania average
	Local	Foreign	Average	Local	Foreign	Average	
Hotels	120	450	285	150	360	255	270
Tour operators	455	820	638	240		240	439
Average	288	635	462	195	360	248	355
Ratio of foreign to local		2.2:1			1.8:1		

Table 13B. Estimates of local linkages of selected products used in the tourism industry (%)

Product/service	Tanzania mainland												Zanzibar												
	Domestic tourism firms			Foreign-owned tourism firms			Domestic tourism firms			Foreign-owned tourism firms		
	Locally bought	Imported	From where purchased	Locally bought	Imported	From where purchased	Locally bought	Imported	From where purchased	Locally bought	Imported	From where purchased
Outsourcing												
Insurance	100	0	Local insurance firm	100	0	Local insurance firm	100	0	Local insurance firm	100	0	Local insurance firm
Telecommunications	100	0	Local suppliers	100	0	Local suppliers	100	0	Local suppliers	100	0	Local suppliers
Security contract service	100	0	SME	100	0	SME	100	0	SME	100	0	SME
Cleaning	100	0	Individuals	100	0	SME	100	0	Individuals	100	0	SME
Laundry	100	0	Individual	100	0	Individual	100	0	Individual	100	0	Individual
Electricity and water	100	0	Public utilities + own supply	100	0	Public utilities + own supply	100	0	Public utilities + own supply	100	0	Public utilities + own supply
Vehicles[a]	100	0	Wholesaler	100	0	Wholesaler	100	0	Wholesaler	100	0	Wholesaler
Petrol/gas	100	0	Wholesaler	100	0	Wholesaler	100	0	Wholesaler	100	0	Wholesaler
Furniture	90	10	SME	15	85	Wholesaler	60	40	SME	10	90	Wholesaler
Fixtures and fittings	95	5	SME	22	78	Wholesaler	85	15	SME	10	90	Wholesaler
Construction materials	97	3	Wholesaler	85	15	Wholesaler	80	20	Wholesaler	75	25%	Wholesaler
Equipment (e.g. refrigerators, cooking ranges, etc)	35	65	Wholesalers/ individual shops	15	85	Wholesaler	45	55	Wholesalers/ individual shops	10	90	Wholesaler
Construction labour	100	0	Contractor	80	20	Contractor	100	0	Contractor	85	15	Contractor
Garments (uniforms)	100	0	SME	72	28	SME	98	2	SME	60	40	SME
Linen	70	30	Wholesaler	45	55	Wholesaler	90	10	Wholesaler	20	80	Wholesaler
Cleaning materials	100	0	Wholesaler	65	35	Wholesaler	100	0	Wholesaler	40	60	Wholesaler
Food items												
Fruit & vegetables	100	0	SME	90	10	SME	98	2	SME	72	28	SME
Beverages	60	40	Wholesaler	30	70	Wholesaler	70	30	Wholesaler	20	80	Wholesaler
Chicken	100	0	SME	85	15	SME	80	20	SME	70	30	SME
Fish	100	0	SME	82	18	SME	100	0	SME	85	15	SME
Beef	100	0	Individual supplier	70	30	Individual supplier	65	35	Individual supplier	30	70	Individual supplier
Lamb and Pork	100	0	Individual supplier	70	30	Individual supplier	80	20	Individual supplier	40	60	Individual supplier
Flour and rice	85	15	Wholesaler	80	20	Wholesaler	65	35	Wholesaler	30	70	Wholesaler

Annex 3. The Kilimanjaro Kempinski Hotel

(i) Establishment and investment level is landmark in Tanzania's hotel industry

Established in 2003, and owned by the Albwardy Group of Dubai, the Kilimanjaro Kempinski Hotel (KKH) is apparently the only (judging by interviews with the hotel managers and other stakeholders) 5-star hotel in the United Republic of Tanzania. Since the hotel rating system is not yet established in Tanzania, this rating is international (and not a local one), as reflected in the amount of investment, the market niche and the services offered or experienced by some clients and suppliers. The hotel is managed by Kempinski group of Hotels, an international hotel management chain. The hotel has 180 rooms, selling at an average of $175 per night (slightly higher than the competing hotels which charge around $135). Exceptional facilities include the presidential and diplomatic suites, executive suites and other deluxe rooms.

The hotel is one of the most successful privatization exercises that has been a significant feature of the hotel industry in Tanzania. Formerly it was known as the Kilimanjaro hotel, a 5-star hotel owned by the State, which was divested in the 1990s along with some others. Its privatization process was somewhat controversial given that some local investors lost their appeal to buy the hotel in favour of the successful buyer from the Middle East, with the management contract given to the Kempinski Group in 2005. The start-up investment made in 2005 was about $40 million, of which construction and renovations cost about $14 million, machinery and equipment $10 million, and operations and logistics about another $10 million, and other costs about $5 million.

(ii) Business performance and prospects

Although it is too early to expect the hotel to have made significant profits, the managers noted the differences in profitability of various services offered by the hotel. Conferences and banqueting are considered the most profitable services, followed by accommodation, while restaurant services were the least profitable. In terms of sales turnover, the following is a rough estimate of the breakdown of earnings for 2005/06: accommodation – 53 per cent, restaurant – 28 per cent, conference services – 12 per cent and other services (e.g. souvenir shop) – 7 per cent.

(iii) Benefit, challenges and obstacles

Clearly, a hotel of this size and rating is likely to have a higher than average import content of its supplies than other foreign-owned hotels. We asked Managers to explain to us where their source of supplies for various requirements (e.g. linen, staff uniforms, construction materials, food and beverage items, utensils, stationeries, etc) and the response was as follows. Based on interviews with the various managers of the hotel, it seems that the share of imported supplies was more than 50 per cent. Of the average room rate mentioned above, only about $15 (about 8 per cent) was spent on local supplies (excluding labour, which is of course a significant expenditure).

The hotel managers identified difficulties in sourcing locally, the most notable being the low quality and lack of standards for most of the supplies, which are important considerations for a hotel of this category that has to be able to provide its customers with world-class standards. The second is the lack of a central procurement facility for hotel supplies in Tanzania, implying that the hotels need to buy from the retail trade instead of in bulk, a practice which adds to transaction costs. It should also be noted that the low level of the manufacturing base and supply chain management in Tanzania has resulted in sustained dependence on imports, which limits the extent to which such investments as the KKH can benefit the economy. To increase spending on local supplies, the hotel recommended deliberate efforts to enhance the capacity of local suppliers to supply to the hotel in order to boost development in Tanzania.

At the time of the survey, the hotel was facing problems with infrastructure especially power, and low level of skills of staff, in addition to the poor quality of supplies. But on the positive side, its management was extremely happy with the way the Government handled the investors, and particularly the successive privatization of the hotel. (This has been documented in detail in MIGA (2006). To increase the impact of tourism investment on the Tanzanian economy, the hotel managers emphasized the need for the Government to address the major challenge of poor infrastructure (e.g. power, water, roads), set up skills development programmes and attract further foreign investments.

The hotel is expected to contribute significantly to the Government's tax revenue: in 2005/06, it paid about $ 1.8 million in taxes. More importantly, the hotel has created employment; in 2005/06 it employed a total of 412 workers, of which 248 (60 per cent) are men and 164 (40 per cent) are women. The relatively higher proportion of men is due to the skill-intensive requirement of the services. The division of employment by skill categories shows that most of the workers (90% per cent) are in the medium-skills category and almost none in the unskilled category. Levels of monthly payments of KKH staff aresimilar to other foreign-owned hotels, but much higher than the locally owned ones. The lowest pay is 100,000 Tanzanian shillings (a little less than $100). Room cleaners/gardeners get only $30 more than this lowest pay (about 130,000 Tanzanian shillings) while housekeepers and managerial posts are paid over one million Tanzanian shillings ($1,000).

(iv) Training is a continuous and strategic intervention

The hotel provides continuous training to its staff to increase their skills in order to provide high quality services. According to the hotel managers, this is an area which has received considerable emphasis. Training is ongoing with almost daily classes for upgrading skills in such areas as English, service standards, customer care, train the trainer and hygiene. The hotel has its own training department, which is quite busy given the tight schedule.

Annex 4. List of people/firms interviewed

I: Zanzibar

No.	Name	Designation	Business name	Address/telephone no.	Ownership	Size[a]
1	Bernard Kitivo	Acting General Manager	Zanzibar Beach Resort Box 2586 Mazizini, Zanzibar	0748-356735	Local	Small
2	Issa Mlingoti	Director, Tourism Planning/ Development	Zanzibar Commission for Tourism Box 1410 Zanzibar	+255- 24- 2233485/6	Institution	
3	Raj Dana	Manager	Mtoni Marine Hotel Zanzibar		Foreign	Small
4	Mustafa Mbinga	Acting Manager	Serena Hotel	Zanzibar 255 272544595	Foreign	Big
5	Ahmada Hassan	Manager	Island Discovery Tours		Local	Small
6	Abdulla S. Abdulla	Tour Manager	Holiday Bookings and Tours Box 2243 Zanzibar	0777 480765	Local	Small
7	Lesse Tareto	Touring Co-ordinator	Oceanic Tours Zanzibar	info@oceantorszanzibar.com	Local	Small
8	Ms Fatma A. Jumbe	Head	ZIPPA Investment Promotion and Marketing and After Care Services		Institution	
9	Adam H.	ZIPPA Statistician	ZIPPA		Institution	
10	Fernandes J.	Assistant Manager	Ras Nungwi Beach Resort	Box 1784, Zanzibar 255 242233767	Foreign	Big

II. Dar es Salaam

No.	Name	Designation	Business name	Address/telephone no.	Ownership	Size
11	Hersi Ilchagi Adam	Operations Manager	Oceanic Bay Hotel	Box 256 Bagamoyo +255-23-2440181-83	Local	Small
12	Agash Gupta	General manager	Millennium Sea Breeze Resort	Box 155 Bagamoyo 023-2440201	Foreign	Big
13	J. Kadu	Manager	Scandinavian Tours Ltd	022861948	Local	Small
14	K. Lyimo	General Manager	Riki Hill Hotel	Dar es Salaam	Local	Big
15	Joybeth Emmanuel	Acting Manager	Peacock Hotel	Dar es Salaam +255 0222114071	Local	Big
16	Edward McAyako	Assistant Manager	Sofia House Hotel	Dar es Salaam	Local	Big
17	Ms A. Nadine	Manager	Sea Cliff Hotel	Dar es Salaam +255 222600380-7	Foreign	Big
18	Mohamed Mohamed	Resident Manager	Paradise Holiday Resort	Bagamoyo +255-23-2440142	Foreign	Big
19	J. Magesa	Administrative & Accounting Officer	Palm Tree Village Resort	Bagamoyo 0744 222340	Local	Small
20	Ms H. Urio	Assistant Manager	Belinda Oceanic Resort	Dar es Salaam +255 22264755	Local	Small

No.	Name	Designation	Business Name	Address/Telephone	Ownership	Size
			III. ARUSHA			
21	Ms Juliana M.	Operations Assistant	Movenpick Royal Palm	Box 791 DSM +255 22 2112416	Foreign	Big
22	Hamis M.	Administrative Assistant	Holiday Inn Dar es Salaam	Box 80022 DSM 255-222137575	Foreign	Big
23	Merghi S.	Administrative Manager	Kunduchi Beach Hotel	Box 361 DSM 255 22 2650050	Local	Big
24	Johnson W.Local.	Assistant Manager	Protea Appartments	DSM 255 22 2666665	Foreign	Big
25	John S. Mmari	Assistant Manager	Ebony Tours & Safaris	Arusha	Foreign	Small
26	Julian Can	Operations Manager	Abercrombie & Kent	Box 427 Arusha +255 272508347	Foreign	Big
27	Arbas Maralina	Acting Operations Manager	Ranger Safaris Ltd	Box 9 Arusha +255 272503023	Foreign	Big
28	Kassim Kindu	Operations Manager	Fortes Safaris Ltd	Box 1364 Arusha 255 2544887	Local	Small
29	Buck Tilley	Manager	Thomson Safaris	Box 6074 Arusha	Foreign	Small
30	Rachesh N.	Accountant	The Arusha Hotel	255 272507777	Foreign	Big
31	Hans Makundi	Operations Manager	New Safari Hotel	255272503261	Local	Big
32	Michael K.	Operations Manager	Kudu Safaris	Box 1404 Arusha 255272506065	Foreign	Big
33	Massawe Ronald.	Administrative Assistant	Capricorn Hotel	Box 938 Marangu 255 272751309	Local	Small

[a]   The size of the surveyed firms is considered small if capital investment in the establishment is less than $ 5 million and big if more than $5 million.

Notes: Entries in the last column are described as: Foreign = Foreign firm; Local = Local firm; Institution = Tourism related (Private or Public) Institution. To conserve space and for anonymity purposes, the above list does not include 96 interviewed workers of different firms and categories.

VI. Uganda country case study[1]

Executive summary

Trends in foreign direct investment (FDI) in the tourism sector in Uganda and its impact on demand, employment and revenues were analysed using two methods: (i) review of secondary data sources, and (ii) a field survey of foreign- and domestic-owned hotels and tour operating firms. The findings are summarized below.

a)   *Trends*

- Uganda's tourism industry suffered greatly during 17 years of political instability starting in 1971. The sector has shown revival and growth since 1992 as a result of the improved political environment. Growth in tourism is evident from: (i) the contribution to the balance of payments by the services sector (mostly tourism) of $115 million relative to Uganda's main export, coffee, which contributed $107 million; and (ii) the number of tourist arrivals, which increased at an annual compound rate of 27 per cent between 2000 and 2004; and (iii) the increasing number of investments in hotel accommodation and tour operations.

- Most of the FDI in tourism has been by individual investors, mainly from, in order, the United Kingdom, Kenya, Canada, South Africa and India.

- Investment by transnational corporations (TNCs) in tourism is still low. Just two of them, the Sheraton Group and Tourism Promotion Services Group, have established hotels. Three international car rental firms (Hertz Rent-a-Car, EuropCar and Avis Rent-a-Car) also have operations in the country. No international tour operators are established in Uganda.

- With respect to the mode of operation of TNC hotels, the Kampala Sheraton Hotel operates as a franchise, as do the three international car rentals. The Kampala Serena Hotel, on the other hand, has signed a 30-year concession lease agreement with the Uganda Government, which is renewable for another 20 years.

- Private individual foreign and domestic investments are made using equity and debt financing, mostly from the European Investment Bank through the Apex loan scheme administered by local financial institutions.

- The main determinants of FDI in tourism include political stability, good infrastructure (e.g. good roads to the tourist attractions), reliability and affordability of inputs for the business, specifically electricity and fuel, and opportunities for investment and growth stemming from high demand and/or limited supply of similar services.

b)   *Impacts*

There is increasing demand for good quality accommodation in Uganda because of the growing number of tourists. This has contributed to boosting FDI in accommodation in the tourist sites by individual investors, which in turn may have led to increasing the number of international visitors.

- The tourism industry has benefited by greater investment in improving the quality of the road infrastructure and Entebbe International airport. However, most of the road infrastructure remains in poor condition. Although the number of international airlines flying into Uganda has increased, respondents noted that competition among airlines is still limited, which contributes to the high cost of air travel to Uganda.

- The Kampala Sheraton Hotel and the Kampala Serena Hotel have invested about $51 million altogether (equivalent to 0.7 per cent of gross domestic product (GDP) at basic prices in 2004) in upgrading to 5-star status. They are also among only four providers of 5-star hotel accommodation facilities in Uganda.

- The international hotels have contributed considerably to job creation. The survey showed that they employed more than 800 staff in total. Their average number of employees was higher than the average number of staff in 15 of 32 manufacturing sub-sectors that were surveyed by the Uganda Bureau of Statistics in 2004. These hotels have also provided demonstration effects to other hotels with respect to customer service and aesthetics. Furthermore, they train individual suppliers on produce handling to enable them to comply with European Union (EU) rules on food hygiene. International hotels appeared to pay wages that were at least 30 per cent higher than the average wages in the industry, and provided more benefits to employees than most other hotels.

- FDI by individual investors in hotels is concentrated in small hotels/guest houses with 30 rooms or less, and in accommodation facilities in the national parks. Conversely, investments by domestic investors are more evenly distributed among the small, medium and large hotel categories. Since most of the domestic-owned hotels are relatively large, in 2005 they generated higher than average revenue and employed more staff (on average).

- The capital investment by foreign-owned tour operators was observed to be about five times higher than the capital invested by their domestic-owned competitors. Foreign-owned tour operators also earned more revenue during 2005 ($870,000 compared to $120,000 for domestic-owned tour operators).

- The number of employees in foreign-owned tour operators was about 50 per cent higher than comparable domestic-owned firms. They were also more likely to provide additional benefits to staff, including medical allowances, social security and other incentives and allowances. Most of the surveyed firms in the sector provided on-the-job training to staff.

- Linkages between hotels and tour operators appeared to be limited. Both the foreign-owned hotels and tour operators surveyed depended more on the Internet for their business, while domestic-owned hotels and tour operators depended more on direct customer links. Foreign and domestic-owned hotels also had linkages with small and medium-sized enterprises that supply items such as uniforms, stationery and fresh milk, and with individual farmers that supply fresh fruit and vegetables and poultry products.

- The survey found notable leakages in the tourism industry because of the relatively underdeveloped manufacturing sector. Firms usually import wines, spirits and specialized food products (e.g. butter, specialty meats) and other manufactured goods. Respondents noted that the local manufacturing sector, specifically agro-processing, faces challenges of producing consistently good quality products.

- The impacts of competition and crowding from tourism appeared to be limited, and not evident, because the industry is still relatively underdeveloped, while the impacts of the tourism industry on poverty were difficult to measure.

c)   *Policies*

The Government of Uganda is cognisant of the need to stimulate investment in tourism. The Ministry of Tourism, Trade and Industry developed a Tourism Policy in 2003 and drafted a Tourism Bill, which has been submitted to the Parliament of Uganda[2].

- Furthermore, in addition to the investment incentives outlined in the Investment Code 1991, the Government has provided specific tax incentives to tour operators and, more recently, to hotels. The tax incentives to hotels were driven by the need to increase the number of quality hotels for the Commonwealth Heads of Government Meeting in 2007.

- Nevertheless, respondents noted the following challenges in the operating environment: unreliable power supply, high costs of fuel and electricity, high taxes, especially on products that are not locally manufactured, poor road infrastructure, limited access to affordable financing, and limited government support in actively marketing Uganda as a tourist destination. It was also noted that implementation of the tourism policy had been slow because of lack of adequate resources.

- The main challenge faced by the Government is to provide an enabling environment that will continue to stimulate investment in sustainable tourism, and to provide adequate resources to facilitate implementation of national policies for the sector in a timely and effective manner.

A. Background

This study was commissioned by the United Nations Conference on Trade and Development (UNCTAD) as part of a wider study on FDI in the tourism sector in developing countries. Country case studies were undertaken in six countries in sub-Saharan Africa.

1. Objectives of the study

The objective of this study is to contribute to existing information on the economic dynamics of FDI in tourism, and to understanding its determinants and its impact on developing country economies such as Uganda. Specifically, the study seeks to provide information on the relative impact of different forms of foreign investment in terms of jobs created, revenues generated, foreign exchange earnings, and the sources and magnitude of value added or "leakages" in Uganda, and how these can change over time.

2. Study methodology and survey sample

This study adopted the following approaches:

(a)   A review of relevant published literature on investment stocks, tourism statistics and government policies relating to tourism.

(b)   Interviews with tourism-related associations, such as the Uganda Hotel Owners Association, and a review of various websites and directories to gather data on the number of hotels, tour operators and car rentals in Uganda.

(c)   Analysis of secondary data on tourism investment projects, tourism statistics and community-driven tourism projects.

(d)   Interviews with policymakers in the tourism sector including the Ministry of Tourism, Trade and Industry, the Uganda Investment Authority and the Uganda Community Tourism Association.

(e)   Telephone interviews with hotels to confirm the number of rooms and kind of ownership, and with safari lodges to gather data on ownership and year of establishment.

(f)   A field survey of a sample of foreign- and domestic-owned tour operators, hotels, safari lodges and car rental firms, using a questionnaire developed by UNCTAD. Respondents were assured of the confidentiality of their answers.

(g)   Interviews with six selected suppliers to hotels.

Duration of the assignment

The study was conducted between 20 June and 8 October 2006. Field interviews were conducted by a consultant assisted by a team of two research assistants who were trained by the consultant to ensure that the data collected were robust and consistent with the requirements of the survey. A feed-back workshop was held in Uganda in December 2007 to present and verify the findings with survey participants and tourism stake-holders, and to promote debate.

Survey of firms

Firms were identified and interviewed as follows: (i) a register of firms in each sub-sector was compiled from several data sources; (ii) subsequently, firms were categorized as either foreign-owned or domestic-owned, based on the consultant's knowledge and other sources; (iii) an equal number of hotels and tour operators were contacted for interviews, ensuring that at least 50 per cent of the firms were foreign-owned and that the major hotels and tour operators were included in the sample; and (iii) firms were interviewed on the basis of their willingness to participate in the survey and their proximity (or the proximity of their head office) to Kampala, Entebbe or Jinja,[3] because of the limited resources available for data collection.

Only hotels and tour operators considered to be major (on the basis of their membership in an industry association or listing in *The Eye* magazine, which targets tourists) were selected for the survey sample (table 1).

Table 1. Size of survey sample by category of accommodation and tour operators

Category[4]	Population Total	Sampled Foreign (owned or managed)	Domestic
5-star hotels	4	2	0
3- or 4-star hotels	13	4	4
Other hotels	120	0	0
Lodges: mid or top market	29	2	2
Lodges: budget or target market not known	7	1	0
Tour operators and car rentals	82	11	10

The data were analysed using the SPSS (Statistical Package for the Social Sciences) analytical programme, using only simple statistical analyses (mean and median) because of the small sample size. The findings of the firm survey are presented in section III of this report.

3. Challenges

- *Survey fatigue*: Several firms contacted were unwilling to participate in the survey citing the large number of surveys that had already been conducted in Uganda without demonstrable value added to the respondents or feedback.

- *Reluctance to provide data*: Most of the respondent firms were unwilling to provide quantitative data. According to these firms, the tourism sector in Uganda is very small and therefore it would be easy to identify specific firms despite the findings being aggregated.

- *Survey timing*: The main survey was conducted during the period June–August, which is also the peak tourism season. Therefore, it was difficult to conduct interviews even when appointments had been confirmed. It took on average three visits before an interview was completed. Interviews with stakeholders were also postponed several times because they were preoccupied with preparations for the meeting of Commonwealth Heads of Government scheduled for November 2007.

- *Sample size*: The survey limited its focus to respondents in Kampala, Entebbe and Jinja towns, so the sample size is small.

4. Report outline

This report is divided into four sections. Section I presents the background and study methodology. Section II provides information on the trends in FDI in tourism in Uganda. The findings of study on the impact of FDI in tourism are discussed in section III, and section IV discusses government policies on FDI in tourism.

B. The changing nature of FDI in tourism

1. FDI in Uganda

The value of total FDI in Uganda was estimated at $237.2 million, which represented 4 per cent of GDP in 2004. These figures are similar to the earnings from traditional export crops (coffee, tea, cotton and tobacco) in 2004. The major sources of foreign direct equity investment (FDEI) in terms of book value[5] were the United Kingdom, the United States, Kenya and Ethiopia: their shares in total FDEI were 52.4 per cent, 19.5 per cent, 15.8 per cent and 12.7 per cent, respectively, during the period 2001–2003.

There was robust growth in FDI, which averaged 30 per cent per annum during the period 1993–2004. The highest average growth rate of 42 per cent per annum was recorded in the period 1996 to 1999. The increased level of foreign private investment during this period could be attributed partly to three initiatives that were implemented to improve the investment climate in Uganda. These initiatives were: introduction of the Investment Code of 1991 on the rights of foreign investors; the return of properties confiscated from Asians during the 1970s;[6] and the revoking, in 1992, of the requirement for majority domestic ownership to qualify for preferences in preferential trade agreements, (Reinikka and Collier, 2001).

Although there was an overall upward trend in total FDI, there was a marginal decline of 0.2 per cent between 1995 and 1996, and a considerable decline of 21 per cent per annum between 1999 and 2001 (annex figure 1A). The downward trend could be attributed to the national presidential and parliamentary elections that were held in 1996 and 2001 and the attendant uncertainty and increased perception of political risk in Uganda. It confirms the importance of political stability in attracting FDI to Uganda.

In the period before 1990, FDI inflows into Uganda were characterized by the following trends:
- An increase in FDI in the period up to 1970, which was attributable to the Government's drive towards industrialization, and the legal protection for FDI provided in the Foreign Investment (Protection) Act 1964;
- A downward trends in the period 1971–1986 resulting from (i) extensive disinvestment during the period 1971–1979 following the expulsion of Asians and expropriation of assets owned by foreign investors in 1972; and (ii) the negative perception of Uganda's investment climate in the subsequent period, 1980–1986, as a consequence of the expropriation and political instability (Obwona,1998).

2. The tourism industry

Tourism is one of the priority industries identified for development by the Government of Uganda. Sustainable and quality tourism is recognized as an important engine for economic growth, livelihood improvement and poverty alleviation (Ministry of Tourism, Trade and Industry, 2003).

Uganda's strategy for tourism is to develop products relating to ecotourism, community tourism, cultural tourism and adventure tourism for the niche market segment of special interest tourists. Products include white-water rafting, bird watching, mountain climbing and nature and cultural walks, among others (box 1). Accordingly, Uganda launched its private-sector-driven geo-tourism strategy in Kampala on 19 July 2006.[7] The strategy seeks to differentiate Uganda among the tourist destinations in the world by incorporating environmental conservation activities and involvement of local communities near the protected wildlife and biodiversity areas in tourism development.

Box 1. Uganda's unique attractions

Gorilla and primate viewing
Uganda's star attraction is the endangered mountain gorilla. There are fewer than 700 mountain gorillas, divided between Bwindi Impenetrable National Park in Uganda and the Virunga Mountains in Rwanda. Within Uganda, five habituated gorilla troops – four in Bwindi and one in Mgahinga National Park - can be visited by a total of 30 tourists daily.

Monkeys are exceptionally well represented in Uganda. Indeed, Kibale Forest boasts the greatest primate variety and density in East Africa. Elsewhere, Mgahinga National Park hosts habituated troops of the rare golden monkey, while Murchison Falls is one of the few East African strongholds for the spindly, plains-dwelling patas monkey.

Bird watching Safaris
Uganda is Africa's most complete bird watching destination, with more than 1,000 species recorded within an area comparable to the size of Great Britain.

White water Rafting
Bujagali Falls, which lies downstream of the Source of the Nile an hour's drive east of Kampala, is the East African counterpart to more southerly 'adrenaline capitals' such as Victoria Falls and Cape Town. Bujagali is the launching point for a commercial white-water rafting route that ranks as one of most thrilling but also one of the safest in the world, passing through three heart-stopping grade five rapids in one day. Other activities at Bujagali include kayaking, mountain biking, quad-biking and a new 44 metre-high bungee jump from a cliff above the Nile.

Excerpts from the Tourism Uganda website: www.visituganda.com

---

The tourism industry suffered greatly during Uganda's long period of political instability (1971–1986), with only 37,000 tourists recorded by the Uganda Bureau of Statistics in the early recovery period in 1992. In response to the improved political climate thereafter, revenue from the services sector (mostly tourism), as indicated in the balance of payments statistics by the Bank of Uganda, increased to $115 million in 2001, ahead of Uganda's main export, coffee, which earned $107 million. The National Tourism Policy 2003 states that tourism has the potential to generate more foreign currency revenue than agriculture and industry combined.

The number of tourists visiting Uganda is still low: about 86,000 holiday tourists in 2004, according to data provided by the Uganda Bureau of Statistics (UBOS, 2005). The target is to increase the number of holiday tourists to approximately 100,000 by 2013. The total number of tourists to Uganda, including business, transit and other visitors was about 512,000 in 2004. Most of the visitors were from Africa (79 per cent), followed by Europe (10 per cent) and North America (5 per cent). The low number of visitors from developed countries (15 per cent) suggests that Uganda is not a magnet for international tourists. For example, net migration from Uganda during 2004, of about 8 per cent, was equivalent to the total visitor arrivals from the United Kingdom and the United States combined. The share of Asia, West Asia and ceania in total tourist arrivals was 6 per cent in 2004 (UBOS, 2005).

It is recognized, however, that tourism in Uganda is on an upward trend. Data from UBOS (2005) show that the number of tourists visiting Uganda increased at an annual compound rate of 27 per cent between 2000 and 2004. Tourists from African countries (mostly Kenya) showed the largest increase (32 per cent), followed by North America (8 per cent), Asia (7 per cent) and Europe (2 per cent). Conversely, the number of tourists from West Asia and Oceania declined by 1 per cent and 7 per cent, respectively. However, the contribution of these regions to total tourist arrivals was very small, at less than 1 per cent in 2004.

3. FDI in tourism in Uganda

Foreign direct investment in tourism is a small but growing component of total FDI. The market value of FDEI in the accommodation and tourism sector was $1.2 million in 2000,[8] or 0.17 per cent of total FDEI stocks (Bank of Uganda, 2002). Among 16 sectors analysed, the contribution of tourism in terms of market value was only higher than that of manufacturing of machinery, motors and equipment (0.01 per cent) and of agriculture, hunting, forestry and fisheries (0.06 per cent) (annex table 1A). Nevertheless, the growth rate of tourism in terms of market value was very high: 464 per cent between 1999 and 2000. There is no outward investment in the tourism sector.

The contribution of transport and storage, which includes tour operators and travel agents in addition to land and air transport services, was higher at 3.05 per cent in 2000. The change in market value of investment in this category was 23 per cent between 1999 and 2000. It was not possible to estimate the contribution of tour operators and travel agents within this category.

Trends in investment in the tourism sector

Uganda's tourism industry can be divided into four main activities: hospitality (including accommodation, restaurants and entertainment facilities), transport (including airlines, car rental services and other transportation), tourist attractions, and community activities.

A first view of trends can be seen by examining aggregate data from the Uganda Investment Authority whose mandate includes maintenance of a database of all foreign projects. The Authority registered about 90 foreign-owned (or managed) tourism projects between 1992 and 2006, the estimated value of which was $190 million.

It is estimated that only about 53 per cent[9] of these projects were actually implemented. Although the reasons for abandoning the projects are not documented, inferences could be drawn from responses given by foreign investors on the main challenges of operating in Uganda. They include:

- Infrastructure problems, in particular the poor state of the roads to tourist attraction sites. For example, it takes about 8 hours (equivalent to one day) to travel to Bwindi Impenetrable Forest National Park for a one-day safari.
- High operating costs, attributed mostly to the high price of fuel[10] and very unreliable and costly electricity supply. For example, power tariffs rose by 37 per cent in June 2006 and were expected to further increase before the end of 2006.
- Perceived insecurity in some parts of Uganda.

Nevertheless, it was noted that the conversion rate of investments in the tourism sector is higher than the average conversion rate for all investments, which was estimated to be in the range of 38–40 per cent between 1993 and 1995 (Obwona, 1998).

Foreign individual investors from five countries implemented 66 per cent of the tourism projects: the United Kingdom (20 per cent), Kenya (17 per cent), Canada (13 per cent), South Africa (9 per cent) and India (7 per cent).

The estimated compound growth rate in the number of implemented foreign-owned tourism projects was 12 per cent per annum for the period 1992–2006, representing an average implementation rate of about three tourism projects annually. Although the growth rate appears to be high, it should be noted that the starting base was low.

A second source of information can be obtained from examinging investment projects in the various activities: hotels, safari lodges, tour operators, travel agencies, airlines and car rental companies.

Hotels

Prior to 1992, most of the major hotels in Uganda were government-owned. Between 1994 and 2000, 16 hotels were divested under Uganda's privatization programme, of which 12 were purchased by Ugandan investors. The four other hotels that were purchased by foreign investors had a total value of $32 million, which was equivalent to 87 per cent of the total value of assets sold (annex table 2A).

Two hotels (Nile Hotel Limited and Apollo Hotel Limited) that had been divested to foreign companies were subsequently repossessed by the Government following the failure of the first owners to fulfil the conditions of their purchase agreements. These hotels now have new management: the Apollo Hotel Limited is now Kampala Sheraton Hotel and Nile Hotel Limited is now Kampala Serena Hotel.

According to the 2005 survey of accommodation facilities conducted by UBOS, the number of gradable accommodation facilities in Uganda was 181 in 2005, 52 per cent of which were concentrated in the major towns of Kampala, Entebbe, Jinja and Mbarara. The survey results further showed the total number of accommodation establishments in Uganda to be 1,310 with a total of 19,381 rooms. Most of these facilities were located in the smaller towns and provided basic services.

Membership of the Uganda Hotel Owners Association (UHOA) in 2005 comprised 99 hotels, motels, campsites and lodges (including nine hotels under construction). The total number of rooms in 2005 was estimated to be close to 4,000. Most of these hotels were purchased by the current owners or constructed after 1980.

At the time of researching this report, international hotel chains with operations in Uganda include the Kampala Sheraton Hotel, which is a member of the Starwood Hotels and Resorts Worldwide Inc. managed by Midroc Africa and headquartered in Saudi Arabia, and Kampala Serena Hotel, opened in mid-2007, which is managed by the Tourism Promotion Services (TPS) Group. A South African chain has signed a management contract with Ugandan private investor (Avemar Group) to manage a $100 million hotel for 15 years - the Protea Hotel Entebbe (U). Two additional international chains set to construct hotels in Uganda included the Kampala Hilton Hotel and Kingdom Hotel Investments. One of the chains described its new hotels in Kampala and Entebbe as being part of its "aggressive African expansion plan"; with the timing of opening encouraged by the Commonwealth Head of Government meeting in November 2007.

Other hotels in Uganda are

primarily either independent units or belong to local chains. Uganda has two domestic hotel chains: the Imperial Group, comprising four hotels, and the Speke Group that comprises three hotels. Ugandans own about 80 per cent of the independent gradable hotels, and the other 20 per cent have foreign ownership.

The data on the gradable hotels further show that foreign-owned major hotels mostly target the middle and upper segments of the market. The average price per room[11] at the time of the survey was $122, with a price range of $39–$319. Most domestic hotels by comparison targeted mainly the low-budget and mid-market segments, at an average price per room of $45 with a range of $20–$180.

Safari lodges

Before 1990, there were just three main lodges located in the national parks, which were owned by the Uganda Government: Mweya Safari Lodge, Para Safari Lodge and Chobe Lodge. These were subsequently divested to private investors between 1995 and 2000. There are now 36 main lodges in or near the major tourist sites, which were constructed or leased from the Government between 1990 and 2006 (annex table 3A).

Foreign individual investors own or are shareholders in 63 per cent of the safari lodges and tented camps (table 2). In many instances they were awarded concessions by the Uganda Wildlife Authority (UWA) to operate in the wildlife protected areas and national parks. The duration of concessions for hotels and lodges is between 20 and 30 years, and for tented camps it is between 10 and 15 years.

Table 2. Period of establishment of major safari lodges and tented camps

Period	Ownership		
	Domestic	Foreign	Government
Before 1990	0	0	3[a]
1990–1995	5	3	0
1996–1999	4	10	0
2000–2005	2	9	0
2006	2	0	0
Total	13	22	3[a]

[a]The three government owned safari lodges have now been divested and are now either foreign or domestic-owned.
Source: Field survey

Tour operators

Tour companies provide ground handling services for tourists. They are engaged in preparing, pricing, marketing and selling of holiday packages for tourists. Their activities include arranging ground transport, tour guide services and accommodation, and identifying attractions for domestic, regional and international tourists.

There are more than 60 main tour operators in Uganda. Although data on the years of establishment of the tour operating firms were not readily available, most of them seem to have been established after 1990.

All foreign-owned tour operating firms (41 per cent of the main tour operators) are owned by individual investors. About 76 per cent of all tour operators are members of the Association of Uganda Tour Operators (AUTO), including 92 per cent of the foreign-owned tour firms and 65 per cent of the domestic-owned tour firms. The requirements for membership in AUTO are as follows: a minimum of two tour vehicles, at least one employee should have earned a degree in tourism, and the company should have office premises and a minimum of two computers.

Tour operations are increasingly becoming vertically integrated, with backward linkages to accommodation (12 tour operating firms) and forward linkages to ticketing services (more than 80 per cent of the tour operating firms). According to the tour operators, the main driver for investment in accommodation is the shortage of quality accommodation, especially in the national parks, which is unable to meet the high demand, thus making this a profitable area for investment. The main attraction in the ticketing business is the predictable margins and the reliable income from outbound tourists, especially during the low season for inbound tourism.

Previously, tour operators focused on selling safari products. However, Uganda faces stiff competition in this area from Kenya and the United Republic of Tanzania, which are more popular tourist destinations for big game viewing. They also have more wildlife than Uganda, as Uganda's wild animals are still recovering following the period of instability. Tour operators have now diversified into selling packages with products that are unique to Uganda (box 2).

Box 2. Tour packages offered by tour operators in Uganda

Attraction	Number of days (package)
Gorilla tracking	3 days (including two days of travelling)
Chimp tracking	3 days (including two days of travelling)
White-water rafting	½ day–1 day
Birding safaris	14–30 days
Mountaineering	7 days

Source: Field survey

Airlines

International airlines

Uganda has one international airport, Entebbe International Airport, from where 11 international airlines operate to different foreign destinations. They include seven regional carriers: Air Rwanda, Kenya Airways, Air Tanzania, Sudan Airways, South African Airways, Ethiopian Airlines and Egypt Air. The international carriers are: British Airways, KLM Royal Dutch Airlines, Emirates Airlines and SN Brussels Airlines. All the international airlines are members of the Board of Airline Representatives (BAR).

During Uganda's period of instability, only four airlines flew into Entebbe International Airport: Uganda Airlines (the national airline at the time), Kenya Airways, Ethiopian Airlines and Sabena Airlines (now SN Brussels) of Belgium. Some of the international airlines that had suspended flights to Entebbe Airport in the 1970s have now resumed operations, the first being British Airways in 1989, followed by KLM in 2005. Emirates Airlines, Gulf Air, South African Airways, AfricaOne, Alliance Air, Air Rwanda, Air Tanzania, Sudan Airways, Egypt Air and East Africa Airlines started operations between 1991 and 2004. However, four of them ceased operations between 1994 and 2003: Gulf Air ceased flying into Uganda in 1994, Alliance Air collapsed in 2000, Uganda Airlines was liquidated in 2001 and AfricaOne Airlines ceased operations in 2003. East African Airlines, which had majority domestic shareholders suspended flights in 2005, was sold to new investors in 2006 and is expected to resume operations soon.

Uganda now has a new national carrier, Victoria International Airlines, in which the Uganda Government has a 25 per cent equity stake. Other members of the consortium include investors from Switzerland and South Africa. Scheduled to launch operations in November 2006, it is expected to contribute to increasing the number of international visitors, including tourists, to Uganda.[12]

Domestic airlines

Uganda has nine privately owned domestic carriers. Four of these carriers, Eagle Air, United Airlines, Dairo Air Services and Bukasa Air Services, are owned by Ugandans. Eagle, United and Dairo operate scheduled flights from Entebbe Airport, while Bukasa Air Services provides only chartered air services. The domestic airlines sector has also attracted five foreign investors that operate chartered flights to different parts of Uganda (annex table 4A).

Travel agents

In Uganda, travel agents specialize in providing ticket handling services for outbound travellers. Their main service is selling air tickets on behalf of the international airlines. They receive commissions of between 3 and 10 per cent of the air ticket price.

Most travel agents are either members of The Association of Uganda Travel Agents (TUGATA) or the International Air Transport Association (IATA). Their membership in either of these associations improves their commissions. Members of IATA earn commissions of up to 8 per cent of the ticket price and members of TUGATA earn 5–6 per cent of the ticket price, compared with non-members that earn commissions of between 3 and 5 per cent of the ticket price.

Uganda-based travel agents do not generally provide ticket handling services for inbound tourists. Their role is usually limited to reconfirming foreign passengers' tickets for their homebound journey, either directly for the tourists or on behalf of the tour operators.

Car rental services

Car rental services in the industry are provided by car rental companies, tour companies and individuals.

There are at least 19 firms operating in the Uganda market: three international franchises (Avis Rent-a-Car, EuropCar and Hertz Rent-a-Car), one foreign-owned company and fifteen domestic-owned companies (*The Monitor Telephone Directory*, 2006). There are also several individuals that provide car rental services. Anecdotal information indicates that most of the car rental firms were established between 1990 and 2006. These firms consider their activities as representing a growing market and therefore an attractive investment. A number of car rental firms have expanded their activities to include tour operating services, thus competing with tour operators. Accordingly, they do not have to rely on the tour operators for customers, and ensure earnings throughout the year by organizing such services as hotel reservations (with commissions of up to 10 per cent of the room rates) and tour guide services.

The survey showed that car rental firms did not seem to have developed alliances with tour operators or the hotels. For example, the Kampala Sheraton Hotel had its own car hire service. Furthermore, only one of the known car hire firms had established formal links with major hotels to provide transportation. Other firms relied on individual customers who contacted them either directly or through the Internet.

According to the Investment Code Act (Cap 92), foreign investors in car rental and taxi services are not eligible for investment incentives.

4. Mode of entry

a.   *Hotels and safari lodges*

International hotel chains

The modes by which foreign tourism investors and enterprises are present in Uganda vary. The Kampala Sheraton Hotel operates as a franchise, while the Kampala Serena Hotel is operating under a lease concession agreement with the Uganda Government tenable for a period of 30 years, starting in 2004. The concession is renewable for another 20 years after that date. Funding for the renovation of the Serena was from shareholder equity[13] and other financing sourced internationally by the shareholders. As part of its concession agreement, the Kampala Serena Hotel is required to pay the Government an annual fee equivalent to 4 per cent of net revenue. The South African hotel chain Protea's new $100 million hotel at Entebbe, by comparison, is owned by a Ugandan private investor (Avemar Group) and Protea has signed a management contract to manage the hotel for 15 years.

Other hotels and safari lodges

According to the survey of firms, most of the other hotels were constructed using equity financing. There appeared to be very small differences between the sources of funding for investment by the foreign and domestic-owned hotels surveyed, as shown in table 3. The implication from the data (and from discussions) is that investors use savings as their principal source of funds for investment in the hotel business.

The major source of debt financing was the European Investment Bank (EIB) – Apex Scheme, which is administered by the Bank of Uganda through selected financial institutions in the country. It provides short-

and long-term financing to selected sectors (including tourism) at rates lower than the prevailing market rates. Foreign-owned and domestic-owned hotels have equal opportunities for accessing this financing if they are able to fulfil the conditions of the lending institution.

Table 3. Financing for hotel construction/upgrading (survey respondents)

Type financing	of Percentage of respondents	By ownership (Percentage of respondents)	
		Foreign owned	Domestic owned
Equity	50	50	50
Debt	25	17	33
Equity and Debt	25	33	17
Total	*100*	*100*	*100*

Source: Field survey

b.   *Tour operators*

Type of investment and nature of operation

The survey of firms showed that tour operators in Uganda financed their investments using mainly equity financing (table 4a).

Table 4a. Nature of financing of tour operating firms (survey respondents)

Type of financing	Percentage of respondents
Equity	95
Franchise	5
Total	100

Source: Field survey

Most tour operators reported working independently, suggesting that this allowed: (i) flexibility, to enable the business to adapt quickly to Uganda's changing business climate, (ii) faster and more efficient decision-making, and (iii) easier sourcing of capital from local banks.

Qualitative findings from the survey showed that a firm operating as a franchise benefited from its association with the international brand for its operations and marketing. Business operational guidelines were provided by the international partner, and the partner also referred customers to the franchisee. Indeed, one of the firms operating as a franchise reported that 80 per cent of its customers were referred by the international chain.

However, there are also challenges in this type of operation in the Ugandan environment. According to the respondents, the high standards demanded by the international partner required more investment and they were therefore required to charge higher prices than competitors. This affected revenues when operating in a business environment with low entry barriers and relatively low volumes of upmarket customers, especially since many customers in the car hire business were price sensitive. Nevertheless, a comparison of three firms in the same line of business showed that although the international franchise charged higher fees than the foreign and domestic-owned firms, its asset utilization (or asset efficiency) was higher and it generated more revenue per customer in 2005 (table 4b).

Table 4b. Comparison of asset utilization and revenue per customer by different tour operators (survey responses)

Type of operation	Asset utilization ratio	Revenue per customer ($)	Fee per day ($)
International franchise	0.5	620	215
Foreign-owned equity firm	0.3	120	150
Domestic-owned equity firm	0.2	50	150

Source: Country case-study field survey

5. Conclusions

The tourism industry in Uganda is growing steadily following 17 years of political instability during the period 1971–1988. Growth in the sector is demonstrated by (i) the increasing contribution of tourism to the balance of payments relative to Uganda's main export, coffee; (ii) the rising number of tourist arrivals; and (iii) the growing number of investors (foreign and domestic) in hotel accommodation, tour operations and airlines.

FDI in accommodation and tour operations is dominated by individual investors. Only two international corporations, the Sheraton Group and Tourism Promotion Services Group, have established hotels. Three international car-hire firms (Hertz Rent-a-Car, EuropCar and Avis Rent-a-Car) also have operations in the country.

Private individual foreign and domestic investors in the sector use mainly equity and debt financing for their investments. With respect to the international hotels, the Kampala Sheraton Hotel operates as a franchise, while the Kampala Serena Hotel has a 30-year concession agreement with the Uganda Government.

C. The impact of FDI in tourism

This section provides information on the impact of foreign investment relative to domestic investment in hotels and tour operations, in terms of demand, revenue, jobs and employment conditions, and on the sources of value-added or leakages, using mostly data from the survey of firms.

1. Capital and infrastructure effects

a. Hotels

International hotel chains

International hotel chains have helped to broaden the range of hotel accommodation that was available in Uganda, especially at the business and high quality sectors of the market. The Kampala Serena Hotel, which was officially opened in November 2006, is one of the largest hotels in Uganda. It, along with the Sheraton hotel, provides the only five-star hotel accommodation currently available in the capital city, and so the international investors have contributed a valuable addition to the accommodation that is provided domestically. The estimated total cost of renovation and upgrading the Kampala Sheraton Hotel and the Kampala Serena Hotel was $51 million, equivalent to about 0.7 per cent of GDP at basic prices in 2004 - which is a significant contribution to the capital base in Ugandan tourism.

Other hotels

FDI in hotels by individual as opposed to chain investors is concentrated in small hotels/guest houses with 30 rooms or less (71 per cent of hotels) and large-size hotels with at least 100 rooms (24 per cent of hotels) (table 5a). By comparison, investment by domestic-owners is more evenly distributed among the different hotel room categories.

Table 5a. Number of rooms in the major hotels, by ownership

No. of rooms	Foreign (owned or managed)		Domestic-owned	
	Per cent of respondents	Cumulative total percentage of respondents	Per cent of respondents	Cumulative total percentage of respondents
10 or less	24	24	11	11
11–20	29	53	17	28
21–30	18	71	27	55
31–50	0	71	21	76
51–100	6	76	10	86
101+	24	100	14	100
Total	**100**		**100**	

Source: UHOA, field survey

The survey findings show that foreign-owned hotels are more likely to be represented in the middle and upper end of the tourist market segments (table 5b). About 65 per cent of foreign-owned firms surveyed charged room rates of more than $90 compared to only about 30 per cent of domestic-owned firms. At the very top end of the market, in the five-star bracket where foreign hotel chains are present, hotel room rates of more than $200 are charged. Since many respondents did not provide data on the amount of capital invested to enable direct comparisons, we used room rates as a proxy for the amount of capital invested (*ceteris paribus*). From this, it could be deduced that foreign-owned hotels had invested comparatively more capital than the domestic-owned hotels.

Table 5b. Room rates in the major hotels, by ownership

Room rates[a] ($)	Foreign (owned or managed)		Domestic-owned	
	Per cent of respondents	Cumulative total percentage of respondents	Per cent of respondents	Cumulative total percentage of respondents
10–30	0	0	21	21
31–50	14	14	37	58
51–70	7	21	5	63
71–90	14	36	8	71
91–100	36	71	3	74
101+	29	100	26	100
Total	**100**		**100**	

Source: Field survey
[a] Per weeknight for an executive or deluxe double room (with bed and breakfast).

b. Safari lodges

Most investors in safari lodges appeared to target the middle and upper end of the tourist market (table 6). The room rates in mid-market safari lodges were in the range of $40–$90 per person, while they were higher in the upmarket lodges. Most of the accommodation (57 per cent) in the national parks was owned by individual foreign investors, rather than chains.

c. Tour operators

The survey of firms found that the value of assets owned by foreign-owned tour operators was $110,000 at the median, with a mean value of $1.3 million. This shows that there are a large number of small firms of relatively small capital value, and then a small number of much larger firms. The value of assets of domestic-owned tour operators was $23,000 at the median (indicating a much smaller firm size than the foreign operators, for the majority of firms) although the mean value was roughly similar at $1.1 million. Their main assets were tour vehicles, which accounted for more than 50 per cent of the total asset value. The average value of assets of foreign-owned tour operators, which was higher, was in line with the requirements of the Investment Code 1991, which stipulates that a foreign investor should invest at least $100,000 in order to qualify for an investment licence.

Table 6. Major safari lodges and their target markets

No.	Location	Number	Foreign-owned Middle and upper segment of market	Foreign-owned Budget	Domestic-owned Middle and upper segment of market	Domestic-owned Budget
1	Murchison Falls N. P	5	4	1	0	0
2	Semuliki N.P.	3	1	0	1	1
3	Kibale N. P	3	2	0	1	0
4	Rwenzori Mountain N. P.	0	0	0	0	0
5	Queen Elizabeth N. P	3	1	0	2	0
6	Bwindi Impenetrable N. P.	6	3	1	0	2
7	Mgahinga Gorilla N.P.	2	2	0	0	0
8	Jinja - Source of the Nile	2	1	0	1	0
9	Lake Mburo N. P.	1	1	0	0	0
10	Sipi Falls, Mt. Elgon	2	1	0	1	0
11	Lake Victoria Islands (Bulago, Bugala, Samuka)	3	2	0	1	0
12	Lake Bunyonyi	3	0	0	3	0
13	Kidepo N. P.	1	1	0	0	0
	Total	**34**	**19**	**2**	**9**	**3**

Source: Field survey

d. Impact on road infrastructure

According to an OECD report (2006), the road network in Uganda is estimated to cover around 72,000 km. Of this total, the national grid accounts for only 15 per cent (10,500 km), community roads for 41 per cent, district roads 38 per cent, urban roads 6 per cent and private roads less than 1 per cent. The quality of the national roads is rated as follows: just 20 per cent are rated "good", 62 per cent "fair" and 18 per cent "poor".

According to the survey, respondents claimed that one of the main constraints of operating in Uganda was the poor state of the roads. However, the country has received large amounts of donor funds to repair most of the rural road infrastructure, with the aim of improving access of rural farmers to markets and thus contributing to economic growth and poverty reduction. For example, the European Commission provided support to the Government of Uganda to rehabilitate the Masaka– Mbarara Road (completed in 1992), upgrade numerous roads in Kampala and its suburbs (1993–1996), maintain the national roads in south-west Uganda (1995–2001) and improve the Malaba border post. The total expenditure on national road improvement and development was $365.8 million during the period 2002/03–2004/05.

The tourism industry has benefited from the improvements to the road infrastructure in terms of better access and reduced travel time to most of the tourist attractions. For example, 8 out of the 13 main tourist sites are in the regions of south/south-west Uganda, which benefited from EU support for road infrastructure during the period 1993 to 2001. Furthermore, the national roads (listed in box 3*)* are at various stages of upgrading or repair and will improve access to the tourist sites shown (Times Journal of Construction and Design, 2006).

Box 3. National roads and major tourist sites

National roads[a]	Tourist site(s)[b]
Karuma – Olwiyo – Pakwach	▪ Murchison Falls and Karuma Falls
Fort Portal – Hima – Kasese - Kikorongo	▪ Rwenzori Mountains
Kasese –Kilembe, Kikorongo –Katunguru	▪ Queen Elizabeth N.P, Bwindi and Kibale N. P.
Equator Road	▪ Maramagambo forest
Busunju-Kiboga - Hoima	▪ Murchison Falls to Kibale N. P.
Kafu - Masindi	▪ Murchison Falls

[a] Budget Speech 2006/07
[b] Field survey

e. The airline industry

Since Uganda is a landlocked country, air transport is a major link with the rest of the world. During the period 1991–2000, the infrastructure and facilities at Entebbe International Airport underwent major repair and renovations (Uganda Investment Authority, 2003?). At the same time there was an increase in the number of international airlines operating from Entebbe, from 4 in 1988 to 12 in 2001, and at the time of the survey there were 11. The number of international tourists using air travel also increased at an annual compound rate of 11.4 per cent, from 35,704 in 1992 to 131,029 in 2004 (UBOS, 2005).

However, respondents to the survey noted that despite the increase in the number of international airlines, competition in the airline industry was still low, thus contributing to the high cost of air travel to Uganda and to making Uganda an expensive tourist destination.

In the budget speech for the financial year 2006/07, the Uganda Government committed to investing in the capitalization of the Civil Aviation Authority to enable the Authority to upgrade facilities at the international airport so as to cope with the growth of international passenger traffic and foster regional competitiveness. Furthermore, airport facilities were to be upgraded as part of preparations for the Commonwealth Heads of Government Meeting scheduled for November 2007.

2. Impact on demand

Data from UBOS on the number of visitors to the national parks show that only 86,111 people visited the 10 major national parks in 2004. Figure 1 compares the number of visitors to selected national parks with the number of major accommodation facilities in the parks in

2004. Establishment of accommodation facilities in these tourist sites appears to have been in response to demand from the increasing number of tourists. Considering that most of the accommodation facilities in the national parks are foreign-owned (annex table 3A), it could be inferred that the rise in the number of tourists is contributing to greater foreign investment in hotels/safari lodges.

Figure 1. Number of accommodation facilities and visitors in selected national parks in 2004

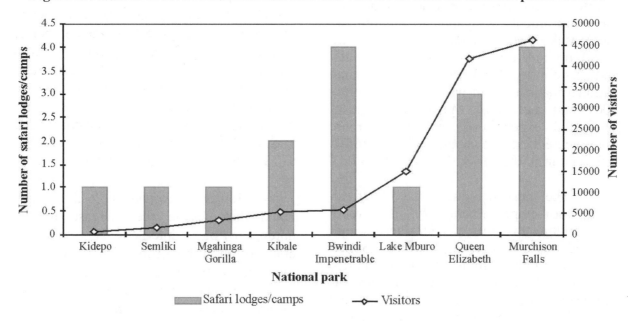

Sources: Field survey for safari lodges/tented camps; Uganda Bureau of Statistics (2005). Migration and tourism, Report IV, 2000–2004, for visitor Data.

a.   *Hotels and safari lodges*

Occupancy rates

The occupancy rates in the hotels increased during the period 2003–2005. The average occupancy rate was estimated at about 70 per cent in 2005. A comparison of the occupancy rates of foreign-owned and domestic-owned hotels shows that the foreign-owned hotels had higher occupancy rates (table 7a). The lower average occupancy rate of 40 per cent in the main safari lodges during 2005 is perhaps a reflection of the still relatively low numbers of tourists visiting the national parks.

Revenue

The revenue earned by the international hotel chains over the period 2003–2005 increased steadily, at an average annual rate of 4 per cent. Their total annual revenues were over $10 million in 2005. Annual revenues of other foreign-owned hotels were lower than those of the domestic-owned hotels in 2005 because most of them were smaller in size on average. The domestic-owned hotels also reported higher revenues per visitor in 2005 (table 7a). On a unit basis, however, the estimated revenue per bed for foreign-owned and domestic-owned hotels was comparable in 2005.

Table 7a. Revenue indicators for hotels, 2005

Indicator	Foreign-owned	Domestic-owned
Occupancy rate		
Mean	79%	61%
Revenue ($)		
Mean	114 160	1 045 429
Median	112 500	210 000
Revenue per customer/day ($)		
Mean	71	118
Median	62	90
Number of rooms		
Mean	34	45
Number of beds		
Mean	45	82
Revenue per bed/night ($)[a]	2 500	2 560
Average length of stay (days)	3	2

Source: Field survey
[a] Median value of sales

Sources of visitors

The source regions for most visitors to hotels in Uganda were Europe (37 per cent), the United States (18 per cent) and the rest of Africa (16 per cent). Just 8 per cent of visitors were from Asia. The major source countries were the United States (18 per cent), the United Kingdom (15 per cent), Kenya (6 per cent) and South Africa (5 per cent). This finding is consistent with a recent study (MoTTI, 2003) that reported that 61 per cent of the tourists in 2003 were from Kenya, South Africa, the United Kingdom and the United States.

Most of the guests at the foreign-owned hotels (44 per cent) made their bookings through the Internet compared to just 13 per cent of those at the domestic-owned hotels in 2005. The main method employed for bookings in domestic-owned hotels was through corporate reservations (37 per cent). Foreign-based tour operators were the least used source of visitors' hotel bookings in 2005 (figure 2).

Payment for services

The survey revealed that, for the most part, tourist transactions in the hotel industry were in foreign currency, although many hotels (foreign and domestic) allowed tourists to pay in the local currency (Uganda shillings). It was noted that more domestic-owned firms (57 per cent) took only foreign currency compared to foreign-owned firms (38 per cent). All payments from abroad were in foreign currency.

Profits

Hotels based in the national parks and targeting the middle to upper segment of the tourist market reported that they did not make any profits on the revenues earned. They cited low visitor occupancy rates and high operating costs, mostly because of high expenditure on generator fuel, which constituted up to 10 per cent of total revenue.

Although most respondents were unwilling to state their profits, 86 per cent of foreign-owned hotels and 71 per cent of domestic-owned hotels indicated that they reinvested their profits mostly in business expansion and facility upgrading. The major sources of profits for hotels in descending order were accommodation, restaurants and other services (e.g. conferences) (table 7b). Foreign-owned hotels reported slightly higher margins for accommodation compared to domestic firms. Domestic-owned hotels reported comparatively higher margins with respect to restaurants and other services.

Taxes

Most firms were unwilling to provide information on taxes paid. However, hotels pay a value-added tax (VAT) of 18 per cent on accommodation and a corporation tax of 30 per cent.

Figure 2. Methods of booking hotel accommodation, 2005

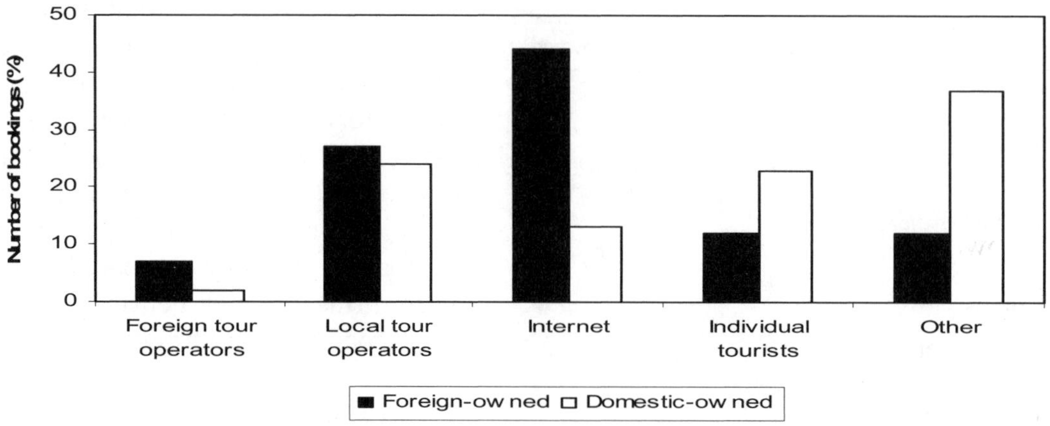

Source: Field survey

Table 7b. Contribution of different services to hotel profits, by hotel ownership (survey respondents) (%)

Financing	Ownership	
	Foreign-owned	Domestic-owned
Accommodation	69	58
Restaurants	26	33
Other (e.g. conference services)	5	8

Source: Field survey

b. Tour operators

Number of tourists and revenue

Tour operating firms with foreign ownership earned more revenue and had more customers than domestic-owned tour operators (table 8). A major reason for this is that foreign tour operators have more tour vehicles; transport is the main source of revenue and profits for these firms.

Table 8. Revenue indicators for tour operators, by ownership (survey respondents)

Indicator	Foreign-owned	Domestic-owned
Revenue ($)		
Mean	1 538 208	1 487 910
Median	870 000	120 000
Total no. of visitors		
Mean	1 931	584
Median	700	312
Revenue per customer in 2005 ($)		
Median	1 240	385
Asset value ($)		
Mean	1 300 000	1 100 000
Median	110 000	23 158

Source: Field survey

Payment for services

Payments to tour operators are often in foreign currency, specifically dollars. Most tour operators (45 per cent of foreign and 60 per cent of domestic) reported accepting only foreign currency. The rest gave their customers the option to pay in local or foreign currency. In 2005, respondent foreign-owned and domestic-owned tour operators earned 69 per cent of their revenue in foreign currency.

Most of the customers paid for services from abroad, with funds transferred to the company's account in Uganda or abroad. The proportions of foreign- and domestic-owned tour operators that reported that services were paid for locally was less than 50 per cent. The proportion of clients paying in local currency was 47 per cent and 41 per cent for foreign-owned and domestic-owned tour operators, respectively.

However, the mode of payment for services depends on the agreed terms and the tourist's preference. Two methods are usually employed: (i) a tourist may be required to pay an initial deposit or commitment fee before the visit and the balance on arrival in Uganda, or (ii) the tourist may negotiate with the tour operator to pay an initial deposit on arrival in Uganda and make the rest of the payment on return to the home country.

Source of tourists

The main individual source countries of customers for the tour operators in descending order were the United Kingdom, the United States, Germany, South Africa and Kenya. Foreign-owned and domestic-owned tour operators attracted customers from similar source countries (figure 3). Most of the visitors using tour operators were from Europe, which accounted for 21 per cent of total customers. Tour operators, regardless of ownership, attracted mostly tourists on holiday (table 9a).

Profits

All of the foreign-owned tour operating firms reported reinvesting their profits in the business, compared to 70 per

cent of domestic-owned firms. The major areas of investment included purchase and maintenance of office equipment and tour vehicles and establishment of hotels (table 9b).

Taxes

Most firms were unwilling to provide information on taxes paid., however tour operators pay a corporation tax of 30 per cent on gross revenue.

Table 9a. Purpose of visit, by ownership of tour operating firm

Ownership of firm	Proportion of tourists (%)			
	Holiday	Business	Other	Total
Foreign-owned	73	10	16	100
Domestic-owned	58	41	1	100
Total	**70**	**17**	**13**	**100**

Source: Field survey.

Table 9b. Distribution of reinvested profits by ownership of firm (%)

Areas for reinvestment	Foreign-owned tour operators	Domestic-owned tour operators
Purchase and maintenance of office equipment	64	33
Purchase of more vehicles	54	78
Hotel construction	38	22
Improving employee salaries and benefits	27	33
Other business owned by the firm	27	0
Promotion activities	18	22
Staff training	0	22

Source: Field survey.

Figure 3. Main source countries/regions of customers of tour operators (survey respondents)

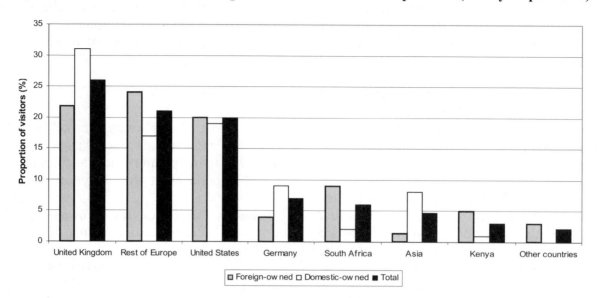

Source: Field survey

3. Impact on human resources

a. *Hotels and safari lodges*

Number of employees

The survey showed that international hotel chains contributed considerably to job creation, and were among the largest employers in Uganda. The two international hotel chains had a combined total of 861 employees. The average number of employees in these hotels was higher than that in 15 of 32 major manufacturing establishments that were surveyed by UBOS in 2004 and this is likely to have increased further since the entry in recent years of additional, large foreign hotels. Up to 95 per cent of the employees were Ugandan nationals. Female employees accounted for 37 per cent of total employees in the hotels surveyed (table 10a).

The survey findings suggest that when hotels of a similar size are compared, domestic-owned hotels employed more staff than their foreign-owned competitors, though foreign-owned hotels had a slightly higher number of employees at the median owing to their larger size (figure 10a). Overall, however, foreign and domestic-owned hotels seemed to have similar characteristics.

The proportion of females employees in hotels and safari lodges was 37 per cent of total employees (28 per cent at the median) and the ratio of management staff to total staff was about 10 per cent (table 10a). However, domestic-owned hotels appeared to employ women mostly at the middle and high-skill levels whereas foreign-owned hotels employed women at all skill levels – low, medium and high.

Expatriates

The survey showed that hotels employed expatriates in high level management positions, which is indicative of a shortage of locally available high-skilled management manpower. Expatriates comprised 50 per cent of managerial staff in foreign-owned hotels, but 36 per cent in domestic-owned hotels (table 10b*)*.

Table 10a. Employment in hotels and safari lodges (survey respondents)

	Foreign-owned		Domestic-owned	
	Number	Share in total (%)	Number	Share in total (%)
Total employees				
Mean	38		116	
Median	40		36	
Female employees				
Mean	14	37	43	37
Median	11	28	10	28
Managerial staff				
Mean	4	10	11	9
Median	4	10	3	8
Female managerial staff				
Mean	2	50	2	18
Median	2		1	33
Medium-level staff				
Mean	10	26	7	6
Median	5	13	6	17
Mid-level staff (female)				
Mean	5	50	3	43
Median	2	40	2	33
Lower level staff				
Mean	24	63	97	84
Median	18	45	28	78
Lower level (female)				
Mean	5	21	13	13
Median	4	22	0	0
Ratio of guests to staff				
Mean	2		4	

Source: Field survey.

Table 10b. Employment of expatriates in hotels and safari lodges, by ownership (survey respondents)

	Foreign-owned	Share in total managerial staff (%)	Domestic-owned	Share in total managerial staff (%)
Number of firms with expatriates in top management positions	8	88	4	57
Expatriates in high-level management				
Mean	2	50	4	
Median	2	50	4	36
Expatriates in middle level management				
Mean	0		1	
Median	0		0	

Source: Field survey

Training

The international hotel chains appeared to train all their staff by sending them on development programmes within the hotel chain.

With respect to the other hotels, the survey findings suggested that it was routine for the hotels and safari lodges in Uganda to move staff within the business to enable them to gain different skills, and training was provided mostly on the job.

The number of staff trained in foreign-owned and domestic-owned hotels was fairly similar: 88 per cent and 86 per cent respectively. Most respondents noted that, in general, employees were recruited without specific training for the hotel industry. Training was therefore provided to the different levels of staff, including medium and high-level management staff, chefs, kitchen staff, waiters and bartenders, room attendants and housekeeping staff, and security and maintenance staff.

Uganda has one national training institution for the sector, the Hotel and Tourism Training Institute in Jinja. However, none of the respondents mentioned sending their employees to that institute for training. This could be attributed to the low quality of training it provides as inferred from the Tourism Policy (2003), which states "the government shall improve the quality of training at the Hotel and Tourism Training Institute through introduction of a certification, diploma and accreditation system". The Ministry of Tourism, Trade and Industry plans to establish training clinics for hotels.

One hotel mentioned hiring staff from the Uganda Management Institute to provide in-house staff training in management. In addition, most local managers received their training and experience in the industry from Canada, India and Kenya.

Wages, staff turnover, pensions and benefits

The international hotel chains reported that they paid wages that were at least 30 per cent higher than the average wages paid in the hotel sector for the different levels of staff employed.

Uganda does not have an official minimum wage. Eighty eight per cent of foreign-owned hotels and 67 per cent of domestic-owned hotels reported that staff wages are dependent on levels of skills and work experience. Of the foreign-owned hotels, 25 per cent reported paying wages that were 25 per cent higher than average wages for their industry. There was a difference of 8 per cent in the number of foreign or domestic hotels that reported paying lower wages than the average for the industry (table 10c), but those that reported paying wages that were 30 per cent lower than the average also said that they provided extra benefits to staff such as lunch and transport to the workplace.

Table 10c. Comparison of wages paid by hotels, by ownership (survey respondents)

Wage level	Hotel ownership	
	Foreign (%)	Domestic (%)
Higher	25	0
Average	50	67
Lower	25	33

Source: Field survey

The international hotels surveyed provided their staff with medical insurance, medical care and social security benefits, and also paid staff a bonus from a 5 per cent levy billed from specific sources of revenue in the hotel. With respect to the independent (i.e. not part of a chain) hotels, it was noted that, in general, more domestic-owned hotels provided benefits to their staff than the foreign-owned hotels (table 10d). The benefits included health insurance (for managerial staff), medical insurance and social security.

Table 10d. Staff benefits provided by independent hotels, by ownership (survey respondents)

Benefits	Foreign-owned	Domestic-owned
Health insurance	38	59
Medical expenses	63	67
Social security	88	100

Source: Field survey.

The survey showed that hotels had a low staff turnover, of less than 1 per cent per annum, partly because of conducive working conditions provided by the employers, comparatively good employment opportunities (as hotels and lodges were often the main employer in the community, especially safari lodges), and limited alternatives because of the high level of unemployment in Uganda. Hotels that operate in the rural areas usually recruit their employees from the nearby communities, which also explains the low staff turnover rate.

Nevertheless, there was a notable link between wages paid and staff turnover, especially for hotels located in Kampala. Seventy-five per cent of hotels that reported paying lower wages than the average for the industry also reported moderate or high staff turnover in 2005. In comparison, just 33 per cent of hotels that paid wages similar to the average had moderate or high staff turnover levels. Overall, 71 per cent of domestic-owned hotels reported low staff turnover rates compared to 62 per cent of foreign-owned hotels.

b. Tour operators

Number of employees

Foreign-owned tour operators were observed to employ up to 50 per cent more staff than the domestic-owned tour operators (table 11a). The proportion of female employees was similar in foreign- and domestic-owned tour operating firms, at about 30 per cent. Women tended to be employed mostly in managerial and high-skilled, non-managerial positions.

Foreign-owned tour operators employed more staff at the lower levels (e.g. as drivers, tour guides) than the domestic tour operators. They had more assets (tour vehicles), as noted earlier, and therefore required more staff on their payroll to operate those assets.

Foreign tour operators preferred to use expatriate staff to manage their businesses, and employed one expatriate on average. Domestic-owned tour operators had Ugandan managers, usually the owners, and did not employ expatriate staff.

Training

It was observed that tour operators tended to move staff within the business to improve their technical versatility. In addition, 90 per cent of foreign-owned tour operators and all domestic-owned tour operators provided on-the-job training to staff.

In 2005, tour operators spent less than 1 per cent of their revenue on formal staff training programmes (i.e. domestic or international courses). However, the survey findings showed that formal training for staff was provided by more foreign-owned tour operators (about 46 per cent) than their

domestic-owned competitors (only 23 per cent). The proportion of staff trained by foreign- and domestic-owned firms was not very different at the median: 27 per cent and 20 per cent respectively.

Table 11a. Employment by tour operators, by ownership (survey respondents)

	Foreign-owned		Domestic-owned	
	Number	Percentage	Number	Percentage
Total employees				
Mean	24		13	
Median	15		10	
Female employees				
Mean	7	29	4	31
Median	5	33	3	30
Managerial staff				
Mean	7	29	3	23
Median	3	30	3	30
Share of female managerial staff in total managerial staff (%)				
Mean	2	29	1	33
Median	1	33	1	33
High-skilled (non-managerial) staff				
Mean	8	33	3	23
Median	5	33	2	20
Share of high-skilled female staff in total high-skilled staff (%)		50		
Mean	4	60	2	67
Median	3		2	100
Other staff				
Mean	5	21	6	46
Median	4	27	4	40

Source: Field survey.

More domestic-owned firms sent their employees to attend national training courses compared to foreign-owned firms (table 11b). The employees sent for training included senior management staff, tour consultants, ticketing staff, accountants and drivers. Ticketing staff and tour consultants usually attend IATA courses provided by TUGATA. Uganda does not have a national accredited institution to train tour operators.

Table 11b. Training provided to staff, by ownership of tour operators (survey respondents)

Variable	Foreign-owned	Domestic-owned
No. of employees trained		
Mean	11	3
Median	4	2
Proportion of firms providing on-the-job training	90%	100%
Proportion of staff attending national courses	55%	70%
Proportion of staff attending international courses	27%	20%
Training budget ($)		
Mean	3 400	375
Median	3 050	175

Source: Field survey.

Wages, pensions and benefits

Most of the tour operators (81 per cent foreign-owned and 70 per cent domestic-owned) had firm-specific minimum wages for different skill levels. The survey findings showed that a high percentage of foreign-owned tour operators (40 per cent) reported paying wages that were higher than the average wages for their industry compared to 10 per cent of domestic-owned firms. The wages were on average 30 per cent higher than the sector average. Nevertheless, the findings also showed that some foreign-owned firms (10 per cent) also paid lower wages than the average for the sector.

Moderate staff turnover was reported by 9 per cent of foreign-owned tour operators, compared with 20 per cent of domestic-owned firms that reported moderate to high staff turnover rates. The major reasons given by firms for the low staff turnover were good staff remuneration, a good working environment and staff training. It should be noted that some firms stated temporarily laying off of staff during the low tourist season, which lasts six months, and rehiring them during the peak season. All firms that paid lower wages for the sector also had a high staff turnover rate

of up to 20 per cent in 2005. Twenty per cent of firms that paid wages comparable to other firms in the industry reported moderate to high staff turnover rates of 10–20 per cent.

Table 11c. Comparison of wages paid by tour operators, by ownership (survey respondents)

Wage Level	Percentage of respondents	
	Foreign (%)	Domestic (%)
Higher	40	10
Average	50	90
Lower	10	0

Source: Field survey

More foreign-owned than domestic-owned tour operators provided staff benefits and contributed to the national pension scheme for staff.

Table 11d. Staff benefits in tour operating firms, by ownership (survey respondents)

Benefits	Percentage of respondents (%)	
	Foreign-owned firms	Domestic-owned firms
Health insurance	36	20
Medical expenses	18	0
Social security	63	30
Incentives and allowances	54	10

Source: Field survey.

4. Linkage effects

a. Hotels and safari lodges

Procurement policy

All of the foreign-owned hotels surveyed had a central procurement policy compared with 71 per cent of domestic-owned hotels. Since most of the hotels are privately owned, capital purchases or purchases above a specified threshold were made by the owner of the business. The general manager or purchasing officer had discretion to purchase most other items, usually food and beverages.

More than 80 per cent of respondents reported experiencing difficulty in procuring some items required for their daily operations, particularly specialty and tinned food items, wine, cleaning chemicals, equipment and fittings (box 4). The hotels either imported the products (e.g. equipment, cleaning chemicals, toiletries and fittings) or purchased them from wholesale suppliers/importers. Since these relatively high value items are not locally produced, the need to import them results in a major leakage from the industry. Hotels usually stock up these items, especially food items, when they become available.

Some of the food items such as butter, ice cream, sausages and bacon are manufactured locally but hotels reported that they tended to import them in practice, because they were often in short supply. Overall, imported products were preferred because the locally manufactured products were reportedly of low or inconsistent quality.

Suppliers

The survey found that most of the purchases made by the hotels were on a cash basis, except in some supermarkets and major beverage depots that allowed the hotels to purchase goods on credit. International chains had accounts with their major suppliers and thus purchased goods on credit.

Most hotels had established direct links with local farmers by purchasing perishable food items directly from them. Farmers were paid cash on supply of the items. A noted indirect link with rural farmers was through purchase of agro-based manufactured products supplied by SMEs, which obtained their raw materials from local farmers. Hotels did not provide data on the value of supplies purchased in 2005.

Box 4. Products that are difficult to procure locally (survey respondents)

Product category	Item	Reason
Food items	▪ Chicken ▪ Fresh milk ▪ Meats (including sausages, bacon) ▪ Ice cream, butter milk, butter ▪ Seafood, tinned foodstuffs ▪ Fresh vegetables	▪ Not available because of bird flu epidemic ▪ Scarcity attributed to foot and mouth disease in south-western Uganda ▪ Hotels prefer the quality of imported products ▪ Not manufactured locally ▪ When out of season
Beverages	▪ Wine	▪ Not manufactured locally and very expensive
Chemicals	▪ Cleaning chemicals	▪ Hotels prefer the quality of imported products
Equipment	▪ Spare parts (e.g. for air conditioners, laundry machines, boats) ▪ Kitchen equipment ▪ Generators	▪ Not manufactured locally, imported products are scarce and expensive.
Fittings	▪ Hotel fittings	▪ Not manufactured locally. Imported products are expensive

Source: Field survey.

Most materials used during construction were purchased locally. One international hotel chain mentioned that all construction and furnishing works were subcontracted. Unique or specialty construction materials (e.g. tents for tented camps or floor tiles) were imported by both the foreign- and domestic-owned hotels. Highly skilled expatriates were usually employed to manage the construction process and to supervise the local labour force employed in construction. Hotels based in Kampala imported most of their furniture and fittings, while safari lodges tended to use local furniture, as they preferred the indigenous, Ugandan look.

Table 12. Suppliers of main products to the major hotels, by ownership (survey respondents)

Supplier	Products		Sources
	Foreign-owned hotels	Domestic-owned Hotels	
Wholesalers	▪ Manufactured food items ▪ Beverages (beer, water, soft drinks, wine) ▪ Stationery ▪ Cleaning chemicals ▪ Cement ▪ Fresh milk ▪ Toilet soap and washing powder ▪ Sugar ▪ Fresh fruit and vegetables	▪ Wines and spirits ▪ Beverages ▪ Manufactured food items ▪ Fuel ▪ Cosmetics ▪ Bed linen ▪ Crockery	▪ Local manufacturers (e.g. beverages, fresh milk, sugar, stationery) ▪ Other products are imports
SMEs	▪ Cosmetics ▪ Bed Linen ▪ Manufactured cereal products e.g. maize flour, ground nuts ▪ Cooking oil ▪ Uniforms ▪ Milk	▪ Cooking oil ▪ Stationery ▪ Coffee and tea ▪ Meat products ▪ Cleaning chemicals ▪ Uniforms	▪ Local manufacturers ▪ Cotton for bed linen supplied by local farmers
Individuals	▪ Services ▪ Beef ▪ Fish and poultry ▪ Vegetables and fruit ▪ Crafts ▪ Perishable products	▪ Vegetables and fruit ▪ Beef, poultry and fish ▪ Perishable products	▪ Local farmers

Source: Field survey.

b. Tour operators

There were similar numbers of foreign-owned and domestic-owned tour operators that did not have ties to any organization, and therefore operated independently: 54 per cent and 50 per cent respectively. Most of the tour operators targeted tourists directly. Some tour operators reported cooperating with wholesalers abroad or having links with the following international organizations: Association of American Travel Agents, the American Public Transport Association (APTA) and VIRTUOSO, a consortium of leisure travel consultants.

The main approach employed by tourists to contact foreign-owned tour operators in 2005 was the Internet. Domestic tour operators were usually contacted directly. The Internet was the method least employed in contacting domestic tour operators. Foreign-based tour operators in general had a limited source of customers for Ugandan-based foreign and domestic-owned tour operators (figure 4).

Most tour operators did not seem to have formal links with the hotels except where they owned the hotel. The tour operators recommended accommodation for tourists according to the price the tourist was willing to pay (budget, middle or upper segment of the market) and the location to be visited. Hotels and safari lodges paid a commission of up to 10 per cent of the room price to the tour operators when they made a reservation.

Figure 4. Methods of booking of tour operators in 2005

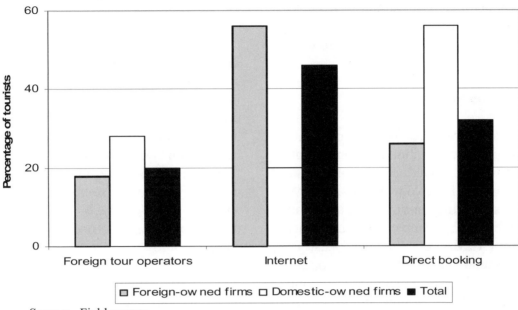

Source: Field survey

c. Crowding out effects

At the macro level it was not possible to determine crowding out effects in the tourism industry, while at the micro level there was no evidence of such effects. During the field survey, no qualitative information was gathered that would suggest crowding out effects in the budget, either in the middle or upper segment of the market for the accommodation and tour operator businesses. Firms were able to invest regardless of ownership. Business performance depends on the operational effectiveness of the firm.

d. Community linkages

More domestic-owned hotels (71 per cent) reported links with the local communities compared to foreign-owned hotels (63 per cent). Most hotels provided services to the local communities as part of their corporate social responsibility policy. The community links included: paying school fees for disadvantaged children, providing social services (e.g. eye clinics, public health project for HIV/AIDS victims

and single mothers), road construction, establishing income-generating projects for the communities (e.g. beekeeping, goat-rearing, jewellery making), donations (e.g. linen and food), and giving priority to the surrounding community in staff recruitment.

Some individual agricultural produce suppliers had benefited from training on product handling provided by one international hotel. The agricultural produce supplied to the hotel must comply with the EU regulations on hygiene, and to make this possible the international hotel had specifically worked with individual smallholder egg suppliers and vegetable growers (mushroom and lettuce producers). The hotel also encouraged the vegetable farmers to introduce new varieties of vegetables which it would purchase.

As far as tour operators were concerned, a slightly higher proportion of domestic-owned tour operators (80 per cent) reported links with the local communities compared to foreign-owned tour operators (72 per cent). The community links included participatory environmental conservation activities, employment and youth training, monetary contributions and funding of community projects.

5. Environmental impact

The international hotel chains stated they complied with national environmental regulations as a matter of policy. For example, the Kampala Sheraton Hotel reported submitting environmental reports to the National Environmental Management Authority (NEMA) on a regular basis. The mission statement of the newly opened Kampala Serena Hotel included implementation of sound environmental protection policies.

Other hotels and safari lodges reported that they complied with national environmental laws relating to waste management, including proper waste collection and disposal, prevention of air and water pollution and conservation of the flora and fauna around the hotel. Hotels and safari lodges located near the national parks reported undertaking an environmental impact assessment (EIA) as part of their concession agreement with the Uganda Wildlife Authority (UWA). They are also required to comply with the rules and regulations of NEMA and UWA.

Seventy-one percent of foreign-owned hotels believed they did more than comparable hotels to protect the environment compared to 57 per cent of domestic-owned hotels. The remainder (29 per cent foreign and 43 per cent domestic-owned) believed they put as much effort in this area as other similar hotels. Just 10 per cent of foreign-owned and domestic-owned hotels were members of Green Globe 21. One of the respondent firms mentioned that it had taken specific steps to introduce the Green Globe 21 certification programme to

Uganda. None of the hotels had an ISO 14000 certificate.

The private sector in the tourism industry has taken specific steps to promote sustainable tourism in Uganda. Individual investors have established ecotourism projects. For example, a foreign-owned hotel was working with the Africa Wildlife Foundation and researchers from an American University to habituate a new group of gorillas in south-western Uganda, and with the Uganda Wildlife Authority to reduce poaching in one of the national parks.

The perception among some tour operators, however, is that some hotels had had a negative impact on the environment. Foreign-owned firms were reported to have had less of a negative impact on waste and littering, noise pollution, the landscape and on water and wetlands than their domestic-owned competitors. However, responses were based mainly on anecdotal information relating to incidents where specific firms had reclaimed wetlands and undertaken deforestation to construct hotels and this may not be representative of the industry as a whole.

6. Indirect effects

Competition effects

According to information from tour operators, hotels and safari lodges, one of the major advantages of operating in the Ugandan market is that the tourism industry is growing and there is limited competition in the sector. Therefore, competition effects are limited.

Demonstration effects

Anecdotal information showed there had been demonstration effects by the international hotel chains in raising the standards of customer service provided by the major independently owned hotels, as well as in terms of aesthetics. The international chains had also attracted some of the better skilled and more experienced personnel in the industry because of the better remuneration they offered. In turn, other hotels had been obliged to improve their own employment conditions in order to retain staff.

Foreign investment in accommodation facilities in the national parks in Uganda has had demonstration effects for domestic firms. All nine concessions for accommodation facilities that were awarded by the Uganda Wildlife Authority (UWA) during the period 1993–2005 went to firms that were classified as foreign-owned.[14] However, in 2006, two domestic-owned firms – Great Lakes Safaris and Mosa Courts – applied for and were awarded concessions to operate in Kibale Forest National Park and Queen Elizabeth National Park respectively.

Anecdotal information showed that domestic-owned tour operators were also increasingly offering specialty tourism products including chimpanzee tracking and birdwatching, following the example of their foreign-owned competitors.

Spillover effects

Fifty-eight per cent of tour operators observed that foreign investment in the rural areas where the national parks and wildlife reserves are located had contributed to improved infrastructure in those areas and better housing in the surrounding communities whose members were employed by the hotels.

The Kampala Serena Hotel is expected to contribute to increased exposure of Ugandan local artists. The hotel's construction is consistent with the Serena philosophy of integrating local art and culture into the design of each hotel,

and showcases the skills of several Ugandan artists in its carved panels, mosaic pillars, copper fretwork and traditional jewellery and wall hangings displayed throughout the hotel.

7. Impact on poverty

The impact of FDI on poverty was difficult to estimate. However, data provided by the Uganda Community Tourism Association (UCOTA), which develops tourism at the grassroots level in Uganda, shows that at least 32 community projects had been established to provide tourist services in some of the tourist sites - with the implication being that as tourism in general is increased, there can be potential spill-over benefits to communities. These services included nature walks, handicrafts, homestead visits, accommodation, food and beverages. The communities had 864 members (90 per cent female). Their total annual revenue, based on estimated earnings for the first quarter of 2006, was expected to be about $20,000. Nevertheless, the benefits of tourism to rural communities are limited. According to NEMA (2005), "While the growth in tourist numbers and earnings in the aggregate is welcome, it also raises equity issues. For example, rural communities are currently receiving minimal benefits from tourism; and their participation in tourism ventures is limited".

8. Conclusions

There is increasing demand for good quality accommodation facilities in Uganda because of the increasing number of tourists. This has contributed to increasing individual FDI in accommodation at tourist sites. At the same time, increasing FDI may also have contributed to the rise in international visitors. The home country of the foreign investor was among the leading sources of visitors to the investors' hotels, according to the responses gathered during the survey.

The tourism industry has benefited from increasing investment in improving the quality of road infrastructure and of Entebbe International airport. However, most of the road infrastructure is still in poor condition. Despite an increase in the number of international airlines flying into Uganda, respondents noted that competition in the sector was still limited, which contributed to the high cost of air travel to Uganda.

The survey showed that international hotels had contributed considerably to job creation, employing about 800 personnel in total. Furthermore, these hotels provided demonstration effects with respect to customer service and aesthetics. They also trained individual suppliers on produce handling to enable them to comply with EU rules on food hygiene. International hotels appeared to pay wages that were at least 30 per cent higher than the average wages in their industry, and they claimed to provide more

benefits to employees than most other hotels.

The number of employees in foreign-owned tour operators was about 50 per cent higher than comparable domestic-owned firms. The foreign-owned tour operators also appeared to provide additional benefits to staff, including medical allowances, social security and other incentives and allowances. Most of the firms provided on-the-job training to staff.

Linkages between hotels and tour operators seemed limited. Foreign-owned hotels and tour operators depended more on the Internet than did the domestic-owned firms, while the latter depended more on customer bookings for their business. There were also linkages with SMEs for the supply of items such as uniforms, stationery and fresh milk, and with individual farmers for the supply of fresh fruit and vegetables and poultry products.

D. National and regional policies

1. Tourism policy, 2003

The general objective of the Tourism Policy, 2003 is to create an enabling environment for growth of the tourism sector in Uganda, and thereby ensure that tourism becomes a vehicle for poverty reduction in line with the Government's overall goal of poverty reduction. The tourism policy covers the areas of economic development, institutional organization, environmental sustainability and cultural promotion.

Stakeholders agree that the tourism policy is all-encompassing and defines the roles of communities, the private sector and the public sector in community development. However, they also note that the policy attempts to address all tourism issues and may not be sufficiently focused. Implementation of the policy is limited because the Ministry of Tourism, Trade and Industry is understaffed and under-resourced. Furthermore, it is argued that the policy gives too much responsibility to the private sector in marketing tourism, which should be the role of the Government.

The Ministry of Tourism, Trade and Industry has also drafted a Tourism Bill that has been submitted to the Parliament of Uganda. This was passed into law in 2008, after the completion of this project.

2. The Investment Code Act Cap 92

The Uganda Investment Authority (UIA) was established in 1991 and aims to be a "one stop facilitator" for investors. Investment in Uganda is governed by the Investment Code Act, which provides for the licensing of investment, protection of foreign investments, and agreements for the transfer of foreign technology and the right to transfer profits and capital earned in

foreign exchange outside the country. Uganda's incentive regime was changed in 1997 to end the 5 year income tax holiday for new investments. The UIA is in the process of updating the Investment Code.

Table 13. Policy measures relating to foreign investment

Policies	Relevant provisions
Investment policy	▪ Foreign investors require a minimum of $100,000 in planned investment in order to secure an investment licence from UIA. For domestic investors, the minimum requirement is $50,000. Local investors, however, may proceed with their investment without licensing with the Authority. ▪ Foreign investors who have invested more than $500,000 may repatriate their investments and dividends and receive foreign exchange to pay debts incurred in the business. *(Source: Investment Code Act, Cap 92)* ▪ Foreign investors in car hire services are not eligible for investment incentives.
Competition policy	▪ Uganda does not have a competition law.
Land Law	▪ Non-citizens can lease land for a period of up to 99 years; ▪ A non-citizen cannot acquire or hold *mailo* land or freehold land. *Mailo* land is registered land held in perpetuity and having roots in the allotment of land pursuant to the 1900 Uganda Agreement; *(Source: The Land Act 1998)*
Taxation and incentives	Uganda's Incentive Allowance Scheme provides for: ● Initial allowances of 50%–70% on plant and machinery depending on location; ● Initial annual allowance of 25% on start up costs for 4 years; ● Initial allowance of 20% on hotel and industry buildings; ● A depreciation rate of 5% for hotels, industrial buildings and hospitals; ● Zero tax on imports of plant and machinery; ● A uniform corporate tax of 30%; ● Possible VAT (18%) deferral. *(Income Tax Act 11 of 1997)*
Treatment of expatriates	▪ Work permits for foreign employees at $1,000. ▪ There are no restrictions on the number of expatriates that can be hired by a firm. *(Source: The Uganda Budget Speech 2006/7)*
Labour laws	▪ The Employment Act 2000 does not have specific provisions relating to foreign-owned companies or expatriate labour.
Revenue sharing	▪ Uganda Wildlife Authority has a revenue-sharing policy, whereby 20% of total gate entry collections are paid to the sub-county, for community development programmes. ▪ UWA is promoting a culture of ensuring that the local people living around parks are given priority for jobs near the national parks.

3. Investment incentives specific to the tourism industry

There are specific incentives provided to investors in the tourism industry that have an investment licence. Most of the incentives relating to removal of taxes for construction and furnishing of hotels were spurred by the need to increase the number of hotels providing quality accommodation in time for the Commonwealth Heads of Government meeting in November 2007. The incentives are:

- Hotels that are in upcountry locations do not pay 18 per cent VAT on hotel rooms.
- Hotels are eligible for incentives such as a VAT refund on building materials during the construction period.
- An initial depreciation allowance of 20 per cent on the cost of an industrial building (including a hotel) is granted in the first year of use, with an annual rate thereafter of 5 per cent.
- Materials for hotel construction or renovation that are not locally produced can be imported duty free subject to approval by the Minister of Tourism, Trade and Industry prior to importation.
- Hotel equipment imported by a licensed hotel for its own use, which has been engraved or printed or marked with the hotel logo, is exempt from duty. Examples include refrigerators and freezers, kitchenware, cookers, air conditioning systems, cutlery, television sets, carpets, curtains, furniture and linen.
- Tax-free diesel is provided for thermal power generation for business operations by hotels. The generator should have a minimum capacity of 100 kVa.

- Specialized tourist trucks can be imported duty free, but are subject to 18 per cent VAT and their import should be approved by the Uganda Tourist Board.

4. Perceptions relating to the investment climate in Uganda

Survey respondent firms indicated the following as the best aspects of the operating environment in Uganda:
- Availability of cheap labour and easy access to land.
- Limited competition in the tourism industry, and the unexploited potential for tourism.
- Limited bureaucracy, although some firms also reported bureaucratic challenges in establishing new projects.
- Relative security in the main towns.
- Easy access to the judicial system.

The challenges that were reported included:
- High fuel and utility costs, especially of electricity. One large hotel mentioned that it spent about $55,000 per month on generator fuel because of the frequent power load- shedding.
- Poor road infrastructure and high costs of air travel to Uganda.
- Limited government support in actively marketing Uganda worldwide as a tourist destination.
- Corruption.
- High taxes on products required by the industry but not produced locally (e.g. an excise tax of 70 per cent on wines and spirits).
- Shortage of qualified skilled staff.
- Limited access to affordable financing, and relatively high bank interest rates.
- Lack of exclusivity zones in the cities.

- Inadequate enforcement of minimum standards for the tour operators.

5. National priorities

National policy is consistent with the priorities of the tourism sector. The Government is cognisant of the requirements for stimulating investment in tourism. For example:

- The tourism policy recommends focusing on the niche market segments (e.g. birdwatching, butterfly safaris, gorilla tracking, white-water rafting, and community and ecotourism).

- The policy further notes the importance of marketing the tourism sector and the need to involve all stakeholders in marketing efforts.

- The tourism policy recognizes that initiatives to stimulate investment in the sector should include reduction of import taxes on capital equipment and zero VAT on tourism services.

- The UIA has in place an investment scheme that allows accelerated depreciation for tax purposes.

The main challenge faced by the Ugandan Government is to provide an enabling environment that will continue to stimulate investment in sustainable tourism, and to provide adequate resources to facilitate the implementation of the national tourism policy in a timely and effective manner.

6. Regional integration

Within the African region, Uganda is a member of the Common Market for Eastern and Southern Africa (COMESA) and the East African Community (EAC).

a. *Common Market for Eastern and Southern Africa*

Uganda is a member of COMESA, which was formed in 1994 and comprises 20 African countries. COMESA's strategy includes removal of trade and investment barriers among member States and progressive integration. To this end, within set timeframes, COMESA member States are required to:

- Implement zero tariffs for all tradable goods among COMESA members;
- Establish a common external tariff, or customs union; and
- Implement programmes to enable free movement of services, labour and capital.

The COMESA strategy for the tourism sector involves encouraging member States to develop a common approach to the promotion and marketing of tourism in the Common Market. COMESA encourages member States to remove restrictions on the movement of tourists within the regional bloc, promote regional tourist circuits and coordinate policies governing the tourism industry.

Impact on Uganda's tourism sector

There was no evidence of investment from COMESA member States (excluding Kenya) in Uganda's tourism industry. Information on investment by Ugandan firms in the tourism sector in COMESA member States was not available.

The contribution of visitors from COMESA member States (excluding Kenya) to total visitor arrivals was 23 per cent in 2005. Most of the visitors (75 per cent of the total) were from Rwanda. In comparison, visitors from African countries that are not members of COMESA constituted 18 per cent of total visitors in 2005. The data thus show that membership of COMESA may not have influenced travel to Uganda by visitors from African countries that are not Uganda's closest neighbours. There were no data available which would show the impact of international visitors travelling to Uganda from COMESA member States on Uganda's tourism sector.

In conclusion, the impact of FDI from COMESA member States (excluding Kenya) on Uganda's tourism sector or vice versa was not evident. Links relating to tourism networks and investment between Uganda and most of the COMESA member States appeared to be very weak. Thus the impact of the COMESA treaty in terms of fostering regional cooperation in tourism among members appeared to be limited.

b. East African Community

The East African Community (EAC), which comprises Kenya, Uganda and the United Republic of Tanzania was formally revived in 2001[15]. Article 5 of the East African Community Free Trade Agreement states that "the objectives of the Community are to develop policies and programmes aimed at widening and deepening co-operation among the Partner States in political, economic, social and cultural fields, research and technology, defence, security and legal and judicial affairs, for their mutual benefit".

Policies specific to the tourism sector

Article 115 of the Agreement required partner States to develop a collective and coordinated approach to the promotion and marketing of quality tourism into and within the Community. Thus, partner States agreed to:

- Coordinate their policies in the tourism industry and to establish a framework of cooperation in the sector that will ensure equitable distribution of benefits;
- Establish a common code of conduct for private and public tour and travel operators, standardize hotel classifications and harmonize the professional standards of agents in the tourism and travel industry within the Community; and
- Develop a regional strategy for tourism promotion whereby individual efforts are reinforced by regional action.

Other related articles of the EAC Agreement:
- Cooperation in trade liberalization and development
- Establishment of a customs union
- Establishment of a common market
- Standardization, quality assurance, metrology and testing

Impact on Uganda's tourism industry
- Following the signing of the EAC Agreement and also in preparation for the Commonwealth Heads of Government Meeting in 2007, Uganda has made progress in implementing the standardized hotel classification system, which is under way.

- As discussed in section II.3.2 of this study, Kenya is one of the main sources of FDI in tourism in Uganda. It is also the main source of tourists to Uganda.

- The EAC Agreement is fostering interregional investment in the sector by TNCs. For example, the Tourism Promotion Services Group, which recently opened the Kampala Serena Hotel, also manages hotels in Kenya and the United Republic of Tanzania. The Agreement seeks to promote free movement of capital, goods and labour, and would thus facilitate movement of staff within the hotel chain and enable the Group to promote East Africa as a single tourist circuit for its customers.

- Joint promotion of East Africa as a single tourist destination would benefit Uganda, which is currently the least known among the three destinations.

- Removal of tariff barriers (e.g. separate visa fees for visitors travelling to each of the countries within East Africa) would facilitate the movement of tourists and could increase the total number of tourists visiting all three countries.

FDI by TNCs in all three East African countries could foster regional integration, through the movement of capital, labour and tourists within the hotel chains and the region and the promotion of the EAC as a single tourist destination. Furthermore, it is expected that investors in the tourism industry will demand accelerated regional integration because such integration offers clear advantages with respect to improved economies of scale and increased tourist traffic from Kenya and the United Republic of Tanzania following the removal of barriers to free movement. In addition the product diversity offe red by the three countries would make the region a more attractive tourist destination.

E. Conclusion

To summarise the findings, foreign direct investment can potentially make an important contribution to the development of the tourism industry in Uganda, to augment the resources that are available domestically. There has already been a significant contribution made by foreign hotels and investors, helping to augment the range and variety of accommodation services, creating jobs and transferring skills, and helping generally to raise the profile of Ugandan tourism through the use of an internationally recognised brand name, etc. There was some evidence of useful linkages between both foreign and domestic hotels with medium-sized enterprises that supply inputs to the hotel industry, however greater efforts will be needed to take full advantage of tourism's unusually long and diverse value-chain. More efforts are needed to promote deeper and more wide-ranging linkages between domestic enterprise and the hotel industry, for example. A major challenge faced by government is to provide an environment that will continue to stimulate investment in sustainable tourism and to provide adequate resources to facilitate implementation of national policies for the sector. The potential benefits of TFDI will not take place automatically, and an active policy response will be needed.

F. References

USAID-SCOPE Project (December 2005). Uganda's Travel and Tourism Industry Competitiveness Plan, Working draft for discussion. (Kampala, Uganda)

Bank of Uganda (2002). Private sector capital flows survey 2001 report. (Kampala: Bank of Uganda)

Bank of Uganda (2006). Report on foreign private capital survey 2004. Bank of Uganda, Uganda Investment Authority, Uganda Bureau of Statistics (Kampala: Bank of Uganda)

Ddumba-Ssentamu J and Mugume A (2001). The privatisation programme and its impact on society. A report for the Uganda National NGO Forum Structural Adjustment Participatory Review Initiative (SAPRI). Makerere University Institute of Economics, Kampala, Uganda

Ministry of Tourism, Trade and Industry, Uganda. (2003). Tourism Policy for Uganda.

The Republic of Uganda (2003). Consolidated low and high expenditure motivation survey report. Ministry of Tourism, Trade and Industry ICB–PAMSU Project, Kampala, Uganda

Monitor Publications (2006). The Monitor Telephone Directory. Monitor Publications Limited, Uganda

NEMA (2005). State of Environment Report for Uganda 2004-05, National Environment Management. Authority, Kampala, Uganda.

The New Vision (2007): Article: "South African firm to manage Bwebajja hotel," *The New Vision*, 5 March 2007: 39.

Obwona B M (1998). Determinants of FDI and their impact on economic growth in Uganda. Economic Policy Research Centre, Uganda

OECD (2006). African Economic Outlook 2005–2006: Uganda. Published by the OECD Development Centre and the African Development Bank, with financial support from the European Commission, Paris.

Reinikka R and Collier P (2001). Uganda's recovery: the role of farms, firms and government. Fountain Publishers, Kampala, Uganda

Republic of Uganda: The Investment Code Act Cap 92

Republic of Uganda: The Income Tax Act 11 of 1997

Republic of Uganda (1998). The Land Act, Act 16.

Republic of Uganda (2000). The Employment Act, revised edition 2000, Chapter 219.

The Aga Khan Development Network (2006). President Museveni and Aga Khan inaugurate Kampala Serena Hotel. Press Release, November 10, 2006. www.akdn.org/news/2006Nov10.html

Times Journal of Construction and Design (May 2006). EU will finance Uganda's road construction. http://www.etconstructionanddesign.com/may_06/news_global.htm

The Republic of Uganda (2006). Budget Speech 2006/07. Ministry of Finance, Planning and Economic Development, Uganda

Uganda Bureau of Statistics (1995). Migration and tourism statistics (Busia, Entebbe and Malaba), vol. 1, *Statistical Bulletin* No. MT/1/1995.

Uganda Bureau of Statistics (2005). Migration and tourism, Report IV, 2000–2004, Uganda Bureau of Statistics, Entebbe, Uganda

Uganda Investment Authority (2003?). The Uganda Transport and Communications Profile. http://www.ugandainvest.com/transport.pdf

The Eye (various). The Insider's Guide to Uganda. The Eye (U) Limited, Kampala, Uganda

Notes

[1]   By Frances Nsonzi, consultant, Uganda.

[2]   This report was completed and draft findings disseminated to tourism-policy-makers in Uganda in 2007, and the Bill was passed in 2008.

[3]   The report of the Consolidated Low and High Expenditure Motivation Survey 2003 by the Ministry of Tourism, Trade and Industry (2003) notes that 75.6 per cent of randomly sampled tourists visited tourist sites in Kampala and Jinja. Therefore, they would have used accommodation facilities in these towns.

[4]   The hotel classification is based on the perceptions in the sector, as the national classification of hotels in Uganda is in progress and has not been finalized

[5]   FDEI stock in book value terms includes paid-up capital, share premium, accumulated retained earnings and revaluations (Bank of Uganda, 2006).

[6]   Between 1991 and March 1996, 1,788 properties were repossessed and returned to their original Asian owners (Obwona, B. M. 1998).

[7]   The private sector developed the geo-tourism strategy in partnership with the USAID-SCOPE (United States Agency for International Development-Strengthening the Competitiveness of Private Enterprise) Project. Key partners in developing the strategy included the Uganda Tourist Board, Uganda Wildlife Authority and the Civil Aviation Authority.

[8]   This was the latest year for which disaggregated data on the market and book value of the contribution of different sectors to total FDEI were available.

[9]   We confirmed that a project is operational or in progress by telephoning the contact person recorded in the Uganda Investment Authority (UIA) database. The existence of some projects could not be confirmed because their contact details could not be traced in existing directories, or the numbers recorded in the UIA database were out of service or belonged to a different institution. These projects were therefore not counted. The UIA is in the process of updating its database.

[10] According to African Econoic Outlook 2005/06 a publication by the OECD Development Centre and the African Development Bank, Uganda had the fifth highest gasoline prices of 25 African countries, and the 23rd highest prices in the world during the period 1998–2002. Fuel represents about 50 per cent of vehicle operating costs compared to 30 per cent in most other countries.

[11] The price is for a double/deluxe room, and includes breakfast and taxes.

[12] Barely two months after its launch in November 2006, however, the airline suspended flights to Nairobi, Juba and South Africa in January 2007, citing poor sales resulting from poor performance of its distribution system. Most of its ticket sales were online.

[13] The shareholders of the Kampala Serena Hotel are: the Aga Khan Fund for Economic Development (AKFED), with 70 per cent ownership, and two government development agencies, PROPACO of France and DEG of Germany, each with 15 per cent ownership.

[14] A concession by Uganda Wildlife Authority is defined as a right to transact business in the Uganda Wildlife Authority property (e.g. national parks and Wildlife Reserves). The current concessions include accommodation facilities in the form of lodge, and tented camps as well as communication facilities.

[15] Burundi and Rwanda joined the EAC in 2007 after this report was prepared. They are not covered in this study.

Selected recent UNCTAD publications on TNCS and FDI
(For more information, please visit www.unctad.org/en/pub)

A. Serial publications

World Investment Reports
(For more information visit www.unctad.org/wir)

World Investment Report 2008. Transnational Corporations and the Infrastructure Challenge. Sales No. E.08.II.D.23. $80. http://www.unctad.org/en/docs//wir2008_en.pdf.

World Investment Report 2008. Transnational Corporations and the Infrastructure Challenge. An Overview. 42 p. http://www.unctad.org/en/docs//wir2008overview_en.pdf.

World Investment Report 2007. Transnational Corporations, Extractive Industries and Development. Sales No. E.07.II.D.9. $80. http://www.unctad.org/en/docs//wir2007_en.pdf.

World Investment Report 2007. Transnational Corporations, Extractive Industries and Development. An Overview. 48 p. http://www.unctad.org/en/docs/wir2007overview_en.pdf.

World Investment Report 2006. FDI from Developing and Transition Economies: Implications for Development. Sales No. E.06.II.D.11. $80. http://www.unctad.org/en/docs//wir2006_en.pdf.

World Investment Report 2006. FDI from Developing and Transition Economies: Implications for Development. An Overview. 50 p. http://www.unctad.org/en/docs/wir2006overview_en.pdf.

World Investment Report 2005. Transnational Corporations and the Internationalization of R&D. Sales No. E.05.II.D.10. $75. http://www.unctad.org/en/docs//wir2005_en.pdf.

World Investment Report 2005. Transnational Corporations and the Internationalization of R&D. An Overview. 50 p. http://www.unctad.org/en/docs/wir2005overview_en.pdf.

World Investment Report 2004. The Shift Towards Services. Sales No. E.04.II.D.36. $75. http://www.unctad.org/en/docs//wir2004_en.pdf.

World Investment Report 2004. The Shift Towards Services. An Overview. 62 p. http://www.unctad.org/en/docs/wir2004overview_en.pdf.

World Investment Report 2003. FDI Policies for Development: National and International Perspectives. Sales No. E.03.II.D.8. $49. http://www.unctad.org/en/docs//wir2003_en.pdf.

World Investment Report 2003. FDI Polices for Development: National and International Perspectives. An Overview. 66 p. http://www.unctad.org/en/docs/wir2003overview_en.pdf.

World Investment Report 2002: Transnational Corporations and Export Competitiveness. 352 p. Sales No. E.02.II.D.4. $49. http://www.unctad.org/en/docs//wir2002_en.pdf.

World Investment Report 2002: Transnational Corporations and Export Competitiveness. An Overview. 66 p. http://www.unctad.org/en/docs/wir2002overview_en.pdf.

World Investment Report 2001: Promoting Linkages. 356 p. Sales No. E.01.II.D.12 $49. http://www.unctad.org/wir/contents/wir01content.en.htm.

World Investment Report 2001: Promoting Linkages. An Overview. 67 p. http://www.unctad.org/wir/contents/wir01content.en.htm.

Ten Years of World Investment Reports: The Challenges Ahead. Proceedings of an UNCTAD special event on future challenges in the area of FDI. UNCTAD/ITE/Misc.45. http://www.unctad.org/wir.

World Investment Report 2000: Cross-border Mergers and Acquisitions and Development. 368 p. Sales No. E.99.II.D.20. $49. http://www.unctad.org/wir/contents/wir00content.en.htm.

World Investment Report 2000: Cross-border Mergers and Acquisitions and Development. An Overview. 75 p. http://www.unctad.org/wir/contents/wir00content.en.htm.

World Investment Directories
(For more information visit http://r0.unctad.org/en/subsites/dite/fdistats_files/WID2.htm)

World Investment Directory 2004: Latin America and the Caribbean. Volume IX. 599 p. Sales No. E.03.II.D.12. $25.

World Investment Directory 2003: Central and Eastern Europe. Vol. VIII. 397 p. Sales No. E.03.II.D.24. $80.

Investment Policy Reviews
(For more information visit
http://www.unctad.org/Templates/Startpage.asp?int
ItemID=2554)

Investment Policy Review – Algeria. 110 p.
UNCTAD/ITE/IPC/2003/9.

Investment Policy Review – Kenya. 126 p. Sales No.
E.05.II.D.21. $25.

Investment Policy Review – Benin. 147 p. Sales No.
F.04.II.D.43. $25.

Investment Policy Review – Sri Lanka. 89 p.
UNCTAD/ITE/IPC/2003/8.

Investment Policy Review – Nepal. 89 p. Sales No.
E.03.II.D.17. $20.

Investment Policy Review – Lesotho. 105 p. Sales No.
E.03.II.D.18. $15/18.

Investment Policy Review – Ghana. 103 p. Sales No.
E.02.II.D.20. $20.

Investment Policy Review – Tanzania. 109 p. Sales No.
E.02.II.D.6 $20.

Investment Policy Review – Botswana. 107 p. Sales No.
E.01.II.D.I. $22.

Investment Policy Review – Ecuador. 136 p. Sales No.
E.01.II D.31. $25.

Investment and Innovation Policy Review – Ethiopia.
130 p. UNCTAD/ITE/IPC/Misc.4.

Investment Policy Review – Mauritius. 92 p. Sales No.
E.01.II.D.11. $22.

Investment Policy Review – Peru. 109 p. Sales No.
E.00.II.D.7. $22.

Investment Policy Review – Egypt. 119 p. Sales No.
E.99.II.D.20. $19.

Investment Policy Review – Uganda. 71 p. Sales No.
E.99.II.D.24. $15.

Investment Policy Review – Uzbekistan.. 65 p.
UNCTAD/ITE/IIP/Misc. 13.

International Investment Instruments
(Fore more information visit
http://www.unctad.org/iia)

International Investment Instruments: A Compendium.
Vol. XIV. Sales No. E.05.II.D.8. 326 p. $60.

International Investment Instruments: A Compendium.
Vol. XIII. Sales No. E.05.II.D.7. 358 p. $60.

International Investment Instruments: A Compendium.
Vol. XII. Sales No. E.04.II.D.10. 364 p. $60.

International Investment Instruments: A Compendium.
Vol. XI. 345 p. Sales No. E.04.II.D.9. $60.
http://www.unctad.org/en/docs//dite4volxi_en.pdf.

International Investment Instruments: A Compendium.
Vol. X. 353 p. Sales No. E.02.II.D.21. $60.
http://www.unctad.org/en/docs/psdited3v9.en.pdf.

International Investment Instruments: A Compendium.
Vol. IX. 353 p. Sales No. E.02.II.D.16. $60.
http://www.unctad.org/en/docs/psdited3v9.en.pdf.

International Investment Instruments: A Compendium.
Vol. VIII. 335 p. Sales No. E.02.II.D.15. $60.
http://www.unctad.org/en/docs/psdited3v8.en.pdf.

International Investment Instruments: A Compendium.
Vol. VII. 339 p. Sales No. E.02.II.D.14. $60.
http://www.unctad.org/en/docs/psdited3v7.en.pdf.

International Investment Instruments: A Compendium.
Vol. VI. 568 p. Sales No. E.01.II.D.34. $60.
http://www.unctad.org/en/docs/ps1dited2v6_p1.en.pdf
(part one).

International Investment Instruments: A Compendium.
Vol. V. 505 p. Sales No. E.00.II.D.14. $55.

International Investment Instruments: A Compendium.
Vol. IV. 319 p. Sales No. E.00.II.D.13. $55.

LDC Investment Guides
(For more information visit
http://www.unctad.org/Templates/Page.asp?intItem
ID=2705&lang=14)

An Investment Guide to Kenya: Opportunities and
Conditions. 92 p. UNCTAD/ITE/IIA/2005/2.

An Investment Guide to Tanzania: Opportunities and
Conditions. 82 p. UNCTAD/ITE/IIA/2005/3.

An Investment Guide to the East African Community:
Opportunities and Conditions. 109 p.
UNCTAD/ITE/IIA2005/4.

An Investment Guide to Mauritania: Opportunities
and Conditions. 80 p. UNCTAD/ITE/IIA/2004/4.

Guide de l'investissement au Mali: Opportunités et
Conditions. 76 p. UNCTAD/ITE/IIA/2004/1.

An Investment Guide to Cambodia: Opportunities and Conditions. 89 p. UNCTAD/ITE/IIA/2003/6. http://www.unctad.org/en/docs//iteiia20036_en.pdf.

An Investment Guide to Nepal: Opportunities and Conditions. 97 p. UNCTAD/ITE/IIA/2003/2. http://www.unctad.org/en/docs/iteiia20032_en.pdf.

An Investment Guide to Mozambique: Opportunities and Conditions. 109 p. UNCTAD/ITE/IIA/4. http://www.unctad.org/en/docs/poiteiiad4.en.pdf.

An Investment Guide to Uganda: Opportunities and Conditions. 89 p. UNCTAD/ITE/IIA/2004/3.

An Investment Guide to Bangladesh: Opportunities and Conditions. 66 p. UNCTAD/ITE/IIT/Misc.29. http://www.unctad.org/en/docs/poiteiitm29.en.pdf.

An Investment Guide to Ethiopia: Opportunities and Conditions. 90 p. UNCTAD/ITE/IIA/2004/2.

Issues in International Investment Agreements
(Fore more information visit http://www.unctad.org/iia)

Investor-State Disputes Arising from Investment Treaties: A Review. 106 p. Sales No. E.06.II.D.1 $15

South-South Cooperation in Investment Arrangements. 108 p. Sales No. E.05.II.D.26 $15.

The REIO Exception in MFN Treatment Clauses. 92 p. Sales No. E.05.II.D.1. $15.

International Investment Agreements in Services. 119 p. Sales No. E.05.II.D.15. $15.

State Contracts. 84 p. Sales No. E.05.II.D.5. $15.

Competition. 112 p. E.04.II.D.44. $ 15.

Key Terms and Concepts in IIAs: a Glossary. 232 p. Sales No. E.04.II.D.31. $15.

Incentives. 108 p. Sales No. E.04.II.D.6. $15.

Transparency. 118 p. Sales No. E.04.II.D.7. $15.

Dispute Settlement: State-State. 101 p. Sales No. E.03.II.D.6. $15.

Dispute Settlement: Investor-State. 125 p. Sales No. E.03.II.D.5. $15.

Transfer of Technology. 138 p. Sales No. E.01.II.D.33. $18.

Illicit Payments. 108 p. Sales No. E.01.II.D.20. $13.

Home Country Measures. 96 p. Sales No.E.01.II.D.19. $12.

Host Country Operational Measures. 109 p. Sales No E.01.II.D.18. $15.

Social Responsibility. 91 p. Sales No. E.01.II.D.4. $15.

Environment. 105 p. Sales No. E.01.II.D.3. $15.

Transfer of Funds. 68 p. Sales No. E.00.II.D.27. $12.

Employment. 69 p. Sales No. E.00.II.D.15. $12.

Taxation. 111 p. Sales No. E.00.II.D.5. $12.

International Investment Agreements: Flexibility for Development. 185 p. Sales No. E.00.II.D.6. $12.

Taking of Property. 83 p. Sales No. E.00.II.D.4. $12.

B. ASIT Advisory Studies (Formerly Current Studies, Series B)

No. 17. *The World of Investment Promotion at a Glance: A survey of investment promotion practices*. UNCTAD/ITE/IPC/3.

No. 16. *Tax Incentives and Foreign Direct Investment: A Global Survey*. 180 p. Sales No. E.01.II.D.5. $23. Summary available from http://www.unctad.org/asit/resumé.htm.

C. Individual Studies

Globalization of R&D and Developing Countries.. 242 p. Sales No. E.06.II.D.2. $35.

Prospects for Foreign Direct Investment and the Strategies of Transnational Corporations, 2005-2008. 74 p. Sales No. E.05.II.D.32. $18.

World Economic Situation and Prospects 2005. 136 p. Sales No. E. 05.II.C.2. $15. (Joint publication with the United Nations Department of Economic and Social Affairs.)

Foreign Direct Investment and Performance Requirements: New Evidence from Selected Countries. 318 p. Sales No. E.03.II.D.32. $35.http://www.unctad.org/en/docs//iteiia20037_en.pdf

FDI in Land-Locked Developing Countries at a Glance. 112 p. UNCTAD/ITE/IIA/2003/5.

FDI in Least Developed Countries at a Glance: 2002. 136 p. UNCTAD/ITE/IIA/6. http://www.unctad.org/en/docs//iteiia6_en.pdf.

The Tradability of Consulting Services. 189 p. UNCTAD/ITE/IPC/Misc.8. http://www.unctad.org/en/docs/poiteipcm8.en.pdf.

Foreign Direct Investment in Africa: Performance and Potential. 89 p. UNCTAD/ITE/IIT/Misc.15. Free of charge. Also available from http://www.unctad.org/en/docs/poiteiitm15.pdf.

TNC-SME Linkages for Development: Issues–Experiences–Best Practices. *Proceedings of the Special Round Table on TNCs, SMEs and Development, UNCTAD X, 15 February 2000, Bangkok, Thailand.*113 p. UNCTAD/ITE/TEB1. Free of charge.

Measures of the Transnationalization of Economic Activity. 93 p. Sales No. E.01.II.D.2. $20.

The Competitiveness Challenge: Transnational Corporations and Industrial Restructuring in Developing Countries. 283p. Sales No. E.00.II.D.35. $42.

FDI Determinants and TNC Strategies: The Case of Brazil. 195 p. Sales No. E.00.II.D.2. $35. Summary available from http://www.unctad.org/en/pub/psiteiitd14.en.htm.

Studies on FDI and Development

TNCs and the Removal of Textiles and Clothing Quotas. 78 p. Sales No. E.05.II.D.20.

Measures of Restrictions on FDI in Services in Developing Countries. 56 p. Sales No. E.06.II.D.13.

D. Journals

Transnational Corporations Journal (formerly *The CTC Reporter*). Published three times a year. http://www.unctad.org/en/subsites/dite/1_itncs/1_tncs.htm.

United Nations publications may be obtained from bookstores and distributors throughout the world. Please consult your bookstore or write:

For Africa, Asia and Europe to:

Sales Section
United Nations Office at Geneva
Palais des Nations
CH-1211 Geneva 10
Switzerland
Tel: (41-22) 917-1234
Fax: (41-22) 917-0123
E-mail: unpubli@unog.ch

For Asia and the Pacific, the Caribbean, Latin America and North America to:

Sales Section
Room DC2-0853
United Nations Secretariat
New York, NY 10017
United States
Tel: (1-212) 963-8302 or (800) 253-9646
Fax: (1-212) 963-3489
E-mail: publications@un.org

All prices are quoted in United States dollars.

For further information on the work of the Division on Investment, Technology and Enterprise Development, UNCTAD, please address inquiries to:

United Nations Conference on Trade and Development
Division on Investment, Technology and Enterprise Development
Palais des Nations, Room E-10054
CH-1211 Geneva 10, Switzerland
Telephone: (41-22) 907-5651
Telefax: (41-22) 907-0498
http://www.unctad.org

Questionnaire

FDI in Tourism: The Development Dimension
East and Southern Africa
Sales No. E.0.II.D.

In order to improve the quality and relevance of the work of the UNCTAD Division on Investment, Technology and Enterprise Development, it would be useful to receive the views of readers on this publication. It would therefore be greatly appreciated if you could complete the following questionnaire and return it to:

Readership Survey
UNCTAD Division on Investment, Technology and Enterprise Development
United Nations Office in Geneva
Palais des Nations, Room E-9123
CH-1211 Geneva 10, Switzerland
Fax: 41-22-917-0194

1. Name and address of respondent (optional):

   _____

   _____

2. Which of the following best describes your area of work?

Government	☐	Public enterprise	☐
Private enterprise	☐	Academic or research institution	☐
International organization	☐	Media	☐
Not-for-profit organization	☐	Other (specify) _____	

3. In which country do you work? _____

4. What is your assessment of the contents of this publication?

Excellent	☐	Adequate	☐
Good	☐	Poor	☐

5. How useful is this publication to your work?

   Very useful ☐   Somewhat useful ☐   Irrelevant ☐

6. Please indicate the three things you liked best about this publication:

   _____

   _____

   _____

7. Please indicate the three things you liked least about this publication:

    _____

    _____

    _____

8. If you have read other publications of the UNCTAD Division on Investment, Enterprise

    Development and Technology, what is your overall assessment of them?

    Consistently good   ☐   Usually good, but with
                                            some exceptions   ☐
    Generally mediocre   ☐   Poor   ☐

9. On the average, how useful are those publications to you in your work?

    Very useful   ☐   Somewhat useful   ☐   Irrelevant   ☐

10. Are you a regular recipient of *Transnational Corporations* (formerly *The CTC Reporter*),
    UNCTAD-DITE's tri-annual refereed journal?

        Yes   ☐   No   ☐

    If not, please check here if you would like to receive a sample copy sent to the name and
    address you have given above   ☐